The Haynes
Computer Codes
& Electronic Engine
Management Systems
Manual

by Robert Maddox
and John H Haynes

Member of the Guild of Motoring Writers

**The Haynes Automotive Repair Manual
for maintaining, troubleshooting and
repairing engine management systems**

(6J14 - 10205)
(2108)

ABCDE
FGHIJ
KLMNO
PQRST 3

Haynes Publishing Group
Sparkford Nr Yeovil
Somerset BA22 7JJ England

Haynes North America, Inc
861 Lawrence Drive
Newbury Park
California 91320 USA

Acknowledgements

We are grateful for the help and cooperation of the Chrysler Corporation, Nissan Motor Company and Robert Bosch Corporation for assistance with technical information and certain illustrations. We also wish to thank Milton Webb for consultation on this project. Technical authors who contributed to this project are Larry Warren, Mark Ryan and Mike Stubblefield.

© **Haynes North America, Inc. 1994, 1997, 2000, 2005**

With permission from J.H. Haynes & Co. Ltd.

A book in the Haynes Automotive Repair Manual Series

Printed in the U.S.A.

ISBN 1 56392 232 0

Library of Congress Catalog Card Number 96-78641

Contents

Chapter 6
Basic troubleshooting

Chapter 7 Part A
Computer trouble code retrieval

Chapter 7 Part B
Computer trouble codes

Chapter 8
Component check and replacement

Introduction

Computerized engine control systems were originally developed to help vehicles meet government emission regulations. A typical system consists of a computer, information sensors and output actuators that interact with each other to collect, store and send data to control virtually every aspect of engine operation.

How does it work?

The information sensors collect data (such as the intake air mass and/or temperature, coolant temperature, throttle position, exhaust gas oxygen content, etc.) and transmit this data, in the form of varying electrical signals, to the computer. The computer compares this data with its programming, which tells what these data should be under the engine's current operating conditions. If the data does not match the programming, the computer sends signals to output actuators (fuel injectors or carburetor mixture control solenoid, Electronic Air Control Valve (EACV), Idle Speed Control (ISC) motor, etc.) which correct the engine's operation to match the programming.

When the engine is warming up (and sensor input is not precise) or there is a malfunction in the system, the system operates in an "open loop" mode. In this mode, the computer does not rely on the sensors for input and sets the fuel/air mixture rich so the engine can continue operation until the engine warms up or repairs are made. **Note:** *The engine's thermostat rating and proper operation are critical to the operation of a computer-controlled vehicle. If the thermostat is rated at too low a temperature, is removed or stuck open, the computer may stay in "open loop" - operation, emissions and fuel economy will suffer.*

Why computerized engine control?

Automobiles and trucks are the number one cause of air pollution in this country; they contribute over half of the airborne pollutants - hydrocarbons, carbon monoxide, oxides of nitrogen and others - collectively referred to as "smog". Once the federal government passed the Clean Air Act restricting the production of these pollutants, the automobile industry had to find a way to reduce them. They found that by using a computerized system to precisely control engine operation, the content of the exhaust could be controlled as well, keeping the level of pollutants within legal limits.

Advantages

Years of refining computerized engine control have allowed the manufacturers to reduce pollutant output by 100-percent over what they were just a few years ago while keeping ahead of ever-tightening regulations. Although originally developed primarily to meet the smog laws, computerized systems have also improved the reliability, efficiency, driveability and responsiveness of modern vehicles.

Driveability

The operation of these systems has become so sophisticated that later models can actually adjust for variables such as engine wear, fuel quality and production variations. This "learning ability" feature keeps the engine running smoothly and efficiently on even a high-mileage vehicle, all the while staying within the program (and smog law) limits.

Ease of diagnosis

For the owner, a major plus of computerized engine control is that it has made finding and fixing problems easier. The computer itself stores easily-accessed codes that pinpoint the area of a malfunction, so zeroing in on the cause can be a simple matter. A brightly lit "Service Engine Soon" light needn't strike fear into an owner's heart - this light is actually the first step to finding and solving the problem.

2 Manufacturers' warranties

Questions and answers

Before you dive under the hood to troubleshoot or fix a problem related to emissions, there are some things you should know about the Federally-mandated extended warranty **(see illustration)** designed to protect you from the cost of repairs to any emission-related failures beyond your control.

There are actually TWO emission control warranties - the "Design and Defect Warranty" and the "Performance Warranty." We will discuss them separately.

Design and Defect Warranty

Basically, the Design and Defect Warranty covers the repair of all emission control related parts which fail during the first five years or the first 50,000 miles of service. **Note**: *This 50,000-mile figure may increase. In fact, under the more stringent California Air Resources Board (CARB) regulations, after the three year, 50,000 miles Performance Warranty has passed, a defective part that causes a smog test failure is warranted for seven years or 70,000 miles.* According to Federal law, the manufacturer must repair or replace the defective part free of charge if:

1. Your car is less than five years old and has less than 50,000 miles;
2. An original equipment part or system fails because of a defect in materials or workmanship; and
3. The failure would cause your vehicle to exceed Federal emissions standards.

If these three conditions are present, the manufacturer must honor the warranty. All manufacturers have established procedures to provide owners with this coverage.

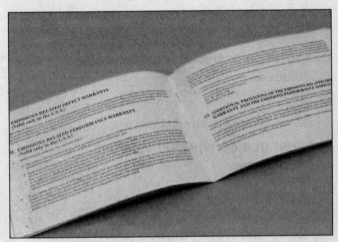

2.1 You'll find the details of your vehicle's Federally-mandated extended warranty coverage in your owner's manual or a separate booklet like this one, in the glove box

The Design and Defect Warranty applies to used vehicles too. It doesn't matter whether you bought the vehicle new or used; if the vehicle hasn't exceeded the warranty time or mileage limitations, the warranty applies.

Note that the length of the warranty is five years and 50,000 miles for cars. The Design and Defect Warranty applies to all vehicles manufactured in the last five years, including cars, pick-ups, recreational vehicles, heavy-duty trucks and motorcycles. The length of the warranty varies somewhat with the type of vehicle. If you own some type of vehicle other than a car, read the description of the emissions warranty in your owner's manual or warranty booklet to determine the length of the warranty on your vehicle.

What parts or repairs are covered by the warranty?

Coverage includes all parts whose primary purpose is to control emissions and all parts that have an effect on emissions. Let's divide these two types of parts in two categories - emissions-control parts and emissions-related parts - then divide the parts within each category into systems. Our list would look something like this:

Primary emissions control parts

Air induction system

1 Thermostatically controlled air cleaner
2 Air box

Air injection system

1 Diverter, bypass or gulp valve
2 Reed valve
3 Air pump
4 Anti-backfire or deceleration valve

Early Fuel Evaporative (EFE) system

1 EFE valve
2 Heat riser valve
3 Thermal vacuum switch

Evaporative emission control system

1 Purge valve
2 Purge solenoid
3 Fuel filler cap
4 Vapor storage canister and filter

Exhaust gas conversion systems

1 Oxygen sensor
2 Catalytic converter
3 Thermal reactor
4 Dual-walled exhaust pipe

Exhaust Gas Recirculation (EGR) system

1 EGR valve
2 EGR solenoid
3 EGR backpressure transducer
4 Thermal vacuum switch
5 EGR spacer plate
6 Sensor and switches used to control EGR flow

Fuel metering systems

1 Electronic control module or computer command module
2 Deceleration controls
3 Fuel injectors
4 Fuel injection rail
5 Fuel pressure regulator
6 Fuel pressure dampener
7 Throttle body
8 Mixture control solenoid or diaphragm
9 Air flow meter
10 Air flow module or mixture control unit
11 Electronic choke
12 Altitude compensator sensor
13 Mixture settings on sealed carburetors
14 Other feedback control sensors, switches and valves

Ignition systems

1 Electronic spark advance

2 High energy electronic ignition
3 Timing advance/retard systems

Miscellaneous parts

Hoses, gaskets, brackets, clamps and other accessories used in these systems

Positive Crankcase Ventilation (PCV) system

1 PCV valve
2 PCV filter

Emissions-related parts

The following parts have a primary purpose other than emissions control, but they still have a significant effect on your vehicle's emissions. If they break or malfunction, your vehicle's emissions may exceed Federal standards, so they're also covered by the Design and Defect Warranty. They include:

Air induction system

1 Turbocharger
2 Intake manifold

Carburetor systems

1 Carburetor
2 Choke

Exhaust system

Exhaust manifold

Fuel injection system

Fuel distributor

Ignition system

1 Distributor
2 Ignition wires and coil
3 Spark plugs

Miscellaneous parts

Hoses, gaskets, brackets, clamps and other accessories used in the above systems.

If - after reading the list above and the manufacturer's description of your warranty coverage in your owner's manual or warranty booklet - you're confused about whether certain parts are covered, contact your dealer service department or the manufacturer's zone or regional representative.

Can any part of a warranty repair be charged to you?

No! You can't be charged for any labor, parts or miscellaneous items necessary to complete the job when a manufacturer repairs or replaces any part under the emissions warranty. For example, if a manufacturer agrees to replace a catalytic converter under the emissions warranty, you shouldn't be charged for the catalyst itself or for any pipes, brackets, adjustments or labor needed to complete the replacement.

How long does the warranty apply?

Parts which don't have a replacement interval stated in the maintenance instructions are warranted for what the EPA calls the "useful life" of the vehicle, which, for cars, is, as stated before, five years or 50,000 miles. For other types of vehicles, read your warranty description in the owner's manual or the warranty booklet to determine the length of the warranty coverage.

Other parts, for example those with a stated replacement interval such as "15,000 miles or 12 months," are warranted only up to the first replacement.

Any parts that are the subject of a maintenance instruction that requires them to be "checked and replaced if necessary," or the subject of any similar requirement, are warranted for the entire period of warranty coverage.

How do you know if you're entitled to coverage?

If you or a reliable mechanic can show that a part in one of the listed systems is defective, it's probably covered under the emissions warranty. When you believe you've identified a defective part that might be covered, you should make a warranty claim to the person identified by the manufacturer in your owner's manual or warranty booklet.

What should you do if your first attempt to obtain warranty coverage is denied?

1 Ask for the complete reason - in writing - for the denial of emissions warranty coverage;
2 Ask for the name(s) of the person(s) who determined the denial of coverage;
3 Ask for the name(s) of the person(s) you should contact to appeal the denial of coverage under the emissions warranty.

Once you've obtained this information, look in your owner's manual or warranty booklet for the name of the person designated by the manufacturer for warranty assistance and contact this person.

How does maintenance affect your warranty?

Performance of scheduled maintenance is YOUR responsibility. You're expected to either perform scheduled maintenance yourself, or have a qualified repair facility perform it for you. If a part failure can be directly attributed to poor maintenance of your vehicle or vehicle abuse (proper operation of the vehicle is usually spelled out in your owner's manual or maintenance booklet), the manufacturer might not be liable for replacing that part or repairing any damage caused by its failure. To assure maximum benefit from your emissions control systems in reducing air pollution, as well as assuring continued warranty coverage, you should have all scheduled maintenance performed, or do it yourself.

Do you have to show any maintenance receipts before you can make a warranty claim?

No! Proof of maintenance isn't required to obtain coverage under the emissions warranty. If a listed part is defective in materials or workmanship, the manufacturer must provide warranty coverage. Of course, not all parts fail because of defects in materials or workmanship.

Though you're not automatically required to show maintenance receipts when you make a warranty claim, there is one circumstance in which you will be asked for proof that scheduled maintenance has been performed. If it looks as if a part failed because of a lack of scheduled maintenance, you can be required to prove that the maintenance was performed.

How is your warranty affected if you use leaded gasoline in your vehicle?

When leaded gas is used in vehicles designed to run on unleaded, the emissions controls - particularly the catalytic converter - can be damaged. And lead deposits inside the engine can lead to the failure of certain engine parts. The emissions warranty does not cover ANY part failures that result from the use of leaded fuel in a vehicle that requires unleaded fuel.

Can anyone besides dealers perform scheduled maintenance recommended by the manufacturer?

Absolutely! Scheduled maintenance can be performed by anyone who is qualified to do so, including you (as long as the maintenance is performed in accordance with the manufacturer's instructions). If you're going to take the vehicle to a repair facility, refer to your owner's manual or maintenance booklet and make a list of all scheduled maintenance items before you go. When you get there, don't simply ask for a "tune-up" or a "15,000 mile servicing." Instead, specify exactly what you want done. Then make sure the work specified is entered on the work order or receipt that you receive. This way, you'll have a clear record that all scheduled maintenance has been done.

If you buy a used vehicle, how do you know whether it's been maintained properly?

Realistically, you don't. But it never hurts to ask the seller to give you the receipts which prove the vehicle has been properly maintained according to the schedule. These receipts are proof that the work was done properly and on time, if the question of maintenance ever arises.

And once you buy a used vehicle, you should continue to maintain it in accordance with the maintenance schedule in the owner's manual or warranty booklet (If the seller doesn't have these items anymore, buy new ones at the dealer).

What should you do if the manufacturer won't honor what you feel is a valid warranty claim?

As we said earlier, if an authorized warranty representative denies your claim, you should contact the person designated by the manufacturer for further warranty assistance. Additionally, you're free to pursue any independent legal actions you deem necessary to obtain coverage. Finally, the EPA is authorized to investigate the failure of manufacturers to comply with the terms of this warranty. If you've followed the manufacturer's procedure for making a claim and you're still not satisfied with the manufacturer's determination, contact the EPA by writing:

Warranty Complaint
Field Operations and Support Division (6406J)
U.S. Environmental Protection Agency
401 M Street SW
Washington, D.C. 20460

California drivers can contact the California Air Resources Board (CARB) at:

California Air Resources Board
9528 Telstar Avenue
El Monte, CA 91731

The Performance Warranty

The Performance Warranty covers those repairs required because the vehicle has failed an emission test. If you reside in an area with an Inspection/Maintenance program that meets Federal guidelines, you may be eligible for this additional Performance Warranty. For more information on the Performance Warranty, ask your local Inspection/Maintenance program official or call or write the nearest EPA office and ask for a copy of the pamphlet "If Your Car Just Failed An Emission Test...You May Be Entitled To Free Repairs," which describes the Performance Warranty in detail.

You may be eligible for coverage under this warranty if:

1   Your 1981 or later car or light truck fails an approved emissions test; and

2   Your state or local government requires that you repair the vehicle; and

3   The test failure didn't result from misuse of the vehicle

or a failure to follow the manufacturer's written maintenance instructions; and

4   You present the vehicle to a warranty-authorized manufacturer representative, along with evidence of the emission test failure, during the relevant warranty period; then . . .

a) for the first two years or 24,000 miles, whichever comes first, the manufacturer must pay for all repairs necessary to pass the emissions test and . . .

b) for the first five years or 50,000 miles, the manufacturer must pay for all repairs to primary emission control parts which are necessary to pass the emissions test.

What vehicles are covered by the Performance Warranty?

The Federally mandated Performance Warranty covers all 1981 and later cars and light duty trucks produced in the last five years. And it doesn't matter whether you bought your vehicle new or used, from a dealer or from a private party. As long as it hasn't exceeded the warranty time or mileage limitations, and has been properly maintained, the Performance Warranty applies.

What types of repairs are covered by the Performance Warranty?

Two types of repairs are covered by the Performance Warranty, depending on the age of your vehicle:

1   Any repair or adjustment which is necessary to make your vehicle pass an approved locally-required emission test is covered if your vehicle is less than two years old and has less than 24,000 miles.

2   Any repair or adjustment of a "primary emissions control" part (see "The Design and Defect Warranty") which is necessary to make your vehicle pass an approved locally required test is covered if your vehicle is less than five years old and has less than 50,000 miles. Although coverage is limited after two years/24,000 miles to primary emission control parts, repairs must still be complete and effective. If the complete and effective repair or a primary part requires that non-primary parts be repaired or adjusted, these repairs are also covered.

What if the dealer claims your vehicle can pass the emissions test without repair?

The law doesn't require you to fail the emissions test to trigger the warranty. If any test shows that you have an emissions problem, get it fixed while your vehicle is still within the warranty period. Otherwise, you could end up failing a future test because of the same problem - and paying for the repairs yourself. If you doubt your original test results or the dealer's results, get another opinion to support your claim.

What kinds of reasons can the manufacturer use to deny a claim?

As long as your vehicle is within the age or mileage limits explained above, the manufacturer can deny coverage under the Performance Warranty only if you've failed to properly maintain and use your vehicle. Proper use and maintenance of the vehicle are your responsibilities. The manufacturer can deny your claim if there's evidence that your vehicle failed an emissions test as a result of:

a) Vehicle abuse, such as off-road driving, or overloading; or

b) Tampering with emission control parts, including removal or intentional damage; or

c) Improper maintenance, including failure to follow maintenance schedules and instructions, or use of replacement parts which aren't equivalent to the originally installed part; or

d) Misfueling: The use of leaded fuel in a vehicle requiring "unleaded fuel only" or use of other improper fuels.

If any of the above have taken place, and seem likely to have caused the particular problem which you seek to have repaired, then the manufacturer can deny coverage.

If your claim is denied for a valid reason, you may have to pay the costs of the diagnosis. Therefore, you should always ask for an estimate of the cost of the diagnosis before work starts.

Can anyone besides a dealer perform scheduled maintenance?

Yes! Scheduled maintenance can be done by anyone with the knowledge and ability to perform the repair. For your protection, we recommend that you refer to your owner's manual to specify the necessary items to your mechanic. And get an itemized receipt or work order for your records.

You can also maintain the vehicle yourself, as long as the maintenance is done in accordance with the manufacturer's instructions included with the vehicle. Make sure you keep receipts for parts and a maintenance log to verify your work.

Why maintenance is important to emissions control systems

Emission control has led to many changes in engine design. As a result, most vehicles don't require tune-ups and other maintenance as often. But some of the maintenance that is required enables your vehicle's emission controls to do their job properly.

Failure to do this emissions-related maintenance can cause problems. For example, failure to change your spark plugs during a 30,000-mile tune-up can lead to misfiring and eventual damage to your catalytic converter.

Vehicles that are well-maintained and tamper-free don't just pollute less - they get better gas mileage, which saves you money. Regular maintenance also gives you better performance and catches engine problems early, before they get serious - and costly.

How do you make a warranty claim?

Bring your vehicle to a dealer or any facility authorized by the manufacturer to perform warranty repairs to the vehicle or its emissions control system. Notify them that you wish to obtain a repair under the Performance Warranty. You should have with you a copy of your emissions test report as proof of your vehicle's failure to pass the emissions test. And bring your vehicle's warranty statement for reference. The warranty statement should be in your owner's manual or in a separate booklet provided by the manufacturer with the vehicle.

How do you know if your claim has been accepted as valid?

After presenting your vehicle for a Performance Warranty claim, give the manufacturer 30 days to either repair the vehicle or notify you that the claim has been denied. If your inspection/maintenance program dictates a shorter deadline, the manufacturer must meet that shorter deadline. Because of the significance of these deadlines, you should get written verification when you present your vehicle for a Performance Warranty claim.

The manufacturer can accept your claim and repair the vehicle, or deny the claim outright, or deny it after examining the vehicle. In either case, the reason for denial must be provided in writing with the notification.

What happens if the manufacturer misses the deadline for a written claim denial?

You can agree to extend the deadline, or it may be automatically extended if the delay is beyond the control of the manufacturer. Otherwise, a missed deadline means the manufacturer forfeits the right to deny the claim. You are then entitled to have the repair performed at the facility of your choice, at the manufacturer's expense.

If your claim is accepted, do you have to pay for either the diagnosis or the repair?

You can't be charged for any costs for diagnosis of a valid warranty claim. Additionally, when a manufacturer repairs, replaces or adjusts any part under the Performance Warranty, you may not be charged for any parts, labor or miscellaneous items necessary to complete the repair. But if your vehicle needs other repairs that aren't covered by your emissions warranty, you can have that work performed by any facility you choose.

What happens to your warranty if you use leaded gasoline?

When leaded gas is used in vehicles requiring unleaded, some emission controls (especially the catalyst) are quickly damaged. Lead deposits also form inside the engine, decreasing spark plug life and increasing maintenance costs.

If your use of leaded fuel leads to an emissions failure, your warranty won't cover the repair costs. So using leaded fuel will not only ruin some of your emission controls, it will cost you money.

Can your regular repair facility perform warranty repairs?

If you want to have the manufacturer pay for a repair under the Performance Warranty, you MUST bring the vehicle to a facility authorized by the vehicle manufacturer to repair either the vehicle or its emission control systems. If your regular facility isn't authorized by the manufacturer, tell your mechanic to get your "go-ahead" before performing any repair that might be covered by the Performance Warranty.

Do you have to provide proof of maintenance when you make a warranty claim?

You're not automatically required to show maintenance receipts when you make a warranty claim. But if the manufacturer feels your failure to perform scheduled maintenance has caused your emissions failure, you can be required to present your receipts or log as proof that the work was in fact done.

If you buy a used vehicle, how do you know whether it's been properly maintained?

When you buy a used vehicle, try to get the maintenance receipts or log book from the previous owner. Also ask for the owner's manual, warranty or maintenance booklet, and any other information that came with the vehicle when it was new. If the seller doesn't have these documents, you can buy them from the manufacturer.

To guarantee future warranty protection for your vehicle, conform to the maintenance schedule provided by the manufacturer.

Does the warranty cover parts that must be replaced as a part of regularly scheduled maintenance?

Parts with a scheduled replacement interval that's less than the length of the warranty, such as "replace at 15,000 miles or 12 months," are warranted only up to the first replacement point. Parts with a maintenance instruction that requires them to be "checked and replaced if necessary," or some similar classification, receive full coverage under the warranty. However, should you fail to check a part at the specified interval, and should that part cause another part to fail, the second part will NOT be covered, because your failure to maintain the first part caused the failure.

The manufacturer may or may not require that such replacement parts be a specific brand. But if a test failure is caused by the use of a part of inferior quality to the original equipment part, the manufacturer may deny your warranty claim.

What if the manufacturer won't honor a claim you believe to be valid?

First, use the information contained above to make your case to the dealer. Then follow the appeals procedure outlined in your vehicle's warranty statement or owner's manual. Every manufacturer employs warranty representatives who handle such appeals. The manufacturer must either allow your claim or give you a written denial, including the specific reasons for denying your claim, within 30 days, or you are entitled to free repairs.

Also, the Environmental Protection Agency is authorized to investigate the failure of manufacturers to comply with the terms of this warranty. If you've followed the manufacturer's procedures and you're still unimpressed with the reason for denial of your claim, contact the EPA at:

Warranty Complaint
Field Operations and Support Division (6406J)
U.S. Environmental Protection Agency
401 M Street SW
Washington, D.C. 20460

California drivers can contact the California Air Resources Board (CARB) at:

California Air Resources Board
9528 Telstar Avenue
El Monte, CA 91731

Finally, you're also entitled to pursue any independent legal actions which you consider appropriate to obtain coverage under the Performance Warranty.

3 Computer basics

Engine control computer

Without the engine control computer, also referred to as a microprocessor, today's cars and trucks could never have met the challenge of complying with the ever-tighter emissions and mileage restrictions imposed by government regulations. Computers have done the job so well that manufacturers are now entrusting them with more vehicle operations. On later models the computer may also control transmission, anti-lock brake, traction control, anti-theft device, air bag system, cruise controls and some other electrical system functions as well. The application of computer controls to modern cars and trucks has, in short, revolutionized their operation.

Computers come in all sizes and shapes and are generally located under the dashboard, around the fenderwells or under the front seat **(see illustration)**. The Environmental Protection Agency (EPA) and the Federal government require all automobile manufacturers to warranty their emissions systems for 5 years or 50,000 miles. This broad emissions warranty coverage will allow most computer malfunctions to be repaired by the dealership at their cost. Keep this in mind when diagnosing and/or repairing any system problems.

While the computer is capable of lightning-fast decision making, it can't actually do anything, and this includes finding out what is going around it. For that, the computer needs a wide array of sensors (described in Chapter 8) to feed it information.

The computer constantly adjusts engine operation while the engine is running, by comparing the stream of data from the sensors with its own programming. This programming consists of two types of information: fixed and variable. Fixed values include computer system operating instructions and vehicle constants such as number of cylinders, emissions equipment and transmission and gear ratios. Variable information is specific to vehicle operation at a given moment and includes engine and vehicle speed, airflow, throttle angle and ignition timing.

3.1 Removed from the vehicle, the computer doesn't look like much but it's the brain that controls your engine and often much more

PROM

On most American vehicles, fixed information is located in the computer controller itself, while variable information is contained on a separate memory chip called the Progammable Read Only Memory (PROM). This is also sometimes referred to as a calibrator or calibration assembly. Some models may use more than one PROM module.

This system allows a manufacturer to save money by using a single computer controller over a wide range of vehicles and then make it model and vehicle specific by inserting the comparatively inexpensive PROM. Since the PROM chip simply plugs into the computer controller, reprogramming of variable information in the field or at the dealer is a simple matter.

EPROM and EEPROM

Great care has to be taken with the fragile PROM chips however, so on later models an erasable PROM (EPROM) is used. On the EPROM, the memory area of the computer is erased by exposing it to ultraviolet light and then reprogrammed. Even later models feature an electrically erasable PROM (EEPROM), allowing a dealership to easily update or change memory to the very latest specification.

Adaptive memory

Later computers have an adaptive memory feature that adjusts for variables such as component wear, fuel quality and production inconsistencies. This adaptive memory feature allows the computer to make minor operating adjustments to compensate and maintain driveability when certain operating values are outside the program parameters.

The adaptive memory changes are stored in the computer Random Access Memory (RAM), and is lost whenever the battery is disconnected. If this happens, the driver simply drives normally for about 20 miles until the computer "relearns" the adaptive memory program changes.

Computer precautions

Computers have delicate internal circuitry which is easily damaged when subjected to excessive voltage, static electricity or magnetism. When diagnosing any electrical problems in a circuit connected to the computer, remember that most computers operate at a relatively low voltage (about 5 volts).

Observe the following precautions whenever working on or around the computer and/or engine control system circuits:

1 Do not damage the wiring or any electrical connectors in such a way as to cause it to ground or touch another source of voltage.

2 Do not use any electrical testing equipment (such as an ohmmeter) that is powered by a six-or-more-volt battery. The excessive voltage might cause an electrical component in the computer to burn or short. Use only a ten mega-ohm impedence multimeter when working on engine control circuits.

3 Do not remove or troubleshoot the computer without the proper tools and information, because any mistakes can void your warranty and/or damage components.

4 All spark plug wires should be at least one inch away from any sensor circuit or control wires. An unexpected problem in computer circuits is magnetic fields that send false signals to the computer, frequently resulting in hard-to-identify performance problems. Although there have been cases of high-power lines or transformers interfering with the computer, the most common cause of this problem in the sensor circuits is the position of the spark plug wires (too close to the computer wiring).

5 Use special care when handling or working near the computer. Remember that static electricity can cause computer damage by creating a very large surge in voltage (see *Static electricity and electronic components* below).

Static electricity and electronic components

Caution: *Static electricity can damage or destroy the computer and other electronic components. Read the following information carefully.*

Static electricity can cause two types of damage. The first and most obvious is complete failure of the device. The other type of damage is much more subtle and harder to detect as an electrical component failure. In this situation the integrated circuit is degraded and can become weakened over a period of time. It may perform erratically or appear as another component's intermittent failure.

The best way to prevent static electricity damage is to drain the charge from your body by grounding your body to the frame or body of the vehicle and then working strictly on a static-free area. A static-control wrist strap properly worn and grounded to the frame or body of the vehicle will drain the charges from your body, thereby preventing them from discharging into the electronic components. Consult your dealer parts department for a list of the static protection kits available.

Remember, it is often not possible to feel a static discharge until the charge level reaches 3,000 volts! It is very possible to be damaging the electrical components without even knowing it!

Computer information sensors

The information sensors are a series of highly specialized switches and temperature-sensitive electrical devices that transform physical properties of the engine such as temperature (air, coolant and fuel), air mass (air volume and density), air pressure and engine speed into electrical signals that can be translated into workable parameters for the computer.

Each sensor is designed specifically to detect data from one particular area of the engine; for example, the Mass Airflow Sensor is positioned inside the air intake system and it measures the volume and density of the incoming air to help the computer calculate how much fuel is needed to maintain the correct air/fuel mixture.

Diagnosing problems with the information sensors can easily overlap other management systems because of the inter-relationships of the components. For instance, if a fuel-injected engine is experiencing a vacuum leak, the computer will often release a diagnostic code that refers to the oxygen sensor and/or its circuit. The first thought would be "Well, I'd better change my oxygen sensor." Actually, the intake leak is allowing more air into the combustion chamber than is desired and the fuel/air mixture has become lean. The oxygen sensor relays the information to the computer which cannot compensate for the increased amount of oxygen and, as a result, the computer will store a fault code for the oxygen sensor. Refer to Chapter 8 for more information on the sensors.

4 Computer Controlled Systems

1 General information

One of the primary values of computers is the ability to integrate the operation of two or more, sometimes many more, individual systems to form a larger and more complex system. For example, we know that centrifugal and vacuum advance mechanisms can control spark timing relative to engine speed and load. We also know that fuel metering is controlled by air flow, and that manifold or ported vacuum can manage basic EGR flow. Integrating such independent systems through a computer, provides faster, more precise regulation of each system, and allows the computer to calculate the effect of changing several variable factors at the same time.

By the late 1970's, many vehicles' ignition systems were controlled by a computer. In quick succession, most other engine systems were also placed under computer control. Since 1980, most vehicles sold in the US have been equipped with computerized engine management systems to help reduce emissions.

No matter how fancy the name, no matter how sophisticated the system, all engine management systems consist of the same three basic types of components: 1) information sensors, 2) a computer and 3) actuators or controls.

1 Every engine management system has a wide variety of

1.1 One of the likely places to find the air temperature sensors is the air cleaner housing, such as this Manifold Air Temperature (MAT) sensor on a Pontiac Fiero - air temperature sensors are also often located in the intake manifold or intake runners

information sensors (as many as a dozen or more) which monitor various operating conditions of the engine (such as coolant temperature, intake air temperature, throttle position angle, engine speed, etc.) **(see illustrations)**.

1.2 How do you know you've got the correct sensor on a vehicle such as this Ford Thunderbird, on which the air temperature sensor is installed right next to another sensor, and they're identical in appearance? Try to determine whether it's installed in a coolant passage in the intake manifold (a coolant temperature sensor) or an air intake runner (an air temperature sensor)

1.3 Coolant temperature sensors, such as this Engine Coolant Temperature (ECT) sensor on a Plymouth Sundance, are usually installed in the thermostat housing

2   The sensors transmit this data, as a variable voltage signal, to a computer (see illustrations) which analyzes this information by comparing it to the "map" inside its memory. The map is simply a program which very specifically details how the engine should be operating under every conceivable operating condition (cold starts, warmups, acceleration, deceleration, etc.).

3   If the computer notes a discrepancy between what's happening and what the map says SHOULD be happening

1.4 This coolant temperature sensor on a Ford Probe is installed in the intake manifold, but note that it's protruding into a coolant passage in the manifold which leads to the thermostat housing in the foreground

1.5 Like air temperature sensors, coolant temperature sensors, such as this one (arrow) between two other sensors on a Pontiac Grand Am, can be difficult to identify - if you're unable to identify the sensor you're looking for using the installation location method, trace the electrical leads back to the main harness or to the device to which they're attached: if that doesn't work, try counting the number and color of electrical leads, then refer to a wiring diagram

1.6 Crankshaft position sensors are installed either in the side of the block, such as this unit on a Chevrolet Beretta, next to the crankshaft at the front of the engine . .

1.7 . . or inside the distributor assembly, such as this unit on a Nissan pickup truck

1.8 Knock sensors, such as this Electronic Spark Control (ESC) sensor on a Chevrolet Corvette, are usually installed in the block, where they can detect harmful detonation in the combustion chamber

1.9 One of the earliest air flow meter designs is the Bosch plate-type unit (arrow) found on all German vehicles with continuous injection (CIS, CIS-E), such as this unit on a VW Fox with Bosch CIS-E; finding the air flow meter on one of these is easy: it's always right next to the fuel distributor, the device with all the braided-stainless-steel fuel lines attached

under a given set of circumstances, the computer transmits commands, again in the form of voltage data, to a smaller group of devices known as actuators, or controls (see illustrations), which alter the operating conditions of the engine (rich or lean the fuel/air mixture, advance or retard the ignition, open or close the EGR valve, open or close the EVAP canister purge valve, etc.).

And that's it! The details vary somewhat from system to system, but not much. All engine management systems use the same three types of components - a bunch of sensors, one computer and several actuators. So don't make engine management systems more complicated than they really are.

1.10 Vane-type air flow meters, such as this unit (arrow) on a Ford Explorer, use a spring-loaded swinging door connected to a variable resistor to send a variable voltage signal to the computer - this type of air flow meter is always located downstream from the air cleaner hosing and upstream from the throttle body

1.11 The latest air flow meters, such as this Mass Air Flow (MAF) unit on a Chevrolet Corsica, use a heated resistance wire to measure air flow by sending a voltage signal to the computer that varies in proportion to the mass of air passing over the wire - this type of air flow meter is also located between the air cleaner housing and the throttle body

1.12 Some air flow meters, such as this unit on a Nissan pickup, are mounted on the right side of the throttle body - these units also use a hot wire to measure air flow mass, but they re-route some of the air entering the throttle into a side passage, where the wire is located

1.13 Manifold Absolute Pressure (MAP) sensor, such as this Chevrolet Corsica unit, are usually a black plastic box located on the firewall, and usually have the same parts:

1   *MAP sensor assembly*
2   *Mounting screws (some units are simply clipped into a bracket)*
3   *MAP sensor vacuum line (goes to intake manifold vacuum)*
4   *MAP sensor electrical connector (usually goes to main harness)*

1.14 Oxygen sensors are easy to find (but not always easy to get to): They're always in the exhaust system, somewhere between the exhaust manifold(s) and the catalytic converter(s)

1.15 The Throttle Position Sensor (TPS) is always mounted on the carburetor or throttle body, usually right on the end of the throttle valve shaft, such as this TBI-mounted unit on a Chevrolet full-size pickup

1.16 Computers can be anywhere there's room, but there are three common locations: Many are installed beneath the right side of the dash - usually right under the glove box, as in this Pontiac Grand Am (arrows point to mounting bolt locations)

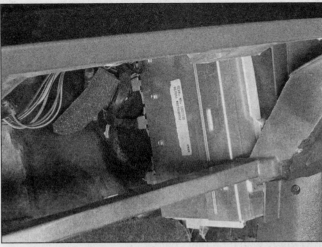

1.17 Another likely location is behind the kick panel (the small triangular area just in front of the door and beneath the extreme right end of the dash) as shown on this Chevrolet Corsica

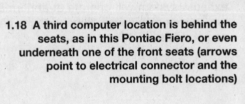

1.18 A third computer location is behind the seats, as in this Pontiac Fiero, or even underneath one of the front seats (arrows point to electrical connector and the mounting bolt locations)

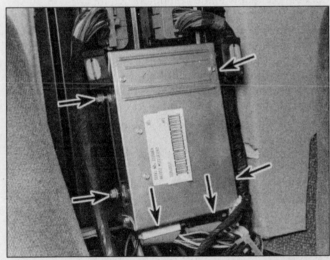

1.19 Ignition system computers, such as this GM Electronic Spark Control (ESC) module on a Chevrolet pickup, are usually on the firewall - but even if they're not, you can always identify them by their large multi-pin connector which connects them to a knock sensor, the ignition coil, the battery, etc. (arrows point to electrical connector and the mounting bolt locations)

1.20 Look for control solenoids in arrays, such as this one on a Dodge Dakota - this computer-controlled switching solenoid controls the vacuum signal to the switch/relief valve on the air injection system

System precautions

When working with the low voltage computer system there are some simple precautions to remember:

1   Never attempt to energize a computer sensor with battery voltage, the sensor and/or the computer will be damaged.

2   Whenever the automobile battery cable(s) are disconnected the memory in the computer will be lost, only driving will allow the computer to relearn on its own. During this relearning period the vehicle may feel kind of sluggish and exhibit poor driveability symptoms. **Caution:** *If the stereo in your vehicle is equipped with an anti-theft system, make sure you have the correct activation code before disconnecting the battery.*

3   Always disconnect the battery cables when charging the battery with a battery charger.

4   Never connect or disconnect the battery cable (s) with the ignition switch in the ON position.

5   Never allow any form of a liquid, (water included) to come in contact with the computer.

6   Never puncture a wire with a test light or volt meter. Puncturing the insulation on a wire can cause poor or intermittent electrical connections. For testing at the connectors, make contact with the metal terminal, between the rubber seal and the wire insulation.

7   Short-circuiting the positive (+) probe between a connector terminal and ground could cause damage to the

1.21 This computer-controlled Auxiliary Air Control (AAC valve is located on the intake manifold on a Nissan Maxima - as coolant temperature rises, the valve gradually closes, restricting auxiliary air flow

vehicle wiring, sensor(s) and computer.

8   Operation of any type, including idling, should be avoided if engine misfiring occurs. Under this condition the exhaust system will operate at abnormally high temperature, which may cause damage to the catalyst or electrical components.

2 Exhaust Gas Recirculation (EGR) system

The EGR system controls nitrogen oxide (NOx) emissions. The system operates by allowing a specific amount of inert exhaust gas to pass from the exhaust manifold into the intake manifold, diluting the air/fuel mixture being delivered to the combustion chambers.

EGR valves are designed specifically to recirculate the exhaust gas into the air/fuel mixture, thereby diluting the air/fuel mixture enough to keep the NOx compounds within breathable limits. It was discovered that short peak combustion temperatures create NOx. By blending an inert gas with the air/fuel mixture, scientists discovered that the rate of combustion slowed down, the high temperatures were reduced and the NOx compounds were kept within limits.

Modern engines are equipped with oxidation/reduction catalysts and feedback carburetion or fuel-injection systems that keep the NOx compounds to a minimum. Even with these newer, more efficient systems, the EGR system is still necessary to reduce the excess emissions.

Early EGR systems are made up of a vacuum-operated valve that admits exhaust gas into the intake manifold (EGR valve), a hose that is connected to a carburetor port above the throttle plates **(see illustration)** and a Thermostatic Vacuum Switch (TVS) spliced into a pipe that is threaded into the radiator or, more typically, into the coolant passage near the thermostat. The TVS detects the operating temperature of the engine.

At idle, the throttle plate blocks the vacuum port so no vacuum reaches the EGR valve and it remains closed. As the throttle uncovers the port in the carburetor or throttle body, the vacuum signal reaches the EGR valve and slowly opens the valve, allowing exhaust gases to circulate into the intake manifold.

Since the exhaust gas causes a rough idle and stalling when the engine is cold, the TVS only allows vacuum to the EGR valve when the engine is at normal operating temperature.

2.1 Some EGR control solenoids are located on small brackets which can be mounted anywhere in the engine compartment - the EGR control solenoid, or vacuum cut solenoid, is on the left on this Nissan Maxima (the control solenoid on the right is for the Air Injection Valve)

2.2 This EGR control solenoid on a Ford Tempo is bolted to a bracket mounted on the left strut tower, another popular mounting point for solenoids

Also, when the pedal is pushed to the floor on acceleration, there is very little ported vacuum available, resulting in very little mixture dilution that will interfere with power output.

The EGR valve on early carbureted engines without computer controls, acts solely in response to the temperature and venturi vacuum characteristics of the operating engine. The EGR valve on engines with computerized controls acts on direct command from the computer, after the computer has determined that all the working parameters (air temperature, coolant temperature, EGR valve position, fuel/air mixture etc.) of the engine are satisfactory. EGR valves on computerized vehicles normally have a computer-controlled solenoid in line between the valve and vacuum source. They also often have a position sensor on the EGR valve that informs the computer what position the EGR valve is in.

There are two common types of EGR valves; ported vacuum EGR valves and backpressure EGR valves. Besides the common ported type EGR valve described in the previous paragraphs, there are basically two types of backpressure EGR valves; The most common type is the positive backpressure valve and the other is the negative backpressure valve. It is important to know the difference between positive and negative backpressure valves because they work differently and they are tested differently. Never substitute a positive for a negative backpressure EGR valve. Always install original equipment from the manufacturer if it is necessary to replace the EGR valve.

Positive backpressure EGR valve

This type of valve is used largely on domestic models. It uses exhaust pressure to regulate EGR flow by means of a vacuum control valve. The stem of the EGR valve is hollow and allows backpressure to bear onto the bottom of the diaphragm. When sufficient exhaust backpressure is present, the diaphragm moves up and closes off the control valve, allowing the full vacuum signal to be applied to the upper portion of the EGR diaphragm. This opens the valve and allows recirculation to occur during heavy loads.

Be careful not to incorrectly diagnose this type of EGR valve. Because backpressure must be present to close the bleed hole, it is not possible to operate the EGR valve with a vacuum pump at idle or when the engine is stopped. The valve is acting correctly when it refuses to move when vacuum is applied or it refuses to hold vacuum. Remember that anything that changes the pressure in the exhaust stream will disturb the calibration of the backpressure system. This includes glass-pack mufflers, headers or even a clogged catalytic converter.

To distinguish this valve, turn the valve upside down and note the pattern of the diaphragm plate. Positive backpressure valves have a slightly raised X-shaped rib. Negative backpressure EGR valves are raised considerably

higher. On some GM EGR valves, the only way to distinguish each type is by a letter next to the date code and part number. N means negative while P means positive.

Negative backpressure EGR valve

In this system, the bleed hole is normally closed. When exhaust backpressure drops (reduced load), the bleed valve opens and reduces the vacuum above the diaphragm, cutting the vacuum to the EGR valve. The negative backpressure EGR valve is similar to the positive backpressure EGR valve but operates in the OPPOSITE way. This type of valve is typically used on engines that have less than natural backpressure such as high-performance vehicles with free-flowing mufflers and large-diameter exhaust tubing.

Other types of EGR valves

Dual-diaphragm EGR valve

This EGR valve receives ported vacuum to the upper portion of the vacuum diaphragm while the lower portion receives manifold vacuum. The simultaneous response characteristics control both throttle position and engine load. The dual-diaphragm system is easily recognized by the two vacuum lines attached to the EGR valve.

Ford air pressure EGR valve

Most commonly installed on 1978 and 1979 Ford EEC-I systems, this type of EGR valve is operated by the thermactor air pump pressure instead of vacuum. Pump output is routed to the underside of the diaphragm. Some models are equipped with an EGR position sensor also.

Ford electronic control EGR valve

This EGR valve resembles the air pressure type but it is dependent on the computer and the EGR position sensors to detect the correct conditions and regulate the EGR valve angle.

Chrysler/Mitsubishi dual EGR valve

Most commonly equipped on the 2.6L silent shaft engine, this type of EGR valve uses both a primary and secondary EGR valve mounted at right angles to each other. This system allows for accurate measurement of the exhaust gases.

Computer controlled EGR valves

On the newer type computerized EGR systems, the EGR valve is regulated by the use of different sensors, transducers or vacuum solenoids directly linked to the EGR valve. Here is a list with a brief explanation for each type:

Remote backpressure transducer

This device is not mounted inside the EGR valve, but instead it is found in the vacuum line leading to the EGR

2.5 This Isuzu pickup backpressure transducer is typical of many models - it's on the intake manifold, near the distributor

2.7 View of an EGR valve equipped with an EGR valve position sensor mounted on the top - the mechanical motion of the pintle is converted to a voltage value and relayed to the computer

valve **(see illustration)**. At idle or light loads, the transducer bleeds off the signal to prevent recirculation to the EGR valve.

Electronic pressure sensor

This capacitive sensor converts exhaust system backpressure into an analog voltage signal that is sent directly to the computer for analysis. This type of pressure sensor is commonly found on newer EEC-IV Ford systems.

Venturi vacuum amplifier

Venturi vacuum from the carburetor indicates engine load and air consumption, but it is inherently too weak to transfer as information to the EGR system. By amplifying the venturi vacuum, the EGR valve is regulated by strong manifold vacuum. These systems also store vacuum in a reservoir for an extra supply when the engine is idling.

Wide open throttle valve

This device is located in-line between the EGR valve and the vacuum source. Controlled by a signal from the carburetor venturi, the wide open throttle valve bleeds off the signal to the EGR valve at wide open throttle to eliminate any mixture dilution and any power loss.

Air cleaner temperature sensor

This sensor cuts off vacuum to the EGR valve until a certain temperature is reached. Instead of reading coolant temperature, the sensor detects air temperature. This is commonly used on carburetor spark port vacuum systems.

Solenoid vacuum valve

This valve works directly with the computer to control the vacuum signal. It is found most commonly on the GM systems and it is referred to as "pulse width modulation."

Electronic vacuum regulator

Instead of the on/off function of a solenoid vacuum valve, the electronic vacuum regulator adjusts vacuum to the EGR valve by way of the pressure sensor and the computer. This device is most commonly found on Ford EEC-III and EEC-IV systems.

Delay timer

This valve interrupts the vacuum to the EGR valve to prevent stalling when the engine is cold. The actual delay time can be anywhere from 30 to 90 seconds after the engine is started. The delay timer works in conjunction with a solenoid vacuum valve.

Charge temperature switch

This switch senses the temperature of the intake system also, but it acts strictly as an ON/OFF switch to prevent current from reaching the delay timer when the temperature is below 60-degrees F. This prevents any EGR mixture and consequently rough idle or stalling when cold. This system is commonly found on Chrysler emissions systems.

EGR valve position sensors

These sensors detect the exact position of the EGR valve and send the information to the computer **(see illustration)**. These sensors are discussed in detail in Section 9.

Electronic EGR valve

Some of the most recent designs (primarily from GM) employ an EGR valve that is not operated by vacuum at all - an electronic solenoid in the valve is operated electrically by the computer. Diagnosing systems with this type of valve requires specialized equipment and is beyond the scope of this manual.

3 Evaporative emissions control (EVAP, EEC or ECS) systems

Evaporating fuel accounts for up to 20% of a vehicle's potential pollution, so since 1971 Federal law has required Evaporative emissions control systems on most vehicles. The system traps fuel vapors that would normally escape into the atmosphere and re-routes them back into the engine where they are burned.

The system consists of a fuel tank with an air space for heat expansion that allows the vapors to collect and flow to the charcoal canister, the tank cap and associated hoses and tubes. The cap contains a check valve to provide pressure and vacuum relief to the system. On carbureted models, the float bowl has a vent which connects to the canister by a tube.

With the engine off, the vapors flow from the tank (and carburetor float bowl, on models so equipped) to the canister where they are absorbed in the charcoal until the engine is started. When the engine is running, the vapors are then purged from the canister and routed to the intake manifold or air cleaner and into the combustion chambers where they are burned.

The system operates using a purge control valve which allows engine vacuum to suck the vapors from the canister at the appropriate time while outside air enters the canister by way of a tube or filter **(see illustration)**. This purge valve is usually mounted on the canister body, but can also be located remotely or in a hose. Some earlier models have an air intake and filter at the bottom of the canister.

The operation of the purge valve is controlled on some models by solenoids and/or delay valves that make sure the vapors will be purged when the engine can burn them most efficiently. On later models, the system is controlled by the computer and operates in slightly different ways, depending on manufacturer.

On Chrysler models with the Single Module Engine Controller (SMEC) system, the controller grounds a solenoid when the engine is below operating temperature so no vacuum can reach the purge valve. When operating temperature is reached, this solenoid is de-energized so vacuum can then purge the fuel vapors through the fuel injection system or carburetor.

The computer on later model GM vehicles also uses a solenoid valve to operate the purge valve when the engine is hot, after it has been running for a specified period, and at certain speeds and throttle positions. The purging increases until the computer receives a rich fuel condition signal from the oxygen sensor (the vapors are burned), then purging regulated until the signal decreases.

Operation of the Ford EEC IV system is similar to the GM system. It purges whenever the engine is at normal operating temperature and off idle.

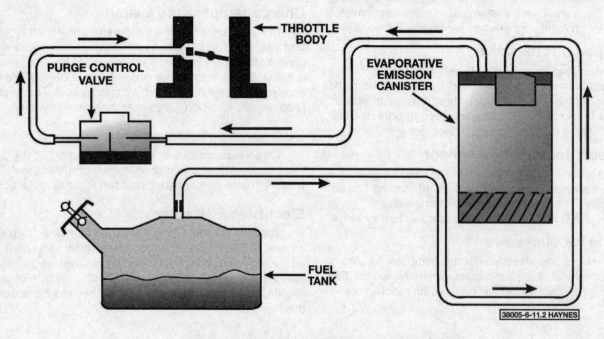

PURGE CONTROL VALVE

THROTTLE BODY

EVAPORATIVE EMISSION CANISTER

FUEL TANK

38005-6-11.2 HAYNES

3.1 A typical Evaporative emissions control system

4 Positive Crankcase Ventilation (PCV) system

When the engine is running, a certain amount of the fuel/air mixture escapes from the combustion chamber past the piston rings into the crankcase as blow-by gases. The Positive Crankcase Ventilation (PCV) system is designed to reduce the resulting hydrocarbon emissions (HC) by routing them from the crankcase to the intake manifold and combustion chambers, where they are burned during engine operation.

The PCV system is basically a check valve with hoses for directing crankcase blow-by back into the combustion chambers in the engine. It consists of a hose which directs fresh air from the air cleaner into the crankcase, the PCV valve (basically a one-way valve that allows the blow-by gases to pass back into the engine) and associated hoses **(see illustration)**. On some models a separate filter for the PCV system is located in the air cleaner housing. Some models have a fixed orifice (usually in a hose) instead of a PCV valve that must be kept clear or rough idling and stalling can result.

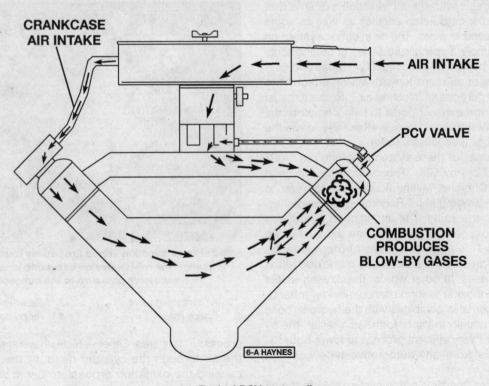

4.1 Typical PCV system flow

5 Air injection systems

This Section deals with the air injection systems that are present on earlier carbureted engines as well as some updated computerized engines. The air injection system on most vehicles is simply a specialized series of components (e.g., an air pump, pulley, drivebelt, injection tubes and several different types of air management valves) attached to the engine for the purpose of injecting air into the exhaust downstream from the exhaust ports to help complete the combustion of any unburned gases after they leave the combustion chamber **(see illustrations)**.

The formal names of these systems include the "AIR" (Air Injection Reaction) by GM, "Thermactor" by Ford and "Air Injection" by Chrysler. Mechanics commonly refer to this system as the "smog pump." Regardless of the names, their functions are the same. The air injection introduces fresh air, high in oxygen content, into the exhaust of an operating engine. This process causes further oxidation (burning) of the hydrocarbons and carbon monoxide left in the hot exhaust gases. In other words, the oxygen unites with the carbon monoxide to form carbon dioxide, a harmless gas. The oxygen also combines with the hydrocarbons to produce water, usually in vapor form. As a result, the air injection system is a very efficient process to lower both HC and CO emissions from any automotive type gasoline engine.

In some vehicles, the air injection system directs the air into the base of the exhaust manifold to assist the oxidation

5.2 The air injection valves are usually found near the air pump - the relief valve on this pump is used to vent excessive pressure to the atmosphere

1	Air switching valve	3	Relief valve
2	Check valve	4	Air pump

process in this area. Other vehicles have systems that inject the air through the cylinder head, at the exhaust ports, causing the oxidation process to begin within this area. Vehicles equipped with three-way catalytic converters often have air injected directly into the converter.

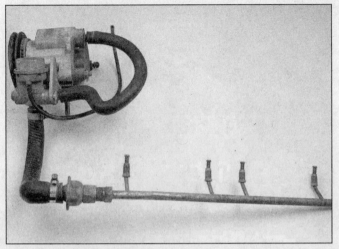

5.3 This is what the air pump and injection lines look like after they have been removed from the engine

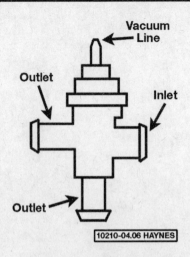

5.5 A typical diverter valve

Air injection systems are less common on modern engines. Manufacturers have designed newer systems that meet emission standards without air injection. Some engines are equipped with a passive (often called Pulse Air) system, which does not use an air pump. In this system, positive and negative exhaust pressures pull air into the exhaust system by way of special reed or check valves.

All things considered, the different systems serve one common purpose: to inject air into the exhaust system and help burn any fuel that did not ignite while in the combustion chamber.

By today's standards, the "smog pump" considerably reduces performance and increases gas mileage. For many years it was quite common to find many of the air injection systems completely removed from the engine and the exhaust ports capped with brass plugs! Eventually, the law required all air injection systems to be intact and ready to perform as originally intended. It became necessary to dig into the garage or even hunt wrecking yards for the pump, hoses and valves that were originally installed on the vehicle.

5.7 Thermactor system with air pump and Electronic Engine Controls (EEC)

1	Vacuum line to control solenoid	
2	Combination air bypass and air control valve hose	
3	Vacuum line to control solenoid	
4	Hose and check valve for catalytic converter (check valve not visible in photo)	
5	Hose and check valve for exhaust manifolds	
6	Air pump	

6 Heated air intake (Thermac and EFE) systems

Although coming under different names and using different techniques, these systems produce the same result: improving engine efficiency and reducing hydrocarbons during the initial warm-up period. Two different methods are used to achieve this goal: Thermostatic air intake (Thermac) and Early Fuel Evaporation (EFE). Thermac warms the air as it enters the air cleaner while EFE heats the air/fuel mixture in the intake manifold. Virtually all later models use some form of Thermac and/or EFE system.

Thermac

The Thermostatic air intake system improves driveability, reduces emissions and prevents carburetor icing in cold weather by directing hot air from around the exhaust manifold to the air cleaner intake **(see illustration)**. The Thermac system is made up of the air cleaner housing, a temperature sensor, a vacuum-operated damper door mechanism in the air cleaner snorkel, a flexible tube connected to the exhaust manifold and associated vacuum hoses **(see illustration)**.

When the engine is cold, the temperature sensor in the air cleaner is closed and full vacuum reaches the vacuum motor which holds the damper door shut so only air heated by the exhaust manifold can enter the snorkel. As the engine warms up, the temperature sensor opens, bleeding off the vacuum motor vacuum and allowing its internal spring to push the door down. This closes off the heated air and allows only cold outside air to enter the snorkel. The vacuum motor spring and vacuum balance one another so the air entering the air cleaner is always at optimum temperature for the best fuel vaporization.

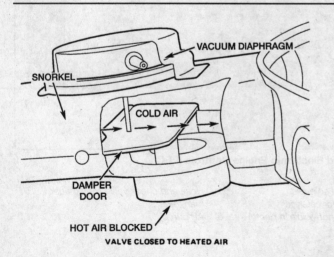

VALVE CLOSED TO HEATED AIR

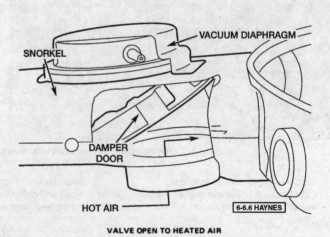

VALVE OPEN TO HEATED AIR

6.1 Thermac system operation: when the engine is cold, the temperature sensor allows intake manifold vacuum to the vacuum motor, which opens the damper door, allowing hot air to be drawn into the air cleaner through the heat cowl and air duct

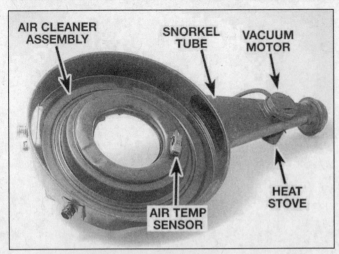

6.2 Typical Thermac system air cleaner components

6.3 The exhaust-type EFE heat valve is located in the exhaust pipe

EFE

Two types of EFE are used to heat the vaporized fuel in the intake manifold for improved driveability and emissions during the warm-up period after the engine is first started. One type routes exhaust heat from the exhaust manifold to warm the intake manifold, while the other electrically heats the fuel/air mixture as it enters the manifold.

The exhaust-type EFE uses a valve in the exhaust manifold to recirculate hot exhaust gases which are then used to pre-heat the carburetor and choke for better driveability and emissions. When the engine is cold, the valve is shut, forcing hot exhaust gases to heat the intake manifold until the engine warms up and the valve opens.

The exhaust-type EFE system consists of a heat riser valve in the exhaust manifold, a thermostatic actuator and heat shroud or duct which directs heat to the intake manifold and carburetor. On some models the actuator is simply a counterweighted heat riser with a thermostatic coil spring that contracts when cold, closing the valve and relaxes and opens it when hot **(see illustration)**. On others the actuator is operated by engine vacuum. On this type, when the engine is cold, the vacuum actuator on the valve is held closed by vacuum from a thermostatic switch in a coolant passage. As the coolant heats up, the switch opens, cutting off the vacuum and the actuator opens the valve.

The electrical-type EFE system is quite simple. It consists of an electrical heating element between the carburetor or fuel injection throttle body which heats and vaporizes the air/fuel mixture as it is drawn into the intake manifold **(see illustration)**. The system is made up of the electrical grid which is activated by a thermostatic switch screwed into a coolant passage or by the computer.

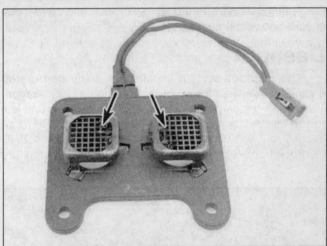

6.4 A typical electric EFE installed between the carburetor and intake manifold - arrows are to the heating grids

7 Carburetor control systems

This Section deals with the carburetor control systems that are installed onto carbureted engines to help control deceleration, acceleration, backfiring and emissions requirements. The carburetor controls installed on various carburetors will vary, but the purpose for each system is essentially similar. Here are some common carburetor control systems along with a brief explanation and some easy checks and adjustments.

Dashpot

The dashpot system installed on early carbureted engines slows the closing of the throttle on deceleration. This allows the carburetor to switch from the main fuel jets to the idle system, thereby preventing stalling due to an excessively rich air/fuel mixture. Also, the amount of HC (hydrocarbons) emissions is reduced. The air/fuel mixture becomes richer when the intake manifold vacuum suddenly rises when the throttle is closed. The high vacuum will draw fuel into the carburetor from the float bowl without any dilution of air from the air horn (venturi).

The dashpot is made up of a small chamber with a spring-loaded diaphragm and a plunger. The dashpot plunger is in contact with the throttle lever during the last stages of deceleration **(see illustration)**. When the lever contacts the plunger on deceleration, the lever exerts force on the plunger and air or hydraulic fluid (depending on the type of dashpot) slowly leaks out of the diaphragm through a small hole. This allows the throttle plate to close slowly.

Some dashpot components are adjustable while others are not **(see illustration)**. Consult a *Haynes Automotive Repair Manual* for the exact procedure. Keep in mind that dashpots are often combined with other throttle devices into the same component **(see illustration 6.3)**.

7.1 A typical carburetor dashpot

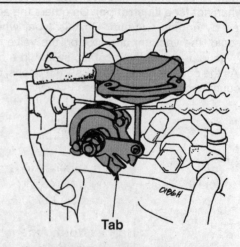

Tab

7.2 The dashpot on 1988 and later Hondas can be adjusted by bending this tab - other types of dashpots use screws for adjustment

Throttle positioner

Throttle positioners are used to control the engine's idle speed under various conditions. Some designs are vacuum actuated and others are electric solenoids. On vacuum-actuated positioners (which usually look the same as dashpots, except there is one or more vacuum hoses connected to it), some use vacuum to turn the positioner on while others use vacuum to turn it off. Be aware of this when checking vacuum conditions.

One basic type throttle positioner functions to prevent dieseling (engine run-on). This type is called a throttle stop solenoid or an idle stop solenoid. When the engine is started, the solenoid is energized and the plunger extends out, pushing against the throttle linkage. This forces the throttle plate to open slightly to the curb idle position. When the ignition switch is turned off, the throttle position solenoid is de-energized and the plunger returns to the normal position. The throttle plate closes completely and the air/fuel supply is cut off, effectively preventing dieseling.

Some throttle positioners are used to increase the curb idle speed to compensate for extra loads on the engine. In this situation, the throttle positioner is referred to as an idle speed-up solenoid or a throttle kicker. This type is often used on air-conditioned vehicles. When the air conditioner is switched on, the relay energizes the solenoid, which extends its plunger farther onto the throttle plate, thereby raising the idle speed. This keeps the engine running at a higher rpm to control emissions levels.

Throttle positioners are also used to control idle speed when the automatic transmission is engaged. A relay in the Park/Neutral switch signals the solenoid to raise the idle speed when the transmission is in gear. This opens the throttle slightly to compensate for the increased load on the engine.

Another type of system is sometimes used on vehicles equipped with power steering. When the steering wheel is turned while the vehicle is stationary and idling, the positioner solenoid raises the idle speed, compensating for the additional load the power steering pump is placing on the engine. This type of system has a switch located on the steering gear, power steering pump or power steering pressure hose. The switch completes the circuit to the solenoid when there's power steering fluid pressure at the switch.

ISC (Idle Speed Control) motor

The ISC motor is a more advanced version of a throttle positioner (see above). The motor is under direct control of the computer, which has the desired idle speed programmed into its memory. The computer compares the actual idle speed from the engine (taken from the distributor or crankshaft position sensor ignition impulses) to the desired rpm reference in memory. When the two do not match, the ISC plunger is moved in or out. This automatically adjusts the throttle to hold an idle speed independent of engine loads.

Many ISC motors have a throttle contact switch at the end of the plunger. The position of the switch determines whether or not the ISC should control idle speed. When the throttle lever is resting against the ISC plunger, the switch contacts are closed, at which time the computer moves the ISC motor to the programmed idle speed. When the throttle lever is not contacting the ISC plunger, the switch contacts are open and the ECM stops sending idle speed commands and the driver controls engine speed.

Fuel deceleration valve

The fuel deceleration valve is designed to prevent backfire during deceleration. This device opens a separate air/fuel mixture passage in the carburetor to dilute the fuel charge with additional air. When the intake manifold vacuum rises, the valve moves up to allow a mixture of air and fuel from the carburetor to flow into the intake manifold (see illustration). The valve provides enough mixture to maintain proper combustion and prevent unburned fuel from being released out the tailpipe.

Some deceleration valves are not attached directly to the carburetor but accomplish the same results (see illustration). This type of valve has a diaphragm housing on one end. A control manifold vacuum line is attached to a port on the lower portion of the valve. Other ports on the valve are connected to the intake manifold and air cleaner. When deceleration causes an increase in manifold vacuum, the diaphragm opens the deceleration valve and allows air to pass from the air cleaner to the intake manifold, leaning out the fuel mixture and preventing exhaust system backfire.

Automatic choke

Automatic choke systems use a bimetal, heat-sensitive element to control choke valve position, and most modern choke systems also have an electric heater to speed warming up the bimetal element (this causes the choke to disengage more quickly, helping reduce emissions). The bimetal element operates a choke valve which closes the carburetor air horn and is synchronized with the throttle plate(s). When the engine is cold, the choke valve closes and the throttle plate opens (operated by the fast idle cam) sufficiently to provide a rich mixture and an increased idle speed for easy starting. Many automatic choke systems are equipped with a choke breaker diaphragm that opens the choke valve when the engine is accelerating and the engine is cold. This prevents the engine from bogging from insufficient airflow.

HIC (Hot Idle Compensator) valve

On some vehicles, when the engine is excessively hot, a hot idle compensator opens an air passage to lean the fuel/air mixture (see illustration). This increases the idle

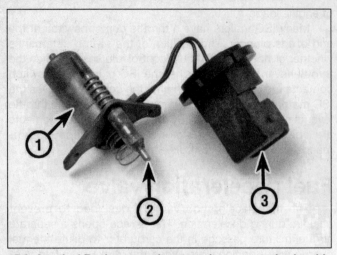

7.9 A typical Rochester carburetor mixture control solenoid assembly consists of:

1 *The mixture control solenoid*
2 *The adjustment screw*
3 *The electrical connector*

Mixture control solenoid

In the late 1970's, the feedback carburetor was introduced to reduce emissions on carbureted vehicles. This system incorporates a computer which controls certain solenoids and valves on the carburetor. The main solenoid controlled by computer is the mixture control solenoid. It is an electronically controlled metering rod that varies the amount of fuel that is allowed to pass into the main fuel jets of the carburetor **(see illustration)**. Some solenoids are mounted vertically and others are mounted horizontally. The computer is programmed to turn the solenoid ON and OFF (cycle) ten times per second. These solenoids are generally referred to as duty-cycle solenoids. Each cycle lasts about 100 milliseconds. The amount of fuel metered into the main fuel jet or passage is directly determined by how many milliseconds the solenoid is ON during each cycle. The solenoid can be ON almost 100% of the time or OFF nearly 100% of the time.

Fuel cut-off solenoid

Fuel cut-off solenoids are mounted onto the carburetor to instantly shut off the fuel to the main jet as the ignition is switched OFF. This prevents engine run-on and unnecessary vibration and backfire.

speed, which in turn cools the engine and prevents excess fuel vaporization and consequently the release of unburned hydrocarbons. The compensator is controlled by a bimetallic strip which bends when it senses high temperatures, thereby opening the air passage.

8 Catalytic converter

The catalytic converter is a unique device because it promotes a reaction which changes the exhaust gases flowing through it without being affected itself. This catalytic reaction reduces the level of three major pollutants: Hydrocarbon (HC), Carbon Monoxide (CO) and Oxides of Nitrogen (NOx). By removing these major pollutants, the catalytic converter system allows the other fuel and emissions systems to be fine-tuned for optimum operation and driveability. These are controlled on later models by the computer and a network of engine sensors. This is called a "feedback" or "closed loop" system.

Catalytic converters are mounted in the exhaust system between the exhaust manifold and the muffler. Because they generate a lot of heat, they are surrounded by heat shields.

The catalytic elements in the converter are palladium, platinum and rhodium. By coating ceramic pellets in the bed of the converter or a ceramic honeycomb, a large surface area is provided for the gases to react on as they pass through the converter.

There are two basic types of converters: oxidation and reduction. On later models, they are combined into one unit called a three-way converter. An oxidation converter uses platinum and palladium to oxidize (add oxygen to) hydrocarbons and carbon monoxide, converting them to water vapor. Since oxidization converters have little effect on NOx, a reduction converter containing rhodium and platinum is used to convert (reduce) the oxygen in the NOx into nitrogen and carbon dioxide.

One stage of a typical three-way converter contains a reduction-oxidation catalyst using rhodium and platinum which controls NOx, HC and CO emissions. The second stage has only a platinum catalyst for controlling the remaining HC and CO emissions. On some models air is pumped directly into a chamber between the two stages **(see illustration)**.

As the gases flow through the converter, they start to burn rapidly at temperatures reaching 1600-degrees F. The extra oxygen needed to support such high temperatures is provided by the air injection system which pumps air into the exhaust system or the converter itself, or by a lean air/fuel ratio. Three-way catalysts use air switching valves to direct air to the manifold during the high-emissions warm-up mode to help burn the HC and CO. It then shifts the air injection to the chamber in the middle of the converter when NOx production begins (normal operating temperature is reached).

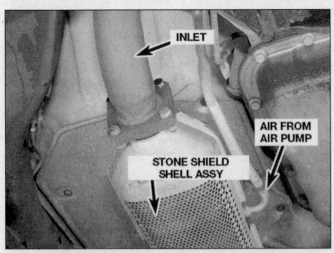

8.1 A typical three-way converter has two stages with air pumped into the chamber between the two

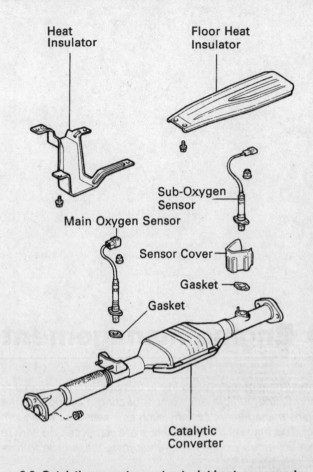

8.2 Catalytic converters put out a lot heat, so properly installed heat shields are very important

About replacement catalytic converters

The Environmental Protection Agency (EPA) closely regulates replacement catalytic converters, so be sure to familiarize yourself with their requirements before starting work. Not following the EPA guidelines is considered "tampering" with the emissions system and is punishable by a hefty fine. The EPA does realize that factory replacement catalytic converters are expensive so they have approved the installation of more reasonably priced aftermarket units under certain conditions.

The EPA says basically that you must use only a factory replacement converter on any vehicle which is still under the federally mandated emissions warranty (in which case the manufacturer would generally replace it at no charge anyway). You can use an approved aftermarket converter on any vehicles which are out of warranty and have damaged or non-functioning units.

Aftermarket converters and installation kits are available at auto parts stores. Also, most auto exhaust shops now install these aftermarket converters. Originally there were only a few "universal" units, but now the full range of aftermarket catalytic converters covers virtually every make and model. Be sure to check with the installer or auto parts store to make sure you are getting the right converter or kit for your car and that everything is in compliance with EPA regulations to avoid trouble later. The auto parts store should have all the necessary information along with advice on the hardware and pipes you'll need to do the job. Remember also that these replacement units come with a mandated lifetime guarantee.

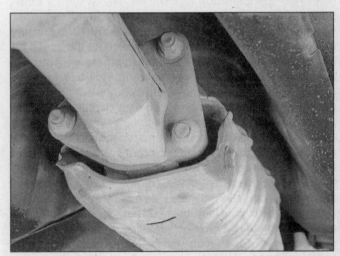

8.3 Most catalytic converters are installed using flanges like this

9 Engine management systems

Note: *Some of the procedures in this Section require you to operate the vehicle after disconnecting a portion of the engine management system (such as a sensor or a vacuum line). This may set trouble codes in the computer. Be sure to clear any trouble codes before returning the vehicle to normal service.*

This Section deals with the engine management systems used on modern, computer-controlled vehicles to meet new low-emission regulations. The system's computer, information sensors and output actuators interact with each other to collect, store and send data. Basically, the information sensors collect data (such as the intake air mass and/or temperature, coolant temperature, throttle position, exhaust gas oxygen content, etc.) and transmit data, in the form of varying electrical signals, to the computer. The computer compares the data with its "map" (the pre-programmed values of the engine's current operating conditions). If the data does not match the map, the computer sends signals to output actuators (fuel injectors or carburetor mixture control solenoid, Electronic Air Control Valve (EACV), Idle Speed Control (ISC) motor, etc.) which correct the engine's operation to match the map.

When the engine is warming up (and sensor input is not precise) or there is a malfunction in the system, the system operates in an "open loop" mode. In this mode, the computer does not rely on the sensors for input and sets the fuel/air mixture rich so the engine can continue operation until the engine warms up or repairs are made. **Note:** *The engine's thermostat rating and proper operation are critical to the operation of a computer-controlled vehicle. If the thermostat is rated at too low a temperature, is removed or stuck open, the computer may stay in "open loop" operation and emissions and fuel economy will suffer.*

The automotive computer

Automotive computers come in all sizes and shapes and are generally located under the dashboard, around the fenderwells or under the front seat. The Environmental Protection Agency (EPA) and the Federal government require all automobile manufacturers to warranty their emissions systems for 5 years or 50,000 miles. This broad emissions warranty coverage will allow most computer malfunctions to be repaired by the dealership at their cost. Keep this in mind when diagnosing and/or repairing any emissions systems problems.

Computers have delicate internal circuitry and are easily damaged when subjected to excessive voltage, static electricity or magnetism. When diagnosing any electrical problems in a circuit connected to the computer, remember that most computers operate at a relatively low voltage (about 5 volts).

Observe the following precautions whenever working on or around the computer and engine management system circuits:

1   Do not damage the wiring or any electrical connectors in such a way as to cause it to ground or touch another source of voltage.

2   Do not use any electrical testing equipment (such as an ohmmeter) powered by a six-or-more-volt battery. The excessive voltage might cause an electrical component in the computer to burn or short. Use only a digital multimeter with ten mega-ohms of internal impedance when working on engine management circuits.

3   Do not remove or troubleshoot the computer without the proper tools and information, because any mistakes can void your warranty and/or damage components.

4   All spark plug wires should be at least one inch away from any sensor circuit or control wires. An unexpected malfunction in a computer circuits can be caused by magnetic fields sending false signals to the computer, frequently resulting in hard-to-identify performance problems. Although there have been cases of high-power lines, transformers or cellular phones interfering with the computer, the most common cause of this problem in the sensor circuits is the position of the spark plug wires (too close to the computer wiring).

5   Use special care when handling or working near the computer. Remember that static electricity can cause computer damage by creating a very large surge in voltage (see Static electricity and electronic components below).

Static electricity and electronic components

Caution: *Static electricity can damage or destroy the computer and other electronic components. Read the following information carefully.*

Static electricity can cause two types of damage. The first and most obvious is complete failure of the device. The other type of damage is much more subtle and harder to detect as an electrical component failure. In this situation the integrated circuit is degraded and can become weakened over a period of time. It may perform erratically or appear as another component's intermittent failure.

The best way to prevent static electricity damage is to drain the charge from your body by grounding your body to the frame or body of the vehicle and then working strictly in a static-free area. A static-control wrist strap properly worn and grounded to the frame or body of the vehicle will drain the charges from your body, thereby preventing damage to the electronic components. Consult an electronics' supply store for a list of the static protection kits available.

Remember, it is often not possible to feel a static discharge until the charge level reaches 3,000 volts! It is very possible to damage the electrical components without even knowing it!

Information sensors

The information sensors are a series of highly specialized switches and temperature-sensitive electrical devices that transform physical properties of the engine such as temperature (air, coolant and fuel), air mass (air volume and density), air pressure and engine speed into electrical signals that can be translated into workable parameters for the computer.

Each sensor is designed specifically to detect data from one particular area of the engine; for example, the Mass Airflow Sensor is positioned inside the air intake system and it measures the volume and density of the incoming air to help the computer calculate how much fuel is needed to maintain the correct air/fuel mixture.

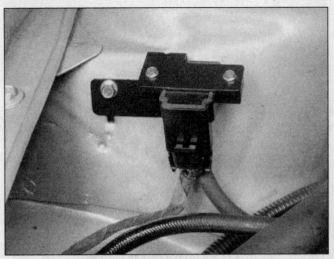

9.2 Here's a typical MAP sensor - this one, on a Plymouth Sundance, is located on the firewall, near the shock tower

Diagnosing problems with the information sensors can easily overlap other management systems because of the inter-relationships of the components. For instance, if a fuel-injected engine is experiencing a vacuum leak, the computer will often release a diagnostic code that refers to the oxygen sensor and/or its circuit. The first thought would be "Well, I'd better change my oxygen sensor." Actually, the intake leak is forcing more air into the combustion chamber than is required and the fuel/air mixture has become lean. The oxygen sensor relays the information to the computer which cannot compensate for the increased amount of oxygen and, as a result, the computer will store a fault code for the oxygen sensor.

MAP (Manifold Absolute Pressure) sensor

The MAP sensor reports engine load to the computer which uses the information to adjust spark advance and fuel enrichment **(see illustration)**. The MAP sensor measures intake manifold pressure and vacuum on the absolute scale (from zero instead of from sea-level atmospheric pressure [14.7 psi] as most gauges and sensors do). The MAP sensor reads vacuum and pressure through a hose connected to the intake manifold. A pressure-sensitive ceramic or silicon element and electronic circuit in the sensor generates a voltage signal that changes in direct proportion to pressure. Under low-load, high-vacuum conditions, the computer leans the fuel/air mixture and advances the spark timing for better fuel economy. Under high-load, low-vacuum conditions, the computer richens the fuel/air mixture and retards timing to prevent detonation. The MAP sensor serves as the electronic equivalent of both a vacuum advance on a distributor and a power valve in the carburetor.

9.3 Here's a typical air flow sensor (this one's from a Nissan Maxima)

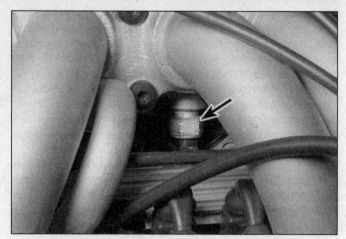

9.5 Here's a typical MAT sensor (this one's on a 1985 Corvette) - it's located in the underside of the air intake plenum

MAF (Mass Air Flow) sensor

The MAF sensor is positioned in the fresh air intake **(see illustration)**, and it measures the amount of air entering the engine. Mass airflow sensors come in two basic varieties; hot wire and hot film. Both types work on the same principle, though they are designed differently. They measure the volume and density of the air entering the engine so the computer can calculate how much fuel is needed to maintain the correct fuel/air mixture.

MAF sensors have no moving parts. Contrary to the vane air flow sensors (see below) that use a spring-loaded flap, MAF sensors use an electrical current to measure airflow. There are two types of sensing elements; platinum wire (hot wire) or nickel foil grid (hot film). Each one is heated electrically to keep the temperature higher than the intake air temperature. With hot-film MAF sensors, the film is heated 170-degrees F warmer than the incoming air temperature. On hot-wire MAF sensors, the wire is heated to 210-degrees F above the incoming air temperature. As air flows past the element it cools the element and thereby increases the amount of current necessary to heat it up again. Because the necessary current varies directly with the temperature and the density of the air entering the intake, the amount of current is directly proportional to the air mass entering the engine. This information is fed into the computer and the fuel mixture is directly controlled according to the conditions.

VAF (Vane Air Flow) sensor

VAF sensors are positioned in the air intake stream ahead of the throttle, and they monitor the volume of air entering the engine by means of a spring-loaded flap **(see illustration)**. The flap is pushed open by the air entering the system and a potentiometer (variable resistor) attached to the flap will vary the voltage signal to the computer according to the volume of air entering the engine (angle of the flap). The greater the airflow, the further the flap is forced open.

VAF sensors are used most commonly on Bosch L-Jetronic fuel injection systems, Nippondenso multi-port fuel injection systems and certain Ford multi-port fuel injection systems (Thunderbird, Mustang and Probe).

Air temperature sensor

The air temperature sensor is also known a Manifold Air Temperature (MAT) sensor, an Air Charge Temperature (ACT) sensor, a Vane Air Temperature (VAT) sensor, a Charge Temperature Sensor (CTS), an Air Temperature Sensor (ATS) and a Manifold Charging Temperature (MCT) sensor. The sensor is located in the intake manifold or air intake plenum **(see illustration)** and detects the temperature of the incoming air. The sensor usually consists of a temperature sensitive thermistor which changes the value of its voltage signal as the temperature changes. The computer uses the sensor signal to richen or lean the fuel/air mixture, and, on some applications, to delay the EGR valve opening until the manifold temperature reaches normal operating range.

TPS (Throttle Position Sensor)

The TPS or Throttle Position Sensor is usually mounted externally on the throttle body or carburetor. Some are inside the throttle body or carburetor. The TPS is attached directly to the throttle shaft and varies simultaneously with the angle of the throttle. Its job is to inform the computer about the rate of throttle opening and relative throttle position. A separate Wide Open Throttle (WOT) switch may be used to signal the computer when the throttle is wide open. The TPS consists of a variable resistor that changes resistance as the throttle changes its opening. By signaling the computer when the throttle opens, the computer can richen the fuel mixture to maintain the proper air/fuel ratio. The initial setting of the TPS sensor is very important because the voltage signal the computer receives, tells the computer the exact position of the throttle at idle.

Oxygen sensor

The oxygen sensor (also known as a Lambda or EGO sensor) is located in the exhaust manifold (or in the exhaust pipe, near the exhaust manifold) and produces a voltage

9.6 Here's a typical TPS (this one's on a Ford). Note there are slots in the sensor at the mounting screws on carbureted models; these allow for adjustment

9.7 This oxygen sensor (arrow) is screwed into the exhaust manifold

signal proportional to the content of oxygen in the exhaust **(see illustration)**. A higher oxygen content across the sensor tip will vary the oxygen differential, thereby lowering the sensor's output voltage. On the other hand, lower oxygen content will raise the output voltage. Typically the voltage ranges from 0.10 volts (lean) to 0.90 volts (rich). The computer uses the sensor's input voltage to adjust the air/fuel mixture, leaning it out when the sensor detects a rich condition or enrichening it when it detects a lean condition. When the sensor reaches operating temperature (600-degrees F), it will produce a variable voltage signal based on the difference between the amount of oxygen in the exhaust (internal) and the amount of oxygen in the air directly surrounding the sensor (external). The ideal stoichiometric fuel/air ratio (14.7:1) will produce about 0.45 volts.

There are basically two types of oxygen sensors on the market. The most popular type uses a zirconia element in its tip. The latest type of oxygen sensor uses a titania element. Instead of producing its own voltage, the titania element resistance will alter a voltage signal that is supplied by the computer itself. Although the titania element works differently than the zirconia element, the results are basically identical. The biggest difference is that the titania element responds faster and allows the computer to maintain more uniform control over a wide range of exhaust temperatures.

Contamination can directly affect the engine performance and life span of the oxygen sensor. There are basically three types of contamination; carbon, lead and silicon. Carbon buildup due to a rich-running condition will cause inaccurate readings and increase the problem's symptoms. Diagnose the fuel injection system or carburetor feedback controls for correct fuel adjustments. Once the system is repaired, run the engine at high rpm without a load (parked in the driveway) to remove the carbon deposits. Avoid leaded gasoline as it causes contamination of the oxygen sensor. Also, avoid using old-style silicone gasket sealant (RTV) around the intake or exhaust system. It releases volatile compounds into the crankcase which eventually wind up on the sensor tip. Always check to make sure the RTV sealant you

are using is compatible with modern emission systems.

Before an oxygen sensor can function properly it must reach a minimum operating temperature of 600-degrees F. The warm-up period prior to this is called "open loop." In this mode, the computer detects a low coolant temperature (cold start) and wide open throttle (warm-up) condition. Until the engine reaches operating temperature, the computer ignores the oxygen sensor signals. During this time span, the emission controls are not precise! Once the engine is warm, the system is said to be in "closed loop" (using the oxygen sensor's input). Some manufacturers have designed an electric heating element to help the sensor reach operating temperature sooner. A typical heated sensor will consist of a ground wire, a sensor output wire (to the computer) and a third wire that supplies battery voltage to the resistance heater inside the oxygen sensor. Be careful when testing the oxygen sensor circuit! Clearly identify the function of each wire or you might confuse the data and draw the wrong conclusions.

EVP (EGR Valve Position) sensors

The EGR Valve Position (EVP) sensor **(see illustration)** monitors the position of the EGR valve and keeps the com-

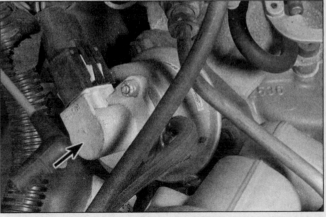

9.8 The EVP sensor is mounted directly on top of the EGR valve

9.9 Typical crankshaft position sensor retaining bolts (arrows) (Ford 5.0L V8 engine shown)

9.10 The crankshaft position sensor pulse rings are mounted on the harmonic balancer (vibration damper)

puter informed on the exact amount the valve is open or closed. From this data, the computer can calculate the optimum EGR flow for the lowest NOx emissions and the best driveability, then control the EGR valve to alter the EGR flow by means of the EGR solenoid.

The EVP sensor is a linear potentiometer that operates very much like a Throttle Position Sensor (TPS). Its electrical resistance changes in direct proportion to the movement of the EGR valve stem. When the EGR valve is closed, the EVP sensor registers maximum resistance. As the valve opens, resistance decreases until it finally reaches a minimum value when the EGR valve is fully open.

Crankshaft position sensor

A crankshaft position sensor works very similarly to an ignition pick-up coil or trigger wheel in an electronic distributor **(see illustration)**. The crankshaft position sensor provides an ignition timing signal to the computer based on the position of the crankshaft. The difference between a crankshaft position sensor and a pick-up coil or trigger wheel is that the crankshaft position sensor reads the ignition timing signal directly off the crankshaft or harmonic balancer instead of from the distributor. This eliminates timing variations from backlash in the timing chain or distributor shaft. Crankshaft position sensors are necessary in most modern distributorless ignition (DIS) systems. Basically, the sensor reads the position of the crankshaft by detecting when pulse rings on the crankshaft or harmonic balancer pass by it **(see illustrations)**.

VSS (Vehicle Speed Sensor)

Vehicle Speed Sensors (VSS) are used in modern vehicles for a number of different purposes. One purpose is to monitor the vehicle speed so the computer can determine the correct time for torque converter clutch (TCC) lock-up. The sensor may also provide input to the computer to control the function of various other emissions systems components based on vehicle speed. On some GM vehicles, the signal from the VSS is used by the computer to reset the Idle Air Control valve as well as the canister purge valve.

Another purpose is to assist with the power steering. Here, the sensor input is used by the electronic controller to vary the amount of power assist according to the vehicle speed. The lower the speed, the greater the assist for easier maneuverability for parking. The higher the speed, the less the assist for better road feel. Another purpose is to change the position of electronically adjustable shock absorbers used in ride control systems. The ride control systems in Mazda 626's and Ford Probes automatically switch the shocks to a "firm" setting above 50 mph in the AUTO mode and "extra firm" in the SPORT mode. Also, vehicle speed sensors replace the mechanical speedometer cable in some modern vehicles.

Knock sensor

The knock sensor (sometimes called an Electronic Spark Control [ESC] sensor) is an auxiliary sensor that is used to detect the onset of detonation **(see illustrations)**. Although the knock sensor influences ignition timing, it doesn't have direct impact on the fuel and emission systems. It affects ignition timing only.

The sensor, which is usually mounted on the intake manifold or engine block, generates a voltage signal when

9.11 On Ford V6 engines, the pulse rings are directly behind the crankshaft pulley, easily detected by the sensor

9.12 Here's a typical knock sensor (Corvette shown here), mounted low on the side of the engine block

9.13 On many GM models, information from the knock sensor is sent to the Electronic Spark Control (ESC) module (arrow), which retards ignition timing if detonation is evident

the engine vibrations are between 6 to 8 Hz. The location of the sensor is very critical because it must be positioned so it can detect any vibrations from the most detonation-prone cylinders. On some engines, it is necessary to install two knock sensors.

When the knock sensor detects a pinging or knocking vibration, it signals the computer to momentarily retard ignition timing. The computer then retards the timing a fixed number of degrees until the detonation stops.

This system is vital on turbocharged vehicles to achieve maximum performance. When the knock control system is working properly, the maximum timing advance for all driving conditions is achieved.

Fuel injectors

Fuel injectors are electro-mechanical devices which both meter and atomize fuel delivered to the engine **(see illustration)**. The injectors on multi-point fuel injection systems are usually mounted in the lower intake manifold **(see illustration)** and positioned so that their tips are directing fuel in front of each engine intake valve. On vehicles equipped with Throttle Body Injection (TBI), the injector(s)

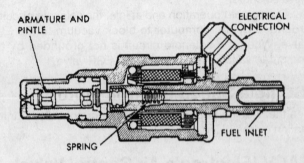

9.14 A cross-sectional view of a typical fuel injector (multi-point type shown here)

are mounted in the throttle body (the carburetor-like device on the intake manifold) **(see illustration)**.

The injector bodies consist of a solenoid-actuated pintle and needle valve assembly. An electrical signal from the computer activates the solenoid, causing the pintle to move inward off the seat and allow fuel to inject into the engine.

9.15 Removing a fuel injector from a typical throttle-body type fuel injection system (GM throttle-body shown)

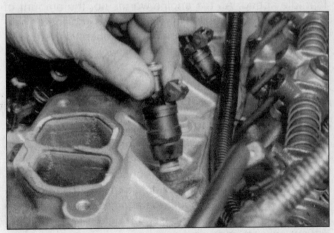

9.16 On multi-point type systems, the injectors are mounted in the intake manifold and spray fuel directly behind the intake valves

Fuel flow to the engine is controlled by how long the solenoid is energized, since the injector flow orifice is fixed and the fuel pressure drop across the injector tip is constant. This duration can be measured electronically and is referred to as the injector pulse width.

EGR valve solenoid

On computer-controlled vehicles, the action of the EGR valve is usually controlled by commanding the EGR control solenoid(s). Refer to the information earlier in this Chapter on EGR valve position sensors for additional information concerning these systems. The EGR valve solenoid is computer controlled and located in the vacuum line between the EGR valve and vacuum source. It opens and closes electrically to maintain finer control of EGR flow than is possible with ported-vacuum-type systems. The computer uses information from the coolant temperature, throttle position and manifold pressure sensors to regulate the EGR valve solenoid.

During cold operation and at idle, the solenoid circuit is grounded by the computer to block vacuum to the EGR valve. When the solenoid circuit is not grounded by the computer, vacuum is allowed to the EGR valve.

ISC (Idle Speed Control) motor

See the heading in Section 6, Carburetor controls for information on the ISC motor.

EACV (Electronic Air Control Valve)

The EACV (sometimes called an Idle Air Control [IAC] valve) changes the amount of air bypassed (not flowing through the throttle valve) into the intake manifold in response to the changes in the electrical signals from the computer. EACVs are usually located on the throttle body, although some are mounted remotely. After the engine starts, the EACV opens, allowing air to bypass the throttle and thus increase idle speed. While the coolant temperature is low, the EACV remains open to obtain the proper fast idle speed. As the engine warms up, the amount of bypassed air is controlled in relation to the coolant temperature. After the engine reaches normal operating temperature, the EACV is opened, as necessary, to maintain the correct idle speed.

TCC (Torque Converter Clutch) solenoid

Lock-up torque converters are installed on newer vehicles to help eliminate torque converter slippage and thus reduce power loss and poor fuel economy. The torque converter is equipped with a clutch that is activated by a solenoid valve. The computer determines the best time to lock up the clutch device based on data it receives from various sensors and switches.

When the vehicle speed sensor indicates speed above a certain range and the coolant temperature sensor is warm, the Throttle Position Sensor (TPS) determines the position of the throttle (acceleration or deceleration) and the transmission sensor relays the particular gear the transmission is operating in to the computer for a complete analysis of operating parameters. If all parameters are within a certain range, the computer sends an electrical signal to the clutch, telling it to lock up. Needless to say, diagnosing a problem in this system can become complicated.

Economy/mileage improvements

In the era before OBD (On-Board Diagnostics), automatic transmissions ranged from two to three speeds and the manual transmissions ranged from three to four speeds.

The manual transmissions were very much as the ones as of today. The automatic transmissions had simple torque converters, gears were shifted by a combination of a vacuum modulator and a governor that was preset to a shift point according to engine load and speed. But for the most part, functions were mechanically controlled.

As engine management gained the ability to handle more information and make a greater number of corrections, manual transmissions grew to be a five speed and in some cases up to six speeds. Today automatic transmissions are equipped with solenoids, actuators, locking torque converters and overdrives and have grown to, in most cases, four speeds with electronically controlled valve bodies and shift points. Automatics had become very fuel efficient and capable of nearly the same mileage as manual transmissions. All this has come about, and improves continuously, because of the ability of modern engine management systems.

Standardization

When we talk about computer systems, take into consideration one very important item. Most of the systems **seem** to be very different from one another. Although the approach taken by different manufactures to energize the computer memory may be different, remember that most of the systems are very similar in the way they respond to temperature, vacuum, voltage signals, etc.

As the early basic computer control systems (which were vastly different between manufacturers) has progressed, to OBD I (On-Board Diagnostics) and currently OBD II, the differences have slowly moved toward similarities in equipment and diagnostics.

With the publication by SAE (Society of Automotive Engineers) of recommended practices, (SAE paper J1934) along with the Clean Air Act (SAE paper J2008 and subsequent amendments J2216 and J2187), the move towards standardization of terminology, hardware and protocol have begun, under the names ODB I and II. Standardization will benefit the manufacturer, independent repair shops and, more importantly, the consumer.

Initial required standardization

The following are the standardized fundamentals which has already taken place and will allow the standardizing of all individual systems in future OBD versions.

Data link connector and protocol (language)
Test modes and trouble codes
Parameter information (specifications of operation)

New requirements

Under OBD II recommendations the following systems will also become standardized among manufacturers:

Catalyst monitor
Misfire detection
Evaporative purge system integrity
Secondary air system function
A/C system refrigerant
Readiness/function code
Tampering deterrence
Stored engine conditions
Comprehensive component monitoring

Notes

5 Tools

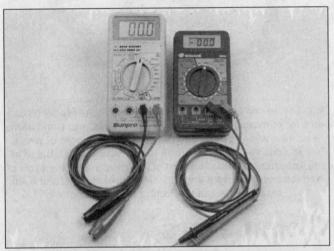

5.1 These two high-impedance digital multi-meters are accurate, versatile and inexpensive, but each unit is equipped with a different type of lead: the one on the left uses insulated alligator clips which don't have to be held in place, freeing your hands for using the meter itself; the unit on the right has a pair of probes, which are handy for testing wires and terminals inside connectors (our advice? Buy both types of leads, or make your own)

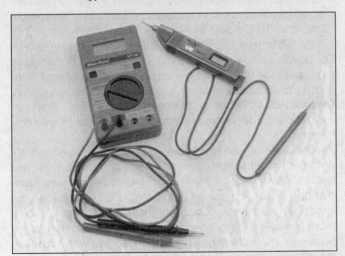

5.2 A probe-style meter like the unit on the right is small and easy to use because one of the probes is integrated into the housing, leaving your other hand free to hold the single ground lead

Lots of interesting high-tech gadgets are available for testing the sensors, actuators, emission control devices and fuel system components involved with a computer controlled engine system. Tools for checking the devices linking the computer to the engine will be the focus here because the computer itself is usually not the problem. Often, the only way to determine that the computer is faulty is to make sure all the other devices and systems are working properly. There are special tools called "scanners" for checking the computer, but these are usually prohibitively expensive and used primarily by dealer mechanics.

Simple visual checks will identify many problems, but there are two tools that are very useful. One of them is a digital multimeter and the other is a hand-operated vacuum pump and gauge. We'll get to the vacuum pump in a minute. First, let's look at the multimeter.

Digital multimeter

The multimeter is a small, hand-held diagnostic tool that combines an ohmmeter and voltmeter (and sometimes an ammeter) into one handy unit. A multimeter can measure the voltage and resistance in a circuit. Many emission and fuel injection devices and systems are electrically powered, so the multimeter is an essential tool.

There are two types of multi-meters: Conventional units (a box with two leads) and probe types (small, hand-held units with a built-in probe and one flexible lead) **(see illustrations)**. Probes - which are about the same size as a portable soldering pen - are easier to use in tight spaces because of their compact dimensions. And you don't need three hands to hold a meter and two test leads all at the same time (you can hold the meter in one hand and the single lead in the other). But probes usually have less features than conventional units.

Why a digital multimeter? Partly because digital meters are easier to read, particularly when you're trying to read tenths of a volt or ohm. But mainly you need a digital meter - instead of an "analog" (needle type) - because digital multi-meters are more accurate than analog meters. More specifically, you need a *high-impedance* digital voltmeter. This kind won't damage sensitive electronic circuits.

5.3 To make a voltage measurement, turn the mode switch or knob on your multimeter to the Volts DC position and hook up the meter in PARALLEL to the circuit being tested; if you hook it up in series, like an ammeter/ohmmeter, you won't get a reading and you could damage something (note how the positive probe is being used to make contact with a wire through the backside of the connector without unplugging the connector)

Using a multimeter to read voltage is simply a matter of selecting the voltage range and hooking up the meter IN PARALLEL **(see illustration)** to the circuit being checked. Older analog (needle-type) meters have always allowed a certain amount of voltage to "detour" through this parallel circuit, which affects the accuracy of the measurement being taken.

This leaking voltage isn't that important when you're measuring 12-volt circuits - and you just want to know if a circuit has 12 or 13 or 14 volts present. If some of the voltage trickles through the meter itself, your judgment call about the health of the circuit is unaffected. But many engine control circuits operate at five volts or less; and some of them operate in the millivolt (thousandths of a volt) range. So voltage readings must be quite accurate - in many cases to the tenth, hundredth or even thousandth of a volt. Even if an older analog meter could measure voltage values this low (and even if you could read them!), the readings would be inaccurate because of the voltage detouring out of the circuit into the meter.

Digital meters have 10-Meg ohms (10 million ohms) resistance built into their circuitry to prevent voltage leaks through the meter. And this is the main reason we specify a digital voltmeter. When you shop around for a good meter, you may find a newer analog type meter with a high-resistance circuit design similar to that of a digital meter, but it will still be difficult to read when performing low-voltage tests, so don't buy it - get a digital model!

Some of the more sophisticated multi-meters **(see illustration)** can perform many of the same functions as scanners, such as checking camshaft and crankshaft position sensors, feedback carburetors, fuel injection on-time, IAC motors, MAF sensors, MAP sensors, oxygen sensors, temperature sensors and throttle position sensors.

5.4 Top-of-the line multi-meters like this Fluke Model 88 can do a lot of things besides just measure volts, amps and ohms - using a wide array of adapters and cables, most of which are included in the basic kit, they can check the status of all the important information sensors, measure the duty cycle of feedback carburetors and idle air control motors, and even measure the pulse width of the fuel injectors

Ohmmeters

So why don't we just specify a digital voltmeter? Because you'll also need to use an ohmmeter a lot too: Most solenoids, sensors and other devices have specific resistance values under specified conditions, so you'll need an ohmmeter to test them. And sometimes the engine won't start, so there's no voltage available to test. When these situations arise, you'll need a good digital ohmmeter to measure resistance (expressed in ohms). But don't buy a separate ohmmeter; get a digital multimeter with an ohmmeter built in.

An ohmmeter has its own voltage source (a low-voltage DC power supply, usually a dry-cell battery). It measures the resistance of a circuit or component and is always connected to an open circuit or a part removed from a circuit. **Caution:** *Don't connect an ohmmeter to a "live" (hot) circuit; current from an outside source will damage an ohmmeter.*

Because an ohmmeter doesn't use system voltage, it's not affected by system polarity. You can hook up the test leads to either side of the part you want to test **(see illustration)**. When you use an ohmmeter, start your test on the lowest range, then switch to a higher range that gives you a more precise reading. Voltage and current are limited by the power supply and internal resistance, so you won't damage the meter by setting it on a low or high scale.

Temperature and the condition of the battery affect an ohmmeter's accuracy. Digital ohmmeters are self-adjusting, but if you're using an analog meter, you must adjust it every

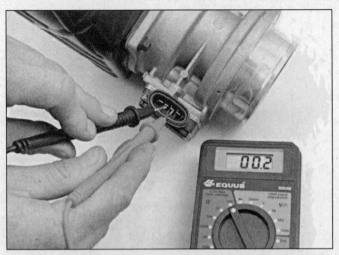

5.5 To measure resistance, select the appropriate range of resistance and touch the meter probes to the terminals you're testing; the polarity (which terminal you touch with which lead) makes no difference on an ohmmeter because it's self-powered and the circuit is turned off

5.6 Get a thermometer with a range from zero to about 220 degrees - there are automotive-specific thermometers available, but a cooking thermometer will work

time you use it:

Simply touch the two test leads together and turn the zero adjustment knob until the needle indicates zero ohms, or continuity, through the meter on the lowest scale.

Thermometer

If you're going to be testing coolant temperature sensors, get a good automotive thermometer **(see illustration)** capable of reading from zero to about 220-degrees F. If you can't find an automotive-specific unit, a good cooking thermometer will work.

Vacuum gauge

Measuring intake manifold vacuum is a good way to diagnose all kinds of things about the condition of an engine. Manifold vacuum is tested with a vacuum gauge **(see illustration)**, which measures the difference in pressure between the intake manifold and the outside atmosphere. If the manifold pressure is lower than the atmospheric pressure, a vacuum exists. Most gauges measure vacuum in inches of mercury (in-Hg). As vacuum increases (or atmospheric pressure decreases), the reading will increase. Also, for every 1000-foot increase in elevation above approximately 2000 feet above sea level, the gauge readings will decrease by about one inch of mercury.

As an example, you would use a vacuum gauge to diagnose a restricted exhaust system with a vacuum gauge. To hook up the gauge, connect the flexible connector hose to the intake manifold, air intake plenum, or any vacuum port below the carburetor or throttle body. On some models, you can simply remove a plug from the man-

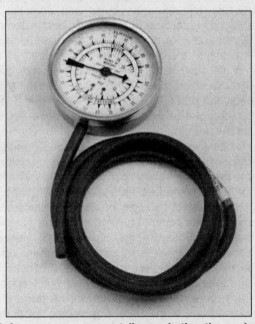

5.7 A vacuum gauge can tell you whether the engine is producing good intake vacuum, help you determine whether the catalytic converter is blocked and help you diagnose a wide variety of engine-related problems

ifold or carburetor/throttle body; on others, you'll have to disconnect a vacuum hose or line from the manifold, carb or throttle body and hook up the gauge inline with a tee fitting (included with most vacuum gauge kits).

A good vacuum reading is about 15 to 20 in-Hg (50 to 65 kPa) at idle (engine at normal operating temperature). Low or fluctuating readings can indicate many different problems. For instance, a low and steady reading may be caused by retarded ignition or valve timing. A sharp vacuum drop at intervals may be caused by a burned intake valve. Refer to the instruction manual that comes with your gauge for a complete troubleshooting chart showing the possible causes of various readings.

Vacuum pump/gauge

Two tools are indispensable for troubleshooting engine control systems. One is a digital multimeter; the other is a hand-operated vacuum pump equipped with a vacuum gauge **(see illustration)**.

Many underhood emission control system components are either operated by intake manifold vacuum, or they use it to control other system components. Devices such as check valves, dashpots, purge control valves, solenoids, vacuum control valves, vacuum delay valves, vacuum restrictors, etc. - all these devices control vacuum in some way, or are controlled by it. They amplify, block, delay, leak, reroute or transmit vacuum. Some of them must control a specified amount of vacuum for a certain period of time, or at a certain rate. A vacuum pump applies vacuum to such devices to test them for proper operation.

Suitable vacuum pump/gauges are sold by most specialty tool manufacturers. Inexpensive plastic-bodied pump/gauges - available at most auto parts stores - are perfectly adequate for diagnosing vacuum systems. Make sure the scale on the pump gauge is calibrated in "in-Hg" (inches of mercury). And buy a rebuildable pump (find out whether replacement piston seals are available). When the seals wear, the pump won't hold its vacuum and vacuum measurements will be inaccurate. At this point, you'll have to rebuild the pump.

Using a vacuum pump is simple enough. Most pump kits include an instruction manual that describes how to use the pump in a variety of situations. They also include a variety of adapters (tee-fittings, conical fittings which allow you to connect two lines of different diameters, etc.) and some vacuum hose, to help you hook up the pump to vacuum, hoses, lines, fittings, pipes, ports, valves, etc. Manufacturers also sell replacements for these adapters and fittings in case they wear out, or you lose them. Sometimes, you may need to come up with a really specialized fitting for a more complicated hook-up. A good place to find weird fittings is the parts department of your local dealer. A well-stocked parts department has dozens of special purpose vacuum line fittings designed for various makes and models. Draw a picture of what you want for the parts man and chances are, he'll have the fitting you need.

Here are a few simple guidelines to keep in mind when using a vacuum pump:

1 When hooking up the pump **(see illustration)**, make sure the connection is airtight, or the test result will be meaningless.

2 Most factory-installed vacuum lines are rubber tubing (some are nylon). Make sure you're using the right-diameter connector hose when hooking up the pump to the device you wish to test. When you attach a connector hose with a larger inside diameter (I.D.) than the outside diameter (O.D.) of the fitting, pipe, port, etc. to which you're attaching it, the vacuum reading will be inaccurate, or you may not get a vacuum reading. If you use a hose or line with a smaller I.D. than the O.D. of the fitting, pipe, port, etc. to which you're

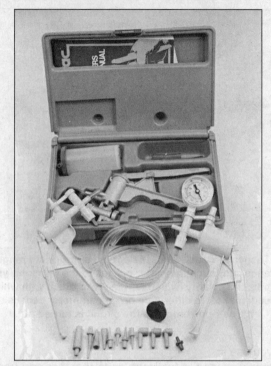

5.8 A hand-operated vacuum pump and gauge tool is indispensable for troubleshooting engine control systems - it can help you track down vacuum leaks and test all vacuum-operated devices; Mityvac pumps (shown) are inexpensive plastic models, like the two in the foreground (one of which can be purchased without a gauge), and sturdier metal units like the one in the box; they come with a variety of fittings and adaptors, and can be used for a host of applications

hooking up the pump, you'll stretch your connector hose and it will be useless in future tests.

3 In general, use as few pieces as possible to hook up the pump to the device or system being tested. The more hoses, adapters, etc. you use between the pump and the

5.9 When connecting a vacuum pump/gauge to a component (such as the Corvette EGR solenoid in this photo), make sure you've got airtight connections at the pump (arrow) and at the fitting or pipe of the device (arrow), or the test results won't mean much

5.10 Scanners like the Actron Scantool and the AutoXray XP240 are powerful diagnostic aids - programmed with comprehensive diagnostic information, they can tell you just about anything you want to know about your engine management system, but they're expensive

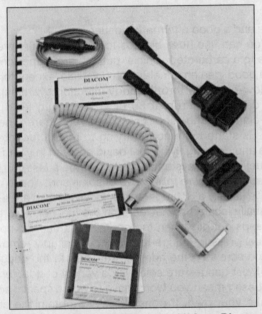

5.11 Diagnostic software, such as this kit from Diacom, turns your IBM compatible computer into the scan tool, saving the extra cost of buying a scanner but providing you with all the same information

5.12 Trouble code tools simplify the task of extracting trouble codes

device or system being tested, the more likely the possibility of a loose connection, and a leak.

4　Don't apply more vacuum than necessary to perform a test, or you could damage something. If the pump won't build up the amount of vacuum specified for the test, or won't hold it for the specified period of time because the piston seal is leaking, discontinue the test and rebuild the pump.

5　When you're done with the test, always break the vacuum in the pump before you detach the line or hose from the system. Breaking a connection while vacuum is still applied could cause a device to suck dirt or moisture into itself when exposed to the atmosphere.

6　Always clean the fitting, pipe or port to which you've hooked up the pump and reattach the factory hose or line. Inspect the end of the factory hose or line. It it's flared, frayed or torn, cut off the tip before you reattach it. Make sure the connection is clean and tight.

7　Clean your pump, adapter fittings and test hose, and put them away when you're done. Don't leave the pump laying around where it could be dropped and damaged.

Scanners, software and trouble-code tools

Scanners (computer analyzers)

Hand-held digital scanners **(see illustration)** are the most powerful and versatile tools for analyzing engine management systems used on later models vehicles. Unfortunately, they're also the most expensive. In this manual, we're going to show you how to troubleshoot sensors and actuators without resorting to analyzers.

Software

Software **(see illustration)** is available that enables your desktop or laptop computer to interface with the engine management computer on many 1981 and later General Motors and Chrysler vehicles.

Such software can output trouble codes, identify problems without even lifting the hood, solve intermittent performance problems and even help you determine the best repair solutions with on-line technical help. We tested Rinda Technology's Diacom software. It runs on any IBM PC, XT, AT or compatible. The kit includes the software, an instruction manual and the interface cables you need to plug in your computer.

Trouble-code tools

A new type of special tool - we'll call it the trouble code tool - has recently become available to the do-it-yourselfer **(see illustration)**. These tools simplify the procedure for extracting trouble codes from your vehicle's engine management computer. Of course, you can extract trouble codes without special tools. And we'll show you how to get those codes with nothing fancier than a jumper wire or an analog multimeter or voltmeter. But trouble code tools do make the job a little easier and they also protect the diagnostic connector terminals and the computer itself from damage.

Fuel injection tools

You don't need a lot of special tools to service fuel injection systems. Most parts and components can be removed and installed with the same tools you use to work on the rest of your vehicle. But there are a few special diagnostic tools that you will need. Here are some of the important ones.

Fuel pressure gauge

In a continuous injection system, the fuel pressure is the critical factor in determining the amount of fuel injected. And fuel pressure is one of the important operating variables in any electronic fuel injection system. So one of the most important tools you'll need for troubleshooting is a good fuel pressure gauge designed for use with fuel injection systems.

Electronic injection

With the exception of some low-pressure systems, the fuel pressure in an electronic fuel injection system is generally higher than the pressure in a carbureted system. In some low-pressure systems (usually throttle-body injection systems), fuel pressure might be only 9 or 10 psi, so a fuel pressure gauge designed for use with a mechanical fuel pump (range of 1 to 15 psi) may be adequate. But most fuel injection systems operate at higher pressures, so you'll need a special gauge designed for higher operating pressures.

A typical fuel-pressure gauge **(see illustration)** for fuel injection work has a range of 1 to 100 psi. The finest quality gauges are available from OEM suppliers such as Kent-Moore, OTC and Miller, and from professional-quality tool manufacturers such as Mac or Snap-On. These generally run from $100 to $200. However, less expensive units, generally under $100, are available at most auto parts stores. These gauges will work just fine for the do-it-yourselfer. They're just not designed for the same level of abuse as a more expensive unit. When buying a gauge, try to verify that at least one of the adapters included with the kit will enable you to hook up the gauge to the system you're going to diagnose. Because Murphy's Law is always an important element of every "adapter search," you'll probably discover that none of the adapters included will fit your system! This is why some people simply pay the piper and purchase a factory gauge, because they know it will fit. But don't despair! You can usually find or make something that will work for far less than the difference between a factory

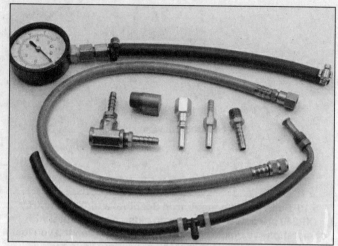

5.13a A fuel pressure gauge is a necessary tool for diagnosing the fuel injection system

gauge and a good aftermarket gauge.

You can use hose clamps to hook up a fuel pressure gauge to a carbureted vehicle, but, generally speaking, this isn't a good idea on a fuel-injected vehicle (except for a few very-low-pressure throttle-body injection systems). Systems designed to run at 30 or 40 psi might leak past a hose-clamp fitting, squirting fuel everywhere when the engine is started. It's no fun trying to read a fuel-pressure gauge and dodging flying fuel being sprayed in your face.

Fuel injection systems usually provide a *test port, pressure tap,* or *pressure relief valve* of some sort. The test port, which is usually a Schrader valve, looks just like a tire valve. It's usually located somewhere on the fuel rail. A screw-off cap keeps out dirt when the port's not in use. To hook up your fuel pressure gauge to a test port, simply remove the cap and screw on the adapter attached to the gauge test hose. Most gauges are sold with a variety of adapters. But that doesn't mean you won't have to buy a special adapter or make your own. If possible, try to obtain the correct adapter for your vehicle when you purchase a gauge.

Adapters

In theory, there should be enough adapters available to provide some means of hooking up virtually any aftermarket fuel pressure gauge to any fuel injection system test port. In practice, this isn't always the case. Test ports are not yet standardized, nor are they even included on every system. Every manufacturer, it seems, has its own way of letting you tap into the system.

Some fuel injection systems have no test port. If the system you're servicing has no port, your only option is to relieve the system fuel pressure, disconnect a fuel line from the fuel rail and hook up the fuel pressure gauge with a "T" type fitting. This can be tricky on some Ford and GM models equipped with spring-lock couplings. If you're servicing one of these models, you'll have to obtain a T-fitting with the special spring-lock couplings on either end, either from the manufacturer or from a specialized tool company that

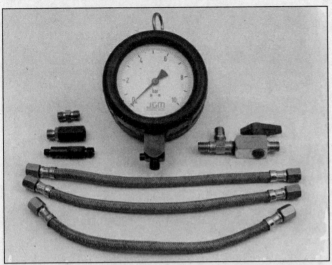

5.13b On high pressure CIS systems, a pressure gauge is a really useful (and often really expensive) tool

5.14 Tools like these are necessary for disconnecting the spring-lock or duckbill type fuel line connectors used on some later models

makes its own line of specialized adapters.

Systems that provide threaded test ports are easier to tap into. These ports are simply a threaded hole in the fuel rail, with a bolt or threaded plug screwed into the hole. The factory gauge for this setup comes equipped with an adapter that screws into the test port. Or, you can purchase the special adapter fitting and hose and use it with your gauge. Or you can fabricate your own adapter by obtaining a bolt with the correct thread diameter and thread pitch and drilling it out on a drill press.

Some systems provide Schrader-valve type test ports. For these systems, all you need to tap into the test port is a test hose with the right threaded adapter on the end that attaches to the Schrader valve. Manufacturers usually sell adapter hoses through their own suppliers, such as OTC, Kent-Moore, Miller, etc. These units are the best quality, but they're often pricey and difficult to obtain unless you're on very good terms with a savvy dealership parts man. There's only one way around this quandary.

It's not that difficult to fabricate your own adapter for this type of fuel injection system. We have fabricated our own adapters here at Haynes for various project vehicles for years. Here's how we do it: Relieve the fuel pressure, remove the Schrader valve, remove the core from the valve stem and install the hollow valve. Now, push a short section of rubber hose down over the valve and clamp it tightly with a hose clamp. Finally, attach the other end of the hose to the fuel pressure gauge and clamp it tightly as well with another hose clamp. You're in business!

Continuous injection

Fuel-pressure gauges for continuous injection systems **(see illustration)** are different from those used on electronic injection systems. First, they're more expensive! Nearly all of them are in the $200 to $300 range. Second, they're more difficult to obtain. You'll have to buy this type of instrument either directly from Robert Bosch or from an aftermarket tool company, such as Assenmacher, that specializes in tools for European vehicles (Assenmacher doesn't sell tools to the public directly; it sells through companies such as Snap-On) Third, not all CIS systems can be accessed with the same adapters. You must obtain special adapters to hook up one of these gauges to certain models. Your local Snap-On dealer can show you an Assenmacher tool catalog with the fittings available for various fuel injection systems. Fourth, you can't use gauges intended for electronic injection systems on CIS. The pressure range for most non-CIS gauges is from 0 to 70 psi. This isn't high enough for CIS work. You need a gauge that reads to 100 psi. But even if you have a conventional gauge that does read to 100 psi, there's no way to safely hook it up to a high-pressure system.

Special tools for disconnecting special connections

The fuel lines on many newer Ford fuel injection systems are now attached to each other and to other components in the fuel injection system with *spring lock couplings*. Some GM vehicles, Saturn for instance, are also starting to use special *duckbill* fuel line connections. If you're servicing a Ford or GM system with funny-looking fuel line connections, do NOT try to disconnect them without a special fuel line disconnect tool **(see illustration)**.

Injector harness testers ("noid" lights)

Noid (short for [injector] solenoid) lights **(see illustration)** tell you whether an injector harness is working prop-

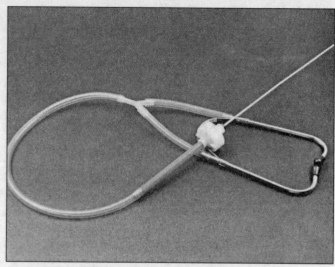

5.15 A noid light provides a quick and easy way to check the electrical signal to the fuel injector

5.16 Use a mechanic's stethoscope to isolate and check the sound made by fuel injectors and other mechanical components

erly or not. To use one, simply unplug the harness connector from the injector, plug the noid light into the connector and run the engine. The noid light will flash on and off as the computer sends pulses to the injector. Or it won't, if there's something wrong with the injector driver or the harness for that injector. Quick and simple. Noid lights are available in a wide variety of configurations for various port and throttle body injectors.

Stethoscope

An automotive stethoscope **(see illustration)** looks just like the one your doctor uses, except that it's equipped with a noise attenuator to dampen the harsh sounds of the engine, and a probe on the end. When you want to isolate the sound of one injector, listen to a fuel pump, an idle speed control motor, etc., a stethoscope is the only way to go.

Fuel tank lock ring wrenches

In-tank fuel pump/sending unit assemblies are usually mounted inside the tank. To remove a defective pump and install a new unit, you must work through a smallish hole in the top of the tank. This hole is sealed with a circular base plate, the flange of which uses a bayonet-type locking ring that must be turned counterclockwise to unlock it before you can remove the fuel pump/sending unit assembly. If you don't mind dropping the fuel tank, this is a fairly simply procedure. In fact, you can knock the locking ring loose with a hammer and a brass punch (*never* use a steel punch

on one of the lock rings - it could cause sparks which could ignite the gasoline in the tank) **(see illustration)**. Nowadays, many vehicles are equipped with an access plate in the floor of the trunk or hatch area that allows you to get at this lock ring/baseplate *without* dropping the fuel tank. Which means you can replace a fuel pump/sending unit without dropping the tank! The trouble is, on many of these vehicles with an access plate, the distance between the access plate and the lock ring/baseplate makes it virtually impossible to knock that ring loose with a hammer and punch. In order to loosen the lock ring through the hole in the trunk, you'll need a special wrench.

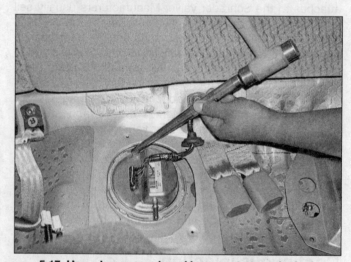

5.17 Use a brass punch and hammer to turn the lock ring counterclockwise

Diagnosing and correcting circuit faults

The goal of electrical diagnosis is to find the faulty component which prevents current from flowing through the circuit as originally designed. As fuel injection systems are equipped with more and more electrical and electronic components, devices and subsystems, the potential for electrical and electronic problems increases dramatically. Because of the complexity of these electrical parts and subsystems, and because of the high cost of replacing them, a "hit-and-miss" approach to troubleshooting is expensive. An organized and logical approach to diagnosis is essential to repair fuel injection electrical circuits in a prompt and cost effective manner.

You'll need a few pieces of specialized test equipment to trace circuits and check components. Accurate methods of measuring current, voltage and resistance are essential for finding the problem without unnecessary parts replacement and wasted time.

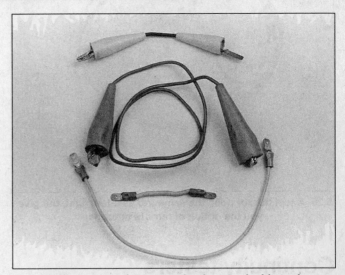

5.18 Jumper wires are a simple yet valuable tool for checking circuits

Jumper wires

Jumper wires **(see illustration)** are used mainly for finding open circuits and for finding excessive resistance by bypassing a portion of an existing circuit. They can also be used for testing components off the vehicle. You can purchase them in completed form, or you can fabricate your own from parts purchased at an automotive or electronics supply store.

Jumper wires can be equipped with various types of terminals for different uses. If you're jumping current from the battery to a component, make sure your jumper wire is equipped with an inline fuse to avoid a current overload, and make sure it has insulated boots over the terminals to prevent accidental grounding. **Warning:** *Never use jumpers made of wire that is thinner (of lighter gauge) than the wiring in the circuit you are testing. Always use a fuse with the same (or lower) rating as the circuit had originally.*

Test lights

Test lights are handy for verifying that there's voltage in a powered circuit. A test light **(see illustration)** is one of the cheapest electrical testing devices available; it should be the first thing you purchase for your electrical troubleshooting tool box. Test lights can also be fabricated from parts purchased at an automotive or electronics supply store. Test lights come in several styles, but all of them have three basic parts: a light bulb, a test probe and a wire with a ground connector. Six, 12, or 24-volt systems may be tested by changing the bulb to the appropriate voltage. Although accurate voltage measurements aren't possible with a test light, large differences can be detected by the relative brightness of the glowing bulb. **Note:** *Before using a test light for diagnosis, check it by connecting it to the battery, ensuring the bulb lights brightly.*

Test buzzers

A test buzzer **(see illustration)** works the same way as a test light; but it offers the advantage of remote operation. For example, one person working alone may test a fuel pump circuit by turning the key to On and listening for the sound of the buzzer connected to the fuel pump circuit. A test buzzer can be fabricated at home from parts purchased at an electronics store or made with jumper wires and a key reminder buzzer. Test buzzers are used in the same manner described for test lights. Additionally, they can be used to find shorts to ground.

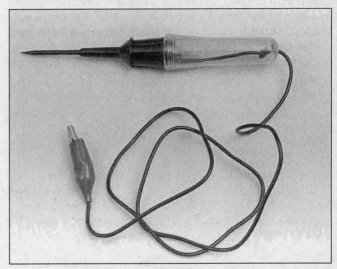

5.19 A test light is an economical and easy to use tool for making sure there is voltage in a powered circuit

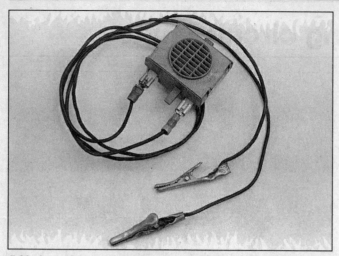

5.20 A test buzzer does the same job as a test light, but gives you the option of remote operation

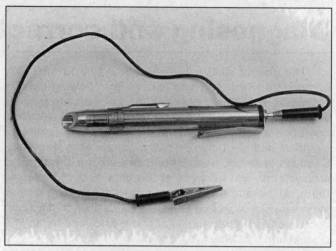

5.21 Use a continuity tester (also called a self-powered test light) to check for open or closed circuits - never use one on circuits with solid state components; it could damage them

Continuity testers

A continuity tester **(see illustration)**, also known as a self-powered test light, is used to check for open or short circuits. The typical continuity tester is nothing more than a light bulb, a battery pack and two wires combined into one unit. These parts can be purchased from any auto parts or electronics store. Continuity testers must be used only on non-powered circuits; battery voltage will burn out a low-voltage tester bulb.

Caution: *Never use a self-powered continuity tester on circuits that contain solid state components, since damage to these components may occur.*

Short finders

A short finder **(see illustration)** is an electromagnetic device designed to trace short circuits quickly and easily. One part of the short finder is a pulse unit, which is installed in place of the fuse for a circuit in which a short is suspected. The other part of the short finder is a hand-held meter which is moved along the faulty wiring harness. Meter deflections indicate the area in the harness where the

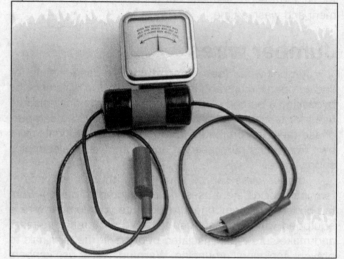

5.22 A short finder simplifies the job of tracing a short circuit

short is located. Short finders are available from most tool manufacturers for a moderate price. The savings from one use usually offsets the purchase price.

6 Basic troubleshooting

1 General information

A malfunctioning fuel injection system or component can cause a variety of problems. While some may be obvious, others are not. The obvious symptoms might include a vehicle that won't start or stay running, sluggish performance or a lack of power, pinging, backfiring or excessive exhaust smoke. Symptoms that are more difficult to diagnose include an occasional fuel smell, an intermittent misfire or decreased fuel mileage.

Many of the symptoms described can also be caused by malfunctions of the basic fuel, ignition or mechanical systems of the vehicle. More often than not, the cause of a problem can be found through inspecting and testing one of these basic systems. You may actually find that performing the basic troubleshooting procedures found in this Chapter may correct the symptoms thought to be fuel injection or computer related.

This Chapter provides a guide to the most common problems, and their corrections, diagnosed with the basic tools common to today's automotive industry.

The fundamentals of all basic engine and fuel systems being dealt with in this Chapter are similar enough, among manufacturers, that the basic tests and specifications given will help you correctly track down the reason(s) for the problem(s) being experienced.

2 Safety precautions

Regardless of how enthusiastic you may be about getting on with the job at hand, take the time to ensure that your safety is not jeopardized. A moment's lack of attention can result in an accident, as can failure to observe certain simple safety precautions. The possibility of an accident will always exist, and the following points should not be considered a comprehensive list of all dangers. Rather, they are intended to make you aware of the risks and to encourage a safety-conscious approach to all work you carry out on your vehicle.

Essential DOs and DON'Ts

DON'T rush or take unsafe shortcuts to finish a job.

DON'T allow children or pets in or around the vehicle while you are working on it.

DON'T start the engine without first making sure that the transmission is in Neutral (or Park where applicable) and the parking brake is set.

DON'T touch any part of the engine or exhaust system until it has cooled sufficiently to avoid burns.

DON'T use poorly maintained trouble lights/shop lights that may have exposed wiring, broken insulation or a bad ground.

DON'T open any connection in the fuel system without properly releasing the pressure.

DON'T siphon toxic liquids such as gasoline, antifreeze and brake fluid by mouth, or allow them to remain on your skin.

DON'T remove the radiator cap from a hot cooling system - let it cool sufficiently, cover the cap with a cloth and release the pressure gradually.

DON'T attempt to drain the engine oil until you are sure it has cooled to the point that it will not burn you.

DON'T use loose fitting wrenches or other tools which may slip and cause injury.

DON'T push on wrenches when loosening or tightening nuts or bolts. Always try to pull the wrench toward you. If the situation calls for pushing the wrench away, push with an open hand to avoid scraped knuckles if the wrench should slip.

DO keep loose clothing and long hair well out of the way of moving parts.

DO get someone to check on you periodically when working alone on a vehicle.

DO carry out work in a logical sequence and make sure that everything is correctly assembled and tightened.

DO keep chemicals and fluids tightly capped and out of the reach of children and pets.

DO remember that your vehicle's safety affects that of yourself and others. If in doubt on any point, seek professional advice.

Gasoline and fuel injection cleaners

Warning: *Gasoline and fuel injection cleaners are extremely flammable, so take extra precautions when you work on any part of the fuel system or hook up external connections to clean the system. Don't smoke or allow open flames or bare light bulbs near the work area, and don't work in a garage where a gas-type appliance (such as a water heater or a clothes dryer) is present. Since gasoline and fuel injector cleaners are carcinogenic, wear latex gloves when there's a possibility of being exposed to fuel, and, if you spill any fuel on your skin, rinse it off immediately with soap and water. The vapors are harmful. Avoid prolonged breathing of vapors or contact with eyes or skin. Use with adequate ventilation. Follow all additional instructions and warning on the product being used. Mop up any spills immediately and do not store fuel-soaked rags where they could ignite. The fuel system on fuel-injected models is under constant pressure, so, if any fuel lines are to be disconnected, the fuel pressure in the system must be relieved first. When you perform any kind of work on the fuel system, wear safety glasses and have a Class B type fire extinguisher on hand.*

Fire

Warning: *We strongly recommend that a fire extinguisher suitable for use on fuel and electrical fires be kept handy in the garage or the workshop at all times. Never try to extinguish a fuel or electrical fire with water. Post the phone number for the nearest fire department in a conspicuous location near the phone.*

A spark caused by an electrical short circuit, by two metal surfaces contacting each other, or even by static electricity built up in your body under certain conditions, can ignite gasoline or battery vapors, which in a confined space are highly explosive. Do not, under any circumstances, use gasoline for cleaning parts. Use an approved safety solvent.

Fumes

Warning: *Certain fumes are highly toxic and can quickly cause unconsciousness and even death if inhaled to any extent. Gasoline vapor falls into this category, as do the vapors from some cleaning solvents. Any draining or pouring of such volatile fluids should be done in a well ventilated area.*

When using cleaning fluids and solvents, read the instructions on the container carefully. Never use materials from unmarked containers.

Never run the engine in an enclosed space, such as a garage. Exhaust fumes contain carbon monoxide, which is extremely poisonous. If you need to run the engine, always do so in the open air, or at least have the rear of the vehicle outside the work area.

If you are fortunate enough to have the use of an inspection pit, never drain or pour gasoline and never run the engine while the vehicle is over the pit. The fumes, being heavier than air, will concentrate in the pit with possibly lethal results.

In the event of an emergency, be sure to post the phone number for poison control in a conspicuous location near the phone.

Battery

Warning: *Never create a spark or allow a bare light bulb near a battery. They normally give off a certain amount of hydrogen gas, which is highly explosive.*

Always disconnect the battery ground/negative(-) cable at the battery before working on the fuel or electrical systems. If disconnecting both cables for any reason, always disconnect the ground/negative cable first, then disconnect the positive cable.

If possible, loosen the filler caps or cover when charging the battery from an external source (this does not apply to sealed or maintenance-free batteries). Do not charge at an excessive rate or the battery may burst.

Take care when adding water to a non maintenance-free battery and when carrying a battery. The electrolyte, even when diluted, is very corrosive and should not be allowed to contact clothing or skin.

Always wear eye protection when using compressed air.

Always wear eye protection when cleaning the battery to prevent the caustic deposits from entering your eyes.

Household current

When using an electric power tool, inspection light, etc., which operates on household current, always make sure that the tool is correctly connected to its plug and that, where necessary, it is properly grounded. Do not use such items in damp conditions and, again, do not create a spark or apply excessive heat in the vicinity of fuel or fuel vapor.

Secondary ignition system voltage

A severe electric shock can result from touching certain parts of the secondary ignition system (such as the spark plug wires, coil, etc.) when the engine is running or being cranked, particularly if components are damp or the insulation is defective. In the case of an electronic ignition system, the secondary system voltage is much higher and could prove fatal.

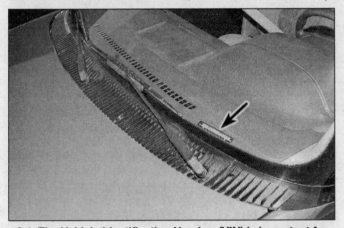

3.1 The Vehicle Identification Number (VIN) is important for identifying the vehicle and engine type - it is on the front of the dash, visible from outside the vehicle, looking through the windshield on the driver's side.

3 Vehicle identification

Changes, modifications and corrections are a continuing process in vehicle and replacement parts manufacturing. Don't rely on information that is 'thought' to be correct, always find the **correct** specification and procedure. It may have been correct for one model year and not the next, even if everything in the vehicle appears the same in all other respects.

Since spare parts manuals and lists are compiled on a numerical basis. The individual vehicle numbers are essential to correctly identify the part needed when going to the local parts store or when checking the specifications to be used.

Vehicle Identification Number (VIN)

This very important identification number is stamped on a plate attached to the left side of the dashboard just inside the windshield on the driver's side of the vehicle (**see illustration**). The VIN also appears on the Vehicle Certificate of Title and Registration. It contains information such as where and when the vehicle was manufactured, the model year and engine codes.

Finding the correct information is the usual starting point and two important pieces to find first are the model year and engine codes. On models through 1980 the VIN has 11, 12 or 13 digits, depending on manufacturer. On Chrysler and General Motors products the engine code is the fifth digit (counting from the left) and the model year code is the sixth digit. On AMC vehicles the second digit is the model year code and the seventh digit is the engine code. On Ford cars the first digit is the model year code and the fifth digit is the engine code. On Ford trucks the fifth digit is the engine code and the sixth digit is the model year code. On Jeep vehicles the second digit is the model year and the sixth digit is the engine code. On 1981 and later models the VIN has 17 digits - the 8th digit is the engine code and the 10th digit is the model year code. The exception to this is on AMC and Jeep vehicles. On these models the fourth digit is the engine code and the tenth digit is the model year code. **Caution:** *It's possible the original engine may have been "swapped" for a different engine somewhere in the life of the vehicle. This information may or may not have been passed on from owner to owner. If the engine has been replaced it will be necessary to know what engine (year, size, emissions, etc.) is in the vehicle, in order to find the correct specifications to use for repairs or adjustments.*

The Vehicle Emissions Control Information (VECI) label

The VECI label **(see illustrations)** identifies the engine, the fuel system and the emission control systems used on your specific vehicle. It also provides essential tune-up specifications, such as the spark plug gap, slow-idle speed, fast-idle speed, initial ignition timing setting (if adjustable) and components that originally came on the vehicle such as Exhaust Gas Recirculation (EGR), Three Way Catalyst (TWC) converter, Fuel Injection (FI), etc.

Some VECI labels simply provide the specifications for these adjustments; others even include brief step-by-step adjustment procedures. Most labels also provide a simplified vacuum diagram of the emissions control devices used on your vehicle and the vacuum lines connecting them to each other and to engine vacuum. You won't find everything you need to know on the VECI label, but it's a very good place to start.

The information on the VECI label is specific to your vehicle. Any changes or modifications authorized by the manufacturer will be marked on the label by a technician making the modification. He may also indicate the change with a special modification decal and place it near the VECI label.

It can't be emphasized enough, DON'T make substitutions for parts or specifications. If the vehicle doesn't run well with all the manufacturer designated parts and specifications used, there is still an unrepaired problem. Trying to

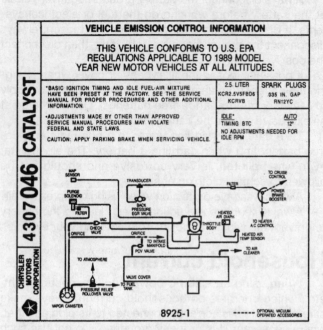

3.2 Here's a typical Vehicle Emission Control Information (VECI) label (this one's from a Chrysler) - note the warning against ignition timing adjustments and the schematic-style vacuum diagram that shows the major emission control components and their relationship to each other, but not their location.

compensate by changing spark plug heat ranges or altering timing doesn't correct the problem and in some cases may actually mask a problem and allow damage to other engine components.

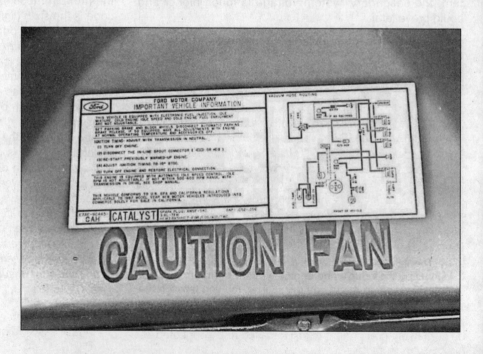

3.3 The Vehicle Emission Control Information (VECI) label, normally located on the top of the cooling fan shroud, contains essential and specific information (like spark plug type, the proper ignition timing procedure for your vehicle and a vacuum hose routing schematic) that applies to the emissions-related devices on your vehicle

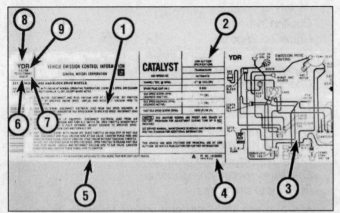

3.4 The vehicle Emission Control Information (VECI) label provides information regarding engine size, exhaust emission system used, engine adjustment procedures and specifications and an emission component and vacuum hose schematic diagram

1   *Adjustment procedures*
2   *Engine adjustment specifications*
3   *Emission component and vacuum hose routing*
4   *Label part number*
5   *Area of certification (California, Federal or Canada)*
6   *Evaporative emission system*
7   *Exhaust emission system*
8   *Label code*
9   *Engine size*

What does a VECI label look like?

The VECI label is usually a small, white, adhesive-backed, plastic-coated label about 4 X 6 inches in size, located somewhere in the engine compartment. It's usually affixed to the underside of the hood, the radiator support, the firewall or one of the inner fender panels.

What if you can't find the VECI label?

If you're not the original owner of your vehicle, and you can't find the VECI label anywhere, chances are it's been removed, or the body part to which it was affixed has been repaired or replaced. Don't worry - you can buy a new one at a dealer parts department. **Note:** *They normally have to be ordered from the assembly plant where the vehicle was manufactured.*

Be sure to give the parts department the VIN number, year, model, engine, etc. of your vehicle; be as specific as possible. For instance, if it's a high-altitude model, a 49-state model or a California model, be sure to tell them, because each of these models may have a different fuel system and a unique combination of emission control devices.

Don't just forget about the VECI label if you don't have one. Intelligent diagnosis of the fuel injection system on your vehicle begins here. Without the VECI label, you can't be sure every component is still installed and connected as originally manufactured.

4 Problem identification

Identifying the problem, or symptom, is the first step in using your time wisely, getting to the basis for the problem quickly and dealing with it effectively.

The most inexpensive and easiest way to keep your vehicle operating properly is simply to check it over on a regular basis. This is the best to way spot individual problems before other component problems occur and compound the symptoms. When maintenance is ignored, over a period of time, multiple repairs usually become necessary. This makes diagnosing the symptoms more difficult than if they had been discovered individually during periodic checks.

The emissions, fuel, ignition, and engine management systems are interrelated, a minor problem in one can have a ripple effect on others. These minor malfunctions among several systems can eventually lead to a breakdown which could have been avoided by a simple check and maintenance program.

When you've taken a vehicle to a dealership or auto shop in the past, you'll probably remember how difficult it was to make the service advisor clearly understand the problem being experienced. Sometimes the written repair order described something completely different than what you were trying to convey. So the explanation and problem, many times, was mis-diagnosed or the problem may not have been addressed completely. A return visit to the shop now becomes necessary. This example of poor communication is the stuff that the highly advertised Customer Satisfaction Index (CSI) ratings are made of. Repeat repairs and return visits to a shop don't make for a happy customer.

Follow simple guidelines like:

- Don't ignore the basics! (spark, fuel, air, etc.).
- Don't overlook the simple or obvious problems that can be found upon visual inspection (vacuum line disconnected, air intake hose cracked, etc.).
- Never assume that someone else's diagnosis is correct.
- Start out the repair procedure correctly by questioning yourself, or the driver that experienced the symptoms, these essential pieces of information:
- **WHAT are the problems or symptoms being experienced?**
- Does the engine stall, surge, misfire, or does it idle rough? . . . etc.
- **WHEN are these symptoms experienced?**
  Is the engine hot or cold? Does the problem happen immediately, or only after an extended drive? Is the vehicle moving at a constant speed or idling at a stop when the problem occurs? Does the problem occur under easy or hard acceleration? Is the weather wet or dry ? . . . etc.

- **WHERE do the symptoms seem to be most obvious or severe?**

    Are they most severe under a load (possibly pulling a trailer or boat), going up a grade, at sea level or high altitude (such as Denver, Albuquerque, etc.)?

- Did the vehicle emit any out-of-the-ordinary noises or unusual smells at the time the problem was being experienced? Noises from pre-ignition (pinging) or the smell of sulfur (rotten eggs) could help pinpoint the problem system or component.

- Has another shop or person worked on the vehicle recently?

    If so ,what problems was the vehicle taken in for? What was the diagnosis? What was actually done to repair the vehicle?

    Everyone has heard, at one time or another, that there is no such thing as a dumb question. Getting all the information possible to repair a problem, in a timely and effective manner, is an instance when that old saying really holds true. Ask all the questions necessary that will help clarify the problem. This can only help narrow the search for the cause of the problem. Even ask questions like; is tire inflation correct? . . . was parking brake applied? . . . what is the quality of gasoline used? . . . when was the last time the vehicle was serviced, and what was done? . . . etc. If you think these questions sound dumb, see how sluggish a vehicle feels with tires at half pressure, or with a parking brake that is partially applied.

5 Basic system checks

General engine condition

The term "tune-up" is used in this manual to represent a combination of individual operations rather than one specific procedure.

If, from the time the vehicle is new, the routine maintenance schedule is followed closely and frequent checks are made of fluid levels and high wear items, as suggested throughout this manual, the engine will be kept in relatively good running condition and the need for additional work will be minimized.

More likely than not, however, there will be times when the engine is running poorly due to lack of regular maintenance. This is even more likely if a used vehicle, which has not received regular and frequent maintenance checks, is purchased. In such cases, an engine tune-up will be needed outside of the regular routine maintenance intervals.

The following general list of components and tests are those most often needed to bring a generally poor running engine back into a proper state of tune:

Air intake system
Cooling system
Under hood hoses
Check all engine-related fluids
Adjustment of the drivebelts
Check engine vacuum and hoses
Clean, inspect and test the battery, cables and starter
Charging system output
Primary ignition system
Secondary ignition system
Computer power and grounds
Emissions related components
Fuel pump pressures

Any of these areas or components found to be excessively worn, damaged or out of specifications should be repaired replaced before proceeding with other diagnosis.

The vehicle being worked on may have a problem with one or more of these items or systems, so take the time to be thorough and use the procedures in the following Sections.

Since you are now at this point in the repair procedure, questions should have been asked and the visual inspection should have been completed. If the symptom or problem still exists, follow the procedures described to more closely examine the individual components making up the fundamental engine systems.

Disable the ignition system, either by grounding the ignition coil or disconnecting the primary (low voltage) wires from the coil, so that the vehicle won't start. **Note:** *If it's not possible to disable the ignition system, many computer-controlled vehicles will not start (only crank) under certain conditions. Turn the ignition on, wait for two seconds, push the accelerator to wide open throttle (WOT), then crank the engine. Try it - it may not work on every vehicle, but if it does work it makes it a little easier to perform checks on the engine systems that require disabling the ignition.*

Crank the engine over and listen to the sound it is making. A smooth, even rhythm to the engine's rotation, with no slowing at spots during cranking, is a good general indicator that there is even compression in all cylinders. High or low compression, in comparison to other cylinders, would cause individual piston strokes to be harder or easier than others, thereby causing uneven rotating speed.

Now this isn't, by any stretch of the imagination, as accurate as actually performing a compression test. For purposes of saving time, finding the source and correcting the problem, this quick check will indicate whether more time should be spent on this area or should you go on to look elsewhere for the source of the driveability problem being experienced.

A good general rule of thumb would be, if fluctuations or surging are noted of more than 40 or 50 rpm, then there is a significant difference between the compression of the cylinders. A more in-depth look at each individual cylinder should be taken with a compression gauge to more accurately determine the cause for the compression differences.

Airflow, filters, hoses and connections

Inspect the outer surface of the filter element. Even if the surface looks fairly clean it needs to checked further. Place a shop light on one side of the element and see if light can be see when looking through the filter towards the light. If it is dirty, replace it. If it is only moderately dusty, it can be reused by blowing it clean, from the back to the front surface, with compressed air. If it is a pleated paper type filter, it cannot be washed or oiled. If it cannot be cleaned satisfactorily with compressed air, discard and replace it.

High temperatures in the engine compartment can cause the deterioration of the rubber and plastic components and/or hoses used for engine, accessory and emission systems operation. Periodic inspection should be made for soft deteriorating hoses, cracks, loose clamps, material hardening and leaks.

Some, but not all, hoses are secured to the fittings with clamps. Where clamps are used, check to be sure they haven't lost their tension, allowing the hose to leak. If clamps aren't used, make sure the hose has not expanded and/or hardened where it slips over the fitting.

Air-leak check

The term "air-leak" refers to outside air that has entered into the system downstream (after) from the airflow meter or mass airflow sensor (where the airflow is metered and fuel flow is calibrated accordingly) in a fuel injected engine or after the throttle plate in a carbureted engine, but before the intake valves. This un-metered air makes the correct air/fuel calculations difficult, if not impossible. The computer can't measure the additional air so it's unable to compensate for the change, which results in a lean air/fuel mixture. Although the oxygen sensor does send a signal to adjust for what is indicated by the exhaust gas, it can't command a large enough adjustment to overcome the problem.

Look for air inlet hoses and flexible ductwork that has broken, split or cracked from age and/or underhood heat. One other possibility may be from a previous repair. Sometimes connections don't always get aligned or reassembled quite right. Handling of original hoses or lines sometimes causes them to crack because they have become so brittle with age and heat.

Check for leaks in the air intake system by spraying water or carburetor cleaner in the area of suspected leaks and listen for a change in engine rpm. **Warning:** *Carburetor cleaner spray is flammable and can ignite if sprayed on hot manifolds or comes in contact with an open spark. For the sake of safety, it's recommended that water be used to check for air leaks.*

Oil level and condition

The proper level of good clean oil must be maintained in the engine at all times for a number of reasons. Everyone knows that the first and foremost reason is lubrication, which prevents engine damage. But dirty oil has an affect on other systems as well.

Poorly maintained engine oil will allow sludge and moisture to build up within the lubrication system. Over a period of time this can lead to blockages in the oil passageways or PCV systems. This can increase crankcase pressure and, as a result, increase blow-by gases. Excessive blow-by combined with marginal ignition parts can combine to create an engine misfire that may be hard to locate.

Many modern vehicles have protection built into the engine management system. If for any reason oil pressure drops below a set lower limit, the oil pressure switch will indicate this lack of pressure and the computer will shut the engine off. Hopefully before any damage can take place.

The lubrication system could often be overlooked as a cause of a stalling problem. Here again, regular maintenance and awareness of the overall condition of the engine may help find a simple solution to a problem, rather than allowing matters to become more complicated than they really are.

Coolant level, condition and circulation

The level, condition and circulation of the coolant has a direct affect on engine operation. Of course, the engine must not be allowed to overheat, but it must also reach the correct operating temperature for proper fuel control to take place. Therefor, a thermostat that operates within the temperature range the vehicle was originally designed for, must be installed in the vehicle at all times. Never install a "cooler" thermostat in your engine in an attempt to solve an overheating problem, and never, ever, completely remove the thermostat. With the thermostat removed, the engine may remain in the "open loop" mode (no computerized fuel control) and fuel economy and performance will suffer.

The cooling system must be maintained properly to keep the engine from overheating. Overheating the engine can cause many problems, none of which would seem to be fuel system related. But when an engine is overheated it can not only damage the engine mechanically, it can also damage sensors, electrical solenoids and output actuators, all of which have a impact on how the computer senses the operating condition of the engine. The damaged condition of these components and the ECM's attempt to manage all the systems, without accurate information, will cause a driveability problem. This is one of those items that, although unrelated, can indirectly affect other systems, such as fuel control, of the vehicle.

The cooling system should be checked with the engine cold. Do this before the vehicle is driven for the day or after the engine has been shut off for at least three hours. Remove the cooling system cap and inspect the condition of the coolant. **Note:** *Some later vehicles no longer have a cap on the radiator itself, In these systems the coolant expansion tank/reservoir is a part of the pressure system.*

The pressure cap is located on the expansion tank. If you hear a hissing sound (indicating there is still pressure in the system), wait until it stops before proceeding with the cap removal.

The coolant inside the radiator will have some color, probably light green or pink, but should be relatively transparent. If it's rust colored, the system should be drained and refilled. If the coolant level isn't up to the proper level, add additional antifreeze/coolant mixture until it is.

Thoroughly clean the cap, inside and out, with clean water. Pressure check the radiator cap to be sure it maintains the specified pressure (14-to-18 lbs, and is usually stamped on the cap). Pressurizing the system allows the operating temperature of the coolant to reach a temperature above the normal boiling point of 212-degrees.

Make sure that all hose clamps are tight. A small leak in the cooling system, if not large enough to have a noticeable drip, will usually show up as white or rust colored deposits on the areas adjoining the leak. If older style wire-type clamps are used at the ends of the hoses, it may be a good idea to replace them with more secure screw-type clamps.

If rust or corrosion is excessive, or if the coolant is due to be replaced, consider flushing the cooling system at this time. If corrosion is found at the connections or at the radiator cap it is an indication that the coolant should be flushed from the engine, and refilled with a fresh coolant/water mixture. Flushing kits and/or cooling system additives to clean the inside of the system, are available at local auto parts stores.

Vacuum hoses, fittings and connections

The fuel control and engine emission systems often use engine vacuum to operate various switches and control devices on the engine. Vacuum may also be used to alter the spark timing at the distributor, if equipped. Accessories such as power brake boosters, automatic transmission vacuum modulators, cruise control systems and heating-ventilation-air conditioning air distribution systems also use engine vacuum to operate their various systems. A vacuum leak in any one of these systems could seriously affect engine performance.

Most emission control systems depend on vacuum for proper operation. These systems use numerous vacuum-operated devices that respond to vacuum to activate and deactivate output actuators which control emissions by altering engine operation in accordance with changing loads and operating temperatures.

It's quite common for vacuum hoses, especially those in the emissions system, to be color coded or identified by colored stripes. Various systems require hoses with different wall thickness, collapse resistance and temperature resistance. When replacing hoses, be sure the new hoses meet the same specifications as the original.

Often, because the routing of the hose may be under other components, the only effective way to check a hose is to remove it completely from the vehicle. If more than one hose is removed, be sure to label the hoses and fittings to ensure correct installation. When checking vacuum hoses, be sure to include all plastic connectors and T-fittings in the inspection. Look at the fittings for cracks, and check the hose where it fits over the fitting for distortion, hardening or cracking, which could cause leakage. Check the entire hose, but especially at spots where the hose may make contact with hot engine components and/or oil leakage areas. A hot engine can melt through or bake a hose until it crumbles, likewise oil leakage will rot a hose until it disintegrates.

The major cause of vacuum-related problems is damaged or disconnected vacuum hoses, lines or tubing. Vacuum leaks can cause many engine performance related problems. It can cause an engine to idle rough or erratic, or misfire. Vacuum leaks in the emission system can cause spark knock or "pinging", or cause an engine to backfire. If a large enough leak is present, the engine may stall repeatedly and of course, fuel economy will suffer drastically.

If you suspect a vacuum problem because one or more of the above symptoms occurs, the following visual inspection may get you to the source of the problem with no further testing:

Make sure all the vacuum hoses are routed correctly - kinked lines block vacuum flow at first, then cause a vacuum leak when they crack and break.

Make sure all connections are tight. Look for loose connections and disconnected lines. Vacuum hoses and lines are sometimes accidentally knocked loose by an errant elbow during an oil change or some other maintenance.

Inspect the entire length of every hose, line and tube for breaks, cracks, cuts, hardening, kinks and tears **(see illustration)**. Replace all damaged lines and hoses.

When subjected to the high underhood temperatures of a running engine, hoses become brittle (hardened). Once

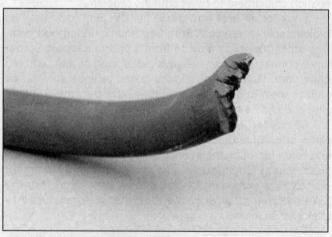

5.1 This vacuum hose was routed too close to an exhaust manifold - after being overheated repeatedly, it finally cracked and broke.

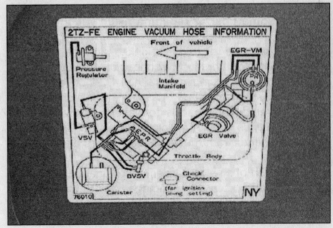

5.2 Raise the hood and find your VECI label - many manufacturers place the vacuum diagram right on the VECI label

they're brittle, they crack more easily when subjected to engine vibrations. When you inspect the vacuum hoses and lines, pay particularly close attention to those that are routed near hot areas such as exhaust manifolds, EGR systems, reduction catalysts (often right below the exhaust manifold on modern front-wheel drive vehicles with transverse engines), etc.

Inspect all vacuum devices for visible damage (dents, broken pipes or ports, broken tees in vacuum lines, etc.)

Make sure none of the lines are coated with coolant, fuel, oil or transmission fluid. Many vacuum devices will malfunction if any of these fluids get inside them.

If none of the above steps eliminates the vacuum leak problem, using a vacuum pump, apply vacuum to each suspect area, then watch the gauge for any loss of vacuum.

And if you still can't find the leak? Well, maybe it's not in the engine control system - maybe it's right at the source, at the intake manifold or the base gasket between the carburetor or throttle body. To test for leaks in this area, spray aerosol carburetor cleaner along the gasket joints with the engine running at idle. If the idle speed smoothes out momentarily, you've located your leak. Tighten the intake manifold or the throttle body fasteners to the specified torque and recheck. If the leak persists, you may have to replace the gasket.

A small piece of vacuum hose (1/4-inch inside diameter) can be used as a stethoscope to detect vacuum leaks. Hold one end of the hose to your ear and probe around vacuum hoses and fittings, listening for the "hissing" sound characteristic of a vacuum leak. **Warning:** *When probing with the vacuum hose stethoscope, watch where you are placing your hands! be very careful not to come into contact with moving engine components such as the drivebelts, cooling fan, etc.*

Where can you find vacuum diagrams?

The quickest way to determine what vacuum devices are used on your vehicle is to refer to the Vehicle Emission Control Information (VECI) label located in the engine compartment. Most vehicles have a vacuum diagram (or "schematic") located on or near the label. The label is usually affixed to the radiator core support, inner fender panel, engine air cleaner assembly or the underside of the hood for convenient reference when working on your vehicle.

Raise the hood and find your VECI label. Most manufacturers place the vacuum diagram right on the VECI label **(see illustration)**. Some put it on a separate label, near the VECI label **(see illustration)**. **Note:** *The diagrams in this manual are typical examples of the type you'll find on your*

5.3 Some manufacturers put the vacuum schematic on a decal by itself and place it near the VECI label

vehicle's VECI label, in a Haynes Automotive Repair Manual or in a factory service manual. But they're instructional - they DON'T necessarily apply to your vehicle. When you're working on emission control systems, if you notice differences between the vacuum diagram affixed to your vehicle and those in the owner's manual, a Haynes Auto Repair Manual for the specific vehicle or a factory manual, always go with the one on the vehicle. It's always the most accurate diagram.

If the VECI label has been removed from your vehicle, replacement labels are available at your authorized dealer parts department. (Of course, as mentioned above, sometimes the vacuum diagram is part of the VECI label, sometimes they're not.)

Repairing and replacing vacuum hose and/or plastic lines

Replace defective sections one at a time to avoid confusion or misrouting. If you discover more than one disconnected line during an inspection of the lines, refer to the vehicle vacuum schematic to make sure you reattach the lines correctly. Route rubber hoses and nylon lines away from hot components, such as EGR tubes and exhaust manifolds, and away from rough surfaces which may wear holes in them.

Most factory-installed vacuum lines are rubber, but some are nylon. Connectors can be plastic, bonded nylon or rubber. Nylon connectors usually have rubber inserts to provide a seal between the connector and the component connection.

Replacing nylon vacuum lines can be expensive and tricky. Using rubber hose may not be as aesthetically pleasing as the OEM nylon tubing, but it's perfectly acceptable, as long as the hoses and fittings are tightly connected and correctly routed (away from rough surfaces and hot EGR tubes, exhaust manifolds, etc.).

Here are some tips for repairing nylon vacuum hoses and lines:

If a nylon hose is broken or kinked, and the damaged area is 1/2-inch or more from a connector, cut out the damaged section (don't remove more than 1/2-inch) and install a rubber union.

If the remaining hose is too short, or the damage exceeds 1/2-inch in length, replace the entire hose and the original connector with rubber vacuum hoses and a tee fitting.

If only part of a nylon connector is damaged or broken, cut it apart and discard the damaged half of the harness. Then replace it with rubber vacuum hoses and a tee.

Battery, cables, electrical connections and grounds

Battery warnings and precautions:

a) Batteries give off hydrogen gas constantly. During charging, they give off even more. Hydrogen gas is highly explosive.

b) Always disconnect the battery cable from the negative battery terminal **first,** and hook it up **last**.

c) Sulfuric acid is the active ingredient in battery electrolyte (the fluid inside the battery). It's a powerful acid that will corrode all common metals, destroy paint finishes and clothing and inflict serious burns when it contacts skin and eyes.

d) If you spill electrolyte on your skin, rinse it off immediately with water.

e) If you get electrolyte in your eyes, flush them with water for 15 minutes and get prompt medical attention.

f) If you accidentally ingest electrolyte, immediately drink large amounts of water or milk. Follow with milk of magnesia, beaten eggs or vegetable oil. Call a doctor immediately.

g) When you service, charge or jump start a battery, make sure the area is well ventilated.

h) Never allow flames, cigarettes or any device that might cause a spark anywhere near a battery being charged or jump started.

i) When inspecting or servicing the battery, always turn the engine and all accessories off.

j) Never break a live circuit at the battery terminals. An arc could occur when the battery, charger or jumper cables are disconnected, igniting the hydrogen gas.

k) Always wear safety goggles when performing any work on the battery.

l) When loosening cables or working near a battery, keep metallic tools away from the battery terminals. The resulting short circuit or spark could damage the battery or ignite the hydrogen gas around the battery.

m) Never move a battery with the vent caps removed. Electrolyte can easily splash out.

n) Always use a battery carrier when lifting a battery with a plastic case or place your hands at the bottom and end of the battery. If you're not careful, too much pressure on the ends can cause acid to spew through the vent caps.

o) Use fender covers to protect the vehicle from acid spillage.

p) Keep sharp objects out of the battery tray to avoid puncturing the case, and don't over-tighten the battery hold-down.

5.7 Battery terminal corrosion usually appears as light, fluffy powder

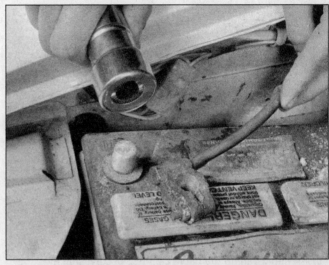

5.8 Regardless of the type of tool used on the battery posts, a clean, shiny surface should be the result

Maintenance

All batteries, although later batteries are called "maintenance free", do require some attention. Poor battery and cable connections **(see illustration)** can cause starting problems and poor operation of the electrical system. The high current requirement of the starting system means that voltage loss through the cables (voltage drop) must be minimized. The voltage drop, caused by the resistance in the cable, the ends and all their connections, reduces the amount of available voltage for cranking, starting and sometimes even computer functions. Inspect the entire length of each battery cable. Inspect the clamps and all connections. Examine the positive and negative terminals and cables for corrosion or loose connections (usually these two problems are found together, so check for both). Clean and/or replace the cables as necessary.

Clean the cable clamps thoroughly with a battery brush or a terminal cleaner **(see illustrations)** and a solution of warm water and baking soda. Wash the terminals and the top of the battery case with the same solution but make sure that the solution doesn't get into the battery. When cleaning the cables, terminals and battery top, wear safety goggles and rubber gloves to prevent any solution from coming in contact with your eyes or hands. Wear old clothes too - even diluted, sulfuric acid splashed onto clothes will burn holes in them. If the terminals have been extensively corroded, clean them with a terminal cleaner. Thoroughly wash all cleaned areas with plain water. **Note:** *Although cables can be repaired and replacement ends are available, it is a good suggestion to replace the entire cable. Replacement cables have connections that are sealed and resist corrosion much better, and thereby give the cable a longer life, than repaired connections.*

Earlier batteries, with removable vent caps, must be checked periodically for low electrolyte (battery fluid) in each of the cells. **Note:** *If you have a maintenance free battery with removable caps, it's a good idea to occasionally check the electrolyte level, regardless of the manufacturers recommendations. If any of the cells are found to be low, water can be added to bring them up to the correct level.*

5.9 When cleaning the cable clamps, all corrosion must be removed (the inside of the clamp is tapered to match the taper on the post, so don't remove too much material)

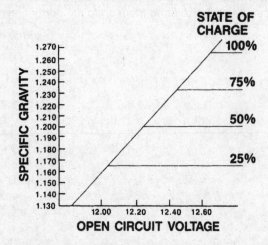

5.10 Use a hydrometer to measure the specific gravity of each individual cell

Battery condition

On models not equipped with a sealed battery, check the electrolyte level of all six battery cells. Remove the filler caps and check the level of each individual cell. - they must be at or near the split ring. If the level is low, add distilled water. Install and securely re-tighten the caps.

Use a hydrometer **(see illustration)**, that can be purchased at local automotive parts stores, and the accompanying chart **(see illustration)**, to check the state of charge of each battery cell.

If the battery has a sealed top and no built-in hydrometer to check the state of the batteries charge, you can hook up a digital voltmeter across the battery terminals to check the charge **(see illustration)**. A fully charged battery should read 12.6 volts or higher (engine off). If the voltage is less than 12.6 volts, charge the battery fully and retest.

5.11 Use the specific gravity to determine the state of charge of the battery

Battery charging

Warning: *Battery handling and servicing involves two hazardous substances: sulfuric acid and hydrogen gas. When batteries are being charged, sulfuric acids creates hydrogen gas, which is very explosive and flammable, is produced. Do not smoke or allow open flames near a charging or a recently charged battery. Wear eye protection when near the battery during charging. Also, make sure the charger is unplugged before connecting or disconnecting the battery from the charger.*

Slow-rate charging is the best way to restore a battery that's discharged to the point where it will not start the engine. It's also a good way to maintain the battery charge in a vehicle that's only driven a few miles between starts. Maintaining the battery charge is particularly important in the winter when the battery must work harder to start the engine and electrical accessories that drain the battery are in greater use.

It's best to use a one or two-amp battery charger (sometimes called a "trickle" charger). They are the safest and put the least strain on the battery. They are also the least expensive. For a faster charge, you can use a higher amperage charger, but don't use one rated more than 1/10th the amp/hour rating of the battery. Rapid boost chargers that claim to restore the power of the battery in one to two hours are hardest on the battery and can damage batteries not in good condition; this type of charging should only be used in emergency situations.

The average time necessary to charge a battery should be listed in the instructions that come with the charger. As a general rule, a trickle charger will fully charge a battery in 12 to 16 hours.

Remove all the cell caps (if equipped) and cover the holes with a clean, damp cloth to prevent spattering electrolyte. Disconnect the negative battery cable and hook the battery charger leads to the battery posts (positive to posi-

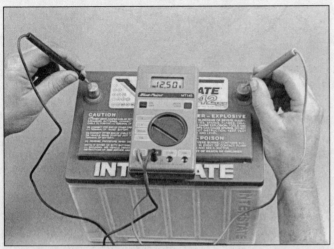

5.12 Measure the battery voltage by using the voltmeter, with a test lead at each battery post, Place the positive lead to the positive post and the negative lead to the negative post

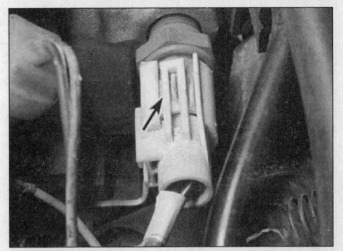

5.13 Most connectors have one or more tabs like this (arrow) that must be lifted before the halves can be separated

tive, negative to negative), then plug in the charger. Make sure it is set at 12 volts, if it has a selector switch.

If you're using a charger with a rate higher than two amps, check the battery regularly during charging to make sure it doesn't overheat. If you're using a trickle charger, you can safely let the battery charge overnight after you've checked it regularly for the first couple of hours.

If the battery has removable cell caps, measure the specific gravity with a hydrometer every hour during the last few hours of the charging cycle. Hydrometers are available inexpensively from auto parts stores - follow the instructions that come with the hydrometer. Consider the battery charged when there's no change in the specific gravity reading for two hours and the electrolyte in the cells is gassing (bubbling) freely. The specific gravity reading from each cell should be very close to the others. If not, the battery probably has a bad cell or cells.

Some batteries with sealed tops have built-in hydrometers on the top that indicate the state of charge by the color displayed in the hydrometer window. Normally, a bright-colored hydrometer indicates a full charge and a dark hydrometer indicates the battery still needs charging. Check the battery manufacturer's instructions to be sure you know what the colors mean.

Cables

Battery cables can be deceptive by their appearance. The obvious signs of cracks or corrosion may not be evident, but the cable can still need replacement. Feel the cable. Has it become extremely hard? Is it no longer flexible? Cut back the insulation at little, near the ends and examine the cable. If it shows signs of corrosion that weren't showing on the outside, replace the cable(s). **Note:** *It is recommended that battery cables be replaced in pairs. If one is bad the other is probably very close to the same condition, or shortly will be.*

Connections and electrical grounds

The electrical grounds, both the battery-to-engine block and the engine block-to-body/chassis, are usually overlooked as a source for problems. Inspect all connections, they must be clean on all contacting surfaces and the connection must be tight. Make sure there is a ground strap from the engine to the body and/or chassis.

Once the battery, cables and connections have been checked, repaired, replaced or cleaned, seal the connections from the elements using either a small amount of petroleum jelly or grease to coat the connections. There are products available at local parts stores made specifically for this purpose.

Check the electrical connections to the computer, all sensors and actuators and all other emissions devices. Make sure they're mated properly and tightly connected. Shake and wiggle the connectors to ensure they're tight. Loose connectors should be unplugged and inspected for corrosion **(see illustrations)**. Look closely at the connector pins and tabs. If corrosion is present, clean it off with a small wire brush and electrical contact cleaner. Some connectors might require use of a special conductive grease to prevent corrosion.

Charging system

Check the alternator drivebelt tension and condition. Replace the belt if it's worn or deteriorated. If the drivebelt tension is correct, try turning the alternator pulley with your hand to see if the belt is slipping **(see illustration)**. If it slips, replace the belt. When replacing a belt, adjust the tension, then make sure the alternator mounting bolts are tight.

Inspect the alternator wiring harness and the connectors at the alternator. They must be in good condition, tight and have no corrosion.

Start the engine and check the alternator for abnormal noises (a shrieking or squealing sound indicates a bad bearing).

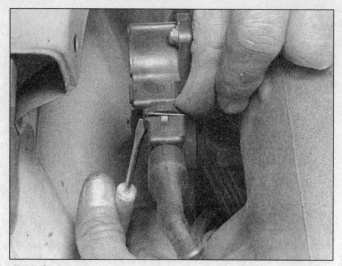

5.14 Some connectors, such as this one on a Toyota throttle position sensor, have a spring clip that must be pried up before the connector can be unplugged

5.15 Many modern engine-management system connectors have flexible seals (arrow) to keep moisture off the terminals and prevent corrosion - make sure the seal isn't damaged in any way

If the alternator is to be replaced, consider a rebuilt unit from the local parts store. Older alternators are rebuildable and most parts are readily available at auto parts stores. Some later model vehicles use alternators, referred to by the manufacturer, and aftermarket parts books, as "non-serviceable". This usually means that parts are only available to an authorized rebuilder. Many times parts are soldered or crimped in place. Some fasteners may even be the type that must be broken to disassemble the unit, requiring the same type fastener for reassembly. Don't just blindly start overhauling your alternator. Check for the availability of parts first!

For specific voltage and amperage tests see Section 8, of this Chapter.

Fuel system

Warning 1: *Gasoline is extremely flammable, so take extra precautions when you work on any part of the fuel system. Don't smoke or allow open flames or bare light bulbs near the work area, and don't work in a garage where a natural gas-type appliance (such as a water heater or a clothes dryer) with a pilot light is present. Since gasoline is carcinogenic, wear latex gloves when there's a possibility of being exposed to fuel, and, if you spill any fuel on your skin, rinse it off immediately with soap and water. Mop up any spills immediately and do not store fuel-soaked rags where they could ignite. The fuel system on fuel injected models is under constant pressure, so, if any fuel lines are to be disconnected, the fuel pressure in the system must be relieved first (see Chapter 4 for more information). When you per-*

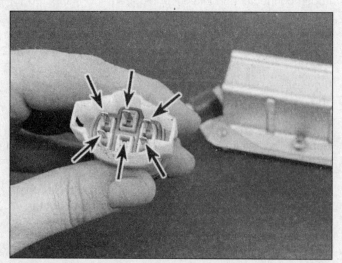

5.16 Check the terminals (arrows) in each connector for corrosion that will cause excessive resistance in the circuit, or even an open circuit

5.17 With your hand, try turning the pulley to see if the belt slips

form any kind of work on the fuel system, wear safety glasses and have a Class B type fire extinguisher on hand.

Warning 2: *Many of the flexible fuel lines/hoses used for fuel injection systems are **high-pressure** lines with special crimped-on connections. When replacing a hose, use only hose that is specifically designed for your fuel-injection system.*

This Section is to be used as a preliminary check of the fuel system before any disassembly or repairs. For more specifics on inspection, depressurization, disconnection, removal and testing refer to Chapters 4 and 6.

If you smell gasoline while driving or after the vehicle has been sitting in the sun, inspect the fuel system immediately.

Remove the gas filler cap and inspect it for damage and corrosion. The gasket should have an unbroken sealing imprint. If the gasket is damaged or corroded, remove it and install a new one.

Inspect the fuel feed and return lines for cracks. Make sure that all the fittings and connectors, which secure the metal fuel lines to the fuel injection system, and the in-line fuel filter (if equipped), are properly connected and/or tightened correctly.

Since some components of the fuel system - the fuel tank and part of the fuel feed and return lines, for example - are underneath the vehicle, they can be inspected more easily with the vehicle raised on a hoist. If that's not possible, raise the vehicle and support it securely on jackstands.

Check all rubber fuel lines for deterioration and chafing. Check especially for cracks in areas where the hose bends and just before fittings, such as where a hose attaches to the fuel filter.

With the vehicle raised and safely supported, inspect the fuel tank and filler neck for punctures, cracks and other damage. The connection between the filler neck and the tank is particularly critical. Sometimes, a rubber filler neck will leak because of loose clamps or deteriorated rubber. These are problems a home mechanic can usually rectify.

Warning: *Do not, under any circumstances, try to repair a fuel tank (except rubber components). A welding torch or any open flame can easily cause fuel vapors inside the tank to explode.*

Carefully check all rubber hoses and metal lines leading away from the fuel tank. Check for loose connections, deteriorated hoses, crimped lines and other damage. Carefully inspect the lines from the tank to the fuel rail or carburetor. Repair or replace damaged sections as necessary.

6 Fuel pressure

Key components of the fuel injection system (if equipped) include the fuel pump and the fuel pressure regulator. Incorrect fuel pressure could cause such symptoms as an engine that is hard to start or won't start, to one that hesitates, surges, or misfires. Any basic troubleshooting procedures should include a fuel pump pressure check.

Fuel pump pressures and testing procedures are covered in the *Haynes Automotive Repair Manual* for your particular vehicle, and also in the *Haynes Fuel Injection Manual*. See Chapter 8 for component and circuit checks related to the fuel injection system.

7 Troubleshooting with a vacuum gauge

General information

A vacuum gauge provides valuable information about what is going on inside the engine at a low cost. You can check for many internal engine problems such as rings and valves, leaking intake manifold gaskets, restricted exhaust, improper ignition or valve timing and ignition problems.

Vacuum system problems can produce, or contribute to, numerous driveability problems. These include, but aren't limited to:

Deceleration backfiring
Detonation
Hard to start
Knocking or pinging
Overheating
Poor acceleration
Poor fuel economy
Rich or lean stumbling
Rough idling
Stalling
Won't start when cold

Unfortunately, vacuum gauge readings are easy to misinterpret, so they should be used in conjunction with other tests to confirm the diagnosis.

Both the absolute readings and the rate of needle movement are important for accurate interpretation. Most gauges measure vacuum in inches of mercury (in-Hg). The following typical vacuum gauge readings assume the diagnosis is being performed at sea level. As elevation increases (or atmospheric pressure decreases), the reading will decrease. From sea level to approximately 2,000 feet, the gauge readings will the remain the same. For every 1,000 foot increase in elevation, above 2,000 feet, the gauge readings will decrease about one inch of mercury. **Example:** *Let's say a vehicle, at sea level, has engine vacuum of 17 to 18 in-Hg. This would be a "normal" reading and not be any indication of internal engine trouble. Now, suppose the same vehicle was driven to Denver, Colorado (5,280 feet above sea level). The vacuum reading would be approximately 14 to 15 in-Hg. This reading would be a concern at sea level, but at a mile above sea level this is an indication of "normal" internal engine vacuum.*

Connect the vacuum gauge directly to intake manifold vacuum, not to ported vacuum. You want to read full engine vacuum, uncontrolled by the throttle body or carburetor. Be sure no hoses are left disconnected during the test or false readings will result.

Before you begin the test, allow the engine to warm up completely. Block the wheels and set the parking brake. With the transmission in neutral (or Park, on automatics), start the engine and allow it to run at normal idle speed. **Warning:** *Keep your hands, the vacuum tester and hose clear of the fan and do not stand in front of the vehicle or in line with the fan when the engine is running.*

Read the vacuum gauge and as a general rule apply the following guidelines:

What is "normal" vacuum?

Internal combustion engines, regardless of four, six or eight cylinders, all have the approximately the same range for acceptable vacuum of about 15 to 20 in-Hg.

At wide-open-throttle (WOT) the vacuum reading will be 0 in-Hg, and on deceleration, vacuum may go as high, very briefly, as 25 to 30 in-Hg.

Vacuum diagnostic checks

Refer to illustrations 7.1, 7.2, 7.3, 7.4, 7.5, 7.6 and 7.7

The following guidelines for vacuum are approximate and will be affected by the overall condition of the engine and related systems:

Cranking vacuum

Disable the ignition system and hold the throttle in the wide open position. Take a reading of the engine vacuum while only cranking the engine, don't start the engine at this time. There should be approximately 1-to-4 in-Hg during cranking.

Operating readings

Start the engine and read the gauge. A healthy engine should produce approximately 15-to-20 in-Hg at idle, with a fairly steady needle.

Raise the engine speed to about 2500 rpm and hold rpm steady, a reading of approximately 19-to-21 in-Hg should be seen on the gauge.

Rev the engine up and down, watch the gauge during both increasing and decreasing rpm. At wide open throttle (hard acceleration), vacuum approaches zero. While on deceleration, the vacuum should jump up to somewhere around 21-to-27 in-Hg as the throttle is released.

If the readings you are seeing aren't at the appropriate level or steady, refer to the following vacuum gauge readings and what they indicate about the engine:

7.1 Low, steady reading

Low steady reading

This usually indicates a leaking gasket between the intake manifold and carburetor or throttle body, a leaky vacuum hose, late ignition timing or incorrect camshaft timing **(see illustration)**. Check ignition timing with a timing light and eliminate all other possible causes, utilizing the tests provided in this Chapter before you remove the timing chain cover to check the timing marks.

7.2 Low, fluctuating needle

Low, fluctuating reading

If the needle fluctuates about three to eight inches below normal **(see illustration)**, suspect an intake manifold gasket leak at an intake port or a faulty injector(s) (on port-injected models only).

Regular drops

If the needle drops about two-to-four inches at a steady rate **(see illustration)**, the valves are probably leaking. Perform a compression or leak down test to confirm this.

7.3 Regular drops

Irregular drops

An irregular down-flick of the needle **(see illustration)** can be caused by a sticking valve or an ignition misfire. Perform a compression or leak down test and read the spark plugs.

7.4 Irregular drops

Rapid vibration

A rapid four in-Hg vibration at idle **(see illustration)** combined with exhaust smoke indicates worn valve guides. Perform a leak down test to confirm this. If the rapid vibration occurs with an increase in engine speed, check for a leaking intake manifold gasket or head gasket, weak valve springs, burned valves or ignition misfire.

7.5 Rapid vibration

Slight fluctuation

A slight fluctuation, say one inch up-and-down, may mean ignition problems. Check all the usual tune-up items and, if necessary, run the engine on an ignition analyzer.

Large fluctuation

If this occurs **(see illustration)**, perform a compression or leak down test to look for a weak or dead cylinder or a blown head gasket.

7.6 Large fluctuation

Slow hunting

If the needle moves slowly through a wide range, check for a clogged PCV system, incorrect idle fuel mixture, carburetor/throttle body or intake manifold gasket leaks.

Slow return after revving

Quickly snap the throttle open until the engine reaches about 2,500 rpm and let it shut. Normally the reading

7.7 Slow return after revving

should drop to near zero, rise above normal idle reading (about 5 in.-Hg over) and then return to the previous idle reading **(see illustration)**. If the vacuum returns slowly and doesn't peak when the throttle is snapped shut, the rings may be worn. If there is a long delay, look for a restricted exhaust system (often the muffler or catalytic converter). An easy way to check this is to temporarily disconnect the exhaust ahead of the suspected part and redo the test.

Restricted or blocked exhaust

When an exhaust system becomes restricted, usually the catalytic converter, it typically causes a loss of power and backfiring through the throttle body or carburetor. A vacuum gauge can be used to check a restricted exhaust by checking for excessive exhaust backpressure and observing any vacuum variation. Follow the steps described:

1   Block the wheels and set the parking brake.
2   Disconnect a vacuum line connected to an intake manifold port and plug the line, so you don't create your own vacuum leak, and install a vacuum gauge to the intake manifold port.
3   Start the engine and record the vacuum at idle. If the vacuum reading slowly drops toward zero, there is a restriction.
4   Gradually increase speed to 2,000 rpm with the transmission in Neutral or Park. The reading from the vacuum gauge should quickly rise above the level recorded at idle, somewhere around 16 in-Hg. If not, there could be excessive backpressure in the exhaust system.
5   While at approximately 2000 rpm, quickly close the throttle. The vacuum reading should return to normal idle vacuum as quickly as it rose above it in the previous step.
6   If the vacuum reading is 5 in-Hg or more higher than the normally observed reading, there is an exhaust restriction.

Once it has been determined that the exhaust system is the cause of the problem, the exact cause must be pinpointed. Perform the following:

7   Turn the ignition key OFF.
8   Disconnect the exhaust system at the exhaust manifold.
9   Start the engine (despite the loud exhaust roar) and gradually increase the engine speed to 2,000 rpm.
10   The reading from the exhaust manifold vacuum gauge should be above 16 in-Hg.
11   If 16 in-Hg. is not reached, the exhaust manifold may be restricted (or the valve timing or ignition timing may be late, or there could be a vacuum leak).

Approximate temperature (degrees Fahrenheit)	Minimum voltage
70	9.6
60	9.5
50	9.4
40	9.3
30	9.1
20	8.9
10	8.7
0	8.5

8.1 Follow this chart to determine the acceptable minimum battery voltage, adjusting for the outside side temperature

12   If 16 in-Hg. is reached, the blockage is most likely in the muffler, exhaust pipes, or catalytic converter. Also, if the catalytic converter debris has entered the muffler, have it replaced also.

8 Starting and charging circuits

Battery

Warning: *Certain precautions must be followed when checking and servicing the battery. Hydrogen gas, which is highly flammable, is always present in the battery cells, so keep all open flames and sparks away from the battery. The electrolyte inside the battery is actually diluted sulfuric acid, which will cause injury if splashed on your skin or in your eyes. It will also ruin clothes and painted surfaces. See additional warnings and precautions in Section 5 of this Chapter.*
Caution: *Overfilling the cells may cause electrolyte to spill over during periods of heavy charging, causing corrosion or damage. When removing the battery cables, always detach the negative cable first and hook it up last!*

Charging and maintenance
See Section 5 of this Chapter.

Cranking voltage

The next check is cranking voltage. Cranking voltage is used to determine if the battery has enough reserve capacity.
1   Disable the ignition.
2   Hook up a voltmeter across the battery **(see illustration 5.12)**. Now, crank the engine for a few seconds and watch the battery voltage. This will use the starter, cranking the engine, as the load for the battery. **Note:** *In a shop the technicians would use a machine to place an artificial load on the battery to duplicate the starter's effect.*
3   The low limit for this test is 9.6 volts. If the voltage falls to the 9.6 volts, or lower, it doesn't have enough reserve power and will never keep up with the demands of the starting system. Replace the battery. **Note:** *The low limit of 9.6 volts is based upon a outside temperature of approximately 70 degrees Fahrenheit. The acceptable voltage goes down as the temperature drops. If, when testing a battery, the temperature is less than 70 degrees F, refer to the table* **(see illustration)** *for the correct minimum voltage.*

Battery ground circuit check

1   The other value to check, while cranking, is the voltage of the battery ground circuit. Hook up the voltmeter positive lead to the battery ground at the engine block or starter and the negative lead to the negative terminal of the battery. **Note:** *Be sure to touch the voltmeter probe directly to the battery post, not the clamp. If touched to the clamp, any additional resistance at that connection to the post would not*

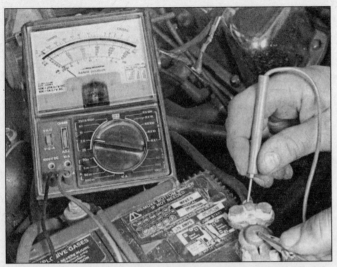

8.2 Here's a battery cable connection being checked for a voltage drop that could be caused by corrosion or a loose connection

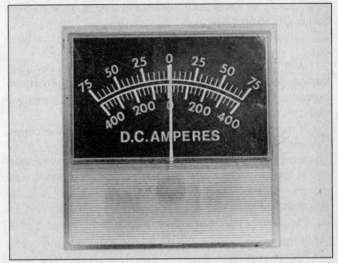

8.3 Simple inductive ammeters like this are available from auto parts stores at reasonable prices

be measured. With the ignition still disabled, crank the engine for a few seconds and note the reading on the voltmeter.

2   Readings will probably be somewhere between 0.1 and 0.3 volts. Anything above 0.3 volts is an indication of a bad ground connection. Inspect, clean and replace parts as necessary.

Voltage drops

1   The next concern is the voltage drop (the amount voltage lost from one point to another in an electrical circuit) in the battery terminals, cables, starter and connections. Hook up a voltmeter so the meter is connected across the connection where the voltage drop is to be checked, example: If the voltage loss between the battery post and connecting clamp is to be checked, the voltmeter probes should be connected to the post and the clamp **(see illustration)**.

2   Have the meter set on the volt scale and read the amount of voltage drop on the gauge, it should be 0.2 volts maximum, across any of the individual connections tested.

3   A greater reading than this would indicate an excessive voltage drop. Caused by a loose connection, corroded end or cable, rusty connection, etc. If found, repair any of these conditions and recheck the connections to be sure the problem has been corrected.

Starter

Cranking amperage (starter draw)

1   Checking the amount of cranking amperage required to operate the starter, will require the use of an inexpensive inductive amp gauge **(see illustration)** which can be found at most auto parts stores.

2   Disable the ignition system, if not already done from previous tests.

3   Place the gauge directly on the battery cable **(see illustration)**. **Note:** *In order for the reading to be accurate, the*

use of this gauge requires that it placed directly on the battery cable with about three-to-four inches of clearance from all other components to avoid magnetic interference.

4   Crank the starter and take a reading after the starter reaches a steady cranking speed. This usually takes about two-to-three seconds. **Caution:** *Don't continuously operate the starter for more than 15 seconds, it can be damaged by overheating.* Compare your readings to these general guidelines:

Four cylinder engine - 120-to-180 amps
Six cylinder engine - 150-to-200 amps
Eight cylinder engine - 180-to-220 amps

Note: *Large cubic inch or high compression eight cylinder engines, as well as engines using high performance starters, may normally use 300-to-350 amps.*

Alternator

1   If a malfunction occurs in the charging system, do not automatically assume the alternator is causing the problem.

8.4 This is another simple inductive ammeter being used to check starter draw while cranking the engine

First check the visual and maintenance items (refer to Section 5, Charging system).

2   Check the battery, as described in the previous Section.

3   With the key off, remove the cable from the negative battery terminal. Connect a test light **(see illustration)** between the negative battery post and the disconnected negative cable clamp:

a   If the test light does not come on, reattach the clamp and proceed to Step 5.

b   If the test light comes on brightly, there is a short (drain) in the electrical system of the vehicle. The short must be repaired before the charging system can be checked.

4   Disconnect the alternator wiring harness:

a   If the light goes out, there's a problem in the alternator. Repair or replace it.

b   If the light stays on, pull each fuse until the light goes out. When the light goes out it indicates which circuit has the problem.

c   Now, replace the fuse and inspect and/or disconnect each individual component of that circuit to find the cause of the current drain **Note:** *Many owners manuals have a section describing the fuse block and list of the components that are handled by each circuit. Repair and/or replace as necessary.*

5   Reconnect the cable to the negative battery terminal. Start the engine, increase engine speed to approximately 2000 RPM and check the battery voltage again. It should now be approximately 13.5 to 14.7 volts.

6   Turn on the headlights. The voltage should drop, and then come back up, if the charging system is working properly.

7   If the voltage reading is more than approximately 14.7 volts, check the regulator ground connection (vehicles with remotely mounted regulators). If the ground is OK, the problem lies in the regulator, the alternator or the wiring between them. If the vehicle has an internal regulator, replace the alternator. If the vehicle has a remotely mounted regulator, remove the electrical connector from the regulator and repeat checking the voltage at 2000 rpm. If the voltage drops with the regulator disconnected, replace the regulator. If the voltage is still high, there's a short in the wiring between the alternator and regulator or there's a short in the rotor or stator within the alternator. Check the wiring. If the wiring is OK, replace the alternator.

8   If the voltage is less than 13 volts, an undercharging condition is present. If the vehicle is equipped with an indicator light, turn the ignition key to ON and see if the light illuminates. If it does, proceed to the next Step. If it doesn't, check the indicator light circuit. In some vehicles, a faulty circuit could cause the alternator to malfunction.

9   If the indicator light circuit is OK, check for a bad ground at the voltage regulator. If the ground is OK, the problem lies in the alternator, regulator or the wiring between them. If the vehicle has an internal regulator,

8.5 To find out whether there's a drain on the battery, simply disconnect the negative battery cable and hook up a test light between the cable clamp an the battery post - if the light comes on brightly, with all the accessories off, there's an electrical drain (the light will glow dimly due to the current draw of the computer, clock and radio memories).

replace the alternator. If the vehicle has a remotely mounted regulator, check the wiring. If necessary, disconnect the cable from the negative battery terminal and check for continuity, using the vehicle's wiring diagram for reference. If the wiring is OK, you'll have to determine whether the problem lies in the alternator or regulator.

10   A good way to determine whether an undercharging problem is caused by the alternator or regulator is with a full-field test. **Caution:** *Full-fielding sends high voltage through the vehicle's electrical system, which can damage components, particularly electronic components. Carefully monitor the charging system voltage during full-fielding to be sure it doesn't exceed 16 volts. Also, do not operate a full-fielded alternator for an extended period of time. Operate it only long enough to take the voltage reading.* Basically, the full-field test bypasses the regulator to send full battery voltage to the alternator's field (the rotor). If the charging voltage is normal when the alternator is "full-fielded," you know the alternator is OK. If the voltage is still low, the problem is in the alternator. It's best to obtain wiring diagrams for the vehicle to determine the best way to send battery voltage to the field. However, the following gives some general guidelines which may help you in determining how to full-field the alternator:

a   On older Delco (GM) alternators with remotely mounted regulators ("B"-circuit type), disconnect the electrical connector from the regulator and connect a jumper wire between the BAT and F terminals of the connector.

b   On Ford Motorcraft alternators with remotely mounted regulators ("B"-circuit type), disconnect the electrical connector from the regulator and connect a jumper wire between the A and F terminals of the connector.

8.6 This is a typical example of how the identifying information will look on an alternator

a To check the condition of the alternator output, even if no symptoms are occurring currently, hook up a volt meter to the alternator output wire and ground. Set the selector to AC voltage. With the engine running there should be no more than 0.5 AC volts. Any reading any higher than .5 volts indicates replacement or repairs to the alternator are necessary.

b Start the engine and see if there is an engine miss. If there is, turn off the engine, and disconnect the alternator output wire (wire from the alternator to the battery). Restart the engine with the wire disconnected. If the miss has stopped, perform a thorough check and test of the charging system.

9 Ignition system

General information

With the introduction of electronic ignition (Breakerless ignition) many of the areas that could create a problem, such as points and condensers, were eliminated. If information on detailed diagnosis, overhaul or removal and installation is needed, refer to the specific *Haynes Automotive Repair Manual* for the vehicle being worked on.

Distributor (if equipped)

The distributor is a key component that determines engine operation and performance. The distributor is made up of a mechanical, electrical and, on some models, a vacuum system. Each of these need to be inspected, repaired and/or replaced as necessary. **Note:** *Many later model vehicles don't use mechanical advance above idle (they do have some mechanical timing built in for initial timing), these vehicles have computer controlled timing advance.*

Make sure the wires are numbered before removal, then remove the spark plug wires from the distributor cap. Remove the distributor cap and rotor and inspect the parts for cracks, carbon tracking between terminals, pitting or corrosion buildup on electrodes, etc. **(see illustrations on the following page).** If any of these are evident replace the necessary parts. **Note:** *Always replace the cap and rotor together as a set. The air gap between the tip of the rotor and the terminal in the cap is critical to delivering correct firing voltage.*

Mechanical advance

1 Most distributors use weights and springs to mechanically advance the ignition timing as rpm increases. Once the cap and rotor are removed, the mounting positions of the weights and springs can be easily seen **(see illustration).**

2 With the rotor removed turn the shaft, it will only move slightly, and let it snap back. If it is operating properly the weights should move out from their rest positions, when turned, and the spring tension should snap them back into

---

c On Chrysler alternators with remotely mounted electronic voltage regulators ("A"-circuit type), disconnect the regulator connector and connect a jumper wire between the green wire terminal of the connector and ground.

11 Make the connections with the ignition turned OFF, then repeat Step 5, above. The voltage reading should be high (about 15 to 16 volts). If it's not, the alternator is faulty. If it is, the regulator is probably bad.

Alternator output amperage

1 To check the amount of output amperage will require the use of an inductive amp gauge. These are inexpensive and can be found at most local auto parts stores. In order for the reading to be accurate, the use of this gauge only requires that it placed on the output wire of the alternator.

2 Place a load on the electrical system of the vehicle. Do this by turning on all lights and accessories for approximately one minute before and during testing.

3 Start the engine and accelerate to about 1500-to-2000 rpm. Hold the gauge in place and read the amps, it should be within a few amps of the rated output of the alternator **(see illustration). Note:** *The output amperage of an alternator is stamped either in the housing or on a tag attached to the housing.*

Alternator voltage - "AC (alternating current) bleed off"

1 A last check is to look for AC voltage "leaks" or voltage "bleed off". **Note:** *Voltage spikes that are cause by a failed or weak diodes can fool the ECM and create an engine misfire.* Diodes in the alternator are supposed to direct all electrical flow into DC (direct current) voltage. A failed or weakened diode can allow small amounts of AC voltage to surge back through the circuit.

2 AC bleed off can be checked for in two ways:

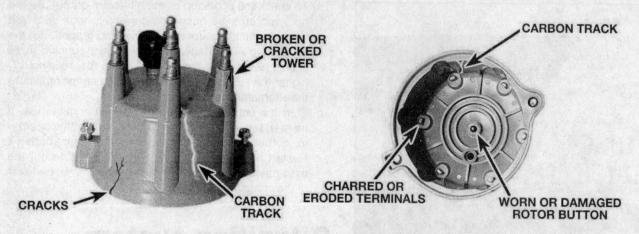

9.1 Shown here are some of the common defects to look for when inspecting the distributor cap (if in doubt about its condition, install a new one)

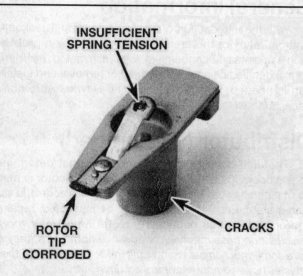

9.2 The ignition rotor should be checked for wear and corrosion as indicated here (if in doubt about its condition, install a new one)

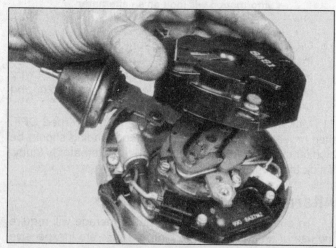

9.3 To detach the rotor, in order to get to the centrifugal weights and springs, remove the two screws on top and lift off the rotor

place when the shaft is released.

3   Watch to make sure the weights don't stick. A very thin film of lubrication between the weights and the top of the shaft should be all that is needed to allow the weights to move freely.

Vacuum advance

Note: *Computer controls have done away with vacuum advance on many later model vehicles. This information only applies to models with vacuum operated advance.*

1   The diaphragm assembly is attached to the distributor breaker plate. A vacuum line attaches the diaphragm housing to a ported vacuum source. As vacuum changes from idle to acceleration through deceleration and back to idle, the timing changes accordingly.

2   With the engine off, check the condition of the vacuum

hose from the distributor to the vacuum source. Make sure the hose is connected and the connections seal well (see Section 5).

3   Disconnect and plug the vacuum hose to the distributor. Connect a vacuum pump to vacuum diaphragm **(see illustration)**. Apply between 15-to-20 in-Hg and make sure the diaphragm assembly holds vacuum. If it bleeds down, replace the diaphragm assembly. **Note:** *This assembly can be replaced without removal of the distributor.*

4   Connect a timing light to the engine according to the manufacturers instructions.

5   Start the engine and allow it to idle. Shine the timing light on the scale and while watching the timing indicator, apply 5-to-10 in-Hg to the diaphragm.

6   As the vacuum is applied, does the timing change? It should, this indicates that the advance is working properly. The engine will probably stumble or stall as more vacuum is applied. If the assembly holds vacuum when applied, but no timing advance takes place, the advance plate inside the

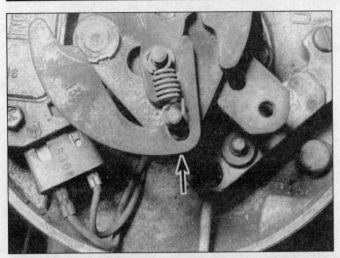

9.4 An example of a worn centrifugal advance weight - note the elongated hole showing the need for replacement

9.5 Apply vacuum to the vacuum advance unit and observe movement of the distributor plate

distributor is stuck.

7 If the vacuum advance is functioning as described, it may be wise to inspect and test other components or systems in this general way first, in order to look for obvious failures. Then if the cause isn't found, inspect different systems with an emphasis on looking for components out of specifications.

Ignition module and coil

1 In the previous tests for available coil voltage and available spark plug firing voltage, the end check for voltages would verify that the components of the ignition system are working properly. If not, there would no voltage readings for any of the tests performed.

2 The condition of the coil and module and any tests to be conducted, although important, are beyond the scope of this manual. If there is no voltage reading the problem(s) will need to be diagnosed further. The primary concern of this manual is engine management system-related problems and corrections. **Note:** *There are many variations of manufacturers wiring, connections, components, locations and appropriate test procedures for ignition modules, coils or Distributorless Ignition Systems (DIS). If further information is needed to diagnose or repair the vehicle electrical system, beyond the information given in Sections 5 and this Section, refer to the specific Haynes Automotive Repair Manual for the vehicle being repaired.*

Spark plug wires

1 The spark plug wires should be checked at the recommended intervals and whenever new spark plugs are installed in the engine.

2 Using a clean rag, wipe the entire length of the wire to remove built-up dirt and grease. Once the wire is clean, check for burns, cracks and other damage. Do not bend the wire sharply, because the conductor might break.

3 Make a visual check of the spark plug wires while the engine is running. In a darkened garage (make sure there is adequate ventilation) start the engine and observe each plug wire. Be careful not to come into contact with any moving engine parts. If there is a break in the wire, you will see arcing or a small spark at the damaged area. If arcing is noticed, stop the engine, allow the engine to cool and replace the necessary parts.

4 The wires should be further inspected, if necessary, one at a time to prevent mixing up the order, which is essential to proper engine operation.

5 Disconnect the plug wire from the spark plug. A removal tool can be used for this purpose or you can grasp the rubber boot, twist the boot half a turn, to break it loose from the spark plug, and pull the boot free **(see illustration)**. Do not pull on the wire itself.

6 Disconnect the wire from the distributor, or coil pack. Again, pull only on the rubber boot.

7 Check inside the boot for corrosion, which will look like a white crusty powder. **Note:** *Don't mistake white, dielectric grease, for corrosion. Many manufacturers use this grease during assembly to prevent corrosion.*

Spark plug wire resistance check

8 Spark plug wires, some times referred to as ignition

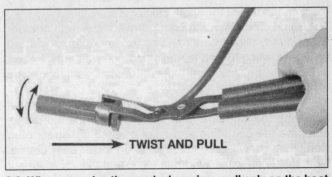

9.6 When removing the spark plug wires, pull only on the boot and twist it back-and-forth - a spark plug wire removal tool makes this job easier and safer

cables, should be checked for continuity to determine if they need replacement. **Note:** *Spark plug wires can be replaced separately. It sometimes is all that is needed to correct a problem. But it is suggested that if any need replacement, they all be replaced as a set. Even if not all wires test bad, their condition is probably very similar to the ones that are already in need of replacement.*

9   There are some general resistance (ohms) values used to test spark plug wires. Remove each spark plug wire, one at a time, and hook up an ohm meter (see Chapter 2). Measure the resistance of each wire. Use the following guidelines for interpreting your vehicle's resistance readings:

a) When measuring the resistance value of the spark plug wires there should be approximately 1K (1,000) ohms per inch of length.

b) There should not be a resistance of more than 30K (30,000) ohms for any complete spark plug wire, regardless of length.

10   These resistance values are for new or used spark plug wires. If your test values are outside these ranges, replace the spark plug wires.

11   Inspect the remaining spark plug wires, making sure that each one is securely fastened at the distributor, or coil pack, and spark plug when the check is complete.

12   Push the wire and boot back onto the end of the spark plug. It should fit tightly onto the end of the plug and 'snap' into place, indicating a proper connection. If it doesn't, remove the wire and use pliers to carefully crimp the metal connector inside the wire boot until the fit is correct.

13   If new spark plug wires are required, purchase a set for your specific engine model. Pre-cut wire sets with the boots already installed are available or spark plug cable and terminal ends of many different angles can be purchased for anyone that wants to route the wires to fit a custom application. Remove and replace the wires one at a time to avoid mix-ups in the firing order.

Spark plugs

Removal

14   The spark plugs provide a sort of window into the combustion chamber and can give a wealth of information about engine operation to a savvy mechanic. Fuel mixture, heat range, oil consumption and detonation all leave their mark on the tips of the spark plugs.

15   Before you begin the check, drive the vehicle at highway speed, allowing it to warm up thoroughly without excessive idling. Shut the engine off and wait until it cools sufficiently so you won't get burned if you touch the exhaust manifolds.

16   Whether you are replacing the plugs at this time, or just removing to inspect, and intend to re-use the old plugs, compare the condition and color of each old spark plug with those shown. **(see illustration on inside rear cover)**. **Note:** *If a spark plug is worn to the extent that replacement is necessary, it's recommended that all spark plugs be replaced at the same time.*

17   If compressed air is available, blow any dirt or foreign material away from the spark plug area before proceeding (a common bicycle pump will also work).

18   Check the spark plug wires to see if they have the cylinder numbers on them. Label them if necessary so you can reinstall them on the correct spark plugs.

19   Never remove the spark plug wire connector from the spark plug by pulling the wire. Be sure, even when grabbing the boot, that the connector is being grasped before pulling it off the plug. There are some helpful spark plug removal tools available at local automotive parts stores.

20   Once the spark plug wires have been disconnected, proceed with removing the spark plug(s).

Heat range

21   Remove the spark plugs and place them in order on top of the air cleaner or on the work bench. Note the brand and number on the plugs. Compare this to the VECI label, which is the manufacturers recommendation for that vehicle, to determine if the correct type and heat range is being used.

22   Spark plug manufacturers make spark plugs in several heat ranges for different vehicle applications and driving conditions. These have been determined by working with the vehicle manufacturers to come up with the proper match of spark plug to engine requirements.

23   The engine must have the correct heat range spark plugs before you can read the tips accurately. Plugs that are too hot will mask a rich fuel mixture reading; conversely, cold plugs will tend to foul on a normal mixture. On most European and Japanese spark plugs, the higher the number, the colder the heat range. American plugs are just the opposite.

24   There are several "old mechanic's tales" about heat range that need to be dispelled. Hotter heat range plugs don't make the engine run hotter, they don't make a hotter spark and they don't increase combustion chamber temperature (unless the colder plug wasn't firing).

25   If a change in spark plug heat range is being considered, first ask - what is causing the engine to run in a way that necessitates a change? Manufacturers go to a great deal of trouble to determine the correct plug type, heat range and gap for every vehicle on the market. It's recommended that the spark plug requirements, found on the VECI label under the hood, should be followed at all times. After the conditions are corrected that were causing the spark plug to fire poorly, the original spark recommendation will work as it was intended. **Note:** *Non-resistor spark plugs can add electrical interference or "noise" to the ECM and/or sensor circuits. This is sometimes referred to as "spark echo" (think of all that static that solid, non-resistor, plug wires caused on the radio of your old hot rod). This can have a direct affect on the low amperage current used by computer control vehicles to monitor and control engine functions, such as fuel ratios, spark timing, etc. or any circuit that is controlled by low voltage impulses.*

9.7 An example of a wire-type gauge for checking the gap - if the wire does not slide between the electrodes with a slight drag, adjustment is required

9.8 To change the gap, bend the side electrode as shown to specification, be careful not to chip or crack the porcelain insulator

Reading spark plugs

26 Examine the plugs for hints about the engine's internal condition and state of tune. If any of the plugs are wet with oil, engine repairs are needed right away. If the plugs have significant gray or white deposits, it means that a moderate amount of oil is seeping into the cylinders and repairs will be needed soon, or you've been doing a lot of short trip driving.

27 The ideal color for plugs used in engines run on leaded gasoline is light brown on the insulator cone and beige on the ground (side) electrode. Engines that run on unleaded gasoline tend to leave very little color on the plugs. Late-model emission-controlled engines run very lean. Normally, the plugs range from almost white to tan on the porcelain insulator cone and the ground electrode should be light brown to dark gray.

28 Excessively rich fuel mixtures cause the spark plugs tips to turn black and lean mixtures result in light tan or white tips. You can tell by the color if the fuel mixture is in the ballpark by reading the plugs.

29 If the engine has a misfire and one or more plugs are carbon fouled, look for an ignition problem or low compression in the affected cylinder(s). Sometimes the spark plugs will vary among each other in color because of improper mixture distribution. Look for a leaky intake manifold gasket if one or more adjoining cylinders are running very lean. If the plugs are burning unevenly, you may have a vacuum leak, or a fuel distribution problem in the fuel injection system.

30 Detonation, preignition and plugs that are too long can result in physical damage to the tip. Check the accompanying photos to help identify these problems.

31 You will also need a gauge, different types are available, to check and adjust the spark plug gap and a torque wrench to tighten the new plugs to the specified torque.

32 If you are replacing the plugs, purchase the new plugs, adjust them to the proper gap and then replace each plug one at a time. **Caution:** *When buying new spark plugs, it's*

essential that you obtain the correct plugs for your specific vehicle. Don't substitute spark plugs, use what was designed for the vehicle. This information can be found on the Vehicle Emissions Control Information (VECI) label located on the underside of the hood or in the owner's manual **(see Section 3).** *Many people, even professionals, sometimes substitute heat ranges for the ones called for by the manufacturer. This is a mistake and misses the underlying reason for the condition of the spark plugs. If the spark plug change is to correct a problem (not just a tune-up) the new plug may mask the real cause of the driveability problem, which still exist. Correct the cause and the recommended spark plugs will work as they were originally designed. Incorrect spark plug selection can cause engine damage.*

33 Inspect each of the new plugs for defects. If there are any signs of cracks in the porcelain insulator of a plug, don't use it. Check the electrode gaps of the new plugs. Check the gap by inserting the gauge of the proper thickness between the electrodes at the tip of the plug **(see illustration).** The gap between the electrodes should be identical to the manufacturers specifications, which are listed on the VECI label. If the gap is incorrect, use the notched adjuster, on a wire type gauge, on the feeler gauge to bend the curved side electrode slightly.

34 If the side electrode is not exactly over the center electrode, use the notched adjuster to align them **(see illustration). Caution:** *If the gap of a new plug must be adjusted, bend only the base of the side electrode, do not touch the tip.*

Installation

35 Prior to installation, apply a light film of anti-seize compound or a drop of oil on the spark plug threads **(see illustration).** It's often difficult to insert spark plugs into their holes without cross-threading them. To avoid this possibility, fit a short piece of rubber hose, or an old spark plug boot, over the end of the spark plug **(see illustration).** The flexible hose, or boot, acts as a universal joint to help align

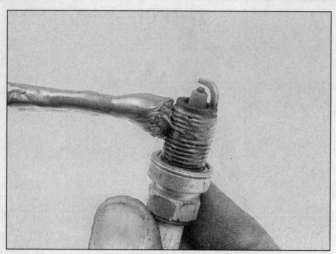

9.9 Apply a very thin coat of anti-seize compound, or a few drops of oil, to the spark plug threads ease in installation and prevent the spark plug from seizing in the cylinder head

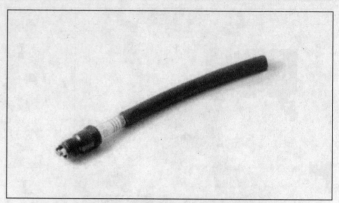

9.10 A length of rubber hose will save time and prevent damaged threads when installing the spark plugs

the plug with the plug hole. Should the plug begin to cross-thread, the hose will slip on the spark plug, preventing thread damage. Follow the manufacturers recommendations for torque when tightening the plugs on installation. If that information isn't readily available, use the following guidelines:

a) Spark plugs with a gasket require only 1/4 additional turn, after the gasket makes contact with the cylinder head, to seal properly.

b) Tapered seat spark plugs, ones that have no gasket, require only 1/16 additional turn, after the spark plug seat contacts the cylinder head, to seal properly.

36   Attach the plug wire to the new spark plug, again using a twisting motion on the boot until it is firmly seated on the end of the spark plug.

37   Follow the above procedure for the remaining spark plugs, replacing them one at a time to prevent mixing up the spark plug wires.

Available spark plug firing voltage

Warning 1: *Before starting these procedures, make sure the vehicle is in park or in neutral with the parking brake set. Always perform all tests while standing to the side of the vehicle - never from the front.*

Warning 2: *To avoid electrical shock,* **always use** *insulated pliers* **(see illustration 9.6)** *when it's necessary to grasp the high voltage spark plug wire, with the engine running, in order to perform tests.*

Note: *The purpose of the following voltage tests are to verify that the ignition system is functioning properly, which must be done before a proper engine management diagnosis can be continued. Although this test would normally be performed on an Engine Analyzer or Oscilloscope, they can successfully be performed with a far less expensive hand-held digital K-V tester with an inductive pick-up.*

1   Spark plug firing voltage is a measurement of the available output of the entire ignition circuit, checked at the spark plugs. Checking for the correct end result, such as the firing voltages within their specifications, is a quick confirmation of all the parts of the primary and secondary ignition circuits are functioning properly.

2   Using an inductive digital K-V tester, attach the meter to each individual spark plug wire, one at a time, perform the tests and record the voltage readings described in the following steps to determine the condition of the entire ignition circuit.

3   Start the vehicle and read the meter at idle while performing a "snap-test". **Note:** *It's called a snap-test because the voltage reading is taken as the throttle is quickly opened and allowed to return to idle ("snapped").* The general guidelines for the voltage readings, of an engine in good operating condition, are:

a) Idle - 10-to-12 kilovolts (kV)

b) Snap-test - 15-to-25kV (up to 30kV on distributorless ignition systems)

4   Look for consistency between cylinders at idle and on the snap-test. Variations would indicate the ignition system components are worn to different degrees. Inspect the components in question and repair or replace as necessary.

5   If there is no voltage reading the problem will need to be diagnosed further, which is beyond the scope of this manual. The primary concern of this manual is engine management related problems and corrections. If further information is needed to diagnose or repair the electrical system beyond the information given in Section 5 and this Section of this manual, refer to the specific *Haynes Automotive Repair Manual* for the vehicle being repaired.

Available coil voltage

1   This test will check the available coil voltage to verify the condition of the coil(s).

2   Attach the inductive K-V tester to one of the spark plug wires as in the previous tests. Disconnect the spark plug wire from the spark plug and secure it away from the

engine. **Caution:** *Never pull the on the spark plug wire itself, it can be internally damaged. Grasp the boot over the tip of the spark plug. The open created by disconnecting the spark plug wire causes the build up of voltage that the coil is trying to send to ground through the spark plug. The available coil voltage goes to maximum buildup when this open in the circuit is made.*

3   Disable the fuel system so the engine won't start (see Chapter 4) and crank the engine over long enough to take the reading.

4   A general guideline of 30-to-50 kilovolts (kV) (30,000-to-50,000 volts) of available coil voltage indicates a coil with sufficient reserve capacity for times of greater demand.

5   If there is no voltage reading the problem will need to be diagnosed further, which is beyond the scope of this manual. The primary concern of this manual is engine management related problems and corrections. If further information is needed to diagnose or repair the electrical system beyond the information given in Section 5 and this Section of the manual, refer to the specific *Haynes Automotive Repair Manual* for the vehicle being repaired.

Rotor tip-to-cap terminal air gap voltage check

1   Another important test to perform is the rotor tip-to-cap terminal air gap voltage (the voltage required for spark to "jump" the air gap between the rotor tip and the distributor cap terminal). This test checks the condition of the distributor cap and rotor without removing the cap. **Note:** *The visual check of parts for cracks, carbon tracking, etc. should have been done in the previous inspection steps.*

2   Different manufacturers have different specifications when manufacturing their parts. So the voltage required to jump the gap inside the distributor cap, even with new parts, can vary. But as a general rule it only takes 2000-to-3000 volts to jump from the rotor tip to the distributor cap terminal. Normally voltages higher than approximately 5000-to-6000 volts would indicate an excessive gap or very pitted, deteriorated condition of the parts. Replace all necessary parts based upon voltage readings and visual inspection.

3   To perform the test attach the inductive K-V tester to the spark plug wires, as in the previous tests, Disable the fuel system so the engine won't start (see Chapter 4).

4   Disconnect the spark plug wire from the spark plug and ground the terminal against the block or cylinder head, crank the engine over and read the voltage on the meter.

5   With the wire connected directly to ground, the only air gap remaining in the circuit is the gap from the rotor tip to the terminal post. So the voltage reading is what is required to bridge the air gap.

Timing and idle speed

1   The first thing to do, before actually pulling out your timing light, is to look up the **correct specifications and adjustment procedures. Caution:** *Don't just read that sentence - it's important to actually follow the procedures to the*

9.11 Align the notch in the pulley with the 0 on the timing scale then check to see if the distributor rotor is pointing to the number 1 cylinder

letter. One of the most overlooked or misadjusted items in the diagnosis of driveability problems or a tune-up, is setting the timing either to the wrong specification or not following the proper steps necessary to correctly set the timing.

2   This information can be found in several places. First find and read the VECI label (see Section 3) under the hood. If this label is affixed to the vehicle, always use this information before any other source. If the label is missing, a possibility if the vehicle has been repaired previously, contact the auto dealership to order another to be put back in the originals place. If more information is needed refer to the specific *Haynes Automotive Repair Manual* that applies to your vehicle.

3   Next, locate the timing marks on the vibration damper and engine cover **(see illustration). Note:** *Some manufacturers have the timing marks on the flywheel, and an inspection cover must be removed to see the marks for Top Dead Center (TDC) location or timing adjustment.* Clean them off so no mistake is made, not even a couple of degrees, when aligning the marks during the timing procedure. If the marks are faint or there are multiple marks to choose from, highlight the correct marks so it will make locating of the correct marks easier when timing is set. Typing correction fluid works great. It has a small brush in the bottle and isn't easily washed off, so it will be there for the next tune-up. Chalk also works.

Base timing (initial advance)

4   Base timing is made up of two forms of advance, base timing and built in mechanical advance. Together they give the engine the base timing, before any centrifugal or computer control timing advance, above idle, is added by the computer.

5   The following guidelines are general and will be close for most vehicles. If more information is needed, refer to the Haynes Automotive Repair Manual specifically for your vehicle:

6   Advance, at idle, will generally be between 15 and 25-

degrees BTDC. This is the advance that is seen at the timing marks with your timing light, and the built in mechanical advance of the distributor.

Total advance

7   Advance at about 2500 rpm will generally be between 30 and 50-degrees BTDC, of total advance. This is the initial, built-in advance plus base timing, and the centrifugal advance of either the mechanical weights and springs, or a computer controlled amount of timing advance.

Timing adjustment and idle speed

Caution: *Misadjusted base ignition timing and idle speed are probably the two major causes for most driveability problems found during a tune-up. The computer system takes many of it's readings and makes it's adjustments using this information as a basis. If these are wrong, the subsequent engine management functions will also be wrong. Many times the end result will appear to be a fuel injection or engine management problem, when in fact it's only a misadjustment of the fundamentals.*

8   Many times, when tuning a vehicle, the timing is adjusted to try and offset some other problem (idles too slow, pings on acceleration, etc.). A slight deviation of approximately 2 or 3-degrees is usually all right. Be careful, if the timing has to be moved, maybe 5-degrees or more, then it should raise a warning flag that there is probably something else to be corrected, or replaced, before the timing changes should even be considered. Again don't take it upon yourself to re-engineer the specifications. Follow the VECI label that is found on the vehicle, and don't deviate.

9   This is one of the most commonly ignored or misadjusted specifications of any repair work done. Some "mechanics" think they know better. Better than the people who designed and tested it? I would question that answer. **Always** adjust the base idle speed, fast idle, minimum air rate, etc. to the specification listed, and follow exactly the procedures outlined on the VECI label of the vehicle being worked on.

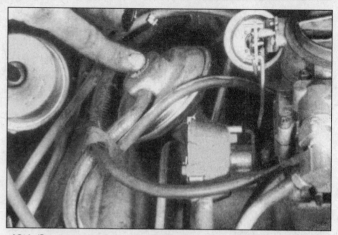

10.1 On most models, the EGR valve is located on the intake manifold, adjacent to the throttle body

10   For correct adjustment procedures and specifications of minimum idle speed, refer to the VECI label of your vehicle and Chapter 6 of this manual.

10 EGR (Exhaust Gas Recirculation) system

General information

To reduce oxides of nitrogen emissions, a small amount of exhaust gas is recirculated through the EGR valve **(see illustration)** into the intake manifold. The introduction of the inert gas lowers the combustion temperatures, which reduces the oxides of nitrogen. The EGR system **(see illustration)** typically consists of the EGR valve, the EGR modulator, vacuum switching valve, the Electronic Control Module (ECM) and the EGR gas temperature sen-

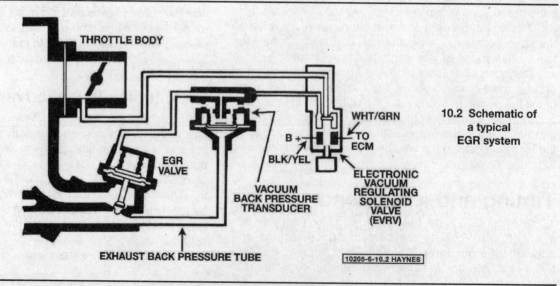

10.2 Schematic of a typical EGR system

10.3 Some EGR solenoids (left arrow) are installed on a bracket near the EGR valve, such as this on a Nissan Maxima. The arrow on the right points to the air injection system solenoid

10.4 Some EGR solenoids are installed on the firewall, in an array of other solenoids, such as these units on a Ford Thunderbird - the vacuum valve (1) supplies vacuum to the electronic EGR valve when energized; when de-energized, the vent valve (2) vents the EGR valve to the atmosphere through a small vent (3)

sor (found on some California models only).

Early EGR systems are made up of a vacuum-operated valve that admits exhaust gas into the intake manifold (EGR valve), and a hose that is connected to a ported vacuum source. A Thermostatic Vacuum Switch (TVS) is spliced into a pipe that is threaded into the radiator or, more typically, into the coolant passage near the thermostat. The TVS detects the operating temperature of the engine and doesn't allow the EGR to operate until the correct temperature is reached.

At idle, the throttle plate blocks the vacuum port - no vacuum reaches the valve, allowing it to remain closed. As the throttle opens and uncovers the port, a vacuum signal is sent to the EGR valve which slowly opens the valve, allowing exhaust gases to circulate into the intake manifold.

Since the introduction of the exhaust gas leans the fuel mixture and causes a rough idle and stalling when the engine is cold, the TVS only allows vacuum to the EGR valve when the engine is at normal operating temperature.

Also, when the throttle is opened on full acceleration, there is little or no ported vacuum available to the EGR, resulting in little or no EGR flow, which would cause mixture dilution and interfere with power output.

On later vehicles there are additional sensors and actuators included in the EGR system. The EGR valve acts on direct command from the computer after it (the computer) has determined that all the working parameters (air temperature, coolant temperature, EGR valve position, fuel/air mixture etc.) are correct.

Later model EGR valves are often controlled by a computer-controlled solenoid in line with the valve and vacuum source **(see illustrations)**. Some models also often have a position sensor on the EGR valve that informs the computer what position the EGR valve is in **(see illustration)**.

The EGR valve could be either a negative or positive backpressure type of valve. For the purposes of replace-

10.5 Some EGR valves are also equipped with a position sensor like this unit on a Ford Thunderbird - the position sensor is almost always mounted on top of the EGR valve

ment you may need to know which type it is, but for a function check it really isn't that important. The biggest concern is that the valve has movement, indicating a good signal to the EGR valve. Also, that with the movement of the EGR the engine rpm is changing, indicating that the EGR command, and exhaust gases are getting to the engine. If more detailed information is needed for any reason, refer to the *Haynes Automotive Emissions Control Manual* or the *Haynes Automotive Repair Manual* for the specific vehicle.

Checking EGR systems

Warning: *Wear gloves whenever it is necessary to touch the EGR valve - they can become very hot during engine opera-*

10.6 Apply vacuum to the EGR valve and check with the tip of the finger for movement of the diaphragm (if the valve is hot be sure to wear a glove). It should move smoothly without any binding with vacuum applied (this check won't work on a positive backpressure type valve unless the engine is running and the exhaust system is artificially restricted).

10.7 With the engine running, check for vacuum to the EGR valve

tion.

1   There are several basic EGR system checks that you can perform on your vehicle to pinpoint problems. To perform these checks you will need a vacuum pump **(see illustration)** and a vacuum gauge.

2   Check for a vacuum source **(see illustration)** by hooking up a vacuum gauge to the line going to the EGR valve.

3   If no vacuum if found, the vehicle may have computer controlled solenoids, which regulate the vacuum to the EGR valve **(see illustrations 10.3 and 10.4)**, depending upon conditions such as the transmission being in drive, engine at operating temperature, open or closed loop computer operation, etc.

4   If the EGR valve diaphragm is accessible, lightly push it up or down slightly (against spring pressure) to see if it can move and operate freely **(see illustration)**.

5   If it is stuck, proceed to Step 13.

6   If the EGR valve stem moves smoothly and the EGR system continues to malfunction, check for a pinhole vacuum leak in the diaphragm of the EGR valve. Obtain a can of spray carburetor cleaner and attach the flexible "straw" to the tip. Aim carefully into the diaphragm areas of the EGR valve and spray around the actuator shaft while the engine is running. Listen carefully for any changes in engine rpm. If there is a leak, the engine rpm will increase and surge temporarily. Then it will smooth back out to a constant idle. The only way to properly repair this problem is to replace the EGR valve with a new unit.

7   After the engine has been warmed up to normal operating temperature, open the throttle to approximately 2,500 rpm and observe the EGR valve stem as it moves with the rise in engine rpm. Use a mirror or even a finger placed on the diaphragm to feel movement, if necessary. If it doesn't move, remove the vacuum hose and check for vacuum with a gauge. Reconnect the hose, raise the rpm of the engine

10.8 Use your finger to check for free movement of the diaphragm within the EGR valve

and see or feel if the valve opens up and/or flutters approximately 1/8 inch. Larger abrupt, jerky movements and/or opening all the way will cause a driveability problem and is not indicative of correct operation. Replace the EGR valve. **Warning:** *A computer-controlled EGR valve needs to have the vehicle placed into gear in order for the computer to signal the valve to work. Block the wheels, have an assistant sit in the vehicle and apply the parking brake **and** press firmly on the brake pedal before placing the vehicle in gear for this check.*

8   This test will tell you if the gas flow passages are open and if the gas flow is proper. Remove the vacuum line from the EGR valve and plug the line. Attach a hand-held vacuum pump to the EGR valve. With the engine idling, slowly apply approximately 8-to-10 in-Hg to the valve and watch the valve stem for movement. **Note:** *If the valve is a positive backpressure type, it will be necessary to create an exhaust restriction. This can be done by folding a thick towel over a few times, soaking it in water then having an assistant hold it*

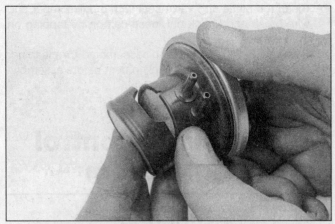

10.9 To remove the EGR vacuum modulator filters (if equipped) for cleaning, remove the cap . . .

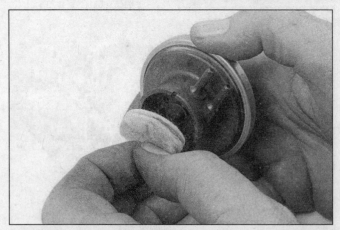

10.10 . . .then pull out the filter(s) and blow it out with compressed air - be sure the coarse side of the outer filter faces the atmosphere (out) when reinstalling the filters

10.11 Depress the EGR valve diaphragm and inspect the full length of the pintle and the seat at its base for carbon deposits

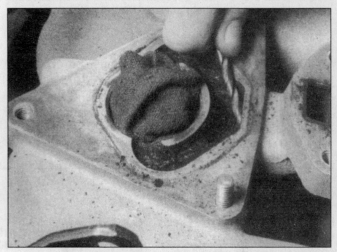

10.12 With a rag in the passage opening, the exhaust gas passages can be scrapped clean of deposits

over the end of the exhaust pipe (don't do this any longer than necessary to perform the test). If the gas flow is good, the engine will begin to idle rough or it may even stall. If the stem moves but the idle does not change, there is a restriction in the valve spacer plate or passages in the intake manifold (see *Cleaning the EGR valve*). If the valve stem does not move or the EGR valve diaphragm does not hold vacuum, replace the EGR valve with a new part.

9   The thermostatic vacuum switch (TVS) should also be checked, if equipped. This switch is usually regulated by a bimetal core that expands or contracts according to the temperature. The valve remains closed and does not operate as long as the coolant temperature is below 115 to 129-degrees F. As the coolant temperature rises, the valve will open and the EGR system will operate. Remove the switch and place it in a pan of cool water and check the valve for vacuum - vacuum should not pass through the valve. Heat the water to the specified temperature (over 129-degrees F) and make sure the valve opens and allows the vacuum to pass. If the switch fails the test, replace it with a new part.

EGR vacuum modulator valve (if equipped)

10   Remove the valve.
11   Pull the cover off and check the filters **(see illustrations)**.
12   Replace the filters or clean them with compressed air, reinstall the cover and the modulator.

Cleaning the EGR valve

13   The bottoms of EGR valves often get covered with carbon deposits **(see illustration)**, causing them to restrict exhaust flow or leak exhaust. The valve must be removed so the bottom of the valve and the passages in the manifold can be cleaned **(see illustration). Caution:** *When removing the EGR valve be sure to replace the gasket upon reassembly* **(see illustration)**. *There is generally more heat at this location, because of exhaust gases, and the gasket deteriorates quickly. If not replaced, the gasket, can be the source of an exhaust leak after reassembly.*

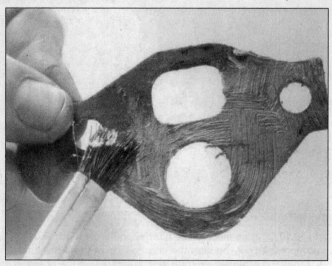

10.13 Coat the new EGR base gasket with a lithium-based grease to help preserve the gasket

14 There are important points that must be observed when cleaning EGR valves:

a) Never use solvent to dissolve deposits on EGR valves unless you are extremely careful not to get any on the diaphragm.

b) Clean the pintle and valve seat with a dull scraper and wire brush and knock out loose carbon by tapping on the assembly.

c) Some EGR valves can be disassembled for cleaning, but be sure the parts are in alignment before assembly.

11 Evaporative emissions control (EVAP) system

General description

The evaporative emissions control system **(see illustration)** stores fuel vapors generated in the fuel tank in a charcoal canister when the engine isn't running. When the engine is started, the fuel vapors are drawn into the intake manifold and burned. The crankcase emission control system works like this: When the engine is cruising, the purge control valve (bypass valve) is opened slightly and a small amount of blow-by gas is drawn into the intake manifold and burned. When the engine is started cold or idling, the bypass valve prevents any vapors from entering the intake manifold, since that would cause an excessively rich fuel mixture.

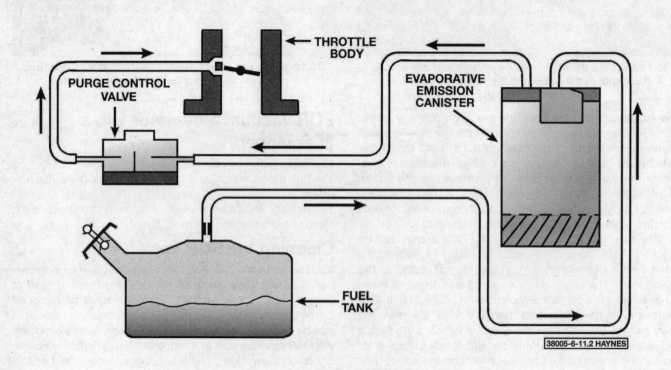

11.1 Typical Evaporative Emission Control System flow diagram

Two types of purge valves or bypass valves are used on these models; an electrically operated valve or a vacuum-operated valve. To find out which type is on your vehicle, follow the hose from the charcoal canister until you locate the purge valve. Some are located on the intake manifold and others near the charcoal canister. Look for an electrical connector **(see illustration)** to the purge valve (electrically operated) or a vacuum line running between the valve and the throttle body (vacuum-operated).

A faulty EVAP system affects the engine driveability only when the temperatures are warm. The EVAP system is not usually the cause of hard cold starting or any other cold running problems.

Check

Vacuum-operated purge valve

1   Remove the vacuum lines from the purge valve and blow into the larger port of the valve. It should be closed and not pass any air. **Note:** *Some models are equipped with a thermo-vacuum valve that prevents canister purge until the coolant temperature reaches approximately 115-degrees F. Check this valve to make sure that vacuum is controlled at the proper temperatures. The valve is usually located in the intake manifold, near the thermo-time switch and the coolant temperature sensor.*

11.2 A common location for the canister purge solenoid valve is on the firewall or an inner fender, where it's often installed as part of an array of other solenoids

2   Disconnect the small vacuum hose from the purge valve and apply vacuum with a hand-held vacuum pump **(see illustration)**. The purge valve should be open and air should be able to pass through.

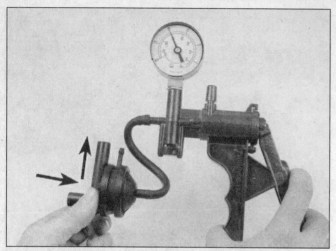

11.3 Apply vacuum and blow air through the purge control valve - air should pass through

11.5 Example of a typical canister location. To remove the charcoal canister, label and detach the vacuum lines, then remove the canister clamp bolt and lift the canister out (some canisters may come out from underneath the vehicle)

3   If the test results are incorrect, replace the purge valve with a new part.

Electrically operated purge valve

1   Disconnect any lines from the purge valve and without disconnecting the electrical connector, place the valve in a convenient spot for testing. Check that the valve makes a "click" sound as the ignition key is turned to the On position.

2   If the valve does not "click", disconnect the valve connector and check for power to the valve using a test light or a voltmeter.

3   If there is battery voltage, replace the purge valve. If there is no voltage present, check the control unit and the wiring harness for any shorts or faulty components.

Canister

1   Label, then detach all hoses to the canister **(see illustration)**.
2   Slide the canister out of its mounting clamp.
3   Visually examine the canister for leakage or damage.
4   Replace the canister if you find evidence of damage or leakage.

12 Computer function

General information

Note: *For more information and testing on this, or other engine management sensors and components, refer to Chapter 8.*

The actual internal functions of the computer can't be checked without expensive diagnostic equipment. Dealerships have the luxury of "replacing with a known good unit", a popular step in factory service manuals, but for practical diagnosis it really doesn't matter. Even dealerships don't "fix" computers, they check power, grounds and closed loop operation. There are simple checks to verify that the computer is functioning properly.

The electronic fuel injection and engine management components are really quite reliable. There are actually many more problems with wiring, vacuum hoses and connections. Even very small amounts of rust, oxidation or corrosion can, and will, interfere with the small milliamp current that is used in computer circuits.

When first assembled and run as a new vehicle, any computer problems would have normally shown up at that time. But over the years, and miles, sometimes failures can occur. Heat, moisture, vibration, corrosive salt air, previous inspections, repair or maintenance could all have an affect on the condition of the computer and related systems.

12.1 Computers can be anywhere there's room, but there are some common locations: Many are installed beneath the right side of the dash - usually right under the glove box as on this Pontiac Grand Am (arrows point to mounting bolt locations)

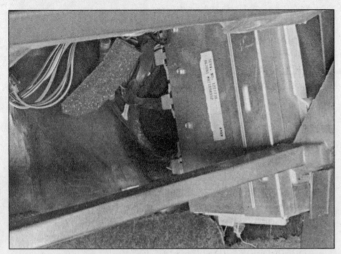

12.2 Another likely location is behind the kick panel (usually the right side) just ahead of the door and underneath the dash, as on this Chevrolet Corsica

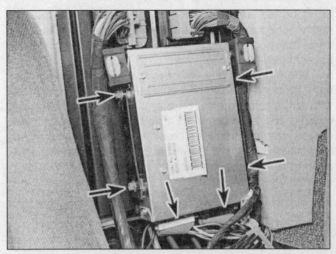

12.3 A third computer location is between the seats, as on this Pontiac Fiero, or even underneath one of the front seats (arrows point to electrical connector and mounting bolt locations)

Locate the computer **(see illustrations)** and check the harness connections and electrical grounds. If necessary, take the connectors apart and check for corrosion or a bent pin. Clean the connectors with electrical contact cleaner and reconnect the computer, making sure that all the terminals are securely seated in the connectors. Check all the computer grounds for corrosion and make sure they're clean, tight and secure.

Refer to Chapter 8 for the oxygen sensor checking procedure, which is a good quick-check to conform that the computer is operating in the closed-loop mode when the engine reaches normal operating temperature.

13 Symptom-based troubleshooting

Note: *The problem symptoms and driveability complaints listed in this Section are primarily related to the fuel, emissions and engine management systems. For other possible causes of vehicle problems, refer to the* Haynes Automotive Repair Manual *for your specific vehicle.*

This Section provides an easy reference guide to the more common problems that may occur during the operation of your vehicle. Various symptoms and their probable causes are grouped under headings denoting components or systems, such as Engine, Cooling system, etc.

Remember that successful troubleshooting isn't a mysterious art practiced only by professional mechanics, it's simply the result of knowledge combined with an intelligent, systematic approach to a problem. Always use a process of elimination starting with the simplest solution and working through to the most complex - and never overlook the obvious. Anyone can run the gas tank dry or leave the lights on overnight, so don't assume that you're exempt from such oversights.

Finally, always establish a clear idea why a problem

12.4 In recent years manufacturers have been placing the computer in the engine compartment (BMW shown here) for ease of access and actually cooler operation than when sandwiched inside an insulated body panel with no air flow

has occurred and take steps to ensure that it doesn't happen again. If the electrical system fails because of a poor connection, check all other connections in the system to make sure they don't fail as well. If a particular fuse continues to blow, find out why - don't just go on replacing fuses. Remember, failure of a small component can often be indicative of potential failure or incorrect functioning of a more important component or system. If, and/or when, a check engine light should appear on the instrument panel of your vehicle, don't automatically assume that the faulty component is the computer. A majority of the driveability related complaints so often turn out to be corrected by simply attending to the basics. Concentrate on fundamental items such as air flow, fuel flow, adequate voltage and good grounds to operate the ignition system and sensor/relay systems, good engine mechanical condition -

i.e. good vacuum, minimal blow by gases, good maintenance schedule for oil and coolant changes, etc. All these items make up the whole picture upon which the computer bases the system operations.

The following is a list of symptoms and driveability complaints, to be used as a guide, most often experienced with engine management systems. The list has been put together to try and cover the majority of all engine management systems. Not all the possibilities listed may apply to all types of systems. Following each symptom are the components and/or general systems to more closely look at in order to correct the problem being experienced:

1 Engine noise

Hiss - vacuum leak(s) (see Section 5)
Electrical arcing (snapping noise) (see Section 9).

2 Engine cranks but won't start

Carbon (charcoal) canister full of fuel (see Section 11).
Faulty MAP, MAF (if equipped) or coolant sensor or circuit (see Chapter 8).
EGR valve stuck open (see Section 10).
Faulty canister vent valve (see Section 11).
Lack of or incorrect fuel pressure (see the *Haynes Fuel Injection Manual* or the *Haynes Automotive Repair Manual* for your particular vehicle).
Fuel tank empty.
Water in fuel.
Cold start injector not opening (see the *Haynes Fuel Injection Manual* or the *Haynes Automotive Repair Manual* for your particular vehicle)
Battery discharged (engine rotates slowly) (see Section 8).
Battery terminal connections loose or corroded (see Section 8).
Water/excessive moisture inside the distributor cap (particularly in foul weather).
Fouled spark plugs or bad spark-plug wires (see Section 9).
Faulty distributor components (see Section 9).
Faulty distributor pick-up coil or ignition module.
Severe vacuum leak (see Sections 5 and 7).
Severely restricted injectors (see Chapter 8)
Broken, loose or disconnected wires in the starting circuit (see Section 8).
Loose distributor (changing ignition timing) (see Section 5).
Jammed or sticking airflow meter (see Chapter 8)
Auxiliary air valve sticking (see Chapter 8)

3 Engine is hard to start - cold

Leaking injectors (see Chapter 8)
Distributor rotor carbon tracked (see Section 9).
Faulty choke operation.

4 Engine is hard to start - hot

Battery discharged or low (see Section 8).
Air filter clogged (see Section 5).
PCV valve stuck open.
Vacuum leak (see Section 7).
Defective coolant sensor or circuit (see Chapter 8).
Defective air temperature sensor or circuit (see Chapter 8).
Defective MAF (if equipped) sensor or circuit (see Chapter 8).
Defective MAP (if equipped) sensor or circuit (see Chapter 8).
Faulty TPS or circuit (see Chapter 8).
Corroded battery connections (see Section 8).
Bad engine ground connection (see Section 8).
Spark plugs fouled (see Section 9).
Fuel pressure incorrect (see the *Haynes Fuel Injection Manual* or the *Haynes Automotive Repair Manual* for your particular vehicle).
Insufficient residual fuel pressure (see the *Haynes Fuel Injection Manual* or the *Haynes Automotive Repair Manual* for your particular vehicle).
Airflow meter faulty (see Chapter 8).
Cold start valve leaking or operating continuously (see the *Haynes Fuel Injection Manual* or the *Haynes Automotive Repair Manual* for your particular vehicle).

5 Engine starts but won't run

Faulty canister vent valve (see Section 11).
EGR valve stuck open (see Section 10).
Loose or damaged electrical connections at distributor, coil or alternator (see Section 9).
Intake manifold vacuum leaks (see Section 7).
Insufficient fuel flow (see the *Haynes Fuel Injection Manual* or the *Haynes Automotive Repair Manual* for your particular vehicle).

6 Engine 'lopes' while idling, rough idle or idles erratically (cold or warm)

Clogged air filter (see Section 5).
Incorrect ignition timing (see Section 9).
Dirty throttle plate or throttle bore (see the *Haynes Fuel Injection Manual* or the *Haynes Automotive Repair Manual* for your particular vehicle).
Minimum idle speed adjustment out of specification (see the *Haynes Fuel Injection Manual* or the *Haynes Automotive Repair Manual* for your particular vehicle).
EGR valve stuck open or leaking (see Section 10).
Vacuum leak (see Section 7).
Air leak in intake duct and/or manifold ("false air") (see Section 5).

Idle system faulty (see Chapter 8)
Lean injector(s) (see Chapter 8).
Rich injector(s) (see Chapter 8).
Fuel pump not delivering sufficient pressure (see the *Haynes Fuel Injection Manual* or the *Haynes Automotive Repair Manual* for your particular vehicle).
Incorrect carburetor adjustment or defective carburetor

Cold only:

PCV valve stuck open or closed.
Heat control valve stuck open (see the *Haynes Automotive Emissions Control Manual* or the *Haynes Automotive Repair Manual* for your particular vehicle).
EFE heater (if equipped) inoperative (see the *Haynes Automotive Emissions Control Manual* or the *Haynes Automotive Repair Manual* for your particular vehicle).

Warm only:

Heat control valve stuck closed (see the *Haynes Automotive Emissions Control Manual* or the *Haynes Automotive Repair Manual* for your particular vehicle).
TPS or circuit malfunctioning or out of adjustment (see Chapter 8).
MAF (if equipped) sensor or circuit out of adjustment or malfunctioning (see Chapter 8).

7 Engine misses at idle speed

Spark plugs fouled, faulty or not gapped properly (see Sections 3 and 9).
Faulty spark plug wires (see Section 9).
Wet or damaged distributor components (see Section 9).
Sticking or faulty EGR valve (see Section 10).
Clogged fuel filter and/or foreign matter in fuel (see Chapter 5).
Vacuum leaks at intake manifold or hose connections (see Section 5).
Incorrect ignition timing (see Section 9).
Low or uneven cylinder compression.
Cold start injector (if equipped) operating incorrectly (see the *Haynes Fuel Injection Manual* or the *Haynes Automotive Repair Manual* for your particular vehicle).

8 Excessively high idle speed

Vacuum leak (see Section 5).
Idle speed incorrectly adjusted (see the *Haynes Automotive Repair Manual* for your particular vehicle).
Sticking throttle linkage (see Section 5).

9 Engine misses throughout driving speed range

Fuel filter clogged and/or impurities in the fuel system (see Chapter 5).
Low fuel pump pressure (see the *Haynes Fuel Injection Manual* or the *Haynes Automotive Repair Manual* for your particular vehicle).
Fouled, faulty or incorrectly gapped spark plugs (see Section 9).
Incorrect ignition timing (see Section 9).
Cracked distributor cap, disconnected distributor wires or damaged distributor components (see Section 9).
Spark plug wires shorting to ground (see Section 9).
Low or uneven cylinder compression pressures.
Weak or faulty ignition system (see Section 9).
Vacuum leaks (see Section 5).
Leaky EGR valve (see Section 10).
Lean injector(s) (see Chapter 8).
Defective carburetor

10 Hesitation, stumbles or stalls on acceleration

Spark plugs fouled (see Section 9).
Fuel filter clogged (see Section 5).
Faulty TPS or circuit (see Chapter 8).
Malfunctioning air temperature sensor or circuit (see Chapter 8).
MAP (if equipped) sensor or circuit faulty (see Chapter 8).
Air leak in intake duct and/or manifold ("false air") (see Section 5).
Faulty MAF (if equipped) sensor or circuit (see Chapter 8).
Ignition timing incorrect (see Section 9).
Dirty throttle plate or throttle bore (see the *Haynes Fuel Injection Manual* or the *Haynes Automotive Repair Manual* for your particular vehicle).
Faulty spark-plug wires, distributor cap or ignition coil (see Section 9).
Low fuel pump pressure (see Chapter 8).
Lean injector(s) (see Chapter 8).
Defective carburetor

11 Engine lacks power or has sluggish performance

Clogged air filter (see Section 5).
Restricted exhaust system (most likely the catalytic converter) (see Section 7).
Vacuum leak (see Sections 5 and 7).
EGR valve stuck open or not functioning properly (see Section 10).
EFE heater (if equipped) inoperative (cold engine) or restricted (see the *Haynes Automotive Emissions*

Control Manual or the *Haynes Automotive Repair Manual* for your particular vehicle).

Heat control valve stuck open (during cold engine operation) (see the *Haynes Automotive Emissions Control Manual* or the *Haynes Automotive Repair Manual* for your particular vehicle).

Heat control valve stuck shut (during warm engine operation) (see the Haynes Automotive Emissions Control Manual or the Haynes Automotive Repair Manual for your particular vehicle).

Incorrect ignition timing (see Section 9).

Low or uneven cylinder compression pressures.

MAP (if equipped) sensor or circuit malfunctioning (see Chapter 8).

Faulty or incorrectly gapped spark plugs (see Sections 3 and 9).

Fuel filter clogged and/or impurities in the fuel system (see Chapter 5).

Vacuum leak at the intake manifold (see Section 7).

Lean injector(s) (see Chapter 8).

Defective carburetor

12 Stalls on deceleration or when coming to a quick stop

EGR valve stuck or leakage around base (see Section 10).

Idle speed incorrect (see Section 6).

TPS misadjusted or defective (see Chapter 8).

Idle Speed Control or Electronic Air Control Valve misadjusted or malfunctioning (see Section 6).

Fuel filter clogged and/or water and impurities in the fuel system (see Chapter 5).

Damaged or wet distributor cap and wires (see Section 9).

Emissions system components faulty.

Faulty or incorrectly gapped spark plugs. Also check the spark plug wires (see Sections 3 and 9).

Vacuum leak (see Section 5).

Defective carburetor

13 Surging at steady speed

Clogged air filter (see Section 5).

Vacuum leak (see Sections 5 and 7).

Air leak in intake duct and/or manifold (False-air) (see Section 5).

EGR valve stuck or leakage around base (see Section 10).

Problem with oxygen sensor or circuit (see Chapter 8).

Misadjusted or defective TPS or circuit (see Chapter 8).

Defective Mass Air Flow (MAF) (if equipped) sensor or circuit (see Chapter 8).

Defective MAP (if equipped) sensor or circuit (see Chapter 8).

Loose fuel injector wire harness connectors.

Torque Converter Clutch (TCC (if equipped) engaging/disengaging (may feel similar to fuel starvation).

Fuel pressure incorrect (see the *Haynes Fuel Injection Manual* or the *Haynes Automotive Repair Manual* for your particular vehicle).

Fuel pump faulty (see the *Haynes Fuel Injection Manual* or the *Haynes Automotive Repair Manual* for your particular vehicle).

Lean injector(s) (see Chapter 8).

Defective computer or information sensors (see Chapter 8).

Defective carburetor

14 Engine diesels (runs on) when shut-off or idles too fast

Vacuum leak (see Sections 5 and 7).

EGR valve not operating properly or stuck closed, causing overheating (see Section 10).

Heat control valve stuck closed (see the *Haynes Automotive Emissions Control Manual* or the *Haynes Automotive Repair Manual* for your particular vehicle).

Idle speed too high - check for correct minimum idle speed (refer to the VECI label under the hood) (see *the Haynes Fuel Injection Manual* or the *Haynes Automotive Repair Manual* for your particular vehicle).

Excessive engine operating temperature, check for causes of overheating (see Section 5).

Ignition timing incorrect (see Sections 3 and 9).

Incorrect spark plug selection (see Sections 3 and 9).

Fuel shut-off system not operating properly.

15 Backfiring (through the intake or exhaust)

Vacuum leak in the PCV or canister purge line (see Section 11).

Vacuum leak at fuel injector(s), intake manifold, air control valve or vacuum lines (see Section 7).

Incorrect ignition timing (see Section 9).

Faulty secondary ignition system, (cracked spark plug insulators, bad plug wires, distributor cap or rotor) (see Section 9).

EGR system not functioning properly (see Section 10).

Emission control system not operating properly.

Faulty air injection valve (see the *Haynes Automotive Emissions Control Manual* or the *Haynes Automotive Repair Manual* for your particular vehicle).

Valve clearances incorrectly set (on some vehicles this is a required maintenance item or is done during tune-up procedures).

Damaged valve springs, sticking or burned valves - a vacuum-gauge check will often reveal this problem.

16 Poor fuel economy

Clogged air filter (see Section 5).

EFE heater (if equipped) inoperative (see the *Haynes Automotive Emissions Control Manual* or the *Haynes Automotive Repair Manual* for your particular vehicle).

Heat control valve stuck open or closed (see the *Haynes Automotive Emissions Control Manual* or the *Haynes Automotive Repair Manual* for your particular vehicle).

PCV problem - valve stuck open or closed, or dirty PCV filter (see Section 11).

Emission system not operating properly.

Defective oxygen sensor (see Chapter 8).

Incorrect ignition timing (see Section 9).

Incorrect idle speed (see the *Haynes Fuel Injection Manual* or the *Haynes Automotive Repair Manual* for your particular vehicle).

Fuel leakage (see Section 5).

Fuel injection internal parts excessively worn or damaged (see Chapter 8).

Cold start injector (if equipped) sticking or leaking/dripping (see the *Haynes Fuel Injection Manual* or the *Haynes Automotive Repair Manual* for your particular vehicle).

Sticking/dragging parking brake (see Section 5).

Low tire pressure (see Section 5).

Defective carburetor

17 Pinging (spark knock)

Ignition timing incorrect.

EGR valve inoperative (see Section 10).

Vacuum leak (see Sections 5 and 7).

Worn or damaged distributor components (see Section 9).

Incorrect or damaged spark plugs or wires (see Sections 3 and 9).

Poor quality fuel

18 Exhaust smoke

Black (overly rich fuel mixture) - Dirty air filter or restricted intake duct (see Section 5).

Blue (burning oil) - PCV valve stuck open or PCV filter dirty (see Section 11).

19 Fuel smell

Fuel tank overfilled (see Section 5).

Fuel tank cap gasket not sealing (see Section 5).

Fuel lines leaking (see Chapter 5).

Fuel injector(s) stuck open (see Chapter 8).

Fuel injector(s) leaks internally (see Chapter 8).

Fuel injector(s) leaks externally (see Chapter 8).

EVAP canister filter in Evaporative Emissions Control system clogged (see Section 11).

Vapor leaks from Evaporative Emissions Control system lines (see Section 11).

Defective carburetor (leaking)

Notes

7 Computer trouble code retrieval

Part A

General information

When diagnosing problems on engines controlled by computer systems, remember that many driveability symptoms and/or problems may not necessarily be caused by the computer. The computer is only responding to the input (or change of input information) of the many sensors controlled by the fundamental systems previously discussed in this Book. Unless all of the basic engine systems are properly functioning, the electronic controls have inaccurate information to manage the engine fuel and emissions systems properly.

Condemning a computer, input sensor or output actuator, before verifying that the fundamental systems are operating correctly usually leads to an incorrect diagnosis. Besides wasting your time, you'll find that the electronic components of engine management systems are generally expensive and usually not returnable, even if a mistake has been made in diagnosis.

Before proceeding to the electronic control system tests make the following general checks:

1 The engine is in good overall mechanical condition, as indicated by compression and vacuum tests.

2 The battery is clean and free of connection corrosion, in good condition and fully charged.

3 The starting and charging systems operate properly.

4 All fuses and fusible links are intact.

5 All electrical connectors are free of corrosion and connected securely.

6 All vacuum lines are in good condition, correctly routed, and attached securely.

7 The air and fuel supply systems are free of restrictions and working properly.

8 The PCV, EGR and EVAP and other emissions systems are working properly and maintained as required.

9 The coolant level and condition is good, and the thermostat is in place and is of the correct operating temperature.

10 The engine oil level and condition are good.

11 The ignition system is in good condition with no signs of cross-firing, mis-firing, carbon tracks, corrosion, or wear.

12 The base timing and idle speed are set to specifications found on the VECI label.

13 The computer is going into closed loop operation.

Note: *If in doubt about the condition of any of these items, refer to the appropriate Sections of Chapter 8 and recheck the component(s) or systems in question.*

On-board computer systems not only control the engine fuel, ignition and emission functions in an attempt to achieve optimum efficiency, but on most systems they also have a built-in diagnostic feature. When the computer detects a fault, it stores a **trouble code** in its memory. The code can usually be retrieved from the computer's memory by following a certain procedure. A trouble code doesn't necessarily indicate the exact cause of a problem, but it will direct you to a particular component, circuit or system, which may simplify diagnosis.

While it may not be possible for the home mechanic to repair all of these faults, the codes can allow you to be better informed when explaining a problem to a mechanic, if the need arises.

Operating modes

If, after all the basic troubleshooting procedures have been performed, the tune-up meets specifications, and the driveability problem still exists, it is time to look more closely at the computer/engine management systems.

Computer controlled engine management takes place in two modes, "open-loop" and "closed-loop". The computer must be able to get from "open-loop" to "closed-loop" operation, in order to properly monitor and control the engine management systems.

Open-loop is the operating mode of the system when the vehicle is first started and the engine and the oxygen sensor are warming up. Until all the required criteria are met, such as time and temperature, the computer will remain in "open-loop". This means that all computer controlled functions will stay "fixed" at the manufacturers predetermined default settings. **Note:** *These default settings may also be used in the event of a component failure. They allow the vehicle to run, although poorly, in the "limp-in" mode until repairs can be made.*

Although previously discussed, closed-loop is the normal operating mode of a warmed-up engine and an oxygen sensor warm enough to generate a working signal to the computer (the system also waits a predetermined amount of time before going into closed-loop even if the engine and oxygen sensor are already at operating temperature).

On some vehicles, a few minutes at idle can cause the oxygen sensor to cool enough to allow the system to return to open-loop; on these vehicles, the system may even switch back and forth as the oxygen sensor temperature rises and falls.

Retrieving codes

There are a variety of methods of trouble code retrieval, depending on the manufacturer. Most systems work in conjunction with a light on the dash which illuminates when a fault is detected and a code is stored. The light is marked - "CHECK ENGINE", "POWER LOSS", "SERVICE ENGINE SOON" - or something similar, and is used to blink the codes stored in the computer when manually triggered through the diagnostic connector, if the vehicles computer allows access to trouble codes in this manner.

On other models, the code can be accessed by connecting a voltmeter to the diagnostic connector and counting the needle sweeps or in an LED readout on the computer itself.

Each manufacturer's procedure for retrieving and clearing trouble codes is described at the beginning of the following tables.

Once the codes are retrieved, check them against the chart for your vehicle. **Caution:** *Because engine management systems may differ by year and model, certain trouble codes indicate different problems, depending on the vehicle being repaired. Since this is the case, it would be a good idea to consult your dealer or other qualified repair shop before replacing any electrical component, as they are usually expensive and can't be returned once they are purchased.*

Some models require a special diagnostic scanner or tool to retrieve the codes. These scanners are easy to use to gather information, and are relatively inexpensive (see Chapter 5).
Note 1: *When the battery is disconnected, vehicle computer and memory systems may lose memory data. Driveability problems may exist until the computer systems have completed a relearn cycle.*
Note 2: *If the stereo in your vehicle is equipped with an anti-theft system, make sure you have the correct activation code before disconnecting the battery.*

OBD II systems

For some years there has been a gradual process of making and enforcing a "universal" set of computer codes that would be applied by all auto manufacturers to their self-diagnostics. One of the first automotive applications of computers was self-diagnosis of system and component failures. While early on-board diagnostic computers simply lit a "CHECK ENGINE" light on the dash, present systems must monitor complex interactive emission control systems, and provide enough data to the technician to successfully isolate a malfunction.

The computer's role in self-diagnosing emission control problems has become so important that such computers are now required by Federal law. The requirements of the "first generation" system, nicknamed OBD I for On-Board Diagnostics, have been incorporated into 1993 through 1995 models. The purpose of On Board Diagnostics (OBD) is to ensure that emission related components and systems are functioning properly to reduce emission levels of several pollutants emitted by auto and truck engines. The first step is to detect that a malfunction has occurred which may cause increased emissions. The next step is for the system to notify the driver so that the vehicle can be serviced. The final step is to store enough information about the malfunction so that it can be identified and repaired.

The latest step has been the establishment of the OBD II system, which further defines emissions performance, and also regulates the code numbers and definitions.

The basic OBD II code is a letter followed by a four-digit number. Most manufacturers also have many additional codes that are *specific* to their vehicles. Although many of the self-diagnostic tests performed by early OBD systems are retained in OBD II systems, they are now more sensitive in detecting malfunctions. Where there may have been only one code for an oxygen sensor malfunction, there are now six codes that narrow down where the performance discrepancy is. OBD II systems perform many additional tests in areas not required under the earlier OBD. These include monitoring for engine misfires and detecting deterioration of the catalytic converter.

OBD II systems started appearing on a few models in 1994, a few more in 1995 and almost all models in 1996. At first, a very expensive scan tool was required to read the codes. Now, however, the aftermarket has come up with inexpensive scan tools for the home mechanic to use (see Chapter 5). For most OBD II vehicles, the scan tool is the only way to extract and clear trouble codes. For some OBD II vehicles, however, the manufacturer has kept the "count-the-blinks" method of using the Malfunction Indicator Light (MIL) or Check Engine Light, in addition to the mandated five-character scanner codes, so these vehicles can still be diagnosed by the do-it-yourself mechanic. However, the blinking light codes will not give the detailed information now available from the mandated Federal OBD II codes.
Note: *To determine if your vehicle is OBD II or not, look at the VECI (Vehicle Emission Control Information) decal on the top of the radiator fan shroud. If it's OBD II, the decal will indicate "OBD II certified".*

Retrieving codes on OBD-II systems

Besides a standardized set of diagnostic trouble codes, the Federal government's OBD-II program mandates a standard 16-pin diagnostic link connector (DLC) for all vehicles. The DLC is also referred to as a J1962 connector (a designation taken from the physical and electrical specification number assigned by the SAE). Besides its standard pin configuration, the J1962 must also provide power and ground circuits for scan tool hook-up. The SAE has also recommended locating the DLC or J1962 connector under the driver's end of the dash. At the time of publication, this is a recommendation, not a requirement. Most - but not all - manufacturers are complying with this recommendation. If you can't find the DLC on your vehicle, refer to your owner's manual.

Now that all new vehicles have a standardized connector and a universal set of diagnostic trouble codes, the same scan tool can be used on any vehicle, and any home mechanic can access these codes with a relatively affordable generic scan tool.

All aftermarket generic scan tools include good documentation, so refer to the manufacturer's hook-up instructions in your scan tool manual. Before plugging a scan tool into the DLC, inspect the condition of the DLC housing; make sure that all the wires are connected and that the contacts are fully seated in the housing. Inside the connector, make sure that there's no corrosion on the pins and that no pins are bent or damaged.

Clearing codes on OBD-II systems

After you've made the necessary repairs, you'll need to "clear" (erase) any stored trouble codes from the PCM. Most OBD-II systems require a scan tool to clear the codes. Refer to the manufacturer's documentation that comes with the aftermarket generic scan tool you're using. It will guide you through the correct procedure for clearing any codes stored in the PCM.

Acura

Retrieving codes

The Engine Control Unit (ECU) stores the codes which are accessed by reading the flashing Light Emitting Diode (LED) on the unit (early models) or the CHECK ENGINE light on the dash (later models). (If the ECU has two LED's, the red one is for codes.) On OBD-II models, the Check Engine light is referred to as a Malfunction Indicator Light (MIL). The ECU on 1990 and earlier Legend sedans and Integra models through 1989 is located under the front passenger seat **(see illustration)**. On Legend coupes, 1991 and later Legend sedans, 1990 through 1994 Integras and all Vigor models, the ECU is found under the dashboard on the passenger's side behind the carpet; 1990 Legends incorporate a flip-out mirror so the LED can be seen. On 1995 through 1999 Integra models, the ECM is located behind the right kick panel. On 1997 2.2CL models, 1998 and 1999 2.3CL models, 1995 through 1999 2.5TL models, 1997 through 1999 3.0CL models, 1996 through 1998 3.2TL models and 1996 through 1999 3.5RL models, the ECM (models with a manual transaxle) or PCM (models with an automatic transaxle) is located below the right (passenger side) front footrest. On 1996 through 1999 SLX models and on 1999 3.2TL models, the PCM is located behind the center of the dash, below the radio.

1990 and earlier Legend, 1991 and earlier Integra

When the ECU sets a code, the Check Engine light on the dashboard will illuminate. To access the codes, turn the ignition switch On, then count and record the number of times the LED flashes. On 1986 through 1989 models, the light will blink a sequence the sum total representing the code number (for example, 14 short blinks is code 14). On 1990 Legends and 1990 and 1991 Integras, the light will hold a longer blink to represent the first digit of a two-digit number and then will blink short for the second digit (1 long and 8 short blinks is 18). If the system has more than one problem, the codes will be displayed in sequence, pause, then repeat.

1991 and later Legend and all 1992 and later models

To access the codes on these models, locate the two-terminal diagnostic connector. On Legend and Integra models it's located under the right side of the dash, behind the glove box. On Vigor models it's located behind the right side of the center console, under the dash. On all other models, it's located under the left end of the dash. With the ignition On (engine not running), bridge the two terminals of the diagnostic connector with a jumper wire. Any stored codes will be displayed on the CHECK ENGINE light on the dash, in a series of flashes. For example, a code 14 would be indicated by one long flash, a pause, then four short flashes. If more than one code is present, the codes will be displayed in numerical order, with a pause between each code. **Note:** *The self-diagnostic system switched to OBD II on some models in 1994, others in 1995, and all are OBD II in 1996, but DTC codes can still be accessed through the malfunction indicator light on the dash.*

Clearing codes
1990 and earlier Legend, 1991 and earlier Integra

To erase the codes after making repairs, remove the Hazard fuse at the battery positive terminal (Integra) or Alternator Sense fuse in the under hood relay box (Legend) for at least ten seconds.

7.1 The ECU on 1990 and earlier Legend sedans and 1989 and earlier Integra models is located under the passenger front seat0

1991 and later Legend and all 1992 and later models

To erase codes after making repair to these models, remove the BACK-UP fuse from the relay box under the hood (Integra, Vigor) or the ACG (fuse no. 15) from the fuse box under the left side of the dash (Legend) for at least 10 seconds. On all other models, erase the codes by removing the ECM fuse from the under-dash fuse/relay panel. On 1995 through 1999 Integra models the fuse/relay panel is located under the left end of the dash. On 1995 through 1999 2.5TL models, the fuse panel is located behind the left end of the dash. On 1997 2.2CL models, 1998 and 1999 2.3CL models and 1997 through 1999 3.0CL models, the fuse/relay panel is located in the left kick panel. On 1996 3.2TL models, the fuse/relay panel is located above the right kick panel. On 1996 through 1999 SLX models, 1997 through 1999 3.2TL models and 1997 through 1999 3.5RL models, the fuse/relay panel is located behind the left kick panel. **Caution:** *If the stereo in your vehicle is equipped with an anti-theft system, make sure you have the correct activation code before removing the fuse.*

Audi

Retrieving codes on pre-OBD-II models

Drive the vehicle for five or more minutes (on turbocharged models, the engine must exceed 3000 rpm and 17psi of boost), and then let it idle. If the vehicle won't start, crank the engine over for at least six seconds and then leave the ignition switch turned to ON. Now, proceed to the instructions below for your specific model. **Note:** *Some models are not included because special (and very expensive) diagnostic tools are needed to access the trouble codes.*

1988 through 1990 models with 1984 cc engine

Note: *On these models, you'll need the special Audi tester (part no. US1115) or a suitable equivalent tool, to access the diagnostic trouble codes.*
1   On models with a diagnostic connector in the engine compartment (next to the fuel distributor), hook up the special Audi tester (part no. US1115) between the diagnostic connector and the positive battery terminal. (On some models, the diagnostic connector is in the fuse panel, on the fuel pump relay).
2   To display a stored trouble code, install the spare fuse in the top of the fuel pump relay for four seconds. The tester will display the code.
3   Repeat this procedure to access each stored code.
4   To erase the stored code(s), install the spare fuse and leave it in for at least 10 seconds.

1987 and 1988 models with turbocharged 2226 cc engine or 2309 cc engine

Note: *On these models, the codes are displayed by a flashing Malfunction Indicator Lamp (MIL).*
1   Bridge the test contacts of the diagnostic trigger on the pump relay for four seconds. The MIL will flash the code.
2   Repeat this procedure to access each stored code.

1989 through 1991 models with 2226 cc SOHC turbocharged engine (one knock sensor) or with 2309 cc engine

Note: *On non-California versions of these models, you'll need the special Audi tester (part no. US1115) or a suitable equivalent tool, to access the diagnostic trouble codes. On California models, the codes are also displayed by a flashing Malfunction Indicator Lamp (MIL).*
1   Hook up the special Audi tester (part no. US1115) between the positive terminals of the dark-colored and the light-colored diagnostic connectors.
2   Using a jumper wire, bridge the negative terminals of the dark-colored and light-colored connectors for four seconds. The tester will display the code or, on California models, the MIL will flash the code.
3   Repeat this procedure to access each stored code.

1990 and 1991 models with 2226 cc SOHC turbocharged engine (two knock sensors)

Note: *On non-California versions of these models, you'll need the special Audi tester (part no. US1115) or a suitable equivalent tool, to access the diagnostic trouble codes. On California models, the codes are also displayed by a flashing Malfunction Indicator Lamp (MIL).*
1   Hook up the special Audi tester (part no. US1115) between positive diagnostic terminals 1 and 3.
2   Using a jumper wire, bridge negative terminals 1 and 2. The tester will display the code or, on California models, the MIL will flash the code.
3   Repeat this procedure to access each stored code.

1990 and 1991 models with 3562 cc V8 engine

1   Bridge the upper terminals of diagnostic connectors 1 and 4 with the special Audi tester (part no. US1115).
2   Crank the engine for five seconds, and then leave the ignition switch turned to ON.
3   Using a jumper wire, bridge the lower terminals of diagnostic connectors 1 and 2. The test light or, on California models, the ENGINE light, will flash the code.
4   Repeat the above procedure to access each stored code.
5   After code 0000 has flashed, all stored codes have been displayed.

BMW

The EFI system control unit (computer) has a built-in self-diagnosis system which detects malfunctions in the system sensors and alerts the driver by illuminating a Check Engine warning light in the instrument panel. The computer stores the failure code until the diagnostic system is cleared by removing the negative battery cable for a period of five seconds or longer. The warning light goes out automatically (after five engine starts) when the malfunction is repaired.

Retrieving codes

There are two types of codes accessible on a BMW. The flash codes (listed here) and trouble codes that can be retrieved only with a BMW tester. This manual only addresses codes accessible without using a special BMW tool.

The Check Engine warning light should come on when the ignition switch is placed in the On position. When the engine is started, the warning light should go out. The light will remain on (with the engine running) once the diagnostic system has detected a malfunction or abnormality in the system. In order to read the codes, it is necessary to turn the key to the On position (engine not running), depress the accelerator pedal 5 times (6 times on 12-cylinder models) within 5 seconds (make sure the pedal reaches wide open throttle each time) and wait for any stored codes to be displayed.

The diagnostic code is the number of flashes indicated on the Check Engine light. If any malfunction has been detected, the light will blink the digit(s) of the code. For example on 1988 3-Series models, code 3 (coolant temperature sensor malfunction) will blink three flashes. There will be a pause (3 seconds) and then any other codes that are stored will be flashed. On 1989 and later 3, 5 and 7-Series models, code 1223 (coolant temperature sensor malfunction) will flash the first digit and then pause, flash the second digit (2 flashes) pause, flash the third digit (2 flashes) pause and finally flash the fourth digit (3 flashes). There will be another pause and the computer will start the next stored trouble code (if any) or it will repeat the code 1223. Once all the codes have been displayed, the Check Engine light will remain on. In order to re-check the codes, simply turn the ignition key Off and then back On (repeat procedure) and the codes will be repeated.

The trouble code tables in Chapter 7B indicate the diagnostic code along with the system or component that is affected **Note:** *Diagnostic codes that are not emissions or engine control related (electronic transmission, ABS, etc.) will not be accessed by this system.*

Clearing codes

Caution: *If the stereo in your vehicle is equipped with an anti-theft system, make sure you have the correct activation code before disconnecting the battery.*

After repairs have been made, the diagnostic code can be canceled by disconnecting the negative battery cable for 5 seconds or longer. After cancellation, perform a road test and make sure the warning light does not come on. If desired, the check can be repeated.

Chrysler, Dodge and Plymouth - domestic cars and light trucks

Note: *On the models covered by this manual, the CHECK ENGINE light, located in the instrument panel, flashes on for three seconds as a bulb test when the engine is started. The light comes on and stays on when there's a problem in the EFI system.*

Retrieving codes

Note: *Later models are all equipped with OBD II engine management systems, but Chrysler has continued the use of blinking light codes in addition to the mandated five-character codes accessible only with a scan tool.*

The self diagnosis information contained in the SBEC or SMEC (computer) can be accessed either by the ignition key or by using a special tool called the Diagnostic Readout Box (DRB II). This tool is attached to the diagnostic connector in the engine compartment and reads the codes and parameters on the digital display screen. The tool is expensive and most home mechanics prefer to use the alternate method. The drawback with the ignition method is that it does not access all the available codes for display. Most problems can be solved or diagnosed quite easily and if the information cannot be obtained readily, have the vehicle's self diagnosis system analyzed by a dealer service department or other properly-equipped repair shop.

To obtain the codes using the ignition key method, first set the parking brake and put the transaxle in Park (automatic) or Neutral (manual).

Raise the engine speed to approximately 2500 rpm and slowly let the speed down to idle.

Cycle the air conditioning system, if equipped (on briefly, then off).

If the vehicle is equipped with an automatic transmission, with your foot on the brake, select each position on the transmission (Reverse, Drive, Low etc.) and bring the shifter back to Park. This will allow the computer to obtain any fault codes that might be linked to any of the sensors controlled by the transmission, engine speed or air conditioning system.

To display the codes on the dashboard (POWER LOSS or CHECK ENGINE light), turn the ignition key On, Off, On, Off and finally On (engine not running). The codes will begin to flash. The light will blink the number of the first digit then pause and blink the number of the second digit. For example: Code 23, throttle body temperature sensor circuit, would be indicated by two flashes, then a pause followed by three flashes.

Certain criteria must be met for a fault code to be entered into the engine controller memory. The criteria may be a specific range of engine rpm, engine temperature or input voltage to the engine controller. It is possible that a fault code for a particular monitored circuit may not be entered into the memory despite a malfunction. This may happen because one of the fault code criteria has not been met. For example; The engine must be operating between 750 and 2000 rpm in order to monitor the Map sensor circuit correctly. If the engine speed is raised above 2400 rpm, the MAP sensor output circuit shorts to ground and will not allow a fault code to be entered into the memory. Then again, the exact opposite could occur: A code is entered into the memory that suggests a malfunction within another component that is not monitored by the computer. For example; A fuel pressure problem cannot register a fault directly but instead, it will cause a rich/lean fuel mixture problem. Consequently, this will cause an oxygen sensor malfunction resulting in a stored code in the computer for the oxygen sensor. Be aware of the interrelationship of the sensors and circuits and the overall relationship of the emissions control and fuel injection systems.

The trouble code table in Chapter 7B is a list of the typical trouble codes which may be encountered while diagnosing the system. If the problem persists after these checks have been made, more detailed service procedures will have to be performed by a dealer service department or other qualified repair shop.

Clearing codes

Caution: *If the stereo in your vehicle is equipped with an anti-theft system, make sure you have the correct activation code before disconnecting the battery.*

Trouble codes may be cleared by disconnecting negative battery cable for at least 15 seconds. However, on OBD II models the codes can only be cleared with the use of a scan tool.

Eagle

Summit and Talon (1988 on)
Retrieving codes

Locate the diagnostic connector in or under the glove compartment. On some late-model Summit models, it may be next to the fuse box **(see illustration)**. Connect an analog voltmeter to the upper right (+) and lower left (-) connector terminals. On 1994 and later Summit models, connect the voltmeter (+) to the upper left terminal of the male, 12-pin connector and (-) to either of the upper-middle two of the female connector (on station wagon models, grounding

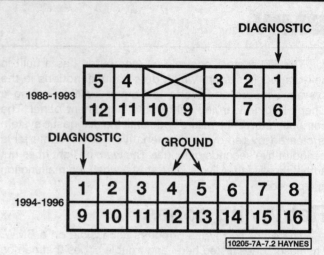

7.2 Diagnostic connectors for Eagle models

the upper left terminal of the 16-pin connector is all that's necessary). Turn on the ignition On (engine Off) and watch the voltmeter needle. It will display the codes as long or short sweeps of the needle. For example, two long sweeps followed by three short sweeps is code 23. Count the number of long and short needle sweeps and write the codes down for reference. Continuous short pulses indicate that all is normal and there are no codes.

In 1995, some models appeared with OBD II systems, while others still had OBD I systems. Some of these models may not display codes on a voltmeter, but grounding the diagnostic connector should still provide codes through the MIL light on the dash. On all OBD II models from 1995 on, the OBD II codes can only be retrieved using a scan tool.

Clearing codes

Caution: *If the stereo in your vehicle is equipped with an anti-theft system, make sure you have the correct activation code before disconnecting the battery.*

After making repairs, disconnect the cable from the negative terminal of the battery to erase codes from the computer memory. **Caution:** *If you disconnect the battery from the vehicle to clear the codes, this will erase stored operating parameters from the computer and may cause the engine to run rough for a period of time while the computer relearns the information.*

Premier (1991 and 1992) and Vision (1993 through 1997)
Retrieving codes

Turn the ignition switch On, Off, On, Off, On and watch the flashes of the Power Loss or Check Engine light on the dash. The codes will blink the number of the first digit, then pause and blink the number of the second digit. For example, Code 23 would be 2 blinks, pause, 3 blinks.

Clearing codes

Caution: *If the stereo in your vehicle is equipped with an anti-theft system, make sure you have the correct activation code before disconnecting the battery.*

After making repairs, disconnect the cable from the negative terminal of the battery to erase codes from the computer memory. **Caution:** *If you disconnect the battery from the vehicle to clear the codes, this will erase stored operating parameters from the computer and may cause the engine to run rough for a period of time while the computer relearns the information.*

Ford, Lincoln and Mercury

Retrieving codes

Note: *Trouble codes are not retrievable on models with an EEC-V engine management system (a special scan tool must be used).*

The diagnostic codes for the EEC-IV systems are arranged in such a way that a series of tests must be completed in order to extract ALL the codes from the system. If one portion of the test is performed without the others, there may be a chance the trouble code that will pinpoint a problem in your particular vehicle will remain stored in the PCM without detection. The tests start first with a Key On, Engine Off (KOEO) test followed by a computed timing test then finally a Engine Running (ER) test. Here is a brief overview of the code extracting procedures of the EEC-IV system followed by the actual test:

Quick Test - Key On Engine Off (KOEO)

The following tests are all included with the key on, engine off:

Self test codes - These codes are accessed on the test connector by using a jumper wire and an analog voltmeter or the factory diagnostic tool called the Star tester. These codes are also called Hard Codes.

Separator pulse codes - After the initial Hard Codes, the system will flash a code 11 (separator pulse) (1990 and earlier) or code 111 (1991 and later) and then will flash a series of Soft Codes.

Continuous Memory Codes - These codes indicate a fault that may or may not be present at the time of testing. These codes usually indicate an intermittent failure. Continuous Memory codes are stored in the system and they will flash after the normal Hard Codes. These codes are either two digit (1988 through 1991) or three digit codes (1992 through 1995). These codes can indicate chronic or intermittent problems. Also called Soft Codes.

Engine running codes (ER)

Running tests - These tests make it possible for the PCM to pick-up a diagnostic trouble code that cannot be set while the engine is in KOEO mode. These problems usually occur during driving conditions. Some codes are detected by cold or warm running conditions, some are detected at low rpms or high rpms and some are detected at closed throttle or wide open throttle.

I.D. Pulse codes - These codes indicate the type of engine (4, 6 or 8 cylinder) or the correct module and Self Test mode access.

Computed engine timing test - This engine running test determines base timing for the engine and starts the process of allowing the engine to store running codes.

Wiggle test - This engine running test checks the wiring system to the sensors and output actuators

Cylinder balance test - This engine running test determines injector balance as well as cylinder compression balance. **Note:** *This test should be performed by a dealer service department.*

Position the parking brake ON, Shift lever in PARK (NEUTRAL in manual transmission vehicles), block the drive wheels and turn off all electrical loads (air conditioning, radio, heater fan blower etc.). Make sure the engine is warmed to operating temperatures (if possible).

Perform the **KOEO tests:**

a) Turn the ignition key off for at least 10 seconds.
b) Locate the diagnostic Test connector inside the engine compartment **(see illustrations)**. Install the voltmeter leads onto the battery and pin number 4 (STO) of the test connector. Install a jumper wire from the test termi-

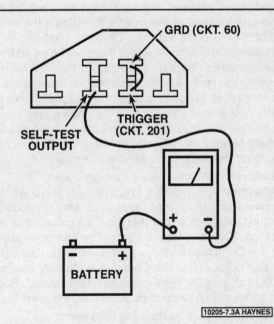

7.3a On 1984 and earlier Ford systems, hook up the volt/ohm meter as shown to read the trouble codes

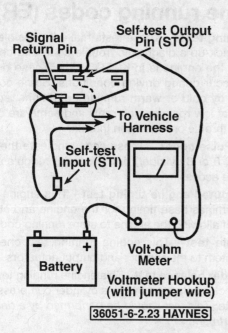

Signal Return Pin

Self-test Output Pin (STO)

To Vehicle Harness

Self-test Input (STI)

Volt-ohm Meter

Battery

Voltmeter Hookup (with jumper wire)

36051-6-2.23 HAYNES

7.3b To output codes on a Ford with the EEC-IV system, connect a voltmeter as shown and, using a jumper wire, bridge the self-test input connector to the signal return pin (terminal 2)

nal to pin number 2 of the Diagnostic Test terminal (STI) **(see illustration)**.

c) Turn the ignition key On (engine not running) and observe the needle sweeps on the voltmeter. For example code 23, the voltmeter will sweep once, pause 1/2 second and sweep again. There will be a two second pause between digits and then there will be three distinct sweeps of the needle to indicate the second digit of the code number. On three digit codes, the sequence is the same except there will be an additional sequence of numbers (sweeps) to indicate the third digit in the code. Additional codes will be separated by a four second pause and then the indicated sweeps on the voltmeter. Be aware that the code sequence may continue into the continuous memory codes (read further). **Note:** *Later models will flash the Check Engine light on the dash in place of the voltmeter.*

Interpreting the continuous memory codes:

After the KOEO codes are reported, there will be a short pause and any stored Continuous Memory codes will appear in order. Remember that the "Separator" code is 11, or 111 on 1992 and later models. The computer will not enter the Continuous Memory mode without flashing the separator pulse code. The Continuous Memory codes are read the same as the initial codes or "Hard Codes". Record these codes onto a piece of paper and continue the test.

Perform the **Engine Running (ER)** tests:

a) Remove the jumper wires from the Diagnostic Test connector to start the test

7.3c This is how it looks on a real vehicle - insert a jumper wire from terminal number 2 (A) to self- test input connector, then install the negative probe of the voltmeter into terminal number 4 (B) and position the positive probe to the battery positive terminal

b) Run engine until it reaches normal operating temperature

c) Turn the engine OFF for at least 10 seconds

d) Install the jumper wire onto Diagnostic Test connector and start the engine.

e) Observe that the voltmeter or Check Engine light will flash the engine identification code. This code indicates 1/2 the number of cylinders of the engine. For example, 4 flashes represent an 8 cylinder engine, or 3 flashes represent a six cylinder engine.

f) Within 1 to 2 seconds of the I.D. code, turn the steering wheel at least 1/2 turn and release. This will store any power steering pressure switch trouble codes.

g) Depress the brake pedal and release. **Note:** *Perform the steering wheel and brake pedal procedure in succession immediately (1 to 2 seconds) after the I.D. codes are flashed.*

h) Observe all the codes and record them on a piece of paper. Be sure to count the sweeps or flashes very carefully as you jot them down.

On some models the PCM will request a Dynamic Response check. This test quickly checks the operation of the TPS, MAF or MAP sensors in action. This will be indicated by a code 1 or a single sweep of the voltmeter needle (one flash on CHECK ENGINE light). This test will require the operator to simply full throttle ("goose") the accelerator pedal for one second. DO NOT throttle the accelerator pedal unless it is requested.

The next part of this test makes sure the system can advance the timing. This is called the Computed Timing test. After the last ER code has been displayed, the PCM will advance the ignition timing a fixed amount and hold it there for approximately 2 minutes. Use a timing light to check the amount of advance. The computed timing should equal the base timing plus 20 BTDC. The total advance should equal 27 to 33 degrees advance. If the timing is out of specification, have the system checked at a dealer service department.

Finally perform the **Wiggle Test:** (This test can be used to recreate a possible intermittent fault in the harness wiring system.)

a) Use a jumper wire to ground the STI lead on the Diagnostic Test connector.

b) Turn the ignition key On (engine not running).

c) Now deactivate the self test mode (remove jumper wire) and then immediately reactivate self test mode. Now the system has entered Continuous Monitor Test Mode.

d) Carefully wiggle, tap or remove any suspect wiring to a sensor or output actuator. If a problem exists, a trouble code will be stored that indicates a problem with the circuit that governs the particular component. Record the codes that are indicated.

e) Next, enter Engine Running Continuous Monitor Test Mode to check for wiring problems only when the engine is running. Start first by deactivating the Diagnostic Test connector and turning the ignition key Off. Now start the engine and allow it to idle.

f) Use a jumper wire to ground the STI lead on the Diagnostic Test connector. Wait ten seconds and then deactivate the test mode and reactivate it again (install jumper wire). This will enter Engine Running Continuous Monitor Test Mode.

g) Carefully wiggle, tap or remove any suspect wiring to a sensor or output actuator. If a problem exists, a trouble code will be stored that indicates a problem with the circuit that governs the particular component. Record the codes that are indicated.

If necessary, perform the Cylinder Balance Test. This test should be performed by a qualified automotive service department.

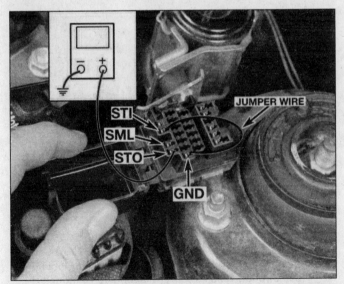

7.3d Diagnostic test connector location and code retrieving terminals (1994 and 1995 Ford Aspire models)

Clearing codes

To clear the codes from the PCM memory, start the KOEO self test diagnostic procedure and install the jumper wire into the Diagnostic Test connector. When the codes start to display themselves on the voltmeter or Check Engine light, remove the jumper wire from the Diagnostic Test connector. This will erase any stored codes within the system.

Caution: *Do not disconnect the battery from the vehicle to clear the codes. This will erase stored operating parameters from the KAM (Keep Alive Memory) and cause the engine to run rough for a period of time while the computer relearns the information.*

Ford imports

Aspire (1.3L), Escort/Tracer (1.8L), Probe (2.5L V6) and Villager (3.0L V6)

These models are equipped with a unique Electronic Engine Control (EEC) system, which differs from Ford EEC-IV and EEC-V systems with respect to the diagnostic connectors and the trouble codes.

Aspire (1.3L)

Retrieving codes

Connect a jumper wire from terminal STI to GND **(see illustration)**. Also, connect a voltmeter from the STO terminal and engine ground. With the ignition key ON (engine not running), watch the sweeps of the voltmeter needle. The voltmeter must be analog to see the movement of the needle as it sweeps across the face of the meter. **Note:** *It is also possible to read the trouble codes from the CHECK ENGINE light on the dash. Simply ground the STI and GND terminals with a jumper wire and watch the light on the dash as it flashes the stored trouble code(s).*

Clearing codes

Remove the jumper wire and close the cover on the DIAGNOSTIC electrical connector. Check the indicated system or component or take the vehicle to a dealer service department or other qualified repair shop to have the malfunction repaired. After repairs have been made, the diagnostic code must be canceled by detaching the cable from the negative terminal of the battery, then depressing the brake pedal for more than five seconds. After cancellation, perform a road test and make sure the warning light does not come on. If the original trouble code is repeated, additional repairs are required.

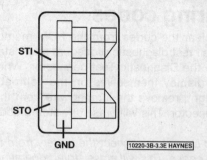

7.3e Diagnostic test connector code retrieving terminals (1993 through 1995 Ford Escort/Mercury Tracer 1.8L models)

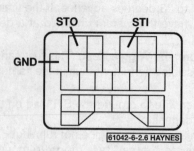

7.3f Diagnostic test connector code retrieving terminals (1993 through 1995 Ford Probe 2.5L V6 models)

Escort/Tracer (1.8L)

Retrieving codes

Locate the EEC diagnostic or self-test connector located behind the battery in the engine compartment. To read the codes with an analog voltmeter, turn the ignition key to the OFF position, connect the voltmeter positive lead to the EEC STO line and the negative lead to ground (see illustration). Connect the EEC STI terminal to ground with a jumper wire. Set the voltmeter on a 20-volt scale. To read the codes with the Check Engine light, connect the EEC STI terminal to ground with a jumper wire.

Clearing codes

Disconnect the jumper wire from the STI terminal and ground. Disconnect the negative battery cable. Depress the brake pedal for 5 to 10 seconds.

Probe (2.5L V6)

Retrieving codes

Connect a jumper wire from terminal STI to GND (see illustration). Also, connect a voltmeter from the STO terminal and engine ground. With the ignition key ON (engine not running), watch the sweeps of the voltmeter needle. The voltmeter must be an analog type to see the movement of the needle as it sweeps across the face of the meter. Note: It is also possible to read the trouble codes from the CHECK ENGINE light on the dash. Simply ground the STI and GND terminals with a jumper wire and watch the light on the dash as it flashes the stored trouble code(s).

Make sure the battery voltage is greater than 11 volts, the transaxle is in Neutral, the accessories are off, the throttle valve is closed and the engine is at normal operating temperature, then turn the ignition switch to the ON position but do not start the engine. The computer will begin outputting or flashing the codes.

Clearing codes

Remove the jumper wire and close the cover on the diagnostic connector. Check the indicated system or component or take the vehicle to a dealer service department or other qualified repair shop to have the malfunction repaired. After repairs have been made, the diagnostic code must be canceled by detaching the cable from the negative terminal of the battery, then depressing the brake pedal for more than five seconds. After cancellation, perform a road test and make sure the warning light does not come on. If the original trouble code is repeated, additional repairs are required.

Villager (3.0L V6)

Retrieving codes

Turn the ignition key ON (engine not running). The CHECK ENGINE light on the dash should remain ON. This indicates that the PCM is receiving power and the CHECK ENGINE light bulb is not defective.

Turn the ignition key to OFF, locate and disconnect the diagnostic connector in the engine compartment (see illustration). (There is a data link connector under the left end of the dash, but it's only for scan tool use.) Turn the ignition key ON (engine not running). Using a suitable jumper wire bridge the appropriate terminals (see illustration). Wait two

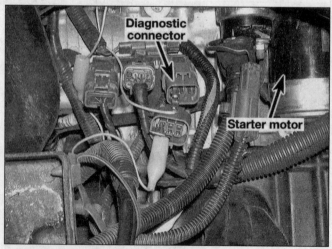

7.3g Engine compartment diagnostic connector location (1993 through 1995 Mercury Villager 3.0L V6 models) (there's another connector under the left end of the dash, but it's only for scan tool use)

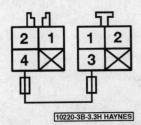

7.3h Diagnostic test connector code retrieving terminals (1993 through 1995 Mercury Villager 3.0L V6 models)

seconds and remove the jumper wire, then reconnect the engine compartment diagnostic connector. **Note:** *Failure to follow this procedure exactly as described may erase stored trouble codes from the PCM memory.*

Carefully observe the CHECK ENGINE light/MIL lamp flashes on the instrument cluster. If everything in the self-diagnosis system is functioning properly, the computer will flash a code 55 (OBD-I). The code will be represented by five long flashes on the CHECK ENGINE light/MIL lamp followed by five short flashes. If the computer has actual trouble codes stored, carefully observe the flashes and record the exact number onto paper. For example, code 43 (throttle position sensor or TPS circuit) is indicated by four long flashes followed by three short flashes.

If the ignition key is turned OFF during the code extraction process and possibly turned back ON, the self-diagnostic system will automatically invalidate the procedure. Restart the procedure to extract the codes. **Note:** *The self-diagnostic system cannot be accessed if the engine is running.*

Clearing codes

Turn the ignition key OFF for at least three seconds. Turn the ignition key back ON and disconnect the diagnostic connector. Using a suitable jumper wire bridge the same two terminals you bridged to retrieve the codes. Wait two seconds and remove the jumper wire, then reconnect the diagnostic connector and turn the ignition key OFF. **Caution:** *Do not disconnect the battery from the vehicle to clear the codes. This will erase stored operating parameters from the memory and cause the engine to run rough for a period of time while the computer relearns the information. If necessary, have the codes cleared by a dealer service department or other qualified repair facility.*

Always clear the codes from the PCM before a new electronic emission control component is installed onto the

7.4a On most GM models (domestic) the ALDL connector is located under the dash, usually on the drivers side - to output trouble codes, jump terminals A and B with the ignition On

engine. The PCM will often store trouble codes during sensor malfunctions. The PCM will also record new trouble codes if a new sensor is allowed to operate before the parameters from the old sensor have been erased. Clearing the codes will allow the computer to relearn the new operating parameters relayed by the new component. During the computer relearning process, the engine may experience a rough idle or slight driveability changes. This period of time, however, should last no longer than 15 to 20 minutes.

General Motors

Domestic cars and trucks (except Geo, Nova and Sprint)

All models except Cadillac with 4.1L, 4.5L, 4.6L, 4.9L and 6.0L engines and Buick Riviera/Oldsmobile Toronado (1986 through 1992)

Retrieving codes

The Check Engine light on the instrument panel will come on whenever a fault in the system has been detected, indicating that one or more codes pertaining to this fault are set in the Electronic Control Module (ECM). To retrieve the codes, you must use a short jumper wire to ground a diagnostic terminal. This terminal is part of an electrical connector known as the Assembly Line Diagnostic Link (ALDL) **(see illustrations)**. On most models the ALDL is located under the dashboard on the driver's side. If the ALDL has a

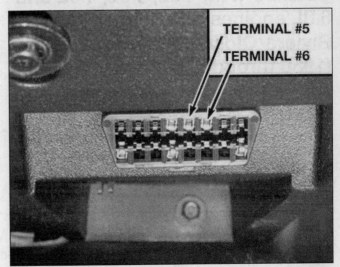

7.4b Some 1995 GM vehicles have the 16-pin connector like the OBD II system, but have accessible OBD I codes (check your emission decal for which system you have) - on this 1995 S-10 pickup with a 16-pin connector, bridge terminals 5 and 6 to extract trouble codes

cover, slide it toward you to remove it. Push one end of the jumper wire into the ALDL diagnostic terminal (B) and the other into the ground terminal (A), except on certain later models (see illustration 7.4b). Caution: *Don't crank the engine with the diagnostic terminal grounded - the ECM could be damaged.*

When the diagnostic terminal is grounded with the ignition On and the engine stopped, the system will enter Diagnostic Mode and the Check Engine (or Service Engine Soon) light will display a Code 12 (one flash, pause, two flashes). The code will flash three times, display any stored codes, then flash three more times, continuing until the jumper is removed.

The new government-mandated OBD II diagnostic system was initially used on some GM models starting in 1994. Some other models switched in 1995, and all models use this system in 1996. This system uses five-character codes which can only be accessed with an expensive scan tool. To know if your model has the OBD II system, look at the VECI emission label on the radiator fan shroud. If it is OBD II, it should say "OBD II certified" somewhere on the decal.

Clearing codes

After checking the system, clear the codes from the ECM memory by interrupting battery power. Turn off the ignition switch (otherwise the expensive ECM will be damaged) disconnect the negative battery cable for at least 30 seconds, then reconnect it. Caution: *If you have an anti-theft radio, make sure you know the activation code before disconnecting the battery. An alternative method of clearing the codes is to disconnect the ECM's fuse from the fuse panel for 30 seconds.*

Cadillac 4.1L, 4.5L, 4.6L, 4.9L and 6.0L engines and Buick Riviera/Oldsmobile Toronado (1986 through 1992)

Obtaining and clearing OBD system codes

The ECM will illuminate the CHECK ENGINE light (also known as the SERVICE ENGINE SOON light) on the dash if it recognizes a component fault for two consecutive drive cycles. It will continue to set the light until the codes are cleared or the ECM does not detect any malfunction for three or more consecutive drive cycles. Note: *Some diagnostic trouble codes will not set the CHECK ENGINE or SERVICE ENGINE SOON light, it is always a good idea to access the self diagnostic system and look for any trouble codes which may exist that have not set the CHECK ENGINE light.*

The diagnostic codes for OBD-I systems can be extracted from the ECM using two methods. The first

7.5a To enter the diagnostic service mode on Cadillac, Buick Riviera and Olds Toronado models, simultaneously press the OFF and WARMER buttons on the climate control panel

method requires accessing the computers self-diagnostic mode with the use of the Electronic Climate Control Panel or CRT display. To extract the diagnostic trouble codes using this method proceed as follows:

Cadillac Deville and Fleetwood models

a) Turn the ignition key ON (engine not running). **Note:** *Before you begin the code extraction process, be sure to obtain a pad of paper and a pencil to write down any stored trouble codes as they're displayed.*

b) Simultaneously press the OFF and WARMER buttons on the electronic climate control panel until "-1.8.8" illuminates on the climate control panel and "8.8.8" illuminates on the fuel data center (see illustrations). **Note:** *If all of the panel segments do not illuminate, it will be necessary to remove the affected display panel and have it serviced at a dealer service department or other qualified repair facility. Burnt out or broken panel segments will lead to incorrect trouble code displays, thereby leading to misdiagnosis of a particular system or component.*

c) After the segment check has been performed, "8.8.8" will be displayed on the fuel data center for approximately two more seconds, this indicates the beginning of the diagnostic trouble codes.

d) ECM trouble codes will now be displayed numerically from the lowest denomination to the highest on the fuel data center in two separate passes. The first pass will contain the ECM history codes and the second pass will contain the ECM current codes. All ECM trouble codes will begin with an "E" prefix.

e) The display ". E" designates the start of ECM history codes (first pass).

f) The display ". E . E" designates the start of ECM current codes (second pass).

ENTERING SERVICE MODE	Turn ignition key to the ON position. Simultaneously press the OFF and WARMER buttons on the electronic climate control panel for three seconds.
SEGMENT CHECK	Visually inspect that "-1.8.8" illuminates on the electronic climate control panel and that "8.8.8" illuminates on the fuel data center after the OFF and WARMER buttons are pressed for three seconds.
DIAGNOSTIC TROUBLE CODE DISPLAY (ECM TROUBLE CODES)	After the service mode has been entered all ECM diagnostic trouble codes will automatically be displayed. ".. E" designates the start of the ECM history codes. ". E . E" designates the start of the ECM current codes. Write down all trouble codes as they're being displayed, if any trouble codes are missed turn the ignition key OFF and restart the procedure.
DIAGNOSTIC TROUBLE CODE DISPLAY (BCM TROUBLE CODES)	After the ECM trouble codes, the BCM trouble codes will automatically be displayed. ".. F" designates the start of the BCM history codes. ". F . F" designates the start of the BCM current codes. Write down all trouble codes as they're being displayed, if any trouble codes are missed turn the ignition key OFF and restart the procedure.
SYSTEM READY MODE	After all diagnostic trouble codes have been displayed or if no codes are present, the fuel data center will display a ".7.0" this indicates that the system is ready for further instructions or testing.
CLEARING CODES	Enable to clear codes, the fuel data center must first display a system ready mode (".7.0"). To clear ECM codes, simultaneously press the OFF and HI buttons on the electronic climate control panel until "E.0.0" is displayed. To clear BCM codes, simultaneously press the OFF and LO buttons on the electronic climate control panel until "F.0.0" is displayed.

7.5b Trouble code extraction process - quick reference chart (Cadillac Deville and Fleetwood models)

g) If no ECM codes are present, the self-diagnostic system will bypass the ECM code symbols (". E" or ". E. E") and begin to display the BCM codes.

h) After the ECM trouble codes, the self diagnostic system will now begin to display the BCM trouble codes numerically from the lowest denomination to the highest on the fuel data center in two separate passes. The first pass will contain the BCM history codes and the second pass will contain the BCM current codes. All BCM trouble codes will begin with an "F" prefix.

i) The display ". F" designates the start of BCM history codes (first pass).

j) The display ". F. F" designates the start of BCM current codes (second pass).

k) When all ECM and BCM codes are finished being displayed or if no codes are present ".7.0" will be displayed. This code indicates a system ready status and the beginning of a switch test mode for various components within the self-diagnostic system. *Note:* Because of the complexity of the remaining OBD system, all further testing of the self diagnostic system is considered beyond the scope of the home mechanic and should be performed by a dealer service department or other qualified repair facility.

l) To clear ECM trouble codes, simultaneously press the OFF and HI buttons on the electronic climate control panel until "E.0.0" is displayed.

m) To clear BCM trouble codes, simultaneously press the OFF and LO buttons on the electronic climate control panel until "F.0.0" is displayed.

n) To exit the self-diagnostic system at any time, press the "AUTO" button and turn the ignition key OFF.

Cadillac Eldorado and Seville, Buick Riviera and Oldsmobile Toronado models

a) Turn the ignition key ON (engine not running). **Note:** *Before you begin the code extraction process, be sure to obtain a pad of paper and a pencil to write down any stored trouble codes as they're displayed.*

b) Simultaneously press the OFF and WARMER buttons (OFF and TEMP UP buttons on 1990 and later Buick models) on the electronic climate control panel until "-1.8.8" illuminates on the climate control panel and all the lights illuminate on the instrument panel cluster (see illustrations). Note 1: *If all of the panel segments do not illuminate, it will be necessary to remove the affected display panel and have it serviced at a dealer service department or other qualified repair facility.*

ENTERING SERVICE MODE	Turn ignition key to the ON position. Simultaneously press the OFF and WARMER buttons on the electronic climate control panel or the climate control page on CRT equipped models for three seconds.
SEGMENT CHECK (NON-CRT MODELS)	Visually inspect that **"-1.8.8"** illuminates on the electronic climate control panel and all the lights on the instrument panel cluster illuminate after the OFF and WARMER buttons are pressed for three seconds.
DIAGNOSTIC TROUBLE CODE DISPLAY	After the service mode has been entered all diagnostic trouble codes will automatically be displayed. Write down all trouble codes as they're being displayed, if any trouble codes are missed turn the ignition key OFF and restart the procedure.
SYSTEM LEVEL MODE (ECM or BCM)	To select a system level, press the fan LO button to scroll to the desired system level, then press the fan HI button to enter your selection. A system level must be selected before the computer can proceed to the next menu. On CRT equipped models use the NO pad on the "SERVICE MODE" page to scroll and the YES pad to enter your selection.
CLEARING CODES	To clear codes, press the fan LO button to scroll to the "CLEAR CODES" menu, then press the fan HI button to enter your selection. A **"CODES CLEAR"** message should appear for approximately three seconds. On CRT equipped models use the NO pad on the "SERVICE MODE" page to scroll and the YES pad to enter your selection.

7.5c Trouble code extraction process - quick reference chart (Cadillac Eldorado and Seville, Buick Riviera and Oldsmobile Toronado models)

Burnt out or broken panel segments will lead to incorrect trouble code displays, thereby leading to misdiagnosis of a particular system or component. **Note 2:** *On vehicles equipped with a CRT display, scroll the CRT menu and select the "CLIMATE CONTROL" page, press the OFF and WARMER buttons until the CRT*

7.5d The Data Link Connector (DLC) (arrow) is located to the left or right of the steering column, depending on the model year of the vehicle (Cadillac, Buick Riviera and Oldsmobile Toronado models)

beeps twice or the "SERVICE MODE" page is present on the CRT screen.

c) After the segment check has been performed, ECM trouble codes will now be displayed numerically from the lowest denomination to the highest on the climate control panel or the instrument panel cluster. ***Note:*** All Cadillac models display the trouble codes on the climate control panel. All Buick and Oldsmobile models display the trouble codes on the CRT (if equipped) or the instrument panel cluster on models without a CRT.

d) All ECM trouble codes will begin with an **"EO"** prefix and will be followed by the suffix **"C "** (current) or **"H"** (history). Suffix **"C"** (current) after the trouble code indicates that the fault was still present the last time the ECM performed a self-diagnostic check. Suffix **"H"** (history) after the trouble code indicates that the fault was not present the last time the ECM performed a self-diagnostic check.

e) If no ECM codes are present, the self-diagnostic system will display a "NO ECM CODES" message or a "NO X CODE" message.

f) After the ECM trouble codes, the self diagnostic system will now begin to display the BCM trouble codes numerically from the lowest denomination to the highest. All BCM trouble codes will begin with a **"B"** prefix and again will be followed by the suffix **"C "** (current) or **"H"** (history) as described in above.

g) If no BCM codes are present, the self-diagnostic system will display a "NO BCM CODES" message or a "NO X CODE" message.

h) When all ECM and BCM codes are finished being displayed the self-diagnostic system will display codes for other subsystems such as the CRT, instrument panel cluster and the SIR system. *Note 1:* Because of the complexity of the remaining OBD system, All further trouble code diagnosis and system testing on the CRT, instrument panel and SIR systems is considered beyond the scope of this manual and should be performed by a dealer service department or other qualified repair facility. *Note 2:* If a "NO X DATA" message appears on the display screen at any time during the trouble code extraction process it signifies that the BCM lost communication with that particular system and cannot retrieve any codes until the communication line or circuit is fixed.

i) To clear trouble codes, you must first select the system level to be cleared. Press the fan LO button on the climate control panel until the system to be cleared ("ECM" or "BCM") is displayed, then press the fan HI button to select (enter) the system.

j) Second you must select the test type. Again press the fan LO button until the **"CLEAR CODES"** menu is displayed, then press the fan HI button to select (enter) the test type. A **"CODES CLEAR"** message should appear for three seconds. *Note 1:* This procedure must be performed for each system level to be cleared. Example: clearing both the ECM and the BCM codes requires performing this procedure twice, once for the ECM system codes and a second time for the BCM system codes. *Note 2:* On models equipped with a CRT display it will be necessary to press the NO button on the "SERVICE MODE" page to scroll through the system levels and the test types and then press the YES button to select (enter) the system levels and **"CLEAR CODES"** menu.

The second method uses a special SCAN tool that is programmed to interface with the OBD-I system by plugging into the DLC **(see illustration)**. When used, the SCAN tool has the ability to diagnose in-depth driveability problems and it allows data to be retrieved from the ECM stored memory. If the tool is not available and intermittent driveability problems exist, have the vehicle checked at a dealer service department or other qualified repair shop.

All models

Always clear the codes from the ECM before a new electronic emission control component is installed onto the engine. The ECM will often store trouble codes during sensor malfunctions. The ECM will also record new trouble codes if a new sensor is allowed to operate before the parameters from the old sensor have been erased. Clearing the codes will allow the computer to relearn the new operating parameters relayed by the new component. During the computer relearning process, the engine may experience a rough idle or slight driveability changes. This period of time, however, should last no longer than 15 to 20 minutes. **Caution:** *Do not disconnect the battery from the vehicle to clear the codes. This will erase stored operating parameters from the memory and cause the engine to run rough for a period of time while the computer relearns the information. If necessary, have the codes cleared by a dealer service department or other qualified repair facility.* **Note:** *If using a OBD-I SCAN tool, scroll the menu for the function that describes "CLEARING CODES" and follow the prescribed method for that particular SCAN tool.*

General Motors imports

Geo (Metro, Prizm, Storm, Tracker)
Chevrolet (Sprint, Nova and Spectrum)
Storm
Retrieving codes

You must use a short jumper wire to ground the white diagnostic connector. This terminal is part of the Assembly Line Diagnostic Link (ALDL), located under the dash near the ECM **(see illustration)**.

Turn the ignition switch to ON (engine not running). Jumper the two outer cavities of the three-terminal connector. The Check Engine light will flash a Code 12 three times, then display the stored codes.

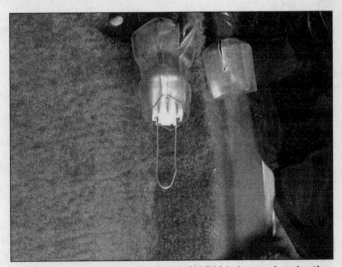

7.6 The Assembly Line Data Link (ALDL) is located under the passenger side glove box behind the kick panel - to activate the diagnostic codes, jump terminals 1 and 3 (the two outer terminals of the *white* connector)

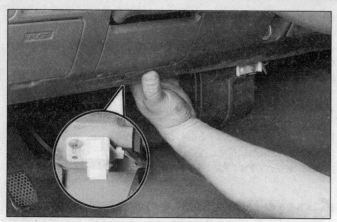

7.7 On 1987 and 1988 Sprint models, the diagnostic switch is located under the instrument panel

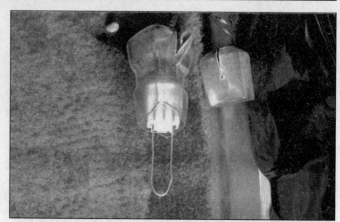

7.8 To display the codes on 1988 Nova (fuel injected) models, insert a jumper wire into the Check Engine connector with the ignition switch in the On position

Clearing codes

After making repairs, clear the memory by removing the ECM fuse for at least ten seconds.

Geo Storm - Electronic Control Module (ECM) - replacement

Note: *This system is equipped with an Engine Control Module (ECM) with an Erasable Programmable Read Only Memory (EEPROM). The calibrations (parameters) are stored in the ECM within the EEPROM. If the ECM must be replaced, it is necessary to have the EEPROM programmed with a special scanning tool (TECH 1) available only at dealership service departments. The EEPROM is not replaceable on these vehicles. In the event of any malfunction with the EEPROM (Code 51), the vehicle must be taken to a dealership service department for diagnosis and repair.*

Sprint

Retrieving codes

With the engine at normal operating temperature, turn the "diagnostic" switch located under the steering column to the On position **(see illustration)**.

The codes will then be flashed by the Check Engine light on the dashboard.

Clearing codes

After checking the system, clear the codes from the ECM memory by turning the "diagnostic" switch Off.

Metro

Retrieving codes

Insert the spare fuse into the diagnostic terminal of the fuse block.

Turn the ignition switch On (engine Off).

Read the diagnostic codes as indicated by the number of flashes of the Check Engine light on the dashboard. Normal system operation is indicated by Code 12. If there are any malfunctions, the light will flash the requisite number of times to display the codes in numerical order, lowest to highest.

Clearing codes

After testing, remove the fuse from the diagnostic terminal and clear the codes by removing the tail light fuse (otherwise the clock and radio will have to be reset).

Nova (fuel-injected models only)

Retrieving codes

With the ignition switch On, use a jumper wire to bridge both the terminals of the Check Engine connector located near the wiper motor **(see illustration)**. The Check Engine light will flash any stored codes.

Clearing codes

After checking, clear the codes by removing the ECM fuse (with the engine Off) for at least ten seconds.

Prizm

Retrieving codes

With the ignition On (engine Off), use a jumper wire to bridge terminals T and E1 of the "diagnostic" connector in the engine compartment **(see illustration)**.

Start the engine; the Check Engine light will then flash any stored codes.

Clearing codes

After checking, clear the codes by removing the ECM fuse (with the engine Off) for at least ten seconds.

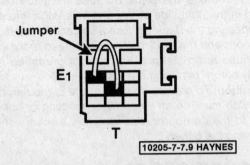

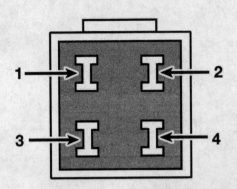

7.9 On 1989 and later Geo Prizm models, insert a jumper wire between terminals T (or TE1) and E1 of the diagnostic connector to retrieve the codes

7.10 Obtain the codes on later Tracker models by using a jumper wire between the number 2 and 3 terminals of the test connector located next to the battery

1	Duty check terminal	3	Ground terminal
2	Diagnostic test terminal	4	Test switch terminal

Tracker

Retrieving codes

On 1989 and 1990 models, insert the spare fuse into the diagnostic terminal of the fuse block.

On 1991 through 1994 (and 1995 TBI) models, use a jumper wire to bridge terminals 2 and 3 of the ECM check connector located in the engine compartment near the battery **(see illustration)**.

On 1995 models with port fuel injection, bridge the diagnostic and ground terminals of the check connector **(see illustration)**.

Turn the ignition switch On (engine Off).

Read the diagnosis codes as indicated by the number of flashes of the Check Engine light on the dashboard. Normal system operation is indicated by Code 12. Code 12 will flash three times, then if there are any malfunctions, the light will flash the requisite number of times to display the codes in numerical order, lowest to highest.

Clearing codes

After testing, remove the fuse or jumper wire and clear the codes by removing the tail light fuse (otherwise the clock and radio will have to be reset).

Honda

Retrieving codes

Accord (1985) and Civic (1985 through 1987)

The computer is located under the passenger's seat and displays the codes on four lights numbered, from left to right, 8-4-2-1. With the ignition On (engine Off), the lights will display the codes in ascending order.

Accord and Prelude (1986 and 1987)

The computer is located under the driver's seat. With the ignition switch On, the red light on the computer will display the codes by blinking (code 12 would be one blink, pause, two blinks) with a two second pause between codes.

Accord, Civic and Prelude (1988 and 1990)

Pull back the carpeting on the passenger's side kick panel for access to the computer.

With the ignition On, the light on the computer will display the codes by flashing.

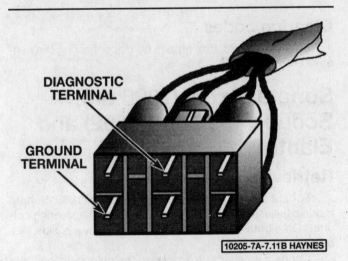

7.11 On 1995 Trackers with port fuel injection, bridge the diagnostic and ground terminals with a jumper wire

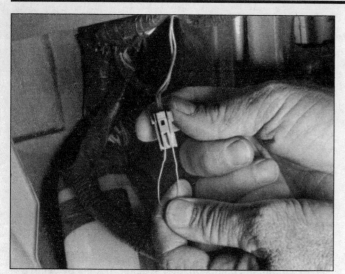

7.12 On most models, the diagnostic connector is located under the passenger side glove box behind the kick panel. To activate the diagnostic codes, bridge the terminals with a jumper wire or paper clip, then turn the ignition to the On position

All later models (1991 through 1995 (except 1995 Accord V6)

Note 1: *The two-digit trouble codes used on 1991 through 1995 models can be retrieved with the following procedures.*

Note 2: *The 1995 Accord V6 and all 1996 and later Honda models are equipped with OBD II diagnostics. The new, five-character codes are accessible only with an OBD II scan tool or Honda factory PGM tester.*

To view self-diagnosis information from the computer memory, install a jumper wire onto the diagnostic terminal **(see illustration)** located in the upper left corner under the dash. **Note:** *On 1991 Prelude models, the diagnostic connector is located in the engine compartment next to the fuse/relay block. On 1992 and later Prelude models, it's located behind the center console, near the accelerator pedal. On Odyssey models it's located behind the center console on the left side.* The codes are stored in the memory of the computer and when accessed, they blink a sequence on the Check Engine light to relay a number or code that represents a system component failure.

With the ignition On, the computer will display the coded flashes in a variety of combinations. The Check Engine light will blink a longer blink to represent the first digit of a two digit number and then will blink short for the second digit (for example, 1 long blink then 6 short blinks for the code 16 [fuel injector]). **Note:** *If the system has more than one problem, the codes will be displayed in sequence then a pause and the codes will repeat.*

When the computer sets a trouble code, the Check Engine light will come on and a trouble code will be stored in the memory. The trouble code will stay in the computer until the voltage to the computer is interrupted. To clear the

memory, remove the Back-Up fuse from the relay box located in the right side of the engine compartment. **Note:** *Disconnecting the Back-Up fuse also cancels the radio pre-set stations and the clock setting. Be sure to make a note of the various radio stations that are programmed into the memory before removing the fuse.*

Caution: *To prevent damage to the computer, the ignition switch must be off when disconnecting or connecting power to the computer (this includes disconnecting and connecting the battery).*

Clearing codes

The procedure for clearing codes is the same for all systems. To clear the codes after making repairs, make sure the ignition is Off, then disconnect the negative battery cable for ten seconds.

Hyundai

1988 Stellar
Retrieving codes

With ignition off, connect an analog voltmeter to the diagnostic connector located in the engine compartment, behind the right strut tower. Turn the ignition On (engine Off) and watch the voltmeter needle.

It will display the codes as sweeps of the needle. The needle will sweep in long or short pulses over a ten-second period with each period separated by six-second intervals.

Short sweep = 0; Long sweep = 1

10000 = 1	00100 = 4	11100 = 7
01000 = 2	10100 = 5	00010 = 8
11000 = 3	01100 = 6	00000 = 9

Clearing codes

Clear the codes after repairs by disconnecting the negative battery cable for 15 seconds.

Sonata, Excel (1990 on), Scoupe 1991 and 1992) and Elantra
Retrieving codes

Locate the diagnostic connector. On 1989 Sonata models this is under the dash, to the left of the steering column. On all other models, it's under the driver's side kick panel.

Connect an analog voltmeter to the diagnostic connector ground terminal and MPI diagnostic terminal **(see illustration)**.

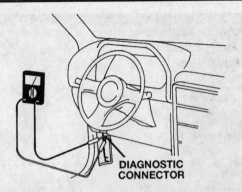

7.13a The self-diagnostic connector is located on the fuse panel (all models except 1989 Sonata)

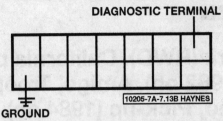

Excel (1990 on), Sonata (1990 on), Scoupe (1991 and 1992) and Elantra

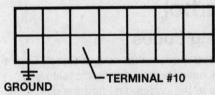

Scoupe (1993 on) and Accent

7.13b Diagnostic terminal positions

Turn the ignition On.

Count the voltmeter needle sweeps and write them down for reference. Long sweeps indicate the first digit in two-digit codes. The short sweeps indicate the second digit. For example, two long sweeps followed by one short sweep indicates a code 21.

Clearing codes

To clear the codes, disconnect the negative battery cable for 15 seconds.

Scoupe (1993 through 1995) and Accent

The diagnostic connector is still in the driver's kick panel area, but on these models, you must ground the #10 wire for three seconds to get the codes to display on the MIL light **(see illustration 7.13b)**. Do not ground for more than 4 seconds. If 4444 is displayed, there are no stored codes. The first stored code will be displayed over and over; to go to the next code, repeat the grounding procedure. Keep going through the procedure until 3333 is displayed which indicates the end of the self-diagnosis (all stored codes have been displayed).

Clearing codes

To clear the codes, disconnect the negative battery cable for 15 seconds.

Infiniti

All models are equipped with a Malfunction Indicator Light (MIL). As a bulb check, the light glows when the ignition is turned on and the engine is not running.

On **California** models, the MIL glows when a fault is detected with the engine running. A corresponding trouble code will set in the computer memory. The MIL also glows if the computer or crankshaft position sensor malfunctions.

On **Federal** models, the MIL glows only when the computer or crankshaft position sensor malfunctions with the engine running.

The self-diagnostic system can detect ECCS malfunctions and store related trouble codes. Intermittent codes are also stored. All codes are stored until cleared from memory. If an intermittent does not reoccur within 50 ignition key cycles, it will be cleared from memory.

Retrieving codes

Turn the ignition to the On position (don't start the engine).

Using a screwdriver, rotate the mode selector on the computer completely clockwise and wait approximately two seconds. After two seconds, turn the selector counterclockwise as far as it will go. This will put the computer in the diagnostic mode, causing the red LED to flash trouble codes, if any are present. For example, two long flashes, pause, followed by four short flashes indicates a code 24. If there is more than one code stored in memory, the codes will be displayed in numerical order; each code will be separated by a two second pause. **Note 1**: *On 1990 to 1995 models, it is the red LED on the computer which will flash. On 1996 models, it is the Malfunction Indicator Light (MIL) that will flash the codes.* **Note 2**: *Be sure the selector is in the fully counterclockwise position before driving the vehicle.*

Computer Location

On G20 models, the computer is located under the dash, in the center console. On J30 and Q45 models, the computer is located behind the right kick panel.

Clearing Codes

Note: *Ensure all diagnostic codes are accessed from the computer memory before disconnecting the battery.*

Stored memory can be erased by disconnecting the negative battery cable.

Isuzu

I-Mark (RWD), California pick-up (1982 on), Amigo, Trooper, Rodeo, Pick-up (1984 on), Impulse (1983 and later non-turbo)

Retrieving codes

The above models that have a Check Engine light on the dash will have the self-diagnostic feature.

To retrieve the codes, first find the diagnostic connectors. These can be located in the engine compartment, under the dash or near the computer. The connectors are usually found behind the drivers trim panel under the dash, on the passenger side, tucked or taped out of the way in the harness.

With the ignition switch On, connect the two leads of the diagnostic connectors together to ground them **(see illustration)**.

Trooper and Rodeo V6 and I-Mark (FWD)

Retrieving codes

To retrieve the codes, use a short jumper wire to ground the diagnostic terminal. This terminal is part of an electrical connector known as the Assembly Line Diagnostic Link (ALDL). The ALDL is usually located under the dashboard or in the console near the computer.

Push one end of the jumper wire into the ALDL diagnostic terminal and the other into the ground terminal.

On I-mark models terminals A and C must be jumpered together (the two outer terminals on the three terminal connector).

On 1989 through 1991 V6 Trooper and Rodeo models, jumper terminals A and B. On 1992 and later models, jumper terminals 1 and 3 (on these models the connector is located to the right of the accelerator pedal).

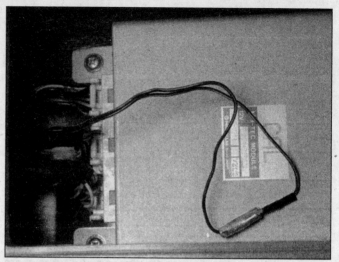

7.15 Typical diagnostic hook-up - make sure the ignition switch is On before connecting the terminals

All of the above models

With the diagnostic terminal now grounded and the ignition on with the engine stopped, the system will enter the Diagnostic Mode and the Check Engine light will display a Code 12 (one flash, pause, two flashes).

The code will flash three times, display any stored codes, then flash three more times, continuing until the jumper is removed.

Note 1: *On feedback carbureted models through 1989, after the code 12 is shown, disconnect the jumper and start the engine to display codes. On some models the codes 13, 15, 31, 44 and 45 will only show after the engine has run for five minutes at part throttle (after already reaching normal operating temperature).*

Note 2: *All 1996 models use the ODB II diagnostic system, which requires an expensive scan tool to access and clear the codes.*

Clearing codes

After checking the system, remove the jumper and clear the codes from the computer memory by removing the appropriate fuse (ECM on four-cylinder models, BLM on V6) for ten seconds.

Jaguar XJS and XJ6 (1988 through 1994)

Note: *Trouble codes are not retrievable on 1995 and later models (a special scan tool must be used).*

All models are equipped with a Check Engine light. When the check engine light remains on, the self-diagnostic system has detected a system failure.

Hard Failures

Hard failures cause the check engine light to glow. Fault codes are stored in the Electronic Control Module (ECM) memory. All codes except Codes 26 and 44 will cause the check engine light to remain illuminated (with the ignition on) until the fault is corrected and the ECM memory is cleared.

Codes 26 and 44 - the check engine light will remain on only until the next ignition on/off cycle. The codes will no longer be indicated by a check engine light, but will still be stored in ECM memory.

If the light comes on and remains on during vehicle operation, the cause of malfunction can be determined using the diagnostic trouble code table.

If a sensor fails, the control unit will use a substitute value in its calculations to continue engine operation. In this condition, the vehicle is functional but poor driveability may occur.

Retrieving codes

To access any stored trouble codes, turn the ignition to the Off position and wait five seconds. Turn the ignition key to the On position, but don't crank the engine.

Locate the Vehicle Condition Monitor (VCM)/trip computer display panel near the speedometer and press the VCM button. Any stored trouble codes will be shown on the display panel. If the engine is started the code will disappear from the display, but the CHECK ENGINE light will stay on. **Note 1:** *On V12 models, the code will display without pushing the button.* **Note 2:** *Not every code is displayed through*

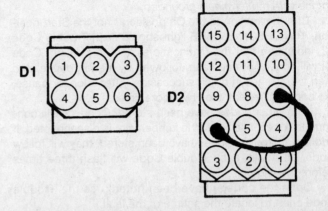

7.17 On 1984 through 1986 four-cylinder and V6 models, jump terminals 6 and 7 of the diagnostic connector to output trouble codes

the dash light, and only the first priority code will display, until it is fixed and cleared. If there is a second code, it will not be displayed until the first is fixed and cleared.

Clearing codes

Turn the ignition key to the Off position, then detach the cable from the negative terminal of the battery for at least 30 seconds.

Jeep

Retrieving codes

1984 through 1986 four-cylinder and V6 models

To extract this information from the ECM memory, you must use a short jumper wire to ground terminals 6 and 7 on the diagnostic connector **(see illustration)**. The diagnostic connector is located in the engine compartment on the left (driver's side) fenderwell. **Caution:** *Do not start the engine with the terminals grounded.*

Turn the ignition to the On position - not the Start position. The CHECK ENGINE light should flash Trouble Code 12, indicating that the diagnostic system is working. Code 12 will consist of one flash, followed by a short pause, and then two flashes in quick succession. After a longer pause, the code will repeat itself two more times.

If no other codes have been stored, Code 12 will continue to repeat itself until the jumper wire is disconnected. If additional Trouble Codes have been stored, they will follow Code 12. Again, each Trouble Code will flash three times before moving on.

Once the code(s) have been noted, use the Trouble Code chart to locate the source of the fault.

It should be noted that the self-diagnosis feature built into this system does not detect all possible faults. If you suspect a problem with the Computer Command Control System, but the CHECK ENGINE light has not come on and no trouble codes have been stored, take the vehicle to a dealer service department or other repair shop for diagnosis.

Furthermore, when diagnosing an engine performance, fuel economy or exhaust emissions problem (which is not accompanied by a CHECK ENGINE light) do not automatically assume the fault lies in this system. Perform all standard troubleshooting procedures, as indicated elsewhere in this manual, before turning to the Computer Command Control System .

Finally, since this is an electronic system, you should have a basic knowledge of automotive electronics before attempting any diagnosis. Damage to the ECM or related components can easily occur if care is not exercised.

1987 through 1990 models

A special scan tool is required to retrieve trouble codes on these models. Take the vehicle to a dealer service department or other qualified shop.

1991 on

The self-diagnostic capabilities of this system, if properly used, can simplify testing. The Powertrain Control module (PCM) monitors several different engine control system circuits.

Hard failures cause the Malfunction Indicator Light (MIL) (may also be referred to as "CHECK ENGINE" Light) to glow and flicker until the malfunction is repaired. If the light comes on and remains on (light may flash) during vehicle operation, determine the cause of malfunction using the self-diagnostic tests. If a sensor fails, the PCM will use a substitute value in its calculations, allowing the engine to operate in a "limp-in" mode. In this condition, the vehicle will run, but driveability may be poor.

Intermittent failures may cause the MIL to flicker or stay on until the intermittent fault goes away. However, the PCM memory will retain a corresponding fault. If a related fault does not reoccur within a certain time frame, the related fault will be erased from PCM memory. Intermittent failures

can be caused by a faulty sensor, bad connector or wiring related problems.

Test the circuits and repair or replace the components as required. If the problem is repaired or ceases to exist, the PCM cancels the fault after 50 ignition on/off cycles. A specific fault results from a particular system failure. A fault does not condemn a specific component; the component is not necessarily the reason for failure. Faults only suggest the probable malfunction area.

Service precautions

1   When the battery is disconnected, vehicle computer and memory systems may lose memory data. Driveability problems may exist until the computer systems have completed a relearn cycle.

2   The vehicle must have a fully charged battery and a functional charging system.

3   Probe the PCM 60-pin connector from the pin side. **Caution:** *Do not back- probe PCM connector.*

4   Do not cause short circuits when performing any electrical tests. This will set additional faults, making diagnosis of the original problem more difficult.

5   When checking for voltage, **do not** use a test light - use a digital voltmeter.

6   When checking for spark, ensure that the coil wire is no more than 1/4-inch from a ground connection. If the coil wire is more than 1/4-inch from ground, damage to the vehicle electronics and/or PCM may result.

7   Do not prolong testing of the fuel injectors, or the engine may hydrostatically (liquid) lock.

8   Always repair the lowest fault code number first.

9   Always perform a verification test after repairs are made.

Retrieving codes

Note 1: *Although other scanners are available, the manufacturer recommends using Diagnostic Readout Box II (DRB-II).The malfunction indicator light (MIL) method can be used, without the need for the diagnostic scanner, but not all trouble codes can be accessed and has limited diagnostic capability. Due to the prohibitive cost of the Diagnostic Readout Box II, only the MIL method will be discussed here.*
Note 2: *Beginning in 1996, all models are equipped with the OBD II diagnostics system. Although a scan tool is required to retrieve and clear the new, five-character codes, the basic two-digit codes can still be retrieved from the MIL light.*

Start the engine, if possible, and shift the transmission through all of the gears. Place the shifter in the Park position, then turn the air conditioning on and off.

Stop the engine, then turn the ignition key to the On position, then Off, then On, then Off, then On again within three seconds. This will cause any stored trouble codes to be displayed by flashing the Malfunction Indicator Light (MIL or CHECK ENGINE light).

Code 55 indicates all of the trouble codes have been displayed.

Clearing codes

Caution: *If the stereo in your vehicle is equipped with an anti-theft system, make sure you have the correct activation code before disconnecting the battery.*

Trouble codes may be cleared by disconnecting the negative battery cable for at least 15 seconds.

Lexus

Retrieving codes

When the system is placed in diagnostic mode, stored fault codes are displayed through a blinking CHECK ENGINE light on the dash. To obtain an output of diagnostic codes, verify first that the battery voltage is above 11 volts, the throttle is fully closed, the transaxle is in Neutral, the accessory switches are off and the engine is at normal operating temperature.

Turn the ignition switch to ON (engine not running). Do not start the engine. Use a jumper wire to bridge terminals TE1 and E1 of the service electrical connector **(see illustration)**. **Note:** *The self-diagnosis system can be accessed by using either test terminal no. 1 (engine compartment) or test terminal no. 2 (under the left end of the dash).*

Read the diagnosis code as indicated by the number of flashes of the "CHECK ENGINE" light on the dash. Normal system operation (no codes found) is indicated by a constant blinking (two times per second). Each code will be displayed by first blinking the first digit of the code, then pause, followed by a pause, followed by blinking the second digit of the code. For example, Code 24 (IAT sensor) will flash two times, pause, and then flash four times. Each flash, and the pause between each flash, is exactly the same length, except for the pause between the flashes for each digit. That pause is longer so that you can distinguish between the first and second digits of the code.

If there are any malfunctions in the system, their corresponding trouble codes are stored in computer memory and the light will blink the requisite number of times for the indicated trouble codes. If there's more than one trouble code in the memory, they'll be displayed in numerical order (from the lowest to the highest) with a 2-1/2 second pause interval between each one. (To ensure correct interpretation of the flashing CHECK ENGINE light, watch carefully for the end of one code and the beginning of the next; otherwise you'll become confused by the apparent number of flashes and will misinterpret the display). After the code with the largest number of flashes has been displayed, there will be another pause and then the sequence begins all over again.

Clearing codes

After the malfunctioning component has been repaired/replaced, the CHECK ENGINE light will reset itself, but the trouble code(s) stored in computer memory must be canceled. To do so, simply turn the ignition to OFF and

7.18 To access the Lexus self-diagnosis system, locate the diagnostic connector under the left end of the dash (shown) or in the engine compartment (not shown) and use a jumper wire or paper clip to bridge terminals TE1 and E1

remove the 20-amp EFI fuse from junction fuse box no. 2. Wait at least ten seconds before reinstalling the fuse. Road test the vehicle and verify that no fault codes are present.

Mazda

All models

Hard Failures

Hard failures cause the Check Engine light to illuminate and remain on until the problem is repaired.

If the light comes on and remains on (light may flash) during vehicle operation, the cause of the malfunction can be determined using the diagnostic code charts.

If a sensor fails, the computer will use a substitute value in its calculations to continue engine operation. In this condition, commonly known as "limp-in" mode, the vehicle will run but driveability will be poor.

Intermittent Failures

Intermittent failures may cause the Check Engine light to flicker or illuminate and go out after the intermittent fault goes away. However, the corresponding code will be retained in the computer memory. If a related fault does not reoccur within a certain time frame, the code will be erased from the computer memory. Intermittent failures may be caused by sensor, connector or wiring related problems.

Retrieving codes

1989 to 1991 models (except Miata); 1992 and 1993 MPV, 1993 and earlier pick-ups

The diagnostic connector is located in the engine com-

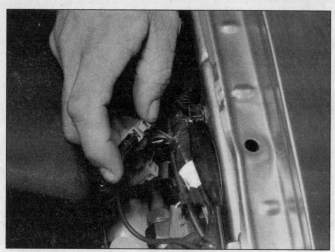

7.19a To retrieve the trouble code, use a jumper wire and ground the green 1-pin connector to a bolt on the body

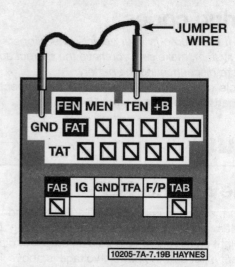

7.19b On 1992 through 1995 Mazdas (except pick-ups), bridge terminals TEN and GND to output trouble codes

partment, back of left front strut tower **(see illustration)**.

Trouble codes are accessed by using a jumper wire to ground the single-pin, green-wire connector.

1990 and 1991 Miata

On these models, a factory diagnostic tool must be used to retrieve codes.

1994 Pick-ups

Refer to the Ford trouble code retrieval procedure, and use the Ford EEC-IV three-digit code list. **Note:** *1995 and later pick-ups use the Ford EEC V engine management system; trouble codes on these models must be retrieved with a special scan tool.*

1992 to 1995 models, except pick-ups

Using a jumper wire, connect the self-diagnostic connector terminal TEN with the ground terminal **(see illustration)**. The connector is located near the left shock tower.

1995 Millennia

These models are equipped with OBD II diagnostic systems, which require the use of an expensive scan tool to retrieve the new, five-character diagnostic codes.

All models

With the ignition On and engine Off, observe the check engine light; any stored trouble codes will be displayed by flashes of the light. For example, two long flashes, pause, followed by four short flashes indicates a code 24.

If the light glows continuously, the check engine light circuit may be grounded or the computer may be defective **Note:** *If there is more than one code stored, they will be displayed in order from the lowest number to the highest number.*

Clearing codes

Disconnect the negative battery cable. Depress the brake pedal for at least 20 seconds. Reconnect the battery cable and reconnect the jumper wire. Turn the key to the ON position for at least six seconds, then start the engine and run it at a high idle (2000 rpm) for at least three minutes. If no codes are displayed on the MIL, the codes have been cleared successfully. Shut the engine off and disconnect the jumper wire.

Mercedes

Before retrieving codes the following pretest conditions must be met:
1   Start and run engine until engine oil temperature is 176°F (80°C).
2   Turn air conditioning **off**.
3   Make sure the shift lever is in **Park**.
4   Check all fuses and replace as necessary.
5   Verify battery voltage is 11-to-14 volts.

Retrieving codes:

HFM-SFI system (except C220, C280, 400, 190E and 500)

Turn the ignition On (engine not running).

Press the non-locking switch, located on diagnostic connector in right rear corner of the engine compartment **(see illustration)**, for 2-to-4 seconds. HFM-SFI control unit will begin output of any fault codes present by flashing the LED light on diagnostic connector.

If the LED only flashes once, this indicates no fault codes are stored. If fault codes are stored, the LED will flash indicating fault code 3.

Press the push-button again for 2-to-4 seconds. If more fault codes are stored, the LED on the diagnostic connector will display the next code.

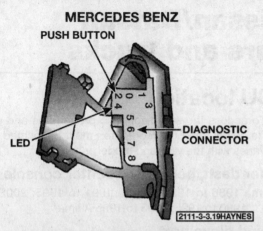

MERCEDES BENZ

7.20 Location of the diagnostic connector is in the right rear corner of the engine compartment

Continue pressing the push-button for 2-to-4 seconds at a time until the LED lights steadily, indicating the end of fault code display.

Record all fault codes and refer to the trouble code identification table. **Note:** *Other 1994 and later models are equipped with OBD II diagnostic systems, which require the use of a special tool to retrieve trouble codes.*

Clearing codes

On Federal vehicles, disconnect the negative battery cable. Stored trouble codes will be erased when the battery is disconnected.

On California vehicles, disconnecting the battery will not erase the codes. Each code that is stored in the CIS-E control unit will have to be erased individually.

Press the non-locking switch located on the diagnostic connector in the right rear corner of the engine compartment for 2-to-4 seconds.

When the fault is displayed, press the non-locking switch for 6-to-8 seconds. That code is now cleared. Repeat the procedure until all stored codes have been erased.

Press the Start button on the pulse counter for 2-to-4 seconds, maximum. The pulse counter will display the fault code. Press the start button again for 6-to-8 seconds. The

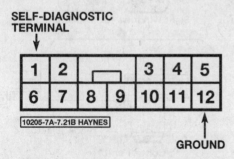

7.21b On 1990 and 1991 Monteros, the connector is slightly different in layout - this one is located in the glove compartment area

fault code is erased when the pulse counter no longer displays the fault code.

Repeat the procedure for other stored fault codes. When the pulse counter displays "1", no faults are stored.

Mitsubishi

Retrieving codes

With the engine Off, locate the diagnostic connector. On most models, an analog voltmeter is connected to the diagnostic connector, the positive lead from the voltmeter to the test terminal, and the ground lead to the ground terminal **(see illustrations)**. **Note:** *On all 1995 models (except the Expo, Summit wagon, and pickup models) the MIL lamp must be used, by jumping the test and ground terminals of the connector with a jumper wire and observing the flashes of the MIL lamp on the dash. The location of the diagnostic connector varies with model and year:*

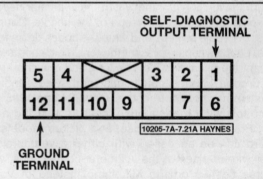

7.21a To put the ECU into code retrieval mode, connect an analog voltmeter to the indicated terminals of the connector - most models have this diagnostic connector

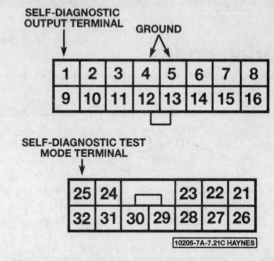

7.21c Location of the self-diagnostic terminals on 1992 and later Mitsubishi models

1983 through 1986 fuel-injected models

The diagnostic connector is located under the battery or on the right side firewall near the computer, depending on model.

1987 through 1989, except Galant and Mirage, 1990 through 1991 Montero

The diagnostic connector is in or under the glove compartment.

1987 through 1991 Galant and Mirage

The connector is behind the left side kick panel.

1990 through 1991 Eclipse and Pick-up, all 1992 through 1995 models

The diagnostic connector is located near the fuse block.

All models

Turn the ignition On and watch the voltmeter needle. It will display the codes as sweeps of the needle. Count the number of needle sweeps and write the codes down for reference. Long sweeps represent the tens digit, short sweeps represent the ones digit, i.e. one long and one short would be DTC code 11. Only continuous short sweeps indicates the system has no stored codes. On 1994 and 1995 models, the following models are accessed by using a voltmeter: Precis, Mirage, Eclipse, and pickup models. The Montero can be accessed with either a voltmeter *or* a jumper wire in place of the voltmeter connections, which indicates flashes on the MIL lamp instead of voltage sweeps. The following models are accessible only through the blinking MIL: Galant, Diamante, and 3000GT. **Note:** *1995 models are equipped with OBD II diagnostic systems, which require the use of an expensive scan tool to retrieve the new, five-character diagnostic codes, however, the basic MIL/voltmeter codes can still be obtained also.*

Clearing codes

Clear the codes by disconnecting the negative battery cable for 30 seconds.

7.22a On all except TBI-equipped pick-ups and 1984 through 1986 300ZX, select the diagnostic mode by turning the ECU mode selector clockwise, gently, until it stops

Nissan/Datsun cars and trucks

ECU location

To access the self-diagnostic procedures and extract trouble codes, the ECU (computer) must be located. Location varies with the year and model as follows:

Under dash, behind the center console
Maxima 1986 to 1994; Sentra 1991 to 1995; 200SX and 300SX, 1990 to 1995; 1993 to 1995 Altima

Behind glove box
Maxima, Quest 1995; 1991 to 1995 300ZX

Under passenger seat
Pick-up and Pathfinder, 1987 to 1995, Pulsar, Stanza, Sentra, 1987 to 1989

Under driver's seat
Stanza wagon, 1987, Sentra 4WD 1990

At kick panel under right side of dash
300ZX, 1986 to 1989; 240SX 1987 to 1995

At kick panel under left side of dash
200SX, 1987 to 1988

Retrieving codes, 1984 to 1989

Remove the computer. **Caution:** *Do not disconnect the electrical connector from the computer or you will erase any stored diagnostic codes.*

Turn the ignition switch to On. **Note:** *On 1984 to 1986 models (except pickups with TBI) start the engine and warm it to normal operating temperature.*

Turn the diagnostic mode selector on the computer fully clockwise or turn the mode selector switch (a hand-operated switch on some models) to On **(see illustrations)**.

Wait until the inspection lamps flash. **Note:** *The LED-*

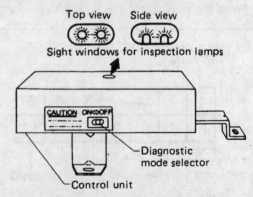

7.22b On TBI-equipped pick-ups, activate the diagnostic mode by pushing the mode switch to the left - the red and green lights should begin flashing

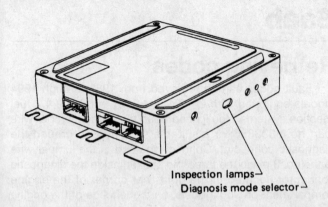

Inspection lamps
Diagnosis mode selector

7.23 On 1984 through 1986 300ZX models, verify the diagnostic mode selector is turned fully counterclockwise using a small screwdriver

type inspection lamps are located on the side or top of the computer **(see illustration)**. The inspection lamps flash once for each level of diagnostics, i.e. one flash is Mode I, two flashes is Mode II. After the inspection lamps have flashed three times (Mode III is the self-diagnostic mode that will display codes), turn the diagnostic mode selector fully counterclockwise or turn the mode selector to Off.

On 1984 to 1986 300ZX models, start the procedure by turning the screw *counter*clockwise, turn the ignition ON, make sure the bulbs stay on, then turn the screw clockwise. Later 300ZX models are diagnosed the same as other models.

The computer is now in the self-diagnostic mode. Now, count the number of times the inspection lamps flash.

First, the red lamp flashes, then the green lamp flashes. **Note:** *The red lamp denotes units of ten, the green lamp denotes units of one. Check the trouble code chart for the particular malfunction. For example, if the red lamp flashes once and the green lamp flashes twice, the computer is displaying the number 12, which indicates the air flow meter is malfunctioning.*

If the ignition switch is turned off at any time during a diagnostic readout, the procedure must be re-started. The stored memory or memories will be lost if, for any reason, the battery terminal is disconnected.

Retrieving codes, 1990 to 1995

Beginning with 1990 models, there are two types of diagnostics systems, the dual-LED type as described above, and a new single-LED system. The dual-LED system works the same as the previous models, with a red and a green light.

The single-LED system (Pathfinder and pick-up models) has only two Modes, with Mode II being the self-diagnostic mode for trouble code retrieval. The red LED will flash a long flash (.6 seconds) for the tens digit and short flashes (.3 seconds) for the single digits.

Note: *All 1995 models have a Malfunction Indicator Lamp (Check Engine light), and instead of using the LED's on the*

computer to read codes, the MIL flashes the codes (except Pathfinder and pick-up models, which still have the dual-LED system). Also, most 1995 models are equipped with OBD II diagnostics systems. Although an expensive scan tool is required to retrieve the new, five-character diagnostic codes, the basic codes can still be obtained using the flashing MIL.

Clearing codes

On early TBI-equipped pick-up models, to erase the memory after self-diagnosis codes have been noted or recorded, turn the diagnostic mode selector to On. After the inspection lamps have flashed four times, turn the diagnostic mode selector to Off Turn the ignition switch to Off.

On all other early models, erase the memory by turning the diagnostic mode selector on the computer fully clockwise. After the inspection lamps have flashed four times, turn the mode selector fully counterclockwise. This will erase any signals the computer has stored concerning a particular component.

Note: *On all models, disconnecting the negative cable of the battery will clear all stored codes. On later models, unless the battery is disconnected, stored codes for problems that have been fixed will remain stored until the vehicle has made 50 restarts.*

Porsche

The vehicle computer, the Digital Motor Electronics (DME) control unit, has the ability to store fault codes related to fuel injection and ignition systems. Detected faults are stored for at least 50 engine starts. If the positive battery cable or the DME control unit connector is disconnected, the fault code memory will be cleared.

Hard Failures

Hard failures cause the Check Engine light to illuminate and remain on until problem is repaired. If the light comes on and remains on (light may flash) during vehicle operation, the cause of malfunction must be determined using diagnostic code tables. If a sensor fails, the control unit will use a substitute value in its calculations to continue engine operation. In this condition, commonly known as limp-in mode, the vehicle will run but driveability will be poor.

Intermittent failures

Intermittent failures may cause the Check Engine light to flicker or illuminate. Light goes out after intermittent fault goes away. However, the corresponding trouble code will be stored in computer memory. If the fault does not reoccur within a certain time frame, related code(s) will be erased from computer memory. Intermittent failures may be caused by sensor, connector or wiring related problems.

Check engine light

The check engine light comes on if a component related to fuel injection and/or ignition system fails.

The check engine light is installed in oil the temperature/pressure gauge cluster. The light comes on as a self-test when the ignition switch is in the On position.

After the engine starts, the throttle valve closes, and the Check Engine light goes out to indicate that there are no codes stored in the computer memory.

If the check engine light remains on, a fault is present (hard failure) in the DME engine management system. If the check engine light comes on, or flickers, while driving, a fault in the DME engine management system has been identified (intermittent failure).

If the idle speed switch is open during the starting sequence, the check engine light will come on. As soon as the idle speed switch closes while driving, the check engine light goes out after a 4-second delay.

If the full throttle switch is faulty (shorted to ground), the check engine light will remain on constantly.

Some fault codes cannot be displayed using the check engine light. In such cases, retrieve the fault code(s) through the diagnostic connector, and repair the condition(s) causing the check engine light to come on.

Retrieving codes

On models with a CHECK ENGINE light, turn the ignition key to the On position, then depress the accelerator pedal to the floor and hold it there for five seconds. The CHECK ENGINE light should go out then come on again. At this point, take your foot off the accelerator pedal; the next series of flashes on the CHECK ENGINE light will represent the first trouble code. Write down the code number, then depress the accelerator pedal again for five seconds, then release the pedal and record the second trouble code. Repeat this procedure until all of the trouble codes have been output and code 1000 is displayed, indicating the end of the sequence.

On models without a CHECK ENGINE light, you'll need a Porsche tester (No. 9288 or 9268) or a suitable aftermarket code reader to display the codes. Plug the factory tester or the code reader into the diagnostic connector, which is located in the right (passenger) footwell on 944 and 968 models, and in the right kick panel on 928 models.

Clearing codes

Ensure the fault that was causing the check engine light to come on has been corrected, then depress and hold the accelerator pedal at wide open throttle (WOT) for more than 12-seconds.

The check engine light will go out briefly after 3, 7 and 10-second intervals to indicate that fault code memory has been cleared.

To clear codes stored in memory, momentarily disconnect the electrical connector from the DME control unit The fault code memory will be cleared.

Saab

Retrieving codes

Fault codes can be retrieved from 1988 through 1994 models equipped with LH 2.4, LH 2.4.1 and LH 2.4.2 fuel injection systems. You'll need Saab's switched jumper wire (part no. 8393886) or a suitable substitute to ground the diagnostic connector. Connect one end of the jumper wire to the no. 3 pin in the three-pin socket inside the diagnostic connector (located in the right rear corner of the engine compartment on 900 models; on the left side of the engine compartment on 9000 models). Connect the other end of the jumper wire to ground. Turn the ignition switch to ON; the CHECK ENGINE light will come on. Set the jumper switch to ON (this grounds ECU pin 16); the CHECK ENGINE LIGHT will go out. Watch the CHECK ENGINE light. After about 2-1/2 seconds, it will flash briefly, indicating that the first diagnostic code is going to be displayed. As soon as the CHECK ENGINE light flashes, turn the jumper switch to OFF.

The first fault code will now be displayed. A single flash, followed by a long pause, indicates the number 1. A single flash, followed by a short pause, another single flash, and a long pause, indicates the number 2. A flash, short pause, flash, short pause, flash, long pause sequence indicates the number 3. Each code has four digits. Each two digits are separated by a longer pause. Each four-digit code is flashed repeatedly until the jumper wire switch is again turned to ON; again, CHECK ENGINE light will flash briefly, after which you turn the jumper wire switch to OFF and the next fault code is displayed. And so on. Repeat this procedure until all fault codes have been displayed and noted. When all stored codes have been flashed, or all faults have been repaired, the CHECK ENGINE light will display an uninterrupted series of flashes. If you want to display the codes again, turn the jumper wire switch to ON. This time watch for *two* short flashes, then turn the jumper wire switch to OFF. Repeat the above procedure.

Clearing codes

Set the jumper switch to ON and watch the CHECK ENGINE light. After three short flashes, turn the jumper wire switch to OFF. The CHECK ENGINE light will either flash a continuous series of long flashes (Code 00000) or it will flash Code 12444 (fault codes stored in memory have been erased).

Saturn

The Computer Command Control (CCC) system consists of an Electronic Control Module (ECM) and information sensors which monitor various functions of the engine and send data back to the ECM.

This system is equipped with an Erasable Programmable Read Only Memory (EEPROM). The calibrations (parameters) are stored in the ECM within the EEPROM. If the ECM must be replaced, it is necessary to have the EEPROM programmed with a special scanning tool called TECH 1 available only at dealership service department. **Note:** *The EEPROM is not replaceable on these vehicles. In the event of any malfunction with the EEPROM (Code 51), the vehicle must be taken to a dealership service department for diagnosis and repair.*

The ECM controls the following systems:

Fuel control
Electronic spark timing
Exhaust gas recirculation
Canister purge
Engine cooling fan
Idle Air Control (IAC)
Transmission converter clutch
Air conditioning clutch control
Secondary air

Retrieving codes

Note: *A special tool is required to retrieve trouble codes on 1996 and later models.*

The CCC system has a built-in diagnostic feature which indicates a problem by flashing a Check Engine light on the instrument panel. When this light comes on during normal vehicle operation, a fault in one of the information sensor circuits or the ECM itself has been detected. More importantly, a trouble code is stored in the ECM's memory.

To retrieve this information from the ECM memory, you must use a short jumper wire to ground the diagnostic terminal. This terminal is part of an electrical connector known as the Assembly Line Data Link (ALDL) **(see illustration)**. The ALDL is located underneath the dashboard, to the left of the driver's foot area.

To use the ALDL, remove the plastic cover and with the electrical connector exposed to view, push one end of the jumper wire into the diagnostic terminal (B) and the other end into the ground terminal (A). When the diagnostic terminal is grounded, with the ignition On and the engine stopped, the system will enter the Diagnostic Mode. **Caution:** *Don't start or crank the engine with the diagnostic terminal grounded.*

In this mode the ECM will display a "Code 12" by flashing the Check Engine light, indicating that the system is operating. A code 12 is simply one flash, followed by a brief pause, then two flashes in quick succession. This code will be flashed three times. If no other codes are stored, Code

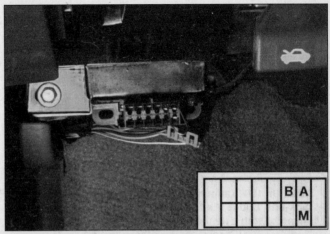

7.24 The Assembly Line Data Link (ALDL) is located under the driver's side dashboard near the kick panel. To activate the diagnostic codes, jump terminals B and A

12 will continue to flash until the diagnostic terminal ground is removed.

After flashing Code 12 three times, the ECM will display any stored trouble codes. Each code will be flashed three times, then Code 12 will be flashed again, indicating that the display of any stored trouble codes has been completed.

When the ECM sets a trouble code, the Check Engine light will come on and a trouble code will be stored in memory. If the problem is intermittent, the light will go out after 10 seconds, or when the fault goes away.

Clearing codes

The trouble code will stay in the ECM memory until the battery voltage to the ECM is interrupted. Removing battery voltage for 10 seconds will clear all stored trouble codes. Trouble codes should always be cleared after repairs have been completed. **Caution:** *To prevent damage to the ECM, the ignition switch must be Off when disconnecting or connecting power to the ECM.*

Subaru

Retrieving codes

There are self-diagnostic connectors on all models which, when connected together with the key ON (engine off) flash diagnostic codes through the LED light on the oxygen monitor on the ECU. The connectors are under the steering wheel, to the left of the module on most models.

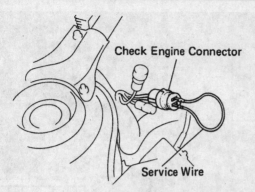

7.26a On 1984 Camrys, 1987 Corollas and 1986 and earlier pick-ups, bridge the terminals of the round Check Engine connector with a jumper wire to obtain the diagnostic codes (Corolla shown, others similar)

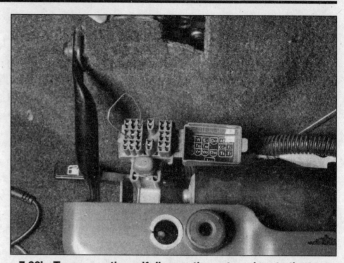

7.26b To access the self diagnostic system, locate the test terminal and using a jumper wire or paper clip, bridge terminals TE1 and E1. On later models, the test terminal is a multi-pin connector, usually with a protective plastic cover over it - using a jumper wire or paper clip, bridge terminals TE1 and E1

On carbureted and SPFI injected 1989 models, the test connectors are located on the engine side of the firewall, on the driver's side. Impreza models have the ECU and test connectors located behind the right side of the dash instead of the left. On SVX models the connectors are located behind the driver's side kick panel.

There are four test modes. With *neither* test connector connected, and the ignition key ON (not running) the light will display codes that relate to starting and driving. With *only* the "Read Memory" connector connected, historic codes will be displayed. With *only* the "Test Mode" connector connected, a dealership technician can perform dynamic tests. The last mode is for clearing codes (see text below).

The codes are displayed as pulses of the Light Emitting Diode (LED) mounted on the module. The long pulses (1.2 seconds) indicate tens and the short pulses (.2 seconds) indicate ones. Pulses are separated by .3-second pauses, and codes are separated by 1.8-second pauses. **Note:** *On 1989 MPFI models, the oxygen sensor monitor light and ECU are mounted under the rear seat package shelf, and are accessible only from the trunk.*

On 1990 models, the trouble codes on the Justy are viewed on the oxygen monitor light only, while on other models, the codes can be viewed on either the oxygen monitor or the Malfunction Indicator Lamp (Check Engine light) on the dash.

1995 Impreza and Legacy models have OBD II diagnostics systems. The OBD II codes can be extracted and cleared with either a Subaru factory tool, called the Subaru Select Monitor, or with a universal OBD II scan tool. Although an expensive scan tool is required to retrieve these new, five-character diagnostic codes, the basic codes can still be obtained using the flashing MIL.

Clearing codes

Codes will clear only when the faulty system or circuit is repaired. After making the repairs, codes can be cleared by connecting *two* pairs of connectors, the self-diagnostic connectors, and the "Read Memory" connectors that are

usually located right next to the diagnostic connectors. To begin, start with a warmed-up engine, turn the engine off, connect both pairs of connectors, then start the engine. This should clear the codes.

Toyota

The Check Engine warning light, which is located on the instrument panel, comes on when the ignition switch is turned to On and the engine is not running. When the engine is started, the warning light should go out. If the light remains on, the diagnosis system has detected a malfunction in the system.

Retrieving codes

To obtain an output of diagnostic codes, verify first that the battery voltage is above 11 volts, the throttle is fully closed, the transaxle is in Neutral, the accessory switches are off and the engine is at normal operating temperature.

Locate the diagnostic connector. The connector is located in several different places, depending on model. In most models it is near the left shock tower in the engine compartment, or near the master cylinder. In Previa models, it is under the driver's seat, In many later vehicles, it is mounted near the fuse/relay box in the engine compartment.

Turn the ignition On (engine not running), then use a jumper wire to bridge the terminals of the service electrical connector **(see illustration)**. Later models use a multi-pin connector **(see illustration)** for use with a factory scan tool, but a jumper wire between the TE1 and E1 terminals will make the MIL blink if there are codes. The connector is

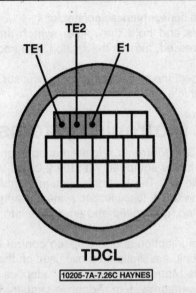

TDCL

10205-7A-7.26C HAYNES

7.26c The 1989 to 1992 Cressida have a different type connector located behind the left dash area, which offers two types of testing modes

usually located in the engine compartment near one of the strut towers, or in the passenger compartment under the dash or near the driver's seat.

The 1989 to 1992 Cressida has a different-shaped connector (see illustration), which performs both static and dynamic (vehicle running, see *Test mode* below) self-diagnostics. The 1993 to 1995 Camry and Supra have the same type connector, and the following 1993 models have the same dual-function self-diagnosis capability, but with a standard-looking connector: Corolla, Land Cruiser, MR2 and T100 (refer to the plastic cover for the positions of terminals TE1 and E1).

Read the basic diagnostic codes on all models by watching the number of flashes of the Check Engine light on the dash. Normal system operation is indicated by Code No. 1 (no malfunctions) for all models. The Check Engine light displays a Code No. 1 by blinking once every quarter-second consistently.

If there are any malfunctions in the system, their corresponding trouble codes are stored in computer memory and the light will blink the requisite number of times for the indicated trouble codes. If there's more than one trouble code in the memory, they'll be displayed in numerical order (from lowest to highest) with a pause interval between each one. The digits are simulated by half-second flashes, with 1.5-second pauses between numbers. For example, two flashes, pause, three flashes will indicate code 23. After the code with the largest number of flashes has been displayed, there will be another pause and then the sequence will begin all over again.

Note: *The diagnostic trouble codes 25, 26, 27 and 71 use a special diagnostic capability called "2 trip detection logic". With this system, when a malfunction is first detected, it is temporarily stored into the ECM on the first test drive or*

"trip". The engine must be turned off and the vehicle taken on another test drive "trip" to allow the malfunction to be stored permanently in the ECM. This will distinguish a true problem on vehicles with these particular codes entered into the computer. Normally the self diagnosis system will detect the malfunctions but in the event the home mechanic wants to double-check the diagnosis by canceling the codes and rechecking, then it will be necessary to go on two test drives to confirm any malfunctions with these particular codes.

To ensure correct interpretation of the blinking Check Engine light, watch carefully for the interval between the end of one code and the beginning of the next (otherwise, you will become confused by the apparent number of blinks and misinterpret the display). The length of this interval varies with the model year.

Beginning in 1994, some Toyota models are equipped with the new OBD II diagnostic system, which requires an expensive Toyota or generic OBD II scan tool to access the new, five-character diagnostic codes. There is no consumer access to the codes through the MIL lamp. 1994 OBD II models include: Camry 3.0L, supercharged Previa, T100 2.7L; 1995 models include the Avalon, Camry 3.0L, Land Cruiser, supercharged Previa, Tacoma, Tercel, and the T100.

"Test" mode diagnostics

Those 1989 through 1993 models mentioned above as having the dynamic testing capability exhibit the standard codes on the MIL with the jumper wire connecting the E1 and TE1 pins. After such a self-diagnosis, turn the key OFF and connect the E1 to the TE2 pin. Now drive the vehicle (above 10 mph) around for about five minutes, trying if you can to simulate the driving conditions under which any driveability problems have occurred in the past.

Stop the vehicle, but keep it running. Switch the jumper wire from the TE2 terminal to the TE1 terminal and read the codes on the MIL. This procedure will self-diagnose some problems which do not show up on the basic static test.

Clearing codes

After the malfunctioning component has been repaired/replaced, the trouble code(s) stored in computer memory must be canceled. To accomplish this, simply remove the 15A EFI fuse for at least 30 seconds with the ignition switch off (the lower the temperature, the longer the fuse must be left out). On Corolla models before 1993, pull the STOP fuse.

Cancellation can also be affected by removing the cable from the negative battery terminal, but other memory systems (such as the clock) will also be canceled.

If the diagnosis code is not canceled, it will be stored by the ECM and appear with any new codes in the event of future trouble.

Should it become necessary to work on engine components requiring removal of the battery terminal, first check to see if a diagnostic code has been recorded.

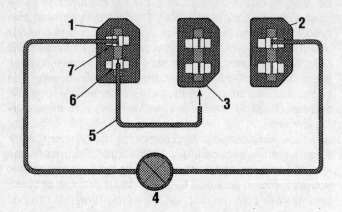

7.27 Here's how to bridge the terminals of the diagnostic connector with a jumper wire and an LED test light to output the codes on a CIS-E Motronic system (the connector is located under the shifter boot)

1	Black connector	5	Jumper wire
2	Blue connector	6	Negative terminal
3	White connector	7	Positive terminal
4	LED test light		

Volkswagen

Digifant I and II systems

Retrieving codes

Some vehicles equipped with the Digifant engine management system and sold in California have control units with a fault diagnosis capability.

This system indicates faults in the engine management system through a combination rocker switch/indicator light located to the right of the instrument cluster. **Note:** *Not all California models are equipped with a fault diagnosis system. Also, there are several variations among those so equipped. We recommend consulting with a VW dealer service department if you have any questions about the specific system used on your model.*

If it's operating properly, the light comes on briefly when you turn on the ignition. After a short period of driving, it also comes on to report any fault codes that might be stored in memory.

To display any stored fault codes, turn on the ignition - but don't start the engine - and depress the rocker switch for at least four-seconds. The indicator will display any stored fault codes in a series of flashes. For example, two flashes, followed by one flash, followed by four flashes, followed by two flashes, indicates the code 2-1-4-2, which means there's a problem with the knock sensor.

Clearing codes

To erase the fault codes from computer memory, make sure the ignition switch is turned off. Unplug the coolant

temperature sensor harness connector.

Depress and hold the rocker switch and, with the switch depressed, turn on the ignition. The codes will then be erased.

Reconnect the coolant temperature sensor. Finally, test drive the vehicle for at least 10 minutes.

CIS-E Motronic systems

The CIS-E Motronic engine management system is used on vehicles equipped with the 2.0L 16-valve engine (engine code 9A). The Motronic system combines the fuel control of the CIS-E fuel injection system with the control of ignition timing, idle speed and emissions into one control unit.

The fuel injection and idle speed control functions of CIS-E Motronic are similar to those used on the CIS-E system. But the Motronic system uses "adaptive circuitry" in its oxygen sensor system. Adaptive circuitry enables the oxygen sensor system to adjust the operating range of fuel metering in accordance with subtle changes in operating conditions caused by such things as normal engine wear, vacuum leaks, changes in altitude, etc.

Retrieving codes

The CIS-E Motronic engine management system can detect faults, store these faults in coded form in its memory and, when activated, display the codes. Each code corresponds to a specific component or function of the Motronic system which should be checked, repaired and/or replaced. When a code is stored on a California vehicle, the "Check" light on the dashboard is illuminated.

You can access trouble codes by using the diagnostic connectors (located under the shifter boot) to activate the memory of the control unit, which displays any stored code(s) on an LED test light **(see illustration)**. Here's how to read the trouble codes on a CIS-E Motronic system.

Make sure the air conditioning is switched off. Verify that fuse numbers 15 (engine electronics), 18 (fuel pump, oxygen sensor) and 21 (interior lights) are good. Inspect the engine ground strap (located near the distributor). Make sure it's in good shape and making a good connection.

Test drive the car for at least five minutes. Make sure the engine speed exceeds 3000 rpm at least once, the accelerator is pressed all the way to the floor at least once and the engine reaches its normal operating temperature.

After the test drive, keep the engine running for at least two minutes before shutting it off. Switch off the ignition. Connect an LED test light to the diagnostic connectors **(see illustration)**. Switch on the ignition.

Any stored fault codes are displayed by the LED as a sequence of flashes and pauses. For example, two flashes, a pause, one flash, a pause, two flashes, a pause and one flash indicates a code 2121, which means there's a problem in the idle switch circuit. A complete guide to the codes, their causes, the location of the faulty component and the recommended repair are contained in the accompanying tables.

To display the first code on 1988 to 1992 models, connect a jumper wire (as shown in illustration) for at least four seconds, then disconnect it. The LED will flash, indicating a four-digit code. To display the next code, connect the jumper wire for another four seconds, then detach it, and so on. Repeat this process until all stored codes have been displayed.

On 1993 and later models, a special scan tool is required to access all of the diagnostic information. However, using a VW jumper harness, the major four-digit codes can be displayed on the MIL.

Clearing codes

To erase trouble codes from the computer memory after all individual codes have been displayed as described in the previous steps, connect the jumper wire for more than four seconds - this erases the permanent fault storage memory of the control unit.

Volvo, all models (1989 on)

There have been two basic systems used on Volvos with self-diagnostics. The 1989 through 1993 models, and some 1994 models, have used a system with a separate ECU for the fuel injection and another for the ignition system. Some 1994 and 1995 models are equipped with the new OBD II diagnostic system, which uses only one central computer.

1989 through 1993 models (and later non-turbo, non-OBD II models)

Locate the diagnostic unit behind left strut tower, and remove its cover. Connect the selector cable to socket number 2, which tests the fuel system for codes. Turn the ignition switch to the On position (engine not running). Enter the diagnostic mode by pressing the push button on the diagnostic unit for at least one second, but not more than three seconds.

Watch the red LED, and count the number of flashes in 3-flash series. Flash series are separated by 3-second intervals. Write down all codes.

If no codes are stored, the LED will flash 1-1-1, indicating the fuel system is operating properly.

To access the ignition codes, repeat the above procedure, but with the selector cable plugged into the number 6 socket on the diagnostic unit. **Note:** *Most turbocharged models have separate codes for the turbo system which are accessed by hooking the diagnostic cable into socket number 5.*

1994 and later models with OBD II

The 850 Turbo and 960 models have the new, five-character OBD II codes, which are accessible only with the Volvo factory scan tool or a generic (still expensive) OBD II scan tool (used only in socket number 2). There are many more specific codes in the OBD II system than the previous three-digit codes. However, the three-digit codes can still be retrieved from the factory diagnostic unit as described above for earlier models.

Clearing codes

Once all the faults have been corrected, turn the ignition switch to the On position (engine not running). Read the codes again, then depress the button for five seconds and release. After three seconds the LED should light up. While the LED is lit, depress the button again for five seconds, after releasing the button the LED should stop shining.

Verify that the memory is erased by depressing the button for more than one second, but not more than three seconds. The LED should flash 1-1-1, indicating the memory is clear.

Notes

7 Computer trouble codes

Part B

Acura

CHECK

MIL

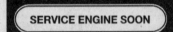
SERVICE ENGINE SOON

CHECK

CHECK ENGINE LIGHT

Code*	Probable cause	Code*	Probable cause
1	Oxygen sensor or circuit (Integra)	18	Ignition timing adjustment
1	Left or front oxygen sensor V6	19	Lock-up control solenoid valve
2	Left or rear oxygen sensor V6	20	Electric load
3	Manifold absolute pressure (MAP) sensor or circuit	21	Front VTEC solenoid valve (NSX)
4	Crank position sensor No. 1	21	Front spool solenoid valve (some models)
5	Manifold absolute pressure (MAP) sensor or circuit	22	Front VTEC pressure switch (NSX)
6	Coolant temperature sensor or circuit	22	Front valve timing oil pressure switch (some models)
7**	Throttle position sensor or circuit	23	Front knock sensor (some NSX, Vigor)
8	TDC sensor or circuit (Integra)	30	A/T FI signal A
9	Crank position sensor or circuit	31	A/T FI signal B
9	Camshaft position sensor	35	TC standby signal
10	Intake air temperature sensor or circuit	36	TC FC signal
12	EGR control system	41	Oxygen sensor heater (Integra)
13	Barometric pressure sensor or circuit	41	Front oxygen sensor heater
14	Idle air control system	42	Rear oxygen sensor heater (Legend, 3.0L)
15	Ignition output signal	43	Fuel supply system (4-cylinder models)
16	Fuel injector	43	Front fuel supply system (V6 models)
17**	Vehicle speed sensor or circuit	44	Rear fuel supply system (V6 models)

Code*	Probable cause
45	Front fuel metering system
46	Rear fuel metering system
47	Fuel pump
50	Mass Air Flow sensor
51	Rear spool solenoid valve (Legend)
51	Rear VTEC solenoid valve (other models)
52	Rear valve timing oil pressure switch (Legend)
52	Rear VTEC pressure switch (other models)
53	Rear knock sensor
54	Crank position sensor
59	No. 1 cylinder position
61	Upstream oxygen sensor, slow response
63	Downstream oxygen sensor, slow response
65	Downstream oxygen sensor heater
67	Low catalytic converter efficiency
70	Transaxle

Code*	Probable cause
71	Misfire, cylinder no. 1
72	Misfire, cylinder no. 2
73	Misfire, cylinder no. 3
74	Misfire, cylinder no. 4
75	Misfire, cylinder no. 5 (V6 models)
76	Misfire, cylinder no. 6 (V6 models)
76	Random misfire (all except 6-cylinder engines)
79	Spark plug voltage detection circuit
80	Low EGR flow
86	Coolant temperature sensor out of range
90	EVAP system leak
92	EVAP purge control solenoid

* If codes other than these are indicated, repeat self-diagnosis. If code(s) reappear, substitute a known good ECM, and recheck codes.

** On Legend models, if S4 on the automatic transaxle indicator panel also blinks, automatic transaxle control unit may require diagnosis.

Audi

   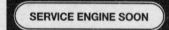

Code	Location or description of fault	Probable cause
1111	ECM	a) Defective ECM unit b) Faulty ECM circuit
1119	Transmission range sensor	a) Defective transmission range sensor b) Faulty transmission range sensor circuit
1213	Vehicle speed sensor	a) Defective speed sensor b) Faulty speed sensor circuit
1231	Vehicle speed sensor	a) Defective speed sensor b) Faulty speed sensor circuit
2111	RPM sensor	a) Defective RPM sensor b) Faulty RPM sensor circuit

Code	Location or description of fault	Probable cause
2112	Timing sensor	a) Defective timing sensor b) Faulty timing sensor circuit
2113	RPM sensor	No signal from Hall sender
2114	Hall reference	Camshaft timing out of phase
2121	Idle switch	a) Defective idle switch b) Faulty idle switch circuit
2122	Hall sender	a) Defective Hall sender b) Faulty Hall sender circuit
2123	Throttle position switch	a) Defective throttle position switch b) Faulty throttle position switch circuit
2132	Control unit	No signal from ignition to injection
2141	Knock control	Excessive detonation signal
2142	Knock control	a) No knock control sensor signal b) Defective knock control sensor c) Faulty knock control sensor circuit
2143	Knock control	Detonation from sensor no. 2, cylinder 4 or 5
2144	Knock control	a) Defective sensor no. 2 b) Faulty sensor no. 2 circuit
2212	Throttle valve	Sensor voltage out of range
2214	RPM signal	Idle speed too high
2214	RPM	Engine over-revved
2221	Vacuum control	No vacuum to control unit
2222	Pressure sensor	Defective control unit pressure sensor
2222	Manifold vacuum	a) Defective vacuum line b) Defective wastegate valve c) Defective turbocharger
2223	Altitude sensor	a) Defective altitude sensor b) Faulty altitude sensor circuit
2224	Manifold pressure	a) Turbo control unit b) Overboost
2224	Boost pressure	a) Air leak b) Defective wastegate valve c) Vacuum leak d) Defective pressure sensor
2231	Air mass sensor	a) Defective air mass sensor b) Faulty air mass sensor circuit
2231	Idle control	Idle speed outside control limits
2231	Idle stabilizer	a) Air leak b) Defective idle stabilizer valve c) Faulty idle stabilizer valve circuit

Code	Location or description of fault	Probable cause
2232	MAF sensor	a) No MAF sensor signal b) Defective MAF sensor c) Faulty MAF sensor circuit
2233	MAF sensor	High reference voltage
2233	Reference voltage	No reference signal to control units
2234	ECM	Low supply voltage
2234	System voltage	Out-of-range system voltage
2242	CO sensor	Low sensor voltage
2312	Engine coolant temperature	a) No engine coolant temperature sensor signal b) Defective engine coolant temperature sensor c) Faulty engine coolant temperature sensor circuit
2314	Signal wire	Short circuit to ground between TCM and ECM
2314	Transmission	Faulty engine-to-transmission circuit
2322	Intake air temperature	a) No intake air temperature sensor signal b) Defective intake air temperature sensor c) Faulty intake air temperature sensor circuit
2324	MAF sensor	a) Defective MAF sensor b) Faulty MAF sensor circuit
2331	Oxygen ratio	a) Defective ignition system b) Defective air/fuel system
2332	Oxygen sensor II	a) Short circuit b) Open circuit
2341	Oxygen sensor	System operating outside control limits
2342	Oxygen sensor	a) No oxygen sensor signal b) Defective oxygen sensor c) Faulty oxygen sensor circuit
2343	Fuel mixture	System running too lean
2344	Fuel mixture	System running too rich
2411	EGR system	System malfunction (California models only)
2413	Mixture control	System running too rich
2413	Fuel pressure	System pressure too low
3424	Fault lamp	System not operating
4312	EGR system	System malfunction (except for California models)
4332	Ignition circuit	a) Open or short to positive b) Open or short to ground

Code	Location or description of fault	Probable cause
4343	EVAP canister purge	a) Defective solenoid sensor circuit b) Faulty solenoid sensor circuit
4411	Fuel injector	a) Check injectors 1 and 5 b) Check circuit for injectors 1 and 5
4412	Fuel injector	a) Check injectors 2 and 7 b) Check circuit for injectors 2 and 7
4413	Fuel injector	a) Check injectors 3 and 6 b) Check circuit for injectors 3 and 6
4413	Fuel injector no. 3	a) Defective injector no. 3 b) Faulty injector no. 3 circuit
4414	Fuel injector	a) Check injectors 4 and 8 b) Check circuit for injectors 4 and 8
4421	Fuel injector no. 5	a) Defective injector no. 5 b) Faulty injector no. 5 circuit
4422	Fuel injector no. 6	a) Defective injector no. 6 b) Faulty injector no. 6 circuit
4423	Fuel injector no. 7	a) Defective injector no. 7 b) Faulty injector no. 7 circuit
4424	Fuel injector no. 8	Listen or feel for pulse at wide open throttle
4431	Idle stabilizer	a) Defective idle stabilizer b) Faulty idle stabilizer circuit
4433	Fuel pump	Listen to see if pump is running (5-cylinder models only)
4442	Wastegate	a) Defective frequency valve b) Faulty frequency valve circuit
4442	Boost pressure	Short circuit
4443	Canister purge	Listen to solenoid to see if it cycles on and off
4444	No faults	Stored memory is clear
0000	End diagnosis	No additional stored codes
16486	MAF sensor	a) Signal from MAF sensor too low b) Air leak c) Plugged air filter d) Faulty MAF sensor circuit
16487	MAF sensor	a) Signal from MAF sensor too high b) Wiring circuit shorted to positive
16500	Coolant temperature sensor	a) Faulty circuit b) Damp circuit
16501	Coolant temperature sensor	a) Short to ground in circuit b) Low signal

Audi (continued)

Code	Location or description of fault	Probable cause
16502	Coolant temperature sensor	a) High signal b) Short to positive in circuit c) Broken wiring
16504	TP sensor	Faulty switch
16505	TP sensor	a) Air leak b) Moisture in wiring
16506	TP sensor	a) Low signal b) Broken wiring c) Short to ground
16507	TP sensor	a) High signal b) Broken wiring c) Short to ground
16514	Oxygen sensor	a) Corrosion in wiring or connectors b) Moisture in wiring or connectors
16516	Oxygen sensor	a) High voltage b) Short to positive c) Defective spark plug d) Faulty connector(s) e) Faulty ignition wire(s) f) Defective sensor
16518	Oxygen sensor	a) Broken wiring b) Defective sensor
16520	Oxygen sensor	Malfunction in bank no. 1, sensor no. 2
16521	Oxygen sensor	Low voltage in bank no. 1, sensor no. 2
16522	Oxygen sensor	High voltage in bank no. 1, sensor no. 2
16524	Oxygen sensor	No activity detected in bank no. 1, sensor no. 2
16534	Oxygen sensor	Moisture in connector
16536	Oxygen sensor	a) High voltage b) Short to positive c) Defective sensor d) Defective spark plug(s) e) Faulty wiring f) Faulty connector(s)
16537	Oxygen sensor	Slow response from bank no. 2, sensor 1
16538	Oxygen sensor	a) Broken wiring b) Defective sensor
16539	Oxygen sensor	Malfunction in bank no. 2, sensor no. 1
16540	Oxygen sensor	Malfunction in bank no. 2, sensor no. 2
16541	Oxygen sensor	Low voltage in bank no. 2, sensor no. 2

Code	Location or description of fault	Probable cause
16542	Oxygen sensor	High voltage in bank no. 2, sensor no. 2
16554	Fuel system	a) Air leak in manifold b) Fuel in engine oil c) False signal from MAF sensor d) Burning oil
16555	Fuel system	a) System too lean b) Air leak to MAF sensor c) Air leak in exhaust system upstream from oxygen sensor d) Low fuel pump quality e) Plugged fuel filter f) Defective fuel pressure regulator g) Sticking EVAP purge solenoid
16556	Fuel system	a) System too rich b) Defective fuel pressure regulator c) Injector(s) not closing
16557	Fuel system	a) Air leak in manifold b) Oil thinning caused by fuel contamination c) Defective MAF sensor d) Oil burning caused by worn or broken piston
16558	Fuel system	a) System too lean b) Air leak to MAF sensor c) Air leak in exhaust system upstream from heated oxygen sensor d) Defective fuel pump e) Plugged fuel filter f) Defective fuel pressure regulator g) Sticking EVAP purge regulator valve
16559	Fuel system	a) System too rich b) Defective pressure regulator c) Injector(s) not closing
16706	Engine speed sensor	a) Short to ground b) Defective engine speed sensor
16711	Knock sensor	a) Corrosion or moisture in connector b) Faulty wiring c) Short to ground d) Defective knock sensor
16716	Knock sensor	a) Corrosion or moisture in connector b) Faulty wiring c) Short to ground or positive d) Defective shielding sensor
16721	Crankcase sensor	a) Low signal b) Bad ground c) Faulty wiring d) Short to ground e) Defective sensor

Code	Location or description of fault	Probable cause
16785	EGR	a) Low throughput b) Defective vacuum hose c) Sticking EGR valve
16786	EGR	a) High throughput b) Sticking or leaking EGR valve
16804	Catalyst system	Bank no. 1 efficiency below threshold
16885	Speed sensor	a) Faulty wiring b) Defective sensor
16955	Cruise/brake switch	Circuit malfunction
16989	Control module	Defective module
17509	Oxygen sensor (bank no. 1)	a) Air leak to MAF sensor b) Air leak in exhaust system upstream from oxygen sensor c) Faulty wiring d) Sticking EVAP canister purge regulator valve e) Plugged fuel filter f) Defective fuel pressure regulator g) Low fuel supply h) Defective oxygen sensor
17514	Oxygen sensor (bank no. 2)	a) Air leak to MAF sensor b) Air leak in exhaust system upstream from oxygen sensor c) Faulty wiring d) Sticking EVAP canister purge regulator valve e) Plugged fuel filter f) Defective fuel pressure regulator g) Low fuel supply h) Defective oxygen sensor
17609	Injector no. 1	a) Short to ground b) Voltage supply problem c) Defective injector
17610	Injector no. 2	a) Short to ground b) Voltage supply problem c) Defective injector
17611	Injector no. 3	a) Short to ground b) Voltage supply problem c) Defective injector
17612	Injector no. 4	a) Short to ground b) Voltage supply problem c) Defective injector
17613	Injector no. 5	a) Short to ground b) Voltage supply problem c) Defective injector

Code	Location or description of fault	Probable cause
17614	Injector no. 6	a) Short to ground b) Voltage supply problem c) Defective injector
17621	Injector no. 1 control circuit	a) Short to positive b) Defective injector c) Injector input problem
17622	Injector no. 2 control circuit	a) Short to positive b) Defective injector c) Injector input problem
17623	Injector no. 3 control circuit	a) Short to positive b) Defective injector c) Injector input problem
17624	Injector no. 4 control circuit	a) Short to positive b) Defective injector c) Injector input problem
17625	Injector no. 5 control circuit	a) Short to positive b) Defective injector c) Injector input problem
17626	Injector no. 6 control circuit	a) Short to positive b) Defective injector c) Injector input problem
17733	Knock sensor (cylinder no. 1)	a) Faulty wiring b) Poor fuel quality (below 95 RON) c) Defective knock control module in ECM d) Damaged engine e) Loose subassembly
17734	Knock sensor (cylinder no. 2)	a) Faulty wiring b) Poor fuel quality (below 95 RON) c) Defective knock control module in ECM d) Damaged engine e) Loose subassembly
17735	Knock sensor (cylinder no. 3)	a) Faulty wiring b) Poor fuel quality (below 95 RON) c) Defective knock control module in ECM d) Damaged engine e) Loose subassembly
17736	Knock sensor (cylinder no. 4)	a) Faulty wiring b) Poor fuel quality (below 95 RON) c) Defective knock control module in ECM d) Damaged engine e) Loose subassembly
17737	Knock sensor (cylinder no. 5)	a) Faulty wiring b) Poor fuel quality (below 95 RON) c) Defective knock control module in ECM d) Damaged engine e) Loose subassembly

Code	Location or description of fault	Probable cause
17738	Knock sensor (cylinder no. 6)	a) Faulty wiring b) Poor fuel quality (below 95 RON) c) Defective knock control module in ECM d) Damaged engine e) Loose subassembly
17747	Crankshaft position/engine speed sensor	Connectors switched
17748	Crankcase/camshaft signal	V-belt off track
17749	Ignition amplifier no. 1 control circuit	a) Short to ground b) Defective ignition coil power output stage
17751	Ignition amplifier no. 2 control circuit	a) Short to ground b) Defective ignition coil power output stage
17753	Ignition amplifier no. 3 control circuit	a) Short to ground b) Defective ignition coil power output stage
17799	Camshaft position sensor	a) Short to ground b) Defective camshaft position sensor
17800	Camshaft position sensor	a) Incorrect voltage or ground supply b) Faulty wiring c) Short to positive d) Defective camshaft position sensor
17801	Ignition amplifier no. 1 control circuit	a) Short to ground b) Defective ignition coil power output stage
17802	Ignition amplifier no. 2 control circuit	a) Short to ground b) Defective ignition coil power output stage
17803	Ignition amplifier no. 3 control circuit	a) Short to ground b) Defective ignition coil power output stage
17808	EGR valve	a) Faulty wiring b) Defective EGR valve c) Incorrect voltage supply to EGR vacuum regulator solenoid valve
17810	EGR valve control circuit	a) Short to positive b) Defective vacuum regulator solenoid valve
17815	EGR temperature sensor	a) Short to ground b) Defective EGR temperature sensor
17816	EGR temperature sensor	a) Incorrect ground supply b) Defective EGR temperature sensor c) Short to positive
17817	EVAP canister purge regulator valve	a) Incorrect voltage supply b) Defective EVAP canister purge regulator valve c) Short to ground
17818	EVAP canister purge regulator valve	a) Defective valve b) Short to positive

Code	Location or description of fault	Probable cause
17819	Secondary air injection (bank no. 2)	a) Defective vacuum hose b) Defective combination valve c) Restricted flow
17822	Secondary air injection (bank no. 2)	a) Leaking combination valve b) Defective combination valve
17828	Secondary air injection control valve	a) Short to ground b) Defective control valve c) Incorrect voltage supply
17830	Secondary air injection control valve	Short to positive
17831	Secondary air injection (bank no. 1)	a) Defective vacuum hose b) Defective combination valve c) Restricted flow
17832	Secondary air injection (bank no. 2)	a) Leaking combination valve b) Defective combination valve
17842	Secondary air system pump relay	a) Short to positive b) Defective relay
17844	Secondary air system pump relay	a) Short to ground b) Incorrect voltage supply c) Defective relay
17908	Fuel pump relay circuit	a) Faulty wiring b) Defective pump relay
17912	Intake system	a) Air leak b) Defective air control valve c) Throttle body second stage not closing
17913	Throttle position switch	a) Floormat pressing on gas pedal b) Throttle misadjusted c) Sticking throttle d) Defective throttle position switch e) Faulty wiring
17914	Throttle position switch	a) Short to ground b) Moisture in connector c) Defective throttle position switch
17918	Throttle position switch	a) Short to positive b) Defective throttle position switch
17919	Intake manifold change-over valve	a) Faulty wiring b) Defective change-over valve
17920	Intake manifold change-over valve	Short to positive
17978	ECM	ECM not adapted
18008	Low voltage at supply terminal	a) Discharged battery b) Bad ground to ECM c) Current drain with ignition turned off
18020	ECM incorrectly coded	a) Manual transmission coded for automatic, or vice versa b) Not coded for Automatic Traction Control (ATC)

BMW

CHECK	MIL	SERVICE ENGINE SOON	CHECK

CHECK ENGINE LIGHT

1988 3-Series

Code	Probable cause
Code 1	Airflow meter or Mass Air Flow sensor
Code 2	Oxygen sensor
Code 3	Coolant temperature sensor
Code 4	TPS

1989 and later 3, 5 and 7-Series

Code	Probable cause
1000, 2000	End of diagnosis
1211, 2211	Electronic Control Unit (ECU)
1215, 2215	Mass Air Flow sensor
1216, 2216	Throttle Position Sensor
1221, 2221	Oxygen sensor
1222	Oxygen sensor control out of range
1222, 2222	Oxygen sensor regulation
1223, 2223	Coolant temperature sensor
1224, 2224	Intake air temperature sensor

Code	Probable cause
1231, 2231	Battery voltage out of range
1232, 2232	Idle switch
1233, 2233	Wide open throttle switch
1251, 2251	Fuel injectors (final stage 1)
1252, 2252	Fuel injectors (final stage 2)
1253	Cylinder no. 3 fuel injector
1254	Cylinder no. 4 fuel injector
1255	Cylinder no. 5 fuel injector
1256	Cylinder no. 6 fuel injector
1261, 2261	Fuel pump relay
1262	Idle speed controller or idle air control valve
1263, 2263	EVAP canister purge valve
1264, 2264	Oxygen sensor heating relay
1444, 2444	No faults in memory

Note: *On 12-cylinder models, codes starting with 1 indicate problems on the right cylinder bank (cylinders 1 through 6). Codes starting with 2 indicate problems on the left cylinder bank (cylinders 7 through 12).*

Chrysler, Dodge and Plymouth - domestic cars and light trucks

CHECK	MIL	SERVICE ENGINE SOON	CHECK

CHECK ENGINE LIGHT

Code	Probable cause
11	No distributor reference signal during engine cranking
12	Battery power to computer disconnected in last 50 to 100 cycles; memory standby power lost (1983 through 1990)

Code	Probable cause
13*	Manifold Absolute Pressure (MAP) sensor vacuum circuit - slow or no change in MAP sensor input and/or output
14*	Manifold Absolute Pressure (MAP) sensor electrical circuit - high or low voltage
15**	Vehicle speed/distance sensor circuit
16*	Loss of battery voltage (1983 through 1989)
16*	Knock sensor (1993 on)
17	Knock sensor circuit open or shorted during engine operation (1985 and 1986 turbo models)
17	Engine running too cold
21**	Oxygen sensor circuit - voltage in neutral zone or above normal range
22**	Coolant temperature sensor unit - high or low voltage
23	Throttle body air temperature sensor circuit - high or low voltage (1987 through 1990 TBI models)
23	Intake air temperature sensor circuit - high or low voltage (1991 through 1998)
24*	Throttle position sensor circuit - high or low voltage
25**	Idle speed control (ISC) or Idle air control (IAC) motor driver - circuit shorted
25**	Automatic idle speed (AIS) motor driver - circuit shorted
26*	Peak injector driver current not reached because of high resistance in circuit
27*	Injector driver not responding correctly to injector control signal
31**	Canister purge solenoid circuit open or shorted
32**	Exhaust Gas Recirculation (EGR) transducer solenoid - circuit open or shorted, or EGR system failed to respond to command (1987 through 1994)
32	Malfunction indicator lamp (MIL) circuit open or shorted (1983 through 1986)
33	Air conditioning clutch relay circuit open or shorted
34	Spare driver circuit open or shorted (1985 models)
34	Open or shorted circuit at the EGR solenoid (1983 through 1985 models)
34	Speed control vacuum or vent solenoid circuit open or shorted
35	Cooling fan relay circuit open or shorted
35	Idle switch circuit open or shorted (1988 through 1994 RWD models)
36	Spare driver circuit open or shorted (1985 models)
36*	Turbocharger wastegate solenoid circuit open or shorted
36*	Air switching solenoid circuit open or shorted
37	Shift indicator lamp circuit open or shorted (1985 and 1986 models with manual transmission)
37	Part-throttle unlock solenoid driver circuit open or shorted (1988 through 1994 models with automatic transmission only)
37	Baro solenoid circuit open or shorted (turbo models)

Code	Probable cause
41	Charging system excess or lack of field current
42	Automatic shutdown driver (ASD) relay circuit open or shorted
43	Ignition coil control circuit or spark interface circuit - output stage not responding to control command
44	Fault in computer (1983 and 1984 models)
44	Battery temperature signal out-of-range (1985 through 1987 and 1992 through 1994 3.3L and 3.8L)
44	No fused circuit voltage at computer connector during engine operation (1987 through 1989 models)
45	Overboost shut-off circuit on MAP sensor reading above overboost limit
45	Overdrive solenoid circuit open or shorted (1989 through 1994 RWD models)
46*	Charging system voltage too high
47*	Charging system voltage too low
51**	Oxygen sensor voltage indicates lean during engine operation
52**	Oxygen sensor voltage indicates rich during engine operation
52	Fault present in computer (1983 through 1986 models)
53	Module internal problem; SMEC/SBEC failure; internal engine controller fault condition detected
54	Problem with the distributor synchronization circuit - no sync pick-up signal detected during operation
55	End of code output
61*	BARO solenoid circuit open or shorted (1989 on turbo models)
62	Emissions maintenance reminder light mileage is not being updated (1989 on)
63	EEPROM write denied - controller failure (1989 on)
64	Speed control vent solenoid no. 1 circuit open or shorted (1990 2.2L turbo)
64	Flexible fuel (methanol) sensor indicates concentration sensor input more than the acceptable voltage
64	Flexible fuel (methanol) sensor indicates concentration sensor input less than the acceptable voltage
65	Manifold tuning valve solenoid circuit open or shorted
65	Power steering switch failure (1996 models)
66	No message from the transmission control module (TCM) to the powertrain control module (PCM)
66	No message from the body control module (BCM) to the powertrain control module (PCM)
71	5-volt PCM output low
72	Catalytic converter efficiency failure
77	Speed control power relay circuit
88	Start of test

*   These codes light up Check Engine light
** These codes light up Check Engine light on vehicles with special California emission controls

Eagle Summit and Talon (1988 through 1998)

Code*	Probable cause	Code*	Probable cause
11	Oxygen sensor	39	Oxygen sensor
12	Airflow sensor	41	Injector
13	Intake air temperature sensor	42	Fuel pump
14	Throttle position sensor	43	EGR
15	Idle speed motor or idle air control position sensor	44	Ignition coil power circuit
21	Coolant temperature sensor	52	Ignition coil (cylinders 2 and 5)
22	Crank angle sensor (crankshaft position sensor)	53	Ignition coil (cylinders 3 and 6)
23	Top dead center sensor (camshaft position sensor)	55	Idle air control valve
24	Vehicle speed sensor	59	Heated oxygen sensor (rear)
25	Barometric pressure sensor	61	ECM-transaxle interlink
31	Knock sensor (turbo models)	62	Warm-up valve position sensor
32	MAP sensor	71	Traction Control vacuum valve solenoid
36	Ignition timing adjustment signal		

Eagle Premier (1991 and 1992) and Vision (1993 through 1997)

  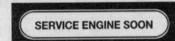

Trouble codes

Note: *Not all trouble codes apply to all models.*

Code 11	No crank reference signal detected during engine cranking. Check the circuit between the crankshaft position sensor and the PCM.
Code 12	Problem with the battery connection. Direct battery input to controller disconnected within the last 50 ignition key-on cycles.
Code 13**	Indicates a problem with the MAP sensor pneumatic (vacuum) system.
Code 14**	MAP sensor voltage too low or too high.

Code 15**	A problem with the vehicle distance/speed signal. No distance/speed sensor signal detected during road load conditions.
Code 16	Loss of battery voltage.
Code 17	Engine is cold too long. Engine coolant temperature remains below normal operating temperatures during operation (check the thermostat).
Code 21**	Problem with oxygen sensor signal circuit. Sensor voltage to computer not fluctuating.
Code 22**	Coolant sensor voltage too high or too low. Test coolant temperature sensor.
Code 23**	Indicates that the air temperature sensor input is below the minimum acceptable voltage or sensor input is above the maximum acceptable voltage.
Code 24**	Throttle position sensor voltage high or low. Test the throttle position sensor.
Code 25**	Idle Air Control (IAC) valve circuits. A shorted condition is detected in one or more of the IAC valve circuits.
Code 26	Peak injector current not reached (1991 and 1992 Premier models)
Code 26	injector circuit (1991 and 1992 Premier models)
Code 27	One of the injector control circuit output drivers does not respond properly to the control signal. Check the circuits.
Code 31**	Problem with the canister purge solenoid circuit.
Code 32**	An open or shorted condition detected in the EGR solenoid circuit. Possible air/fuel ratio imbalance not detected during diagnosis.
Code 33	Air conditioning clutch relay circuit. An open or shorted condition detected in the compressor clutch relay circuit.
Code 34	Open or shorted condition detected in the speed control vacuum or vent solenoid circuits.
Code 35	Open or shorted condition detected in the radiator fan low speed relay circuit.
Code 41**	Problem with the charging system. Occurs when battery voltage from the ASD relay is below 11.75-volts.
Code 42	Auto shutdown relay (ASD) control circuit indicates an open or shorted circuit condition.
Code 43**	Peak primary circuit current not achieved with the maximum dwell time.
Code 44	Battery temperature sensor volts malfunction. Problem with the battery temperature voltage circuit in the PCM.
Code 46**	Charging system voltage too high. Computer indicates that the battery voltage is not properly regulated.
Code 47**	Charging system voltage too low. Battery voltage sense input below target charging voltage during engine operation and no significant change in voltage detected during active test of alternator output.
Code 51*	Oxygen sensor signal input indicates lean fuel/air ratio condition during engine operation.
Code 52**	Oxygen sensor signal input indicates rich fuel/air ratio condition during engine operation.
Code 53	Internal PCM failure detected.
Code 54	No camshaft position sensor signal at PCM. Problem with the camshaft position sensor synchronization circuit.
Code 55	Completion of fault code display on CHECK ENGINE lamp. This is an end of message code.

Code 62	Unsuccessful attempt to update EMR mileage in the controller EEPROM.
Code 63	Controller failure. EEPROM write denied. Check the PCM.
Code 64**	The Flexible Fuel sensor voltage is low. Methanol concentration sensor input below the maximum acceptable voltage requirements.
Code 65	An open or shorted condition detected in the Manifold Tuning Valve (MTV) solenoid circuit.
Code 66	PCM is not receiving CCD Bus signals.
Code 77	Speed Control Power relay circuit is open or shorted.

** These codes light up the CHECK ENGINE light on the instrument panel during engine operation once the trouble code has been recorded.

Ford, Lincoln and Mercury

  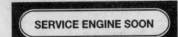

2-digit trouble codes

Code No.	Test condition*	Probable cause
10	R	Cylinder no. 1 low during cylinder balance test
11	O,R,C	System PASS
12	R	Cannot control rpm during high rpm test
13	R	Cannot control rpm during low rpm test
13	O	D.C. motor doesn't move (1987 through 1990 1.9L CFI and 2.3L CFI)
13	C	D.C. motor doesn't follow dashpot (1987 through 1990 1.9L CFI and 2.3L CFI)
14	C	PIP circuit failure
15	O	EEC Read Only Memory (ROM) failed, or Keep Alive Memory (KAM) in continuous
15	C	EEC Keep Alive Memory (KAM) failed (1990)
16	R	ISC rpm exceeds self-test range (1987 through 1989 1.9L and 2.5L)
16	R	Idle rpm too high with ISC retracted (1990 1.9L and 2.5L)
16	O	Ignition Diagnostic Module (IDM) signal not received (1990 and 1991 3.0L, 1991 4.0L truck)
16	R	Idle rpm too low to perform EGO test (2.3L OHC and 5.0L SFI) or HEGO test (5.0L car)
16	R	Air/fuel mixture not within self-test range
17	R	ISC rpm exceeds self-test range (1987 through 1989 1.9L and 2.5L)

*0 = Key On, Engine Off; C = Continuous Memory; R = Engine Running

2-digit trouble codes (continued)

Code No.	Test condition*	Probable cause
17	R	Idle rpm too low with ISC retracted (1990 1.9L and 2.5L)
17	R	Air/fuel mixture not within self-test range (1985 3.0L and 5.0L CFI)
18	R,C	Loss of TACH input to ECA - SPOUT circuit grounded (1984 on)
18	C	SPOUT circuit open (1987 on)
19	O	Failure in EEC reference voltage circuit (1986 through 1989, except 1.9L, 2.3L, 3.0L MA and 3.8L SC)
19	R	RPM for EGR test too low (1988 through 1990 1.9L CFI)
19	R	Engine stumble during hard idle test set (1988 through 1990 1.9L PFI)
19	C	CID circuit failure - DIS (1989 through 1991 3.0L MA, 3.8L SC and 4.0L)
20	R	Cylinder no. 2 low during cylinder balance test
21	O,R	ECT out of range during self test
22	O,C,R	MAP/BP sensor out of range during self test (through 1991)
23	O,R	TP sensor out of range during self test
24	O,R	VAT sensor out of range during self test (1.6L PFI and 2.3L Turbo)
24	O,R	ACT sensor out of range during self test (except 1.6L PFI, 1.9L PFI and 2.3L Turbo)
25	R	Knock not sensed during dynamic response test
26	O,R	VAF sensor out of range during self test (1.6L PFI, 1.9L PFI and 2.3L Turbo, through 1990)
26	O,R	MAF/VAF sensor out of range during self test (1988 1.9L PFI, 2.3L Turbo and 5.0L PFI)
26	O,R	MAF sensor out of range during self test (1989 through 1991 2.3L PFI, 2.9L PFI, 3.0L SHO, 3.8L SC, 4.0L SEFI and 5.0L SEFI)
26	O,R	TOT sensor out of range during self test (1989 and later 5.8L, 7.3L diesel and 7.5L trucks with E4OD)
27	C	Insufficient input from vehicle speed sensor (1987 through 1989 2.3L Turbo)
27	R	Servo leaks down during integrated vehicle speed control test (1987 through 1990)
28	R	Servo leaks up during integrated vehicle speed control test (1987 through 1990)
28	O,R	Intake air temperature at VAF meter out of range during self test
28	C	Loss of (right) primary TACH (1989 and 1990 dual-plug DIS)
30	R	Cylinder no. 3 low during cylinder power balance test
31	O,C,R	EVP voltage out of range during self test (1983 through 1988, 1991 and 1992 2.3L OHC and 3.8L CFI)

*O = Key On, Engine Off; C = Continuous Memory; R = Engine Running

Code No.	Test condition*	Probable cause
31	O,C,R	PFE/EPT/EVP below minimum voltage (1987 through 1990 and 1993)
32	R	EGR not controlling (1983 through 1990 2.3L OHC and 3.8L CFI)
32	C,R	EGR valve not seated (1991 1.9L, 2.3L HSC and 3.0L SHO)
32	O,C,R	EGR/EVP closed voltage too low (1991 on)
33	C,R	EGV valve not seated (1983 through 1989 1.9L CFI, 2.3L OHC, 3.0L and 3.8L SFI)
33	C,R	EGR valve not opening, or opening not detected (1985 through 1990 PFE and Sonic)
33	R	EGR valve not returning to closed position (1990 2.3L OHC)
33	C,R	Insufficient EGR flow detected (191 on PFE and Sonic)
33	C	Throttle position noise (1993 7.3L diesel)
34	R	EVP voltage out of range during self test
34	O	Defective PFI/EPT sensor (1985 through 1989 1.9L CFI, 2.9L and 3.0L)
34	C,R	Exhaust pressure high, or defective PFE/EPT sensor (1985 through 1991)
34	O,C,R	EVP voltage above closed limit (1986 through 1990)
35	R	RPM too low to perform EGR test (1983, 1987 through 1990)
35	R	Exhaust pressure high, defective EPT sensor (1984)
35	O,C,R	PFE/EPT/EVP circuit above maximum voltage (1985 on)
36	R	Insufficient rpm increase during integrated vehicle speed control test (1987 through 1991)
37	R	Insufficient rpm decrease during integrated vehicle speed control test (1987 through 1991)
38	C	ITS circuit open (1987 through 1990 1.9L CFI, 2.3L CFI and 2.5L CFI)
39	C	Automatic transaxle lock-up circuit failed (1986 through 1990 3.0L cars)
40	R	Cylinder no. 4 low during cylinder balance test
41	C,R	EGO sensor indicates system lean (1983 through 1990)
41	C	No EGO sensor switching detected (1987 through 1990)
42	C,R	EGO sensor indicates system rich (1983 through 1990)
42	C	No EGO sensor switching detected (1987 through 1990)
43	C	EGO lean at wide open throttle (1987 through 1990 1.9L PFI and 2.3L Turbo)
44	R	Thermactor air system or secondary air injection system inoperative
45	R	Thermactor air upstream during self test (through 1992)
46	R	Thermactor air not bypassed during self-test
50	R	Cylinder no. 5 low during cylinder balance test
51	O,C	ECT sensor circuit open or ECT indicates -40 degrees F (through 1991)

0 = Key On, Engine Off; C = Continuous Memory; R = Engine Running

2-digit trouble codes (continued)

Code No.	Test condition*	Probable cause
52	O	Power steering pressure switch open (1985 on)
53	O,C	TP sensor circuit open (1983) or above maximum voltage (1984 on)
54	OC	VAT sensor circuit open (1985 and 1986 1.6L PFI, 1.9L PFI and 2.3L turbo)
54	O,C	ACT sensor circuit open or ACT indicates -40 degrees F (1985 through 1991, except 1.6L PFI, 1.9L PFI and 2.3L turbo)
55	O,C,R	Key power circuit low (1985 through 1990 1.9L CFI, 2.3L CFI and 2.5L CFI)
56	O,C	MAF/VAF circuit above maximum voltage (1983 through 1990 1.6L PFI, 1.9L PFI, 2.3L turbo, 3.0L SHO, 3.8L SC and 5.0L PFI)
56	O,C	TOT sensor circuit open or -40 degrees F. indicated by TOT (1989 on with transmission oil temperature sensor)
57	C	NPS circuit failed open (1986 through 1990 3.0L car)
58	R	ITS stuck closed or circuit grounded (1987 through 1990 1.9L CFI, 2.3L CFI and 2.5L CFI)
58	O	ITS circuit open (1987 through 1990 1.9L CFI, 2.3L CFI and 2.5L CFI)
58	O,C	VAT sensor circuit open or -40 degrees F. indicated by VAT (1987 through 1990 1.9L CFI)
58	O	Crank fuel delay service pin in use or circuit grounded (1990 2.9L)
59	C	Automatic transaxle 4/3 circuit failed open (1986 through 1990 3.0L and 3.8L)
59	C	2/3 shift error (1991 on 7.3L diesel, 5.8L and 7.5L with E4OD)
59	C	AXOD 4/3 circuit failed closed
60	R	Cylinder no. 6 low during cylinder balance test
61	O,C,R	ECT sensor circuit grounded or below minimum voltage
62	O,R	Automatic transaxle 3/2 or 4/3 circuit grounded (1986 through 1990 3.0L)
62	C	Converter clutch error (1989 through 1991 5.8L, 7.3L diesel and 7.5L with E4OD)
63	O,C	TP sensor circuit below minimum voltage (through 1991)
63	O,C	Fuel injector pump lever circuit below minimum voltage (1989 through 1991 7.3L diesel with E4OD)
64	O,C	ACT sensor out of range during self test (1983 2.3L turbo and 2.8L)
64	O,C	VAT sensor grounded (1984 through 1986 1.6L PFI, 1.9L PFI and 2.3L turbo)
64	O,C	ACT sensor circuit grounded, or 254 degrees F indicated by ACT/VAT sensor (1984 through 1991, except 1.6L PFI, 1.9L PFI and 2.3L turbo)
65	C,R	Key power low (1984 and 1985 2.8L, 3.8L CFI and 5.0L CFI)

*0 = Key On, Engine Off; C = Continuous Memory; R = Engine Running

Code No.	Test condition*	Probable cause
65	R	Overdrive cancel switch not changing status (1989 5.8L, 7.3L diesel and 7.5L with E4OD)
65	C	System did not go into closed loop (1988 through 1990 1.9L PFI and 2.3L turbo)
66	O,C	VAF sensor circuit input voltage below minimum (1983 through 1990 1.6L PFI, 1.9L PFI and 2.3L turbo)
66	C	MAF sensor circuit input voltage below minimum (1989 through 1991 3.0L SHO, 3.8L SC, 4.0L and 5.0L SEFI)
66	O,C	290 degrees F indicated by TOT sensor or circuit grounded (1989 and 1990 4.9L, 5.0L, 5.8L, 7.3L diesel and 7.5L with E4OD)
66	O,C	TOT sensor circuit below minimum voltage (1991 and later 7.3L diesel, 5.8L and 7.5L)
67	O	NDS circuit open with A/C on during self-test (1983 through 1991)
67	C	A/C clutch energized during self test (1983 2.3L turbo)
68	O	RPM not within self-test range (1983 through 1986)
69	C	Automatic transaxle 3/2 input circuit failed open (1986 through 1990 3.0L and 3.8L)
69	C	Automatic transaxle 3/2 input circuit failed closed (1988 and 1989 3.8L)
69	C	Automatic transaxle 3/4 shift error (1989 on 5.8L, 7.3L diesel and 7.5L with E4OD)
70	R	Cylinder no. 7 low during cylinder balance test
70	C	Data Communication Link (DCL) or ECA circuit failure (1989 and 1990 3.8L)
71	C	Software reinitialization detected (1987 through 1990 1.9L PFI and 2.3L turbo)
71	C	ITS circuit shorted to ground on pre-position (1987 through 1990 1.9L CFI and 2.3L CFI)
72	R	Insufficient MAF/MAP change during dynamic response test (1983 2.3L HSC and 2.8L; 1987 through 1990; 1993 on)
73	R	Insufficient TPS change during dynamic response test (1983 through 1991; 1993 on)
74	R	Brake on/off (BOO) switch circuit open or circuit failure (1985 on)
75	R	Brake on/off (BOO) switch circuit closed or ECA input open (1985 through 1991)
76	R	Insufficient VAF change during dynamic response test (1983 through 1990 1.6L PFI, 1.9L PFI and 2.3L turbo)
77	R	Operator error during dynamic response test or cylinder balance test (1983 through 1991)
77	R	Insufficient rpm change during self test, invalid cylinder balance test (caused by moved throttle), or CID sensor circuit failure (1992 on)
78	R	Power interrupt detected (1987 and 1988 2.3L CFI and 2.5L CFI)
79	O	A/C on during self test (1987 through 1990 2.3L PFI, 2.9L PFI, 3.0L SHO, 3.8L PFI, 4.0L PFI, 5.0L PFI and 5.0L SFI)
80	R	Cylinder no. 8 low during cylinder balance test
81	O	Air management no. 2 circuit failure (1984 through 1992)
81	O	Boost circuit failure (1987 and 1988 2.3L turbo)

0 = Key On, Engine Off; C = Continuous Memory; R = Engine Running

2-digit trouble codes (continued)

Code No.	Test condition*	Probable cause
81	O	Speed control vent circuit failure (1987 through 1991)
82	O	Speed control vent circuit failure (1987 through 1991)
82	O	Electro drive fan (EDF) circuit failure (1987 and 1988 2.3L turbo)
82	O	Supercharger bypass solenoid circuit failure (1989 and 1990 3.8L SC)
83	O	EGR control circuit failure (1984 through 1990)
83	O	High speed electro drive fan circuit failure (1986 through 1991 2.5L CFI and 3.0L)
84	O	EGR circuit, vent, shut-off or vacuum regulator failure (1984 on)
85	O,R	Canister purge circuit failure (1984 on)
87	O,C,R	Primary fuel pump or fuel pump relay circuit failure (1984 on)
87	O	Temperature compensated pump fault (1984 and 1985 2.8L)
88	O	Idle speed not within self test range (1983 through 1985 5.0L CFI)
88	O	Electric cooling fan circuit failure (1983 through 1986 3.0L V6)
88	O	Variable voltage choke circuit failure (1983 through 1986 2.8L)
88	O	Clutch converter override circuit failure (1987 and 1988 2.3L turbo)
89	O	Clutch converter override circuit failure (2.3L PFI , 2.8L and 5.0L CFI)
89	O	Exhaust heat crossover circuit failure (1984 through 1987 3.8L CFI and 5.0L CFI)
89	O	Lock-up solenoid circuit failure (1986 through 1990 3.0L, 3.8L and 4.0L)
90	R	Pass cylinder balance test
91	R	Air/fuel mixture not within self test range (1984 through 1986 3.8L CFI and 5.0L)
92	R	Air/fuel mixture not within self test range (1984 through 1986 3.8L CFI and 5.0L)
94	R	Air/fuel mixture not within self test range (1984 through 1986)
94	R	Thermactor air system inoperative (1985 on 3.8L CFI and 5.0L)
95	R	Air/fuel mixture not within self test range (1984 through 1986)
95	R	Thermactor air system inoperative (1985 3.8L CFI and 5.0L)
96	R	Air/fuel mixture not within self test range (1984 through 1986)
96	R	Thermactor air system inoperative (1985 3.8L CFI and 5.0L)
96	O,C	Fuel pump circuit open - battery to ECA (1988 on)
97	R	Air/fuel mixture not within self test range (1985 3.8L CFI)

*0 = Key On, Engine Off; C = Continuous Memory; R = Engine Running

Code No.	Test condition*	Probable cause
98	R	Air/fuel mixture not within self test range (1985 3.8L CFI)
98	R	Hard fault present (1986 through 1991 2.3L OHC, 2.9L, 3.0L, 4.9L, 5.0L and 7.5L)
98	O	Electronic pressure control (EPC) driver open in ECA (1989 on)
99	R	Idle not learned (1986 through 1990 1.9L CFI, 2.3L CFI and 2.5L CFI)
99	O,C	Electronic pressure control (EPC) circuit failure (1989 on)

3-digit trouble codes

Code No.	Test condition*	Probable cause
111	O,C,R	Pass
112	O,C,R	ACT/VAT sensor circuit grounded or 254 degrees F indicated by ACT/VAT sensor (1990)
112	O,C,R	ACT/IAT sensor circuit below minimum voltage (1991 on)
113	O,R	ACT/VAT sensor circuit open, or -40 degrees F indicated by ACT/VAT sensor (1990)
113	O,C,R	ACT/IAT sensor circuit above minimum voltage (1991 on)
114	O,R	ACT/VAT sensor out of range during self test (1990 through 1992)
114	O,R	IAT sensor out of range during self test (1993 on)
116	O,R	ECT sensor out of range during self test (1990 on)
117	O,C,R	ECT sensor circuit grounded or 254 degrees F indicated by ECT (1990)
117	O,C,R	ECT sensor circuit below minimum voltage or 254 degrees F indicated by ECT (1991 on)
118	O,C,R	ECT sensor circuit open or -40 degrees F indicated by ECT (1990)
118	O,C,R	ECT sensor above maximum voltage or -40 degrees F indicated by ECT (1991 on)
121	O,C,R	TP sensor voltage out of range during self test (1990)
121	O,C,R	Closed TP sensor voltage out of range during self test (1991 on)
121	O,C,R	TP sensor voltage not consistent with air meter input (1993 on)
122	O,C,R	TP sensor circuit below minimum voltage (1990 on)
123	O,C,R	TP sensor circuit above maximum voltage (1990 on)
124	O,C,R	TP sensor voltage higher than expected (1991 on)
125	O,C,R	TP sensor voltage lower than expected (1991 on)
126	O,C,R	MAP/BARO sensor voltage higher than expected (1990 on)
128	O,C,R	MAP/BARO sensor vacuum hose damaged or disconnected (1991 on)
129	O,C,R	Insufficient MAP/MAF sensor voltage change during dynamic response check

*0 = Key On, Engine Off; C = Continuous Memory; R = Engine Running

3-digit trouble codes

Code No.	Test condition*	Probable cause
136	R	HEGO sensor indicates lean condition, cylinder bank no. 2 (1991 on)
137	R	HEGO sensor indicates rich condition, cylinder bank no. 2 (1991 on)
139	C	No HEGO sensor switching detected, cylinder bank no. 2
144	C	No HEGO sensor switching detected, cylinder bank no. 1
157	R	MAF sensor below minimum voltage (1991 on)
158	R	MAF sensor above maximum voltage (1991 on)
159	R	MAF sensor out of range during self test (1991 on)
167	C,R	Insufficient TP sensor change during dynamic response check (1990 on)
171	C,R	HEGO sensor unable to switch, cylinder bank no. 1; fuel system at adaptive limit (1990 on)
172	O,R	HEGO sensor indicates lean condition, cylinder bank no. 1 (1990 on)
173	O,R	HEGO sensor indicates rich condition, cylinder bank no. 1 (1990 on)
174	C	HEGO sensor switching too slow, cylinder bank no. 1 (1990)
175	R	HEGO sensor unable to switch, cylinder bank no. 2; fuel system at adaptive limit (1990 on)
176	R	HEGO sensor indicates lean condition, cylinder bank no. 2 (1990 on)
177	R	HEGO sensor indicates rich condition, cylinder bank no. 2 (1990 on)
178	C	HEGO sensor switching too slowly
179	R	Adaptive fuel lean limit reached at part throttle, system rich, cylinder bank no. 1 (1990 on)
181	R	Adaptive fuel rich limit reached at part throttle, system lean, cylinder bank no. 1 (1990 on)
182	R	Adaptive fuel lean limit reached at idle, system rich, cylinder bank no. 1 (1990 through 1992)
183	R	Adaptive fuel rich limit reached at idle, system lean, cylinder bank no. 1 (1990 through 1992)
184	R	MAF higher than expected (1991 on)
185	R	MAF lower than expected (1991 on)
186	R	Injector pulse width higher than expected, with BP/BARO sensor (1991 on)
187	R	Injector pulse width lower than expected, with BP/BARO sensor (1991 on)
188	R	Adaptive fuel lean limit reached at part throttle, system rich, cylinder bank no. 2 (1991 on)
189	R	Adaptive fuel rich limit reached at part throttle, system lean, cylinder bank no. 2 (1991 on)
191	R	Adaptive fuel lean limit reached at idle, system rich, cylinder bank no. 2 (1991 on)
192	R	Adaptive fuel rich limit reached at idle, system lean, cylinder bank no. 2 (1991 on)

*0 = Key On, Engine Off; C = Continuous Memory; R = Engine Running

Code No.	Test condition*	Probable cause
193	O,C	Flexible fuel (FF) sensor circuit fault (1993 on)
211	C	PIP sensor circuit fault (1990 on)
212	C	Loss of TACH input to ECA, SPOUT circuit grounded (1990)
212	C	Loss of IDM input to ECA (1991 on)
213	R	SPOUT circuit open (1990 on)
214	R	Cylinder identification (CID) circuit fault (1991 on)
215	R	EEC processor/ECA detected coil no. 1 primary circuit fault (1991 on)
216	R	EEC processor/ECA detected coil no. 2 primary circuit fault (1991 on)
217	R	EEC processor/ECA detected coil no. 3 primary circuit fault (1991 on)
219	R	Spark timing defaulted to 10 degrees, SPOUT circuit open (1991 on)
221	R	Spark timing error (DIS/EDIS) (1991 on)
222	R	Loss of IDM signal, right side (dual plug DIS) (1991 on)
223	R	Loss of dual plug inhibit control (dual plug DIS) (1991 on)
224	R	EEC processor/ECA detected coil 1, 2, 3 or 4 primary circuit fault (dual plug DIS) (1991 on)
225	R	Knock not detected during dynamic response test (1991 on)
226	R	IDM signal not received (DIS/EDIS) (1991 on)
232	R	EEC processor/ECA detected coil 1, 2, 3 or 4 primary circuit fault (DIS/EDIS) (1991 on)
233	R	Spark angle pulse width error (EDIS) (1991 and 1992)
238	R	EEC processor/ECA detected coil 4 primary circuit fault (DIS/EDIS) (1991 on)
239	O,C,R	CPS signal received with engine off (1991 and 1992)
241	O,C,R	EDIS-to-ECA IDM pulse width transmission error (1991 on)
242	O,C,R	Operating in DIS failure mode (1991 and 1992)
243	O,C,R	Secondary circuit fault code 1, 2, 3 or 4 (DIS) (1991 and 1992)
244	R	CID circuit fault present during cylinder balance test (1993 on)
311	R	Thermactor air system inoperative (right side on dual EGR systems)
313	R	Thermactor air not bypassed during self-test (1990 on)
314	R	Thermactor air system inoperative (cylinder bank no. 2 with dual HEGO) (1990 on)
326	O,C,R	EGR (EPT) circuit voltage lower than expected (PFE) (1991 on)
327	O,C,R	EGR (EVP/EPT) circuit voltage below minimum voltage (Sonic PFE) (1990 on)
328	O,C,R	EGR (EVP) closed valve voltage below closed limit, or lower than expected (1990 on)
332	C,R	EGR valve opening not detected (1990 Sonic PFE)

*0 = Key On, Engine Off; C = Continuous Memory; R = Engine Running

3-digit trouble codes

Code No.	Test condition*	Probable cause
334	O,C,R	EVP voltage above closed limit (1990 Sonic), or EGR (EVP) closed valve voltage higher than expected (1991 on Sonic)
335	O	EGR (EPT) sensor voltage out of range during self test (1991 on)
336	R	Exhaust gas pressure high/EGR (EPT) circuit voltage higher than expected (1991 on)
337	O,C,R	EGR (EVP/EVT) circuit above maximum voltage (1990 on Sonic/PFE)
341	O,C,R	Octane adjust service pin in use (1991 on)
381	C	Frequent A/C clutch cycling (1993 on)
411	R	Unable to control rpm during low-rpm self test (1990 on)
412	R	Unable to control rpm during high-rpm self test (1990 on)
415	R	ISC system at minimum learning limit (1993 on)
416	R	IAC system at maximum learning limit (1993 on)
452	O,C,R	No input from VSS (1990 on)
453	O	Servo leaking down during self test (1993 on)
454	O	Servo leaking up during self test (1993 on)
455	R	Insufficient rpm increase during self-test (1993 on)
456	R	Insufficient rpm decrease during self-test (1993 on)
457	O	Speed control command switch(es) circuit not functioning during self test (1993 on)
458	O	Speed control command switch(es) stuck, or circuit grounded, during self-test (1993 on)
459	O	Speed control ground circuit open during self-test
511	O	Read Only Memory test failed; replace ECA
512	O,C,R	Keep alive memory (KAM) test failed
513	O,C,R	Internal voltage fault in ECA
519	O,C,R	PSPS circuit open (1991 on)
521	R	PSPS circuit does not change states during self-test (1991 on)
522	O	P/N switch indicates vehicle in gear with A/C on (1991 and 1992)
522	O	Vehicle not in Park or Neutral during self test (1993 on)
525	O,C,R	Indicates vehicle in gear (1991 and 1992)
528	O,C,R	Clutch switch circuit fault (1991 on)
529	O,C,R	DCL or ECA circuit fault (1991 on)
532	O	CCA circuit fault (1993 on)

*0 = Key On, Engine Off; C = Continuous Memory; R = Engine Running

Code No.	Test condition*	Probable cause
533	O,C,R	DCL or EIC circuit fault (1993 on)
536	R	BOO switch circuit fault/not activated during KOER test (1990 on)
538	R	Operator error during dynamic response or cylinder balance test (1990)
538	R	Insufficient rpm change during KOER dynamic response test (1991 on)
538	R	Invalid cylinder balance test caused by CID sensor circuit fault (1991 on)
539	O	A/C or DEFROST on during KOEO test (1991 on)
542	O,C	Fuel pump circuit open, ECA to pump motor ground (1990 on)
543	O,C	Fuel pump circuit open, battery to ECA (1990 on)
551	O,C	IAC circuit fault in KOEO self test (1991 on)
552	O,C,R	Air management no. 1 circuit fault (1991 and 1992)
552	O	Secondary air injection bypass circuit fault (1993 on)
553	O,C,R	Air management no. 2 circuit fault (1990 through 1992)
553	O	Secondary air injection diverter circuit fault (1993 on)
554	O,C,R	Fuel pump pressure regulator control circuit fault (1993 on)
556	O,C	Primary fuel pump circuit fault (1990)
556	O,C	Fuel pump relay primary circuit fault (1991 on)
557	O,C	Low speed fuel pump primary circuit fault (1993 on)
558	O,C,R	EGR (EVR) circuit fault (1990 on)
559	O	A/C ON relay circuit fault (1993 on)
562	O,C,R	AEDF circuit fault (1991 and 1992)
563	O	HEDF circuit fault (1992)
563	O	High fan control circuit fault (1993 on)
564	O,C,R	EDF circuit fault (1991 and 1992)
564	O	Fan control circuit fault (1993 on)
565	O	Canister purge circuit fault (1990 on)
566	O	3/4 shift solenoid circuit fault (A4LD transmission) (1993 on)
567	O	Speed control vent circuit fault (1993 on)
568	O	Speed control vacuum circuit fault (1993 on)
569	O	Auxiliary canister purge circuit fault (1991 on)
571	O	EGRA solenoid circuit fault during KOEO test
572	O	EGRV solenoid circuit fault during KOEO test
578	O,C,R	A/C pressure sensor circuit shorted (VCRM) (1993 on)

0 = Key On, Engine Off; C = Continuous Memory; R = Engine Running

3-digit trouble codes

Code No.	Test condition*	Probable cause
579	O,C,R	Insufficient A/C pressure change (VCRM) (1993 on)
581	O,C,R	Power to fan circuit over current (VCRM) (1993 on)
582	O,C,R	Fan circuit open (VCRM) (1993 on)
583	O,C,R	Power to fuel pump over current (VCRM) (1993 on)
584	O,C,R	VCRM power ground circuit open (VCRM, Pin 1) (1993 on)
585	O,C,R	Power to A/C clutch over current (VCRM) (1993 on)
586	O,C,R	A/C clutch circuit open (VCRM) (1993 on)
587	O,C,R	VCRM communication failure (1993 on)
617	O,C,R	1-2 shift error (1990 on)
618	C	2-3 shift error (1990 on)
619	C	3-4 shift error (1990 on)
621	O,C	Shift solenoid no. 1 circuit fault (1990 on)
622	O	Shift solenoid no. 2 circuit fault (1990 on)
623	O	Transmission control indicator light circuit fault
624	O,C,R	EPC circuit fault (1990 on)
625	O,C,R	EPC driver open in ECA (1990 on)
626	O,C,R	Coast clutch/converter clutch solenoid circuit fault (1990 on)
627	O,C,R	Converter clutch control solenoid circuit fault (1990 on)
628	O,C,R	Excessive converter clutch slippage (1990 on)
629	O,C	Converter clutch control circuit fault (1991 on)
631	O,C,R	Transmission control indicator lamp circuit fault during KOEO test
632	R	Overdrive cancel switch circuit does not change during KOEO test (1990 on)
633	O	4 X 4 switch closed during KOEO test (1990 on)
634	O,C,R	MLP sensor voltage higher or lower than expected (1990 on)
636	O,R	TOT sensor voltage higher or lower than expected (1990 on)
637	O,C,R	-40 degrees F indicated by TOT sensor, or sensor circuit above maximum voltage, or sensor circuit open (1990 on)
638	O,C,R	290 degrees F indicated by TOT sensor, or sensor circuit below minimum voltage, or sensor circuit shorted (1990 on)
639	O,C,R	Insufficient input from TSS (1991 on)

*0 = Key On, Engine Off; C = Continuous Memory; R = Engine Running

Code No.	Test condition*	Probable cause
641	O,C	Shift solenoid no. 3 circuit fault (1991 on)
643	O,C	Shift solenoid no. 4 circuit fault (1992 on)
645	C	Incorrect gear ratio obtained for first gear
646	C	Incorrect gear ratio obtained for second gear
647	C	Incorrect gear ratio obtained for third gear
648	C	Incorrect gear ratio obtained for fourth gear
649	O,C,R	EPC higher or lower than expected (1992 on)
651	O,C,R	EPC circuit fault (1992 on)
653	R	Transmission control switch did not change states during KOER test
652	O,C,R	Modulated lock-up solenoid circuit fault (1992)
652	O,C,R	Torque converter clutch solenoid circuit fault (1993 on)
654	O	MLP sensor not indicating PARK during KOEO test (1991 on)
656	O,C,R	Torque converter clutch control continuous slip error (1992 on)
657	C	Transmission over temperature condition occurred
659	C	High vehicle speed in PARK indicated
667	C	Transmission range sensor circuit voltage below minimum voltage
668	C	Transmission range circuit voltage above maximum voltage
675	C	Transmission range sensor circuit voltage out of range
998	O	Hard fault present - FMEM mode activated

Ford Imports

  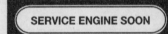

1994 and 1995 Aspire (1.3L)

Code No.	Test condition*	Probable cause
02	O, R	Crankshaft position sensor circuit
03	O, R	Camshaft position sensor circuit
04	O, R	Crankshaft position sensor circuit
06	O, R	Vehicle speed sensor circuit

*0 = Key On, Engine Off; C = Continuous Memory; R = Engine Running

1994 and 1995 Aspire (1.3L) (continued)

Code No.	Test condition*	Probable cause
08	O, R	Mass airflow sensor circuit
09	O, R	Engine coolant temperature sensor circuit
10	O, R	Intake air temperature sensor circuit
12	O, R	Throttle position sensor circuit
15	O, R	Oxygen sensor circuit fault (voltage below 0.55 volt)
16	O, R	EGR valve position sensor circuit
17	O, R	Oxygen sensor defective (voltage doesn't change)
25	O, R	EVAP canister purge solenoid circuit
26	O, R	EGR control (EGRC) solenoid circuit
28	O, R	EGR vent (EGRV) solenoid circuit
29	O, R	Idle air control (IAC) solenoid circuit
34	O, R	Idle air control (IAC) solenoid circuit

1993 through 1995 Escort/Tracer (1.8L)

Code No.	Test condition*	Probable cause
01	C	Ignition diagnostic monitor circuit
02	C	Crankshaft position sensor circuit
03	C	Cylinder identification 1 circuit
08	C	Vane airflow sensor circuit
09	C	Engine coolant temperature sensor circuit
10	C	Intake air temperature sensor circuit
12	C	Throttle position sensor circuit
14	C	Barometric pressure sensor circuit
15	C	Oxygen sensor circuit
17	C	Oxygen sensor signal too rich or too lean
25	C	Fuel pressure regulator solenoid circuit
26	C	Canister purge solenoid circuit
34	C	Idle speed control valve circuit
41	C	Variable inertia charging system solenoid circuit

*0 = Key On, Engine Off; C = Continuous Memory; R = Engine Running

1993 through 1995 Probe (2.5L V6)

Code No.	Test condition*	Probable cause
02	C	Crankshaft position sensor no. 2 circuit
03	C	Cylinder identification circuit
04	C	Crankshaft position sensor no. 1 circuit
05	C	Knock sensor circuit
08	C	Measuring-core vane airflow sensor circuit
09	C	Engine coolant temperature sensor circuit
10	C	Intake air temperature sensor circuit
12	C	Throttle position sensor circuit
14	C	Barometric pressure sensor circuit
15	C	Left oxygen sensor circuit
16	C	EGR valve position sensor circuit
17	C	Right oxygen sensor circuit
23	C	Feedback system fault (left oxygen sensor)
24	C	Feedback system fault (right oxygen sensor)
25	C	Fuel pressure regulator solenoid circuit
26	C	Canister purge solenoid circuit
28	C	EGR vacuum control circuit
29	C	EGR vent control solenoid circuit
34	C	Idle speed control valve circuit
41	C	Variable resonance induction system solenoid no 1 circuit
46	C	Variable resonance induction system solenoid no. 2 circuit
67	C	Cooling fan relay circuit
69	C	Engine coolant temperature fan circuit

1993 through 1995 Villager (3.0L V6)

Code No.	Test condition*	Probable cause
11	C	Crankshaft position sensor circuit
12	C	Mass airflow sensor circuit
13	C	Engine coolant temperature sensor circuit
14	C	Vehicle speed sensor circuit

*0 = Key On, Engine Off; C = Continuous Memory; R = Engine Running

1993 through 1995 Villager (3.0L V6) (continued)

Code No.	Test condition*	Probable cause
21	C	Ignition signal circuit
31	C	PCM internal fault
32	C	EGR control solenoid circuit
33	C	Heated oxygen sensor circuit
34	C	Knock sensor circuit
35	C	EGR vent solenoid circuit
43	C	Throttle position sensor circuit
45	C	Fuel injector leak detected
51	C	Fuel injector signal fault detected
55		EEC system pass code

*0 = Key On, Engine Off; C = Continuous Memory; R = Engine Running

General Motors
domestic cars and trucks (except Geo, Nova and Sprint)

  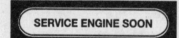

Code	Probable cause
12	No spark reference from ignition control module or distributor (Cadillac)
12	No TACH signal to ECM - system normal
13	Oxygen sensor (right sensor on 1990 and later models) malfunction or circuit fault (Cadillac)
13	Oxygen sensor circuit fault (driver's side on two-sensor systems)
14	ECT sensor indicates high temperature, or ECT sensor circuit shorted
15	ECT sensor indicates low temperature, or ECT sensor open
16	DIS circuit fault
16	Distributor ignition system or Opti-Spark ignition timing system, low resolution pulse
16	Missing 2X reference circuit

Code	Probable cause
16	Transmission speed error (models with 4L60-E transmission or 4.3L S and T vehicle with manual transmission)
16	System voltage out of range
17	Oxygen sensor (left sensor on 1990 and later models) malfunction or circuit fault (Cadillac)
17	Crank signal circuit shorted, or defective ECM
17	Camshaft position sensor (1993 and 1994 with SFI)
17	Spark reference signal fault (Buick and Oldsmobile)
18	Crank signal circuit open, or faulty ECM
18	Injector circuit(s) (engine VIN code P - 5.7L)
18	Cam and crank sensor sync error (1988 through 1993 models with DIS ignition)
19	Fuel pump circuit shorted
19	Crankshaft position sensor circuit (1988 through 1991)
19	Intermittent 7X reference circuit
20	Fuel pump circuit open
21	TPS circuit shorted (Cadillac)
21	TPS circuit open, or voltage out of range (probably high)
21	Grounded wide-open-throttle circuit
22	TPS circuit open (Cadillac)
22	Grounded wide-open-throttle circuit
23	Open or grounded M/C solenoid (feedback carburetors)
23	IAT or MAT sensor circuit out of range, or low temperature indicated (Buick and Oldsmobile)
23	EST or IC circuit fault (Cadillac DFI)
24	VSS defective or circuit faulty
25	MAT sensor defective, sensor circuit out of range (probably high) or circuit shorted
25	Modulated displacement failure (1981 Cadillac V8-6-4)
25	EST (Cadillac HT4100)
26	Quad driver circuit (dealer serviced)
26	Transaxle gear switch circuit
26	EVAP purge solenoid circuit (VIN P - 5.7L)
26	TPS circuit shorted

Code	Probable cause
26	ECM failure (Buick and Oldsmobile)
26	Idle speed control (ISC) motor/throttle switch circuit shorted
27	TPS circuit open
27	2nd gear switch circuit fault (Buick and Oldsmobile)
27	EGR vacuum control solenoid circuit (VIN P - 5.7L)
27	Quad-driver circuit fault (VIN P - 5.7L)
27	Idle speed control (ISC) motor/throttle switch circuit open
28	3rd or 4th gear switch circuit fault (Cadillac)
28	Third gear switch circuit fault (Buick and Oldsmobile)
28	Quad-driver circuit fault (VIN P - 5.7L)
28	Transaxle pressure switch problem (Cadillac)
28	Transmission range pressure switch (V8)
29	Transaxle shift B solenoid problem (Cadillac)
29	Fourth gear switch circuit fault
29	Secondary AIR pump circuit (VIN P - 5.7L)
30	ISC circuit problem (Cadillac TBI)
30	RPM error (Cadillac MFI)
31	Wastegate circuit signal (turbo models)
31	PNP switch or circuit fault (Buick and Oldsmobile)
31	MAT sensor or circuit (Cadillac DFI)
31	EVAP canister purge solenoid circuit (carbureted models)
31	Camshaft sensor or circuit fault
31	EGR circuit (1988 through 1990 TBI)
31	MAP sensor circuit shorted (Cadillac)
32	BARO or altitude sensor or circuit (carbureted models)
32	EGR vacuum control system failure (Buick and Oldsmobile)
32	Digital EGR circuit (3.1L)
32	MAP sensor circuit open (Cadillac)

Code	Probable cause
33	Extended travel brake switch input circuit problem (Cadillac)
33	MAP sensor or circuit (low vacuum)
33	MAF sensor or circuit voltage out of range, probably high
33	MAP sensor signal voltage out of range (Cadillac)
34	MAF sensor or circuit fault (Buick and Oldsmobile)
34	MAP sensor out of range (Cadillac)
35	Ignition ground voltage out of range (Cadillac)
35	ISC or IAC valve or circuit
35	ISC throttle switch or circuit shorted (feedback carburetor)
35	BARO sensor or circuit shorted (Cadillac DFI)
36	EGR pintle valve position out of range (Cadillac)
36	BARO sensor or circuit open (Cadillac DFI)
36	MAF sensor burn-off circuit (1988 through 1990)
36	DIS (Quad-4)
36	Transaxle shift control (3.8L)
36	Closed throttle shift control (1991)
36	24X signal error circuit (1993 through 1995 with SFI)
36	DIS ignition circuit (Corvette and VIN P - 5.7L)
37	IAT or MAT sensor circuit shorted (Cadillac)
37	MAT sensor temperature high (1984 to 1986)
37	Brake switch stuck on (4L60-E transmission)
38	IAT or MAT sensor circuit open (Cadillac)
38	Brake light switch circuit (1988 and later Buick and Oldsmobile)
38	MAT sensor temperature low (1984 to 1986)
38	Brake switch stuck off (4L60-E transmission)
39	TCC engagement problem (Cadillac)
39	TCC signal error
39	Clutch input circuit fault
39	Knock sensor circuit shorted (4.3L engine with manual transmission, "S" and "T" truck models)

Code	Probable cause
40	Power steering pressure switch circuit open (Cadillac)
40	Power steering pressure switch circuit fault
41	No distributor signals to ECM, or faulty ignition module
41	Cam sensor circuit fault or ignition control reference pulse error
41	Cylinder select error
41	Quad-4 engine 1X reference pulse error
41	EST circuit open or shorted (Cadillac)
41	Opti-Spark EST circuit open or grounded (5.7L "F" and "Y" bodies)
42	Opti-Spark EST circuit grounded (5.7L "F" and "Y" bodies)
42	EST circuit fault (Buick and Oldsmobile)
42	Left oxygen sensor signal lean (1990 and later Cadillac)
43	ESC unit circuit fault (Buick and Oldsmobile)
43	TPS out of adjustment
43	Left oxygen sensor signal rich (1990 and later Cadillac)
43	Knock sensor signal error
44	Oxygen sensor no. 2 lean exhaust signal (Cadillac)
44	Oxygen sensor or circuit, lean exhaust detected (driver's side on two-sensor system)
45	Oxygen sensor no. 2 rich exhaust signal (Cadillac)
45	Oxygen sensor or circuit, rich exhaust detected (driver's side on two-sensor system)
46	Power steering pressure switch open (Buick and Oldsmobile)
46	Vehicle Anti-Theft System (VATS) or Personal Automotive Security System (PASS Key II)
46	Left bank-to-right bank fueling imbalance (Cadillac)
47	ECM - body control module (BCM) or IPC/PCM data fault (Cadillac)
47	A/C clutch and cruise circuit fault
47	PCM/BCM data circuit fault
48	Misfire detected (Buick and Oldsmobile)
48	EGR control system fault (Cadillac)
50	2nd gear pressure circuit fault (Cadillac)

Code	Probable cause
51	Faulty MEM-CAL, faulty EEPROM, ECM problem or calibration error
52	ECM memory reset indicator or PCM keep-alive memory reset (Cadillac)
52	Engine oil temperature sensor circuit, low temperature indicated
52	CALPAK missing or incorrect (Buick and Oldsmobile)
52	Over-voltage condition
52	EGR circuit fault
53	Spark reference signal interrupt from IC module (Cadillac)
53	System over-voltage (ECM over 17.7 volts)
53	EGR system (carbureted models)
53	Distributor signal interrupt (1983 and later Cadillac HT4100)
53	Alternator voltage out of range
53	Vehicle anti-theft (PASS-Key) circuit (5.0L TBI)
53	EGR fault (3.8L)
54	Mixture control solenoid circuit shorted (feedback carburetor system)
54	Fuel pump circuit, low voltage indicated (3.1L and 3.4L)
54	EGR fault (3.8L)
55	Closed throttle angle out of range or TPS incorrectly adjuster (Cadillac)
55	Grounded voltage reference, faulty oxygen sensor or fuel lean (feedback carburetor system)
55	ECM/PCM error, or not grounded (except 5.7L PFI systems, fuel lean monitor 5.7L - "F" and "Y" bodies)
55	ECM fault (Buick and Oldsmobile)
55	TPS out of range or out of adjustment (Cadillac)
55	Fuel lean monitor (Corvette and F-body VIN P - 5.7L)
55	EGR fault (3.8L)
56	Transaxle speed sensor input circuit fault (Cadillac)
56	Vacuum sensor circuit
56	Vacuum sensor circuit
56	Quad driver no. 2 circuit (3.8L)
56	Secondary air inlet valve actuator vacuum sensor circuit signal high (5.7L VIN J)
56	Anti-theft system (Cadillac)

General Motors - domestic (continued)

Code	Probable cause
57	Transaxle temperature sensor circuit shorted (Cadillac)
57	Boost control problem
58	Personal Automotive Security System (PASS) control fault (Cadillac)
58	Vehicle anti-theft system (PASS-Key) fuel enable circuit fault
58	Transmission code - TTS high temperature (sensor or signal wire grounded)
59	Transmission code - TTS low temperature (sensor or signal wire open)
60	Cruise control system - transaxle/transmission not in drive (Cadillac)
61	Oxygen sensor signal degraded or faulty
61	Cruise control system vent solenoid circuit fault (3.8L)
61	Secondary port throttle valve system fault (VIN J 5.7L)
61	A/C system performance (5.7L)
61	Transaxle gear switch signal
62	Transaxle gear switch signal circuit fault (3.1L V6 and Quad-4)
62	Engine oil temperature sensor, high temperature indicated (5.7L)
62	Cruise control system vacuum solenoid circuit fault (3.8L)
63	Cruise control system problem (difference between vehicle speed and set speed) (Cadillac)
63	EGR system fault (1990 and earlier Buick and Oldsmobile)
63	MAP sensor voltage out of range, probably high
63	Oxygen sensor circuit open, right side (5.7L)
63	Cruise control system problem (speed error)
64	Cruise control system, vehicle acceleration too high (Cadillac)
64	EGR system fault (1990 and earlier Buick and Oldsmobile)
64	MAP sensor voltage low
64	Oxygen sensor, lean exhaust indicated (right side on dual sensor models)
65	EGR system fault (1990 and earlier Buick and Oldsmobile)
65	Oxygen sensor, rich exhaust indicated (right side on dual sensor models)
65	Cruise servo position sensor circuit fault
65	Fuel injection circuit, low current (Quad-4)

Code	Probable cause
66	Cruise control system, engine rpm too high (Cadillac)
66	A/C pressure sensor circuit fault, probably low pressure
66	Engine power switch, voltage high or low, or PCM fault (VIN J 5.7L)
67	Cruise control system, SET/COAST or RESUME/ACCEL input shorted (Cadillac)
67	A/C pressure sensor circuit, sensor or A/C clutch circuit fault (Chevrolet)
67	Cruise switch circuit
68	Cruise Control Command (CCC) fault or servo position out of range (Cadillac)
68	A/C relay circuit (Chevrolet)
68	A/C compressor relay circuit shorted
68	Cruise system problem
69	Traction control active in cruise mode (Cadillac)
69	A/C clutch circuit fault, or head pressure too high (Chevrolet)
69	A/C head pressure switch circuit fault
69	Transmission code - torque converter stuck on (4L60-E)
70	TPS signal intermittent (Cadillac)
70	A/C refrigerant pressure sensor circuit, high pressure indicated (Chevrolet)
71	MAP sensor signal intermittent (Cadillac)
71	A/C evaporator temperature circuit, low temperature
72	Gear selector switch circuit (Chevrolet)
72	Transmission code - VSS signal loss (4L60-E)
73	ECT sensor signal intermittent (Cadillac)
73	A/C evaporator temperature sensor circuit, high temperature indicated
74	IAT sensor signal intermittent (Cadillac)
74	TCS circuit voltage low (1995 F-body VIN P)
75	Digital EGR no. 1 solenoid circuit fault
75	VSS signal intermittent (Cadillac)
75	EGR circuit (1995)
75	System voltage low (charging system problem)
75	Transmission system voltage low (1995 F-body VIN P)

Code	Probable cause
76	Transaxle pressure control solenoid circuit malfunction (Cadillac)
76	Digital EGR no. 2 solenoid circuit fault
77	Digital EGR no. 3 solenoid circuit fault
79	Transmission fluid temperature high (4L60-E)
79	VSS circuit signal high
80	TPS idle learn not complete (Cadillac 4.6L)
80	Fuel system rich (Cadillac)
80	Transmission converter clutch slipping excessively (F-body 3.4L)
80	VSS circuit signal high
81	Cam-to-4X reference correlation problem (Cadillac)
81	Transmission code - QDM solenoid A (1st and 2nd gear) current error
81	Brake input circuit fault or torque converter clutch signal
82	Reference signal high (Cadillac)
82	Transmission code - QDM solenoid B (2nd and 3rd gear) current error
82	IC 3X signal error
83	Transmission code - QDM torque converter circuit fault (4L80-E)
83	24X reference signal high (Cadillac)
83	Reverse inhibit system (F-body, manual transmission, 5.7L)
85	Idle throttle angle high (Cadillac 4.6L)
85	Throttle body service required (Cadillac)
85	PROM error (1995 3.4L)
86	Undefined gear ratio (Cadillac)
86	Transmission code - low gear ratio (4L80-E)
86	Analog-to-digital ECM error
87	Transmission code - high gear ratio (4L80-E)
87	EEPROM error (1995 3.4L)
88	TCC not disengaging (Cadillac)
89	Long shift and maximum adapt (Cadillac)
90	TCC solenoid circuit (manual transmission)

Code	Probable cause
90	VCC brake switch input fault (Cadillac)
91	Skip shift lamp circuit (1995 F-body, VIN P)
91	P/N switch fault (Cadillac)
92	Heated windshield fault (Cadillac)
93	PCS circuit current error (1995 3.4L)
93	Traction control system PWM link failure (Cadillac)
94	Transaxle shift A solenoid problem (Cadillac)
95	Engine stall detected (Cadillac)
96	Transmission system voltage low (1995 F-body 3.4L)
96	Torque converter overstress (Cadillac)
97	VSS output circuit (1995 F-body VIN P)
97	P/N to Drive or Reverse at high throttle angle (Cadillac)
98	Invalid PCM program (1995 F-body 3.4L)
98	High rpm P/N to Drive or Reverse shift under idle speed control (Cadillac)
99	Power management, cruise control system
99	TACH output circuit (1995 F-body VIN P)
99	Invalid PCM program
99	Cruise control servo not applied in cruise (Cadillac)
102	Shorted brake booster vacuum sensor (Cadillac)
103	Open brake booster vacuum sensor (Cadillac)
105	Brake booster vacuum too low (Cadillac)
106	Stop lamp switch input circuit fault (Cadillac)
107	PCM/BCM data link problem (Cadillac)
108	PROM checksum mismatch (Cadillac)
109	PCM keep-alive memory reset (Cadillac)
110	Generator L-terminal circuit fault (Cadillac)
112	Total EEPROM failure (Cadillac)
117	Shift A or shift B circuit output open or shorted (Cadillac)
131	Knock sensor failure (Cadillac)
132	Knock sensor failure (Cadillac)

General Motors imports
Geo (Metro, Prizm, Storm, Tracker), Sprint, Nova and Spectrum

Geo (Metro, Prizm, Storm, Tracker), Sprint, Nova and Spectrum

Code	Circuit or system	Probable cause
Code 12	No distributor reference pulses to ECM	This code will flash whenever the diagnostic terminal is grounded with the ignition turned On and the engine not running. If additional trouble codes are stored in the ECM they will appear after this code has flashed three times. If this code appears while the engine is running, no reference pulses from the distributor are reaching the ECM.
Code 13	Oxygen sensor circuit	Check for a sticking or misadjusted throttle position sensor (TPS). Check the wiring and connectors from the oxygen sensor. Replace the oxygen sensor.*
Code 14	Coolant sensor - high or low temp	If the engine is experiencing cooling system problems the problem must be rectified before continuing. Check all wiring and connectors associated with the coolant temperature sensor. Replace the coolant temperature sensor.*
Code 21	Throttle position sensor - voltage high or low	Check for a sticking or misadjusted TPS plunger. Check all wiring and connections between the TPS and the ECM. Adjust or Replace the TPS.*
Code 23	Intake Air Temperature (IAT) sensor circuit voltage high or low	Check for continuity in the signal wire and the ground wire. Check the operation of the IAT sensor.
Code 24	Vehicle speed sensor	A fault in this circuit should be indicated only when the vehicle is in motion. Disregard Code 24 if it is set when the drive wheels are not turning. Check the connections at the ECM. Check the TPS setting.
Code 32	EGR (Exhaust Gas Recirculation)	EVRV shorted to ground on start-up, switch not closed after the ECM has commanded the EGR for a specified period of time or the EGR solenoid circuit is open for specified period of time. Replace the EGR valve.*
Code 33	MAP sensor voltage high or low	Check the vacuum hoses from the MAP sensor. Check the electrical connections at the ECM. Replace the MAP sensor.*
Code 42	Electronic Spark Timing circuit	Electronic Spark Timing (EST) bypass circuit or EST circuit is grounded or open. A malfunctioning HEI module can cause this code.
Code 44	O2 sensor indicates lean exhaust (heated type)	Check the ECM wiring connections. Check for vacuum leakage at the throttle body base gasket, vacuum hoses or the intake manifold gasket. Replace the oxygen sensor.*

Code	Circuit or system	Probable cause
Code 45	O2 sensor indicates rich exhaust	Possible rich or leaking injector, high fuel pressure or faulty TPS. Also, check the evaporative charcoal canister and its components for the presence of fuel. Replace the oxygen sensor.*
Code 51	ECM or EEPROM	Be sure that the ECM ground connections are tight. If they are, Replace the ECM.*

Component replacement may not cure the problem in all cases. For this reason, you may want to seek professional advice before purchasing replacement parts.

Spectrum (non-turbo)

Code	Probable cause
12	No distributor reference pulses to ECM
13	Oxygen sensor or circuit
14	Coolant sensor or circuit (shorted)
15	Coolant sensor circuit (open)
16	Coolant sensor circuit (open)
21	Idle switch out of adjustment (or circuit open)
22	Fuel cut off relay or circuit (open)
23	Open or grounded Mixture Control (M/C) solenoid or circuit
25	Open or grounded vacuum switching valve or circuit
42	Fuel cut off relay or circuit
44	Oxygen sensor or circuit - lean exhaust indicated
45	Oxygen sensor or circuit - rich exhaust indicated
51	Faulty or improperly installed PROM
53	Shorted switching unit or faulty ECM
54	Mixture Control (M/C) solenoid or circuit shorted, or faulty ECM
55	Faulty ECM

Spectrum (turbo)

Code	Probable cause
12	No distributor reference pulses to ECM
13	Oxygen sensor or circuit
14	Coolant sensor or circuit (shorted)
15	Coolant sensor or circuit (open)
16	Coolant sensor or circuit (open)

Code	Probable cause
21	Throttle Position Sensor (TPS) voltage high
22	Throttle Position Sensor (TPS) voltage low
23	Intake Air Temperature (IAT), Manifold Air Temperature (MAT) sensor or circuit
24	Vehicle Speed Sensor or circuit
25	Air Switching Valve (ASV) or circuit
31	Wastegate control
33	Manifold Absolute Pressure (MAP) sensor voltage high
34	Manifold Absolute Pressure (MAP) sensor voltage low
42	Electronic Spark Timing (EST) circuit
43	Detonation (knock) sensor or circuit
45	Oxygen sensor - rich exhaust
51	Faulty PROM or ECM

Sprint (non-turbo)

Code	Probable cause
12	Diagnostic function working
13	Oxygen sensor or circuit
14	Coolant temperature sensor or circuit
21	Throttle position switches or circuit
23	Intake air temperature sensor or circuit
32	Barometric pressure sensor or circuit
51	Possible faulty ECM
52	Fuel cut solenoid or circuit
53	Secondary air sensor or circuit
54	Mixture control solenoid or circuit
55	Bowl vent solenoid or circuit

General Motors - imports (continued)

1987 and 1988 Sprint Turbo, 1989 and later Metro, Tracker, Sunrunner, Storm, Sunfire

Code	Probable cause
12	Diagnostic function working
13	Oxygen sensor or circuit
14	Coolant temperature sensor or circuit (open)
15	Coolant temperature sensor or circuit (shorted)
21	Throttle position sensor or circuit (open)
22	Throttle position sensor or circuit (shorted)
23	Intake air temperature sensor or circuit (open)
24	Vehicle Speed Sensor (VSS) or circuit
25	Intake air temperature sensor or circuit (shorted)
31	High turbocharger pressure (1987 and 1988 models)
31	MAP or Barometric pressure sensor or circuit (1989 through 1995 models)
32	MAP or Barometric pressure sensor or circuit (1989 through 1995 models)
32	EGR system (1991 through 1993 models)
33	Air flow meter (turbo models)
33	Manifold Absolute Pressure (MAP) sensor (1990 through 1992 models)
41	Ignition signal problem
42	Crank angle sensor (except Storm, Sunfire)
42	Camshaft position sensor circuit (1994-1995)
42	Electronic Spark Timing (EST) (Storm, Sunfire)
44	ECM idle switch circuit open (1988 and 1989)
44	Idle switch circuit (1992 Tracker, Sunrunner
44	Oxygen sensor or circuit - lean exhaust
45	Oxygen sensor or circuit - rich exhaust
45	Idle switch circuit grounded (1992 Tracker, Sunrunner)

Code	Probable cause
46	Idle speed control motor
51	EGR system (except Storm, Sunfire)
51	ECM (Storm)
53	ECM ground circuit
On Steady	ECM fault

Prizm and Nova (with electronic fuel injection)

Code	Probable cause
Continuous Flashing	System normal
12	RPM signal
13	RPM signal
14	Ignition signal
16	PCM control circuit
21	Oxygen sensor or circuit
22	Coolant temperature sensor or circuit
24	Intake Air Temperature or Manifold Air Temperature sensor or circuit
25	Air/fuel ratio lean
26	Air/fuel ratio rich
27	Sub-oxygen sensor
31	Mass Air Flow (MAF) sensor or circuit
41	Throttle Position Sensor (TPS) or circuit
42	Vehicle Speed Sensor (VSS)
43	Starter signal
51	Air Conditioning Switch signal
52	Knock sensor circuit
53	ECM failure
71	EGR system

Honda

1985 through 1987 models

	LED display	Symptom	Possible cause
1	(Dash warning light on)	Engine will not start	Check for a disconnected control unit ground connector. Also check for a loose connection at the ECU main relay resistor. Possible faulty ECU
2	(Dash warning light on)	Engine will not start	Check for a short circuit in the combination meter or warning light wire. Also check for a disconnected control unit ground wire. Possible faulty ECU
3	1	System does not operate	Faulty ECU
4	2	System does not operate	Faulty ECU
5	2 1	Fuel-fouled spark plugs, engine stalls, or hesitation	Check for a disconnected MAP sensor coupler or an open circuit in the MAP sensor wire. Also check for a faulty MAP sensor
6	4	System does not operate	Faulty ECU
7	4 1	Hesitation, fuel-fouled spark plugs or the engine stalls frequently	Check for disconnected MAP sensor vacuum hose
8	4 2	High idle speed during warm-up, continued high idle or hard starting at low temperature	Check for a disconnected coolant temperature sensor connector or an open circuit in the coolant temperature sensor wire. Also check for a faulty coolant temperature sensor
9	4 2 1	Poor engine response when opening the throttle rapidly, high idle speed or engine does not rev-up when cold	Check for a disconnected throttle angle sensor connector. Also check for an open circuit in the throttle angle sensor wire. Possible faulty throttle angle sensor
10	8	Engine does not rev-up, high idle speed or erratic idling	Check for a short or open circuit in the crank angle sensor wire. Spark plug wires interfering with the crank angle sensor wire. Also the crank angle sensor could be faulty
11	8 1	Same as above	Same as above
12	8 2	High idle speed or erratic idling when very cold	Check for a disconnected intake air temperature sensor or an open circuit in the intake air temperature sensor wire. Possible faulty intake air temperature sensor

Honda (continued)

1985 through 1987 models (continued)

	LED display	Symptom	Possible cause
13	8 · 2 1	Continued high idle speed	Check for a disconnected idle mixture adjuster sensor coupler or an open circuit in the idle mixture adjuster sensor wire. Possible faulty idle mixture adjuster sensor
14	8 4 · ·	System does not operate at all	Faulty ECU
15	8 4 · 1	Poor acceleration at high altitude when cold	Check for a disconnected atmospheric pressure sensor coupler or an open circuit in the atmospheric pressure sensor wire. Possible faulty atmospheric pressure sensor
16	8 4 2 ·	System does not operate at all	Faulty ECU
17	8 4 2 1	Same as above	Same as above

1988 through 1995 models (except 1995 Accord V6)

Code	Probable cause
0	Faulty ECU
1	Left (front) oxygen sensor malfunction or circuit fault
2	Right (rear) oxygen sensor malfunction or circuit fault
3	MAP sensor or circuit electrical fault
4	Crank angle sensor malfunction or circuit fault
5	MAP sensor mechanical fault
6	Engine coolant temperature sensor malfunction or circuit fault
7	Throttle angle sensor malfunction or circuit fault
8	TDC sensor (crank/cylinder/TDC sensor) malfunction or circuit fault
9	Cylinder sensor (crank/cylinder sensor) malfunction or circuit fault
10	Intake air temperature sensor or circuit fault
11	Idle mixture adjuster sensor malfunction or circuit fault
12	EGR lift sensor malfunction or circuit fault
13	BARO or PA sensor malfunction or circuit fault
14	Electronic Air Control Valve (EACV) malfunction or circuit fault
15	No ignition output signal (possible faulty igniter)
16	Fuel injector circuit fault
17	Vehicle speed sensor malfunction or circuit fault
18	Ignition timing or adjuster sensor malfunction or circuit fault
19	Lock-up control solenoid valve (automatic transmission)
20	Electric load detector - possible open or grounded circuit in ECU wiring
21	VTEC spool solenoid valve malfunction or circuit fault
22	VTEC oil pressure switch malfunction or circuit fault
23	Left knock sensor malfunction or circuit fault
30	A/T control unit ECM fuel injection signal "A" (Accord and Prelude)
31	A/T control unit and ECM circuit signal "B" (Accord and Prelude)

Code	Probable cause
41	Left (front) heated oxygen sensor malfunction or circuit fault
42	Right (rear) heated oxygen sensor malfunction or circuit fault
43	Left (front) fuel supply system circuit fault (except D15Z1 engine)
44	Right (rear) fuel supply system circuit fault (except D15Z1 engine)
45	Left (front) air/fuel ratio out of range - rich or lean
46	Right (rear) air/fuel ratio out of range - rich or lean
48	Heated oxygen sensor circuit (D15Z1 engine)
48	Linear air/fuel sensor malfunction or circuit fault
50	Mass air flow sensor malfunction or circuit fault
53	Right knock sensor malfunction or circuit fault
54	Crank angle sensor no. 2 malfunction or circuit fault
59	Cylinder position sensor no. 2 malfunction or circuit fault

Code	Probable cause
61	Front oxygen sensor - slow response
63	Rear oxygen sensor circuit voltage out of range
65	Rear oxygen sensor circuit fault
67	Catalytic converter efficiency low
70	Automatic transaxle problem
71	Cylinder misfire
72	Cylinder misfire
73	Cylinder misfire
74	Cylinder misfire
75	Cylinder misfire
76	Cylinder misfire
80	Insufficient EGR flow
86	Engine coolant temperature sensor circuit
92	Evaporative emission purge flow problem

Hyundai

1988 Stellar

Code	Probable cause
1	Oxygen sensor or circuit
2	Ignition signal
3	Airflow sensor or circuit
4	Atmospheric pressure sensor or circuit
5	Throttle position sensor or circuit
6	Idle Speed Control (ISC) motor position sensor or circuit
7	Coolant temperature sensor or circuit
8	TDC sensor or circuit
9	Normal

Sonata, Excel (1990 on), Scoupe (1991 and 1992), Elantra

Code	Probable cause
1	Electronic Control Unit (ECU) (one long needle sweep)
9	ECU normal state
11	Oxygen sensor or circuit
12	Airflow sensor or circuit
13	Intake air temperature sensor or circuit
14	Throttle Position Sensor (TPS) or circuit
15	Motor position sensor or circuit
21	Coolant temperature sensor or circuit

Sonata, Excel (1990 on), Scoupe (1991 and 1992), Elantra (continued)

Code	Probable cause
22	Crank angle sensor or circuit
23	TDC sensor or circuit
24	Vehicle Speed Sensor or circuit
25	Barometric pressure sensor or circuit
41	Fuel injector or circuit
42	Fuel pump or circuit
43	EGR system
44	Ignition coil
59	Oxygen sensor

Scoupe (1993 through 1995) and Accent

Code	Probable cause
1122	ECM failure (ROM/RAM)
1169	ECM failure
1233	ECM failure (ROM)
1234	ECM failure (RAM)
2121	Turbo boost sensor control valve
3112	No. 1 fuel injector
3114	Idle Air Control (opening failure)
3116	No. 3 fuel injector
3117	Mass Airflow sensor
3121	Turbo boost sensor failure
3122	Idle Air Control (closing failure)
3128	Heated oxygen sensor

Code	Probable cause
3135	EVAP purge control solenoid valve
3137	Alternator output low
3145	Engine coolant temperature (ECT) sensor
3149	Air conditioning compressor
3152	Turbocharger overboost
3153	Throttle position switch (TPS)
3159	Vehicle speed sensor
3211	Knock sensor
3222	Phase sensor
3224	ECM failure (knock evaluation circuit)
3232	Crankshaft position sensor
3233	Same as code 3224
3234	No. 2 fuel injector
3235	No. 4 fuel injector
3241	ECM failure (injector or purge solenoid)
3242	ECM failure (IAC or air conditioning relay)
3243	ECM failure
4133	ECM failure
4151	Air/fuel control
4152	Air/fuel adaptive failure
4153	Air/fuel multiple adaptive failure
4154	Air/fuel additive adaptive failure
4155	ECM failure (A/C relay, IAC, PCV or injector)
4156	Same as code 3121
4444	Normal
3333	End of trouble codes

Infiniti

G20, J30 and Q45 models

Code	System Affected	Probable Cause
11 (1)	Crankshaft Position Sensor	(2) No crank signal
12	Mass Airflow Sensor Circuit	Open/shorted circuit
13	Engine Coolant Temp Sensor	Open/shorted circuit
14	Vehicle Speed Sensor (VSS)	No VSS signal
16 (1)	Traction Control System	Open/shorted circuit
21 (1)	Ignition signal circuit	(2) Open/shorted circuit
31	ECM	Signals not normal
32 (3)	EGR function	No EGR operation
33	Oxygen sensor (Left)	Open/shorted circuit - high oxygen sensor signal
34 (1)	Knock sensor	Open/shorted circuit
35 (3)	EGR temperature sensor	Open/shorted circuit
42	Fuel temperature sensor	Open/shorted circuit
43	Throttle Position Sensor	Open/shorted circuit
45 (3)	Injector leak	Leak at injectors
46 (1) (Q45 models with TCS)	Secondary Throttle Position Sensor	Open/shorted circuit
51	Injector circuit	Injector does not work
53	Oxygen sensor (right)	Open/shorted circuit - high for oxygen signal
54 (1)	Automatic transmission signal	Open signal - Transmission Control Unit
55 (1)	No malfunction	Normal condition

(1) Trouble code will not activate Malfunction Indicator Light (MIL)
(2) If codes 11 and 21 are present at the same time, check items causing a malfunction of the crankshaft position sensor circuit
(3) California models

Isuzu

 CHECK   MIL   **SERVICE ENGINE SOON**   CHECK   CHECK ENGINE LIGHT

Note: *To determine which models a code applies to, refer to the parenthetical reference (A, B and/or C) following the probable cause, then cross-reference the letter(s) with their corresponding models at the end of this chart.*

Code	Probable cause
12	Idle switch not turned on (1982 through 1984 1.8L with feedback carburetor)
12	No TACH signal to ECM (A, B and C)
13	Idle switch not turned off (1982 through 1984 1.8L with feedback carburetor)
13	Oxygen sensor or circuit (A, B and C)
14	Wide open throttle switch not turned on (1982 through 1984 1.8L with feedback carburetor)
15	Wide open throttle switch not turned off (1982 through 1984 1.8L with feedback carburetor)
14	Engine coolant temperature (ECT) sensor shorted (A) or grounded (B) or out of range (C)
15	Engine coolant temperature (ECT) sensor - open circuit (A)
15	Engine coolant temperature (ECT) sensor - incorrect signal (B); open circuit on 1988 through 1994 2.6L)
16	Engine coolant temperature (ECT) sensor - open circuit (B)
21	Output transistor is not turned on (1982 through 1984 1.8L with feedback carburetor)
21	Idle switch - open circuit; or Wide Open Throttle (WOT) switch - short circuit (A)
21	Throttle Valve Switch (TVS) system - idle contact and full contact made simultaneously (B)
21	Throttle position sensor (TPS) - voltage high (C)
21	Throttle position sensor (TPS) - out of range (D)
22	Output transistor not turned on (1982 through 1984 1.8L with feedback carburetor)
22	Fuel cut solenoid circuit open or grounded (A)
22	Starter - no signal input (B)
22	Throttle position sensor (TPS) signal - voltage low (C)
23	Abnormal oxygen sensor (1982 through 1984 1.8L with feedback carburetor)
23	Mixture control solenoid circuit failure (A)
23	Ignition power transistor circuit - output terminal grounded (B)
23	Intake Air Temperature (IAT) sensor voltage - high temperature indicated (C)
23	Intake Air Temperature (IAT) sensor - out of range (D)
24	Coolant temperature sensor malfunction (1982 through 1984 1.8L with feedback carburetor)
24	Vehicle speed sensor (VSS) circuit fault (A and C)

Code	Probable cause
24	Vehicle speed sensor (VSS) - no input signal (D)
24	Pressure regulator vacuum switching valve (1988 through 1994 2.3L)
25	Random Access Memory (RAM) (1982 through 1984 1.8L with feedback carburetor)
25	Air Injection Reactor(AIR) vacuum switch valve (VSV) circuit fault (1987 through 1989 1.5L; A and B)
25	Intake air temperature (IAT) - high temperature indicated (C)
26	Canister vacuum switching valve (VSV) system for canister purge - circuit open or grounded (A and B)
27	Vacuum switching valve (VSV) - constant high voltage to ECM (A)
27	Canister purge vacuum switching valve (VSV) - faulty transistor or bad ground circuit (B)
31	No ignition reference to ECM (A)
31	Wastegate control circuit fault - turbo models (C)
32	Exhaust Gas Recirculation (EGR) system failure (C)
33	Fuel injector circuit fault - output terminal open or grounded (B)
33	Manifold Absolute Pressure (MAP) sensor - voltage high (C)
33	Manifold Absolute Pressure (MAP) sensor - out of range (D)
34	Exhaust Gas Recirculation (EGR)/vacuum switching valve (VSV) - output terminal open or grounded (B)
34	Manifold Absolute Pressure (MAP) sensor - voltage low (C)
34	Exhaust Gas Recirculation (EGR) temperature sensor - electronic idle control circuit fault (A)
35	Ignition power transistor - open circuit (B)
41	Crank angle sensor (CAS) - no signal or faulty signal (B)
42	Electronic spark timing circuit fault (C)
42	Fuel cut-off relay malfunction or circuit fault (A)
43	Electronic spark control (ESC) - knock circuit fault (C)
43	Throttle valve switch - idle switch always closed (B)
44	Oxygen sensor - lean condition indicated (all models)
45	Oxygen sensor - rich condition indicated (all models)
51	Fuel cut-off solenoid circuit shorted, or faulty ECM (A)
51	Bad Programmable Read-Only Memory (PROM) or incorrect PROM installation (1985 through 1989 1.5L I-Mark; C)
51	Electronic Control Module (ECM) failure (B and D)
52	Electronic Control Module (ECM) failure (A and B)
52	CALPAK error - faulty, incorrectly installed or wrong CALPAK (C)
53	Faulty Electronic Control Module (ECM), or shorted air switching solenoid (ASS) or air injection system (A)
53	Vacuum switching valve (VSV) - grounded or faulty power transistor (B)
54	Fuel pump circuit - low voltage (C)

Code	Probable cause
54	Ignition power transistor - grounded or faulty power transistor (B)
54	Shorted mixture control solenoid, or faulty ECM (1987 through 1989 1.5L I-Mark; A)
55	Faulty Electronic Control Module (ECM) (A, B and C)
61	Air flow sensor (AFS) circuit fault - grounded, shorted or open HOW wire (B)
62	Air flow sensor (AFS) circuit fault - broken COLD wire (B)
63	Vehicle speed sensor (VSS) circuit - no signal input (B)
64	Fuel injector driver transistor circuit - grounded or faulty circuit (B)
65	Throttle valve switch always on (B)
66	Knock sensor failure - grounded or open circuit (B)
71	Throttle position sensor (TPS) - turbo control system signal abnormal (B)
72	Exhaust Gas Recirculation (EGR) vacuum switching valve (VSV) - faulty transistor or ground system (B)

A   1985 through 1989 1.5L engine (VIN 7) with feedback carburetor (FBC); 1983 1.8L truck engine with FBC; 1983 through 1986 2.0L engine (VIN A) with FBC; 1986 through 1994 2.3L engine (VIN L) with FBC

B   1985 through 1987 2.0L electronic fuel-injected (EFI) turbo engine (VIN F); 1983 through 1989 2.0L EFI engine (VIN A); 1988 and 1989 2.3L EFI (VIN L) engine; 1988 through 1994 2.6L EFI engine (VIN E)

C   1987 through 1989 1.5L electronic fuel-injected (EFI) turbo engine (VIN 9); 1989 1.6L EFI engine (VIN 5); 1991 and 1992 1.6L EFI turbo engine (VIN 4); 1989 through 1991 2.8L throttle body injection (TBI) engine (VIN R); 1991 through 1994 3.1L TBI engine (VIN Z)

D   1990 and 1991 1.6L electronic fuel-injected (EFI) engine (VIN 7); 1992 through 1994 1.8L EFI engine (VIN 8); 1991 through 1994 2.3L EFI engine (VIN 5, VIN 6); 1992 through 1994 3.2L EFI engine (VIN V, VIN W)

Jaguar

 CHECK MIL 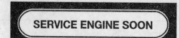 SERVICE ENGINE SOON CHECK   CHECK ENGINE LIGHT

1988 and 1989 models

Code	System affected	Probable cause
1	Oxygen sensor	Open oxygen sensor circuit
2	Airflow sensor circuit	Not in operating range
3	Coolant temperature sensor	Not in operating range
4	Oxygen sensor	System indicates full rich
5	Throttle potentiometer/airflow sensor	Low throttle potentiometer signal with high airflow sensor signal

Code	System affected	Probable cause
6	Throttle potentiometer/airflow sensor	High throttle potentiometer signal with low airflow sensor signal
7	Throttle potentiometer	Idle fuel adjustment failure
8	Intake air temperature sensor	Open or shorted circuit in IAT sensor harness

All other models

Code	System affected	Probable cause
11	Idle potentiometer	Not in operating range
12	Airflow sensor	Not in operating range
13	PCME	No vacuum signal from pressure sensor, incorrect fuel pressure or PCME failure
14	Coolant temperature sensor	Not in operating range
16	Air temperature sensor	Not in operating range
17	Throttle potentiometer	Not in operating range
18	Throttle potentiometer/airflow sensor	Signal resistance low at wide open throttle
19	Throttle potentiometer/airflow sensor	Signal resistance high at idle
22	Heated oxygen sensor	Open or short circuit
22	Fuel pump circuit	Open or short circuit
23	Fuel supply	Rich exhaust indicated
23	Fuel supply (rich or lean)	Open or short in fuel supply circuit; restricted fuel line or injectors (5.3L)
24	Ignition amplifier circuit	Open or short circuit
26	Oxygen sensor circuit	Lean exhaust/vacuum leak
29	ECU	Self-check
33	Fuel injector circuit	Open or short circuit
34	Fuel injector circuit	Faulty injected indicated
34	Bank A (right) injectors	Open or short circuit; faulty or restricted fuel injectors (5.3L)
36	Bank B (left) injectors	Open or short circuit; faulty or restricted fuel injectors (5.3L)
37	EGR solenoid circuit	Short or open circuit
39	EGR circuit	Faulty system operation
44	Lambda (oxygen) sensor (right)	Circuit feedback out of control - rich or lean condition
45	Lambda (oxygen) sensor (left)	Circuit feedback out of control - rich or lean condition
46	Idle speed control valve (coil 1)	Open or short circuit
47	Idle speed control valve (coil 2)	Open or short circuit
48	Idle speed control valve	Not within specification
49	Fuel injection ballast resistor	Open circuit or faulty resistor (5.3L)

Jaguar (continued)

Code	System affected	Probable cause
66	Secondary air inception relay	Voltage out of range
68	Road speed sensor	Incorrect signal voltage
69	Neutral safety switch circuit	Engine cranks in drive (adjust or replace switch)
89	Purge control valve circuit	Open or short circuit

Jeep

 CHECK   MIL   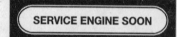 SERVICE ENGINE SOON   CHECK   CHECK ENGINE LIGHT

1984 through 1986 V6 models

Trouble Code	Circuit or system	Probable cause
12 (one flash, pause, two flashes)	No reference pulses to ECM	This code should flash whenever the test terminal is grounded with the ignition On and the engine not running. If additional trouble codes are stored (indicating a problem), they will appear after this code has flashed three times. With the engine running, the appearance of this code indicates that no references from the distributor are reaching the ECM. Carefully check the four terminal EST connector or the distributor.
13 (one flash, pause, three flashes)	Oxygen sensor circuit	Check for a sticking or misadjusted throttle position sensor. Check the wiring and connectors from the oxygen sensor. Replace oxygen sensor.*
14 (one flash, pause, four flashes)	Coolant sensor circuit (high temperature indicated)	If the engine is experiencing overheating problems the problem must be rectified before continuing. Check all wiring and connectors associated with the sensor. Replace the coolant sensor.*
15 (one flash, pause, five flashes)	Coolant sensor circuit (low temperature indicated)	See above.
21 (two flashes, pause, one flash)	TPS circuit (signal voltage high)	Check for sticking or misadjusted TPS. Check all wiring and connections at the TPS and at the ECM Adjust or replace TPS.*
23 (two flashes, pause, three flashes)	Mixture Control (M/C)	Check the electrical connections at the M/C solenoid. If solenoid circuit OK, clear the ECM memory and recheck for code(s) after driving the vehicle. Check wiring connections at the ECM. Check wiring from M/C solenoid.

Trouble Code	Circuit or system	Probable cause
34 (three flashes, pause, four flashes)	Manifold Absolute Pressure	Check the hose to the MAP sensor for a leak. Check the wiring from (MAP) sensor circuit the MAP sensor to the ECM. Check the connections at the ECM and the sensor. Replace the MAP sensor.*
41 (four flashes, pause, one flash)	No distributor signals	Check all wires and connections at the distributor. Check distributor pick-up coil connections.
42 (four flashes, pause, two flashes)	Bypass or EST problem	If the vehicle will start and run, check the wire leading to ECM terminal 12. An improper HEI module can also cause this trouble code.
44 (four flashes, pause, four flashes)	Lean exhaust	Check for a sticking M/C solenoid. Check ECM wiring connections. Check for vacuum leakage at carburetor base gasket, vacuum hoses or intake manifold gasket. Check for air leakage at air management system- to-exhaust ports and at decel valve. Replace oxygen sensor.*
44 and 45 at the same time	Oxygen sensor or circuit	Check the oxygen sensor circuit. Replace the oxygen sensor.*
45 (four flashes, pause, five flashes)	Rich exhaust	Check for a sticking M/C solenoid. Check wiring at M/C solenoid connector. Check the evaporative charcoal canister and its components for the presence of fuel. Replace oxygen sensor.*
51 (five flashes, pause, one flash)	PROM problem	Diagnosis should be performed by a dealer service department or other repair shop.
54 (five flashes, pause, four flashes)	Mixture control (M/C) solenoid	Check all M/C solenoid and ECM wires and connections. Replace the M/C solenoid.*
55 (five flashes, pause, five flashes)	Reference voltage problem	Check for a short to ground on the circuit to ECM. Possible faulty ECM or oxygen sensor.

* Component replacement may not cure the problem in all cases. For this reason, you may want to seek professional advice before purchasing replacement parts.

1991 on
Trouble codes

Note: Not all trouble codes apply to all models.

Code 11	No distributor reference signal detected during engine cranking. Check the circuit between the distributor and the PCM.
Code 12	Problem with the battery connection. Direct battery input to controller disconnected within the last 50 ignition key-ons.
Code 13**	Indicates a problem with the MAP sensor pneumatic (vacuum) system.
Code 14**	MAP sensor voltage too low or too high.
Code 15**	A problem with the vehicle distance/speed signal. No distance/speed sensor signal detected during road load conditions.
Code 16	Loss of battery voltage.

1991 on

Code	Description
Code 17	Engine is cold too long. Engine coolant temperature remains below normal operating temperatures during operation (check the thermostat).
Code 21**	Problem with oxygen sensor signal circuit. Sensor voltage to computer not fluctuating.
Code 22**	Coolant sensor voltage too high or too low. Test coolant temperature sensor.
Code 23**	Indicates that the air temperature sensor input is below the minimum acceptable voltage or sensor input is above the maximum acceptable voltage.
Code 24**	Throttle position sensor voltage high or low. Test the throttle position sensor.
Code 25**	Idle Air Control (IAC) motor circuits. A shorted condition is detected in one or more of the IAC motor circuits.
Code 27	One of the injector control circuit output drivers does not respond properly to the control signal. Check the circuits.
Code 31**	Problem with the canister purge solenoid circuit.
Code 32**	An open or shorted condition detected in the EGR solenoid circuit. Possible air/fuel ratio imbalance not detected during diagnosis
Code 33	Air conditioner clutch relay circuit. An open or shorted condition detected in the air conditioning clutch relay circuit.
Code 34	Open or shorted condition detected in the speed control vacuum or vent solenoid circuits.
Code 37	Torque converter clutch solenoid circuit. An open or shorted condition detected in the torque converter part throttle unlock solenoid circuit (automatic transmissions models only).
Code 41**	Problem with the charging system. Occurs when battery voltage from the ASD relay is below 11.75-volts.
Code 42	Auto shutdown relay (ASD) control circuit indicates an open or shorted circuit condition.
Code 44	Battery temperature sensor volts malfunction. Problem with the battery temperature voltage circuit in the PCM
Code 45	Overdrive solenoid. Problem detected in the overdrive solenoid circuit.
Code 46**	Charging system voltage too high. Computer indicates that the battery voltage is not properly regulated.
Code 47**	Charging system voltage too low. Battery voltage sense input below target charging voltage during engine operation and no significant change in voltage detected during active test of alternator output.
Code 51*	Oxygen sensor signal input indicates lean fuel/air ratio condition during engine operation.
Code 52**	Oxygen sensor signal input indicates rich fuel/air ratio condition during engine operation.
Code 53	Internal PCM failure detected.
Code 54	No camshaft position sensor signal from distributor. Problem with the distributor synchronization circuit.
Code 55	Completion of fault code display on CHECK ENGINE lamp. This is an End of message code.
Code 62	Unsuccessful attempt to update EMR mileage in the controller EEPROM.
Code 63	Controller failure. EEPROM write denied. Check the PCM.

** *These codes light up the CHECK ENGINE light on the instrument panel during engine operation once the trouble code has been recorded*

Lexus

  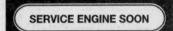

Code	Circuit or system	Trouble area
1	Normal	This code appears when the system is operating satisfactorily
12	RPM signal	The rpm NE, G1 or G2 signal to the ECU is missing for 2 or more seconds after the engine is cranked. Check the distributor and circuit, the igniter and circuit, the starter circuit, and the ECU
13	RPM signal	No NE signal to the ECU with an engine speed of more than 1000 rpm. Check the distributor circuit, the igniter and circuit, and the ECU
14	Ignition signal	Igniter IGF1 signal to ECU missing for eight successive ignitions. Check the igniter circuit, the igniter and the ECU
15	Ignition signal	Igniter IGF2 signal to ECU missing for eight consecutive ignitions. Check the igniter circuit, the igniter and the ECU
16	ECT control signal	Normal signal missing from ECT CPU (1990 through 1994 models)
16	A/T control signal	Normal signal missing between engine CPU and A/T CPU in the ECU (1995 models). Check the ECU
17	No. 1 cam position sensor	G1 signal to ECU missing. Check cam position sensor and circuit between sensor and ECU
18	No. 2 cam position sensor	G2 signal to ECU missing. Check cam position sensor and circuit between sensor and ECU
21*	Main oxygen sensor signal (left)	Signal voltage stays between 0.35 and 0.70 volts for 1 minute or more at 40 to 50 mph, with A/C on and ECT in 4th gear. Or sensor heater circuit open or shorted. Check sensor and circuit
22	Coolant temperature sensor	Open or short in the coolant temperature sensor, circuit or ECU
24	Intake air temperature sensor	Open or short in the intake air sensor circuit
25*	Air/fuel ratio lean malfunction	Air/fuel ratio feedback correction value or adaptive control value continues at the upper (lean) or lower (rich) limit for a certain period of time. Check the injector, injector circuit, oxygen sensor, sensor circuit, ECU, fuel line pressure (injector blockage or leakage), coolant temperature sensor or sensor circuit; air temperature sensor or sensor circuit; airflow meter; air intake system; ignition system. Look for an air leak.
26*	Air/fuel ratio rich malfunction	Air/fuel ratio is overly rich, or there's an open or short circuit in the oxygen sensor. Check the injector and circuit; coolant temperature sensor and circuit; air temperature sensor and circuit; airflow meter; oxygen sensor and circuit; cold start injector; and ECU
27*	Sub-oxygen sensor signal (left)	Open or shorted circuit in the sub-oxygen sensor or circuit. Check the sub-oxygen sensor and circuit, and the ECU

Code	Circuit or system	Trouble area
28*	Main oxygen sensor signal (right)	Signal voltage stays between 0.35 and 0.70 volts for 1 minute or more at 40 to 50 mph, with A/C on and ECT in 4th gear. Or sensor heater circuit open or shorted. Check sensor and circuit
29*	Sub-oxygen sensor signal (right)	Open or shorted circuit in the sub-oxygen sensor or circuit. Check the sub-oxygen sensor and circuit, and the ECU
31	Airflow meter circuit signal to ECU	Airflow meter circuit signal to ECU missing for 2 seconds with engine speed over 300 rpm. Look for an open or short in the airflow meter circuit to the ECU
32	Airflow meter circuit	E2 circuit open or VC and VS shorted. Look for an open or short circuit in the airflow meter or circuit
35	HAC sensor circuit	Open or short for 0.5 seconds or more, or BARO sensor failure. Check the HAC sensor and circuit, or the BARO sensor and circuit
41	Throttle position sensor signal	Open or short in the throttle position sensor or circuit, or in the ECU
42	Vehicle speed sensor circuit	Engine speed over 2350 rpm but VSS indicates 0 mph. Check VSS and circuit
43	Starter signal	No starter signal to the ECU. Check the starter signal circuit, the ignition switch, the main relay switch and the ECU
47	Sub-throttle position sensor signal	Open or short for 0.5 seconds or more in the sub-throttle position sensor circuit (VTA2), or signal outputs exceed 1.45 volts with idle contacts on. Check the VTA2 circuit
51	Switch condition signal	A/C signal on when IDL contacts off, or shift in R, D, 2 or 1 range, during test mode. Check the A/C switch and circuit; A/C amplifier; neutral start switch (automatics); throttle position sensor; and ECU
52	No. 1 knock sensor signal	Knock sensor signal missing from ECU for 3 revolutions with engine speed between 1600 and 5200 rpm. Look for an open or short circuit in knock sensor circuit. Check the knock sensor and the ECU
53	Knock control signal	Problem with knock control system in ECU with engine speed between 650 and 5200 rpm. Check the ECU
55	No. 2 knock sensor signal	Knock sensor signal missing from ECU for 3 revolutions with engine speed between 1600 and 5200 rpm. Look for an open or short circuit in knock sensor circuit. Check the knock sensor and the ECU
71*	EGR gas temperature signal	EGR system gas temperature signal too low (below 149 degrees F for at least 90 seconds while under EGR control). Check the EGR valve, hoses, etc.; EGR gas temperature sensor or circuit; vacuum switching valve for the EGR circuit; ECU
78*	Fuel pump control signal	Open or short in the fuel pump control circuit

A single occurrence of this code will only be stored temporarily in computer memory, and the CHECK ENGINE light won't come on until the fault has been detected a second time during a separate ignition cycle.

Mazda

Code	Probable cause
1	Engine speed (1984 and 1985 2.0L)
1	Crank angle sensor (1984 through 1987 RX-7)
1	Ignition coil - trailing (1988 through 1991 RX-7)
1	No ignition pulse signal (1988 through 1994 1.6L, 1.8L, 2.0L, 2.2L, 2.5L, 2.6L and 3.0L)
2	Coolant thermosensor (1984 and 1985 2.0L)
2	Air flow meter (1984 through 1987 RX-7; 1986 and 1987 1.6L, 2.0L and 2.2L)
2	NE-2 signal - crankshaft (1992 and 1993 1.8L V6, 1994 2.0L and 1992 through 1994 3.0L)
3	Oxygen sensor (1984 and 1985 2.0L)
3	Coolant thermosensor (1984 through 1987 RX-7; 1986 and 1987 1.6L, 2.0L and 2.2L)
3	Crank position sensor - G1 signal/cam position sensor (2.2L turbo, 1988 through 1991 3.0L)
3	Crank angle sensor - G signal (1988 through 1991 RX-7)
4	Vacuum sensor (1984 and 1985 2.0L)
4	Intake air temperature sensor - in airflow meter (1984 through 1987 RX-7)
4	Intake air thermosensor (1986 and 1987 1.6L, 2.0L and 2.2L)
4	Crank position sensor (G2 signal) (2.2L turbo, 1988 through 1991 3.0L); distributor (NE1) signal (1992 through 1994 1.8L V6, 1994 2.0L, 1992 and 1993 3.0L)
5	EGR position sensor (1984 and 1985 2.0L)
5	Oxygen sensor (1984 through 1987 RX-7)
5	Feedback system (1986 and 1987 1.6L, 2.0L and 2.2L)
5	Left knock sensor, or control unit (1992 through 1994 3.0L)
5	Knock sensor (1993 RX-7)
6	Throttle sensor (1984 through 1987 RX-7)
6	Atmospheric pressure sensor (1986 and 1987 1.6L, 2.0L and 2.2L)
6	Speedometer sensor (1988 through 1994 1.6L, 1.8L, 2.0L, 2.2L, 2.5L, 2.6L and 3.0L)
6	Speedometer sensor (1993 RX-7)

Mazda (continued)

Code	Probable cause
7	Right knock sensor (1992 through 1994 3.0L)
7	Boost sensor/pressure sensor (1984 through 1987 RX-7 turbo)
8	EGR position sensor (1986 and 1987 1.6L, 2.0L and 2.2L)
8	Airflow meter (1988 through 1991 RX-7)
9	Atmospheric pressure sensor (1984 through 1987 RX-7)
9	Atmospheric pressure sensor (1986 and 1987 1.6L, 2.0L and 2.2L)
9	Coolant thermosensor (1988 through 1994 RX-7)
10	Intake air thermosensor - in airflow meter (1988 through 1991 RX-7)
10	Intake air thermosensor (1988 through 1994 1.6L, 1.8L, 2.0L, 2.2L and 2.5L)
11	Intake air thermosensor (1988 through 1993 RX-7)
11	Intake air thermosensor - dynamic chamber (1988 through 1994 2.6L and 3.0L)
12	Coil with igniter - trailing ((1984 through 1987 RX-7)
12	Throttle sensor - wide open throttle (1988 through 1994 RX-7)
13	Intake manifold pressure sensor (1988 through 1994 RX-7)
14	Atmospheric pressure sensor (1988 through 1994 2.6L and 1994 2.5L) (inside the ECU on these models)
14	Atmospheric pressure sensor (1988 through 1994 RX-7) (inside the ECU on 1993 models)
15	Intake air temperature sensor - in dynamic chamber (1984 through 1987 RX-7)
15	Oxygen sensor (1988 through 1994 1.6L, 1.8L, 2.0L, 2.2L, 2.5L, 2.6L, 3.0L and RX-7)
15	Left oxygen sensor (1992 through 1994 1.8L V6, 1994 2.5L and 1990 through 1994 3.0L)
16	EGR position sensor (1988 through 1994 1.6L, 1.8L, 2.0L, 2.2L, 2.5L, 2.6L and 3.0L)
16	EGR switch (1993 California RX-7)
17	Feedback system (1988 through 1994 1.6L, 1.8L, 2.0L, 2.2L, 2.5L, 2.6L, 3.0L and RX-7)
17	Left feedback system (1992 through 1994 1.8L V6, 1993 and 1994 2.5L and 1990 through 1994 3.0L)
18	Throttle sensor - narrow range (1988 through 1994 RX-7)
20	Metering oil pump position sensor (1988 through 1994 RX-7)
22	No. 1 cylinder sensor (1986 and 1987 2.2L turbo)
23	Right heated oxygen sensor (1992 through 1994 1.8L V6, 1994 2.5L and 1990 and 1991 3.0L)

Code	Probable cause
23	Fuel thermosensor (1993 RX-7)
24	Right feedback system (1992 through 1994 1.8L V6, 1993 and 1994 2.5L and 1990 through 1994 3.0L)
25	Solenoid valve - pressure regulator control (1988 through 1994 1.6L, 1.8L, 2.0L, 2.2L, 2.5L, 2.6L and 3.0L)
25	Solenoid valve - pressure regulator control (1993 RX-7)
26	Purge control solenoid valve no. 2 (1988 and 1989 3.0L)
26	Purge control solenoid valve (1988 through 1994 1.6L, 1.8L, 2.0L, 2.2L, 2.5L, 2.6L and 3.0L)
26	Metering oil pump stepping motor (1993 RX-7)
27	Purge control solenoid valve no. 1 (1988 and 1989 3.0L)
27	Purge control solenoid valve no. 2 (1989 1.6L)
27	Metering oil pump - step motor (1988 through 1991 RX-7)
27	Metering oil pump (1993 RX-7)
28	EGR solenoid valve (1993 RX-7)
28	Solenoid valve - EGR vacuum (1988 through 1994 1.6L, 1.8L, 2.0L, 2.2L, 2.5L, 2.6L and 3.0L)
29	Solenoid valve - EGR vent (1988 through 1994 1.6L, 1.8L, 2.0L, 2.2L, 2.5L, 2.6L and 3.0L)
30	Relay (or cold start injector, on 3.0L) (1988 through 1994 1.6L, 1.8L, 2.0L, 2.2L, 2.5L, 2.6L and 3.0L)
31	Solenoid valve - relief no. 1 (1988 through 1994 RX-7)
32	Solenoid valve - switching (1988 through 1994 RX-7)
33	Solenoid valve - port air bypass (1988 through 1994 RX-7)
34	Solenoid valve - bypass air control (1988 through 1991 RX-7)
34	Solenoid valve - idle speed control (1993 RX-7)
34	ISC valve (1988 through 1994 1.6L, 1.8L, 2.0L, 2.2L, 2.5L, 2.6L and 3.0L)
34	Idle air control valve (1993 and 1994 2.0L, 2.5L, 1.6L, 1.8L, 2.6L and 3.0L)
36	Oxygen sensor heater relay (1990 3.0L)
36	Right oxygen sensor heater (1992 through 1994 3.0L)
37	Left oxygen sensor heater (1992 through 1994 3.0L)
37	Metering oil pump (1988 through 1993 RX-7)
37	Coolant fan relay (1988 through 1994 1.6L, 1.8L, 2.0L, 2.2L, 2.5L, 2.6L and 3.0L)
38	Solenoid valve accelerated warm-up system (1988 through 1994)
39	Solenoid valve - relief 2 (1993 RX-7)

Code	Probable cause
40	Solenoid (triple induction system) and oxygen sensor relay (1988 and 1989 3.0L)
40	Auxiliary port valve (1988 through 1991 RX-7)
40	Oxygen sensor heater relay (1991 3.0L)
40	Solenoid valve - purge control (1993 RX-7)
41	Solenoid valve - variable dynamic effect intake control (1988 through 1991 RX-7)
41	Solenoid valve - VRIS (1989 through 1994 3.0L MPV)
41	Solenoid valve VRIS 1 (1992 through 1994 1.8L V6 and 1993 2.5L)
41	Variable inertia charging system (VICS) (3.0L only)
42	Solenoid valve - turbo boost pressure regulator (1988 through 1991 RX-7)
42	Solenoid valve - turbo pre-control (1993 RX-7)
43	Solenoid valve - wastegate control (1993 RX-7)
44	Solenoid valve - turbo control (1993 RX-7)
45	Solenoid valve - charge control (1993 RX-7)
46	Solenoid valve - VRIS 2 (1992 through 1994 1.8L V6, and 1993 2.5L)
46	Solenoid valve - charge relief control (1993 RX-7)
50	Solenoid valve - double-throttle control (1993 RX-7)
51	Fuel pump relay (1988 through 1994 RX-7)
54	Air pump relay (1993 RX-7)
65	Air conditioning signal - PCMT (1992 through 1994 3.0L)
67	Coolant fan relay no. 1 (1993 2.5L)
67	Coolant fan relay no. 2 (1992 through 1994 1.8L V6)
68	Coolant fan relay no. 2 (no. 3 on automatics) (1993 2.5L)
69	Engine coolant temperature sensor - fan (1992 through 1994 1.8L V6; 1993 2.0L and 2.5L)
71	Injector - front secondary (1988 through 1994 RX-7)
73	Injector - rear secondary (1988 through 1994 RX-7)
76	Slip lock-up off signal (1993 RX-7)
77	Torque reduced signal (1993 RX-7)

Mercedes

  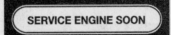

1990 through 1993 - 190E and 300 series (2.3L)

No.of Flashes	Probable cause
1	No System Malfunction
2	Throttle Valve Switch
3	Coolant Temperature Sensor
4	Airflow Sensor Position Indicator
5	Oxygen Sensor
6	Not Used
7	Td Signal
8	Altitude Correction Capsule
9	Electro-Hydraulic Actuator (EHA)
10	Throttle Valve Switch and/or Idle Speed Contact
11	Not Used
12	EGR Temperature Sensor

1991 and later - 300 series (2.8L and 3.2L)

No.of Flashes	Probable cause
1	No faults in system
2	Oxygen Sensor Inoperative
3	Lambda Control Inoperative
4	Air Injection inoperative
5	Exhaust Gas Recirculation (EGR) inoperative
6	Idle Speed Control Inoperative
7	Ignition System Failure
8	Coolant Temperature Sensor - Open Or Short Circuit
9	Intake Air Temperature Sensor - Open Or Short Circuit
10	Voltage At Air Mass Sensor Too High Or Low
11	TN (RPM) Signal Defective
12	Oxygen Sensor Heater Open Or Short Circuit
13	Camshaft Position Sensor Signal From - EZL/AKR Ignition Control Unit Defective
14	Intake Manifold Pressure At Start Too Low
15	Full Throttle Information Defective
16	Idle Speed Information Defective
17	Controller Area Network (CAN) Data Exchange - Malfunction Between Control Units
18	Adjustable Camshaft Timing Solenoid - Open Or Short Circuit
19	Fuel Injectors- Open Or Short Circuit, or Emission Control System Adaptation at Limit
20	Speed Signal Missing
21	Purge Switchover Valve - Open Or Short Circuit
22	Camshaft Position Sensor Signal Defective
23	Intake Manifold Pressure With Engine Running Too Low
24	Starter Ring Gear Segments Defective
25	Knock Sensors Defective
26	Upshift Delay Switch over Valve - Open Or Short Circuit
27	Coolant Temperature Sensor Deviation Between Sensor Circuit No. 1 and Sensor Circuit No. 2
28	Coolant Temperature Sensor (Coolant Temperature Change Monitor)

Mercedes (continued)

1991 through 1993 - 190E and 300 series (2.6L and 3.0L)

No.of Flashes	Probable cause
1	No faults in system
2	Throttle Valve Switch (Full Throttle Contact)
3	Coolant Temperature Sensor
4	Airflow Sensor Potentiometer
5	Oxygen Sensor
6	Not assigned
7	TNA (Engine RPM) Signal
8	Altitude Pressure Signal From EZL Ignition Control Unit
9	Current To Electro-hydraulic Actuator
10	Throttle Valve switch (Idle Contact)
11	Air Injection System
12	Absolute Pressure Valves From EZL Ignition Control Unit
13	Intake Air Temperature Signal
14	Road Speed Signal At CIS-E Control Unit
15	Not assigned
16	Exhaust Gas Recirculation (EGR)
17	Oxygen Sensor Signal

No.of Flashes	Probable cause
18	Current To Idle Speed Air Valve
19	Not assigned
20	Not assigned
21	Not assigned
22	Oxygen Sensor Heating Current
23	Short Circuit To Positive In Regeneration Switch over Valve Circuit
24	Not assigned
25	Short Circuit To Positive in Start Valve Circuit
26	Short Circuit To Positive In Shift Point Retard Circuit
27	Data Exchange Fault Between CIS-E Control Unit and EZL Ignition Control Unit
28	Loose Contact In Coolant Temperature Sensor Circuit
29	Difference In Coolant Temperatures Between CIS-E Control Unit and EZL Ignition Control Unit
30	Not assigned
31	Loose Contact In Intake Air Temperature Sensor Circuit
32	Not assigned
33	Not assigned
34	Faulty Coolant Temperature Sensor Signal from EZL Ignition Control Unit

Mitsubishi

  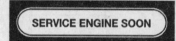

All 1984 through 1988 models (except 1988 Galant)*

Code	Probable cause
1	Exhaust gas sensor and/or ECU
2	Crankshaft angle sensor or ignition signal
3	Air flow sensor

Code	Probable cause
4	Atmospheric/Barometric pressure sensor
5	Throttle position sensor
6	Idle Speed Control (ISC) Motor Position Sensor (MPS)
7	Engine coolant temperature sensor
8	Top Dead Center (TDC) sensor or vehicle speed sensor
9	Top Dead Center (TDC) sensor

1988 Galant uses 1989 two-digit codes.

All 1989 through 1995 fuel-injected models (including 1988 Galant)

Code	Probable cause
1	Electronic Control Unit (ECU) (one long needle sweep)
9	Normal state (continuous short flashes)
11	Oxygen sensor or circuit
12	Air flow sensor or circuit
13	Intake air temperature sensor or circuit
14	Throttle Position Sensor (TPS) or circuit
15	Idle speed control (ISC) motor position sensor or circuit fault
21	Engine coolant temperature sensor or circuit
22	Crank angle sensor or circuit
23	No. 1 cylinder Top Dead Center (camshaft position) sensor or circuit
24	Vehicle Speed Sensor or circuit
25	Barometric pressure sensor or circuit
31	Detonation (knock) sensor
32	Manifold Absolute pressure (MAP) sensor faulty
36	Ignition timing adjustment signal fault
39	Front oxygen sensor (rear sensor on turbo models)
41	Fuel injector failure
42	Fuel pump or circuit
43	Exhaust Gas Recirculation (EGR) system (California models)
44	Ignition coil (except 3.0L DOHC V6)
44	Power transistor for coil (cylinders 1 and 4) (3.0L DOHC V6)

Mitsubishi (continued)

Code	Probable cause
52	Ignition coil (except 3.0L DOHC V6)
52	Power transistor for coil (cylinders 2 and 5) (DOHC V6)
53	Ignition coil (except 3.0L DOHC V6)
53	Power transistor for coil (cylinders 3 and 6) (3.0L DOHC V6)
55	Idle air control (IAC) valve position sensor fault
59	Heated oxygen sensor fault
61	ECM and transmission interlock
62	Induction control valve position sensor
69	Right rear oxygen sensor
71	Traction control vacuum valve solenoid fault
72	Traction control vent valve solenoid fault

Nissan/Datsun cars and trucks

 CHECK MIL 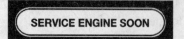 SERVICE ENGINE SOON CHECK CHECK ENGINE LIGHT

1984 and later

Code	Probable cause
11	Crank angle sensor/circuit (1988 to 1990); Camshaft position sensor (1991 to 1996)
12	Air flow meter/circuit open or shorted
13	Cylinder head temperature sensor (Maxima and 300ZX models); coolant temperature sensor circuit (all other models)
14	Vehicle speed sensor signal circuit is open (1988 on)
15	Mixture ratio is too lean despite feedback control; fuel injector clogged (1988)
21	Ignition signal in the primary circuit is not being entered to the ECU during cranking or running
22	Fuel pump circuit (Maxima and 1987 and later 300ZX models); idle speed control valve or circuit (all other models)
23	Idle switch (throttle valve switch) signal circuit is open
24	Park/Neutral switch malfunctioning (1984 through 1987)

Code	Probable cause
24	Fuel switch circuit or overdrive switch circuit
25	Idle speed control valve circuit is open or shorted
25	Auxiliary air control (AAC) valve circuit (1988 through 1991)
26	Turbo boost
28	Cooling fan
29	Fuel system rich
31	1984 through 1986 EFI models: Problem in air conditioning system; all other models: ECU control unit problem
32 (California)	1984 through 1986 EFI models: check starter system. All other models: EGR function
33	Oxygen sensor or circuit (300ZX left side) - all other models: EGR function
34	Detonation (knock) sensor
35 (California)	Exhaust gas temperature sensor
36	EGR transducer
37	Closed loop control/front oxygen sensor (Maxima)
41	Maxima and 1984 through 1987 300ZX models: fuel temp sensor circuit. All other models: air temperature sensor circuit
42	1988 and later 300ZX models: fuel temperature sensor circuit; all other models: throttle sensor circuit open or shorted
43 (1986 and 1987 models)	Fuel injector or circuit
43 (all others)	Throttle position sensor circuit is open or shorted
44	No trouble codes stored in ECU
45 (California)	Injector fuel leak
51 (California)	Fuel injector circuit open
53	Oxygen sensor (300ZX right side)
54	Short between automatic transmission control unit and ECU
55	Normal engine management system operation is indicated
63	Misfire detected - cylinder no. 6
64	Misfire detected - cylinder no. 5
65	Misfire detected - cylinder no. 4
66	Misfire detected - cylinder no. 3
67	Misfire detected - cylinder no. 2
68	Misfire detected - cylinder no. 1
71	Misfire detected (random)

Code	Probable cause
72	Catalytic converter malfunction (right side)
74	EVAP pressure sensor
75	EVAP leak
76	Fuel injection system
77	Rear oxygen sensor
81	Vacuum cut bypass valve
82	Crankshaft sensor
84	Automatic trans-to-fuel injection communication
85	VTC solenoid
87	EVAP canister purge control
91	Front oxygen sensor
95	Crankshaft sensor
98	Coolant temperature sensor
101	Camshaft sensor
103	Park/neutral switch
105	EGR and canister control valve
108	EVAP volume control

Porsche

  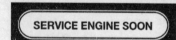

911 Carrera 4, 1989 928CS, 1989 through 1992 928GT, 1987 through 1992 928S4, 1987 through 1991 944S and 1986 through 1990 944 Turbo models

Code	System affected	Probable cause
1000		End of output
1111	ECM power supply	System voltage out of range (less than 10 volts)
1112 (2)	Throttle position (TP) switch	Idle switch contact grounded
1113	Throttle position (TP) switch	Full-load switch contact grounded
1114 (2)	Engine temperature sensor circuit	Open circuit

Code	System affected	Probable cause
1121 (2)	Mass airflow (MAF) sensor signal	Signal not plausible (3)
1122 (2)	Idle control circuit	Signal not plausible (3)
1123 (2)	Oxygen sensor	Air/fuel mixture too rich (928)
1123 (2)	Oxygen sensor	Signal out of range - control circuit fault (944S and 944 Turbo)
1124 (2)	Oxygen sensor	Air/fuel mixture too lean (928)
1124 (2)	Oxygen sensor	Control circuit fault (944S and 944 Turbo)
1125	Oxygen sensor	Open or short circuit or faulty sensor (928)
1125	Intake air temperature sensor	Open or short circuit (911 Carrera 4, 944S and 944 Turbo)
1131	Knock sensor no. 1	Signal not present (3) (944S and 944 Turbo)
1132	Knock sensor no. 2	Signal not present (3) (944S and 944 Turbo)
1133	Knock control regulation circuit	Knock computer faulty (944S and 944 Turbo)
1134	Camshaft position sensor	Open or short circuit (944S)
1134	Engine speed (rpm) sensor	Open or short circuit (944 Turbo)
1141 (2)	ECM	Faulty unit (944S and 944 Turbo)
1142	Fuel pump relay circuit	Open or short circuit (944S and 944 Turbo)
1143	Fuel tank vent solenoid	Open or short circuit (944S and 944 Turbo)
1145	MIL lamp	Open circuit
1151 (2)	Fuel injector no. 1	Open or short circuit (911 Carrera 4)
1152 (2)	Fuel injector no. 2	Open or short circuit (911 Carrera 4)
1153 (2)	Fuel injector no. 3	Open or short circuit (911 Carrera 4)
1154 (2)	Fuel injector no. 4	Open or short circuit (911 Carrera 4)
1155 (2)	Fuel injector no. 5	Open or short circuit (911 Carrera 4)
1156 (2)	Fuel injector no. 6	Open or short circuit (911 Carrera 4)
1311	Injectors	Open or short circuit (944 Turbo)
1321	Idle speed control	Open or short circuit (944 Turbo)
1322	EVAP canister purge (EVAP) valve	Open or short circuit (944 Turbo)
1334	A/C signal to ECM terminal 41	Open or short circuit (944 Turbo)
1335	A/C signal to ECM terminal 40	Open or short circuit (944 Turbo)
1500 (2)	System operating correctly	No fault codes stored in memory

Porsche (continued)

1992 through 1995 968, 1995 911 Carrera, 911 with Tiptronic transmission

Code	Fault
11	ECM supply voltage (all models)
13	Supply voltage (911 with Tiptronic)
14	Engine coolant temperature (ECT) sensor (968, 1995 911 Carrera)
14	Supply voltage
15	Throttle potentiometer (1995 911 Carrera)
16	Throttle position (TP) sensor (968)
18	RPM signal (968 and 1995 911 Carrera)
19	Vehicle speed sensor (VSS) (968 and 1995 911 Carrera)
21	Mass air flow (MAF) sensor (968 and 1995 911 Carrera)
21	RPM signal (911 with Tiptronic)
22	Oxygen sensor signal (1995 911 Carrera)
22	Load signal (911 with Tiptronic)
23	Oxygen regulation/oxygen sensor (968 and 1995 911 Carrera)
24	Heated oxygen sensor (HO2S) (968 and 1995 911 Carrera)
24	Change of ignition timing (911 with Tiptronic)
25	Intake temperature sensor (1995 911 Carrera)
25	Throttle potentiometer (911 with Tiptronic)
26	Ignition timing change (968 and 1995 911 Carrera)
27	Idle air control (IAC) valve (968)
27	Opening winding of idle stabilizer (1995 911 Carrera)
28	Idle air control (IAC) valve (968)
28	Closing winding of idle stabilizer (1995 911 Carrera)
31	Knock sensor (KS) 1 (968 and 1995 911 Carrera)
31	Solenoid valve 1 (911 with Tiptronic)
32	Knock sensor (KS) 2 (968 and 1995 911 Carrera)

Code	Fault
32	Solenoid valve 2 (911 with Tiptronic)
33	Engine control module (ECM) (968 and 1995 911 Carrera)
33	Torque converter clutch solenoid valve (911 with Tiptronic)
34	Hall signal (968 and 1995 911 Carrera)
34	Pressure regulator (911 with Tiptronic)
35	Camshaft position (968)
35	Selector lever switch (911 with Tiptronic)
36	Idle CO potentiometer (968 and 1995 911 Carrera)
36	Transmission speed sensor (911 with Tiptronic)
41	Engine control module (ECM) (968 and 1995 911 Carrera)
42	Fuel pump relay (968 and 1995 911 Carrera)
42	Control unit faulty (911 with Tiptronic)
43	Evaporative emission canister purge (EVAP) valve (968)
43	Tank ventilation relay (1995 911 Carrera)
43	Control unit faulty (911 with Tiptronic)
44	Air pump (1995 911 Carrera)
44	Control unit faulty (911 with Tiptronic)
45	Check Engine warning lamp (1995 911 Carrera)
45	Downshift protection (911 with Tiptronic)
46	Rev limiter (911 with Tiptronic)
51	Injector valve, cylinder no. 1 (968 and 1995 911 Carrera)
51	Manual program switch (911 with Tiptronic)
52	Injector valve, cylinder no. 2 (968)
52	Injector valve, cylinder no. 6 (1995 911 Carrera)
52	Up/down shift tip switch (911 with Tiptronic)
53	Injector valve, cylinder no. 3 (968)
53	Injector valve, cylinder no. 2 (1995 911 Carrera)
53	Kickdown switch (911 with Tiptronic)
54	Injector valve no. 4 (968 and 1995 911 Carrera)

Code	Fault
54	Transverse acceleration sensor (911 with Tiptronic)
55	Injector valve, cylinder no. 3 (1995 911 Carrera)
55	Speed signal 1 (ABS) (911 with Tiptronic)
56	Injector valve, cylinder no. 5 (1995 911 Carrera)
56	Combi-instrument input (911 with Tiptronic)
59	R-position switch (911 with Tiptronic)
60	Reverse light relay (911 with Tiptronic)
67	Ground and plug connections
69	Ground and plug connections

(1) *Except for codes 1000 and 1500, the second digit of all other codes can be a 2, indicating that the fault didn't exist during the last vehicle operation*

(2) *On 1991 and later models, these codes can also be displayed by* **check engine light**. *Other flashing codes are also possible but do not represent a warning regarding the check engine light*

(3) *Signal of a monitored component is not conforming with memory contents of DME control unit. The control unit recognizes that there is a faulty signal, but cannot always recognize the cause of the faulty signal*

Code	System affected	Probable cause
00000		No more fault codes or fault codes not detected
12111	Oxygen sensor adaptation fault	Air/fuel mixture during idling
12112	Oxygen sensor adaptation fault	Air/fuel mixture with engine running
12113	Idle air control (IAC) adaptation fault	Pulse ratio too low
12114	Idle air control (IAC) adaptation fault	Pulse ratio too high
12211	Incorrect battery voltage	Below 10 volts or above 16 volts
12212	Throttle position sensor	Faulty idle contacts (grounded when throttle is open)
12213	Throttle position sensor	Faulty full-throttle contacts (signal below 90 or above 160 degrees F)
12214	Coolant temperature sensor	Faulty signal (below -90 degrees or above 160 degree C)
12221	Mass Air Flow (MAF) sensor	Signal missing
12222	Idle Air Control (IAC) valve	Incorrect idle adjustment
12223	Air/fuel mixture	Too lean
12224	Air/fuel mixture	Too rich
12225	Heated oxygen sensor	Faulty sensor or preheater
12231	No ignition signal (engine switched off)	
12232	ECM	Memory voltage greater than one volt

Code	System affected	Probable cause
12233	EPROM	Incorrect EPROM (or ROM in 1992 and later models)
12241	Fuel injector	Injector malfunction (1992 and later models)
12242	Mass Air Flow (MAF) sensor	No filament burn-off (1992 and later models)
12243	Vehicle Speed Sensor (VSS)	Signal missing
12244	Transmission	No DRIVE signal to ECM (1992 and later automatics)
12245	Exhaust Gas Recirculation (EGR)	Faulty EGR operation
12251	Throttle Position (TP) sensor	Faulty sensor operation (1992 and later models)
12252	EVAP canister purge valve	Faulty valve operation (1992 and later models)
12253	Pre-ignition signal	Stays on more than 20 seconds (1992 and later models)
12254	Engine rpm signal	Signal missing (1992 and later models)

Saturn

  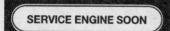

Code	Circuit or system	Probable cause
Code 11	Transaxle codes present	This indicates that there are trouble codes for the transaxle unit stored in the PCM. Read the codes after the engine code sequence on the SHIFT TO D2 light (1991 and 1992 models) or HOT light (1993 and later models).
Code 12	Diagnostic check only	Indicates the system is ready (ALDL grounded) and ready to flash the engine codes.
Code 13	Oxygen sensor circuit	Possible oxygen sensor ground loose; check the wiring and connectors from the oxygen sensor; replace the oxygen sensor.*
Code 14	Coolant sensor/high temperature	If the engine is experiencing cooling system problems, the problem must be rectified before continuing; check all the wiring and the connectors associated with the coolant temperature sensor; replace if necessary*.
Code 15	Coolant sensor/low temperature	See above, then check the wiring harness connector at the PCM for damage.
Code 17	PCM fault - Pull-up resistor	Faulty PCM resistor in PCM; replace PCM.
Code 19	6X signal fault (1992 to 1995 models)	PCM and/or ignition module may be defective; check all connections and grounds.

Code	Circuit or system	Probable cause
Code 21	Throttle position sensor voltage high	Check for a sticking or misadjusted TPS plunger; check all the wiring and connections between the TPS and the PCM; adjust or replace the TPS.*
Code 22	Throttle position sensor voltage low	Check the TPS adjustment; check the PCM connector; replace the TPS.*
Code 23	IAT circuit low	Intake air temperature sensor and/or circuit may be faulty; check sensor and replace if necessary.
Code 24	VSS circuit - no signal	A fault in this circuit should be indicated only when the vehicle is in motion. Disregard code 24 if it is set while the drive wheels are not turning (test situation) - check TPS and PCM.
Code 25	IAT circuit - temperature out of high range	Temperature range excessive causing a misreading by the PCM check IAT sensor.
Code 26 or code 27	Quad driver output fault	The PCM detects an improper voltage level on the circuit that is connected to the Quad Driver Module.
Code 32	EGR system fault	Vacuum switch shorted to ground on start-up, switch not closed after the PCM has commanded the EGR for a specified period of time or the EGR solenoid circuit is open for a specified amount of time; replace the EGR valve.*
Code 33	MAP circuit - voltage out of range high	Check the vacuum hoses from the MAP sensor - check the electrical connections at the PCM; replace the MAP sensor.
Code 34	MAP circuit - voltage out of range low	Signal voltage from MAP sensor too low - check MAP sensor circuit also TPS circuit.
Code 35	Idle air control (IAC) - rpm out of range	IAC motor possibly defective; idle control is high or low, possible PCM problem have the system diagnosed by a dealer service department.
Code 41	Ignition control circuit open or shorted	Possible defective ignition module. Also check circuit to PCM from ignition module.
Code 42	Bypass circuit - open or shorted	Bypass circuit from ignition module to PCM possibly open or shorted.
Codes 41 and 42	IC control circuit grounded/bypass open	Bypass circuit and/or ignition control circuit shorted causing no feedback pulses for the ignition cycle.
Code 43	Knock sensor circuit - open or shorted	Possible loose or defective knock sensor, also check knock sensor circuit.
Code 44	Oxygen sensor indicates lean exhaust	Check for vacuum leaks near the throttle body gasket, vacuum hoses or the intake manifold gasket. Also check for loose connections on PCM, oxygen sensor etc. Replace oxygen sensor if necessary.*
Code 45	Oxygen sensor indicates rich exhaust	Possibly rich or leaking injector, high fuel pressure or faulty TPS or MAP sensor; also, check the charcoal canister and its components for the presence of fuel; replace the oxygen sensor if necessary.*
Code 46	Power steering pressure circuit (1991 models only) - open or shorted	Possible defective power steering pressure switch, also check the circuit to the switch.

Saturn (continued)

Code	Circuit or system	Probable cause
Code 49	High idle indicates vacuum leak	Check all hoses to MAP sensor, PCV valve, brake booster, fuel pressure regulator, throttle body, intake manifold gasket and any other vacuum line.
Code 51	PCM memory error	Possible defective EEPROM, RAM or EPROM - have the vehicle diagnosed by a dealer service department or other qualified repair shop.
Code 53	System voltage error	Check charge voltage. If OK, have vehicle diagnosed by a dealer service department or other repair shop.
Code 55	A/D error	Defective PCM - have the vehicle diagnosed by a dealer service department or other qualified repair shop.
Code 58	Transmission fluid temperature too high	Sensor or signal wire grounded, radiator restricted
Code 59	Transmission fluid temperature too low	Sensor or signal wire open
Code 66 Or 67	A/C pressure sensor	Have the vehicle diagnosed by a dealer service department or other qualified repair shop
Code 81	ABS message fault	Defective ABS controller - have the vehicle diagnosed by a dealer service department or other qualified repair shop.
Code 82	PCM internal communication fault	Defective PCM - have the vehicle diagnosed by a dealer service department or other qualified repair shop.
Code 83	Low engine coolant	

Component replacement may not cure the problem in all cases. For this reason, you may want to seek professional advice before purchasing replacement parts.

Subaru

1983 carbureted models

Code	Probable cause
11, 12, 21, 22	Ignition pulse system
14, 24, 41, 42	Vacuum switches stay on or off
15, 51, 52	Solenoid valve stays on or off
23	Oxygen sensor or circuit
32	Coolant temperature sensor or circuit
33	Main system in feedback
34,43	Choke power stays on or off
42	Clutch switch or circuit

1984 through 1988 carbureted models

Code	Probable cause
11	Ignition pulse system
22	Vehicle Speed Sensor (VSS) or circuit
23	Oxygen sensor or circuit
24	Coolant temperature sensor or circuit
25	Manifold vacuum sensor or circuit (coolant temperature sensor or circuit on 1984 models)
32	Duty solenoid valve or circuit

Code	Probable cause
33	Main system in feedback
34	Back up system
42	Clutch switch or circuit
52	Solenoid valve control system
53	Fuel pump or circuit
54	Choke control system
55	Upshift control
62	Exhaust Gas Recirculation (EGR) solenoid valve control
63	Canister solenoid valve or circuit
64	Vacuum line control valve or circuit
65	Float chamber vent control valve or circuit
71, 73, 74	Ignition pulse system

1983 through 1985 carbureted models

Code	Probable cause
14	Duty solenoid or circuit (fuel control)
15	Coasting Fuel Cut (CFC) system
16	Feedback system
17	Fuel pump and automatic choke
21	Coolant temperature sensor or circuit
22	VLC solenoid valve or circuit
23	Pressure sensor or circuit
24	Idle-up solenoid valve or circuit
25	Float chamber vent solenoid valve or circuit
32	Oxygen sensor or circuit
33	Vehicle speed sensor or circuit
34	EGR solenoid or circuit
35	Canister purge control solenoid or circuit
41	Feedback system (California models)

Code	Probable cause
46	Radiator fan control
52	Clutch switch
53	Altitude compensator switch
55	EGR sensor
56	EGR system
62	Idle-up system (lighting and defogger switch)
63	Idle-up system (fan motor switch)

1984 through 1986 fuel-injected models

Code	Probable cause
11	Ignition pulse
12	Starter switch off
13	Starter switch on
14	Airflow meter or circuit
15	Atmospheric pressure switch - fixed value
16	Crank angle sensor or circuit
17	Starter switch or circuit
21	Seized air flow meter flap
22	Pressure or vacuum switches - fixed value
23	Idle switch - fixed value
24	Wide open throttle switch - fixed value
25	Throttle sensor idle switch or circuit
31	Speed sensor or circuit
32	Oxygen sensor or circuit
33	Coolant sensor or circuit
34	Abnormal aspirated air thermosensor (in airflow meter)
35	Air flow meter or EGR solenoid switch or circuit
41	Atmosphere pressure sensor or circuit
42	Fuel injector - fixed value
43, 55	KDLH control system

1984 through 1986
fuel-injected models (continued)

Code	Probable cause
46	Neutral or parking switch or circuit
47	Fuel injector
53	Fuel pump or circuit
57	Canister control system
58	Air control system
62	EGR control system
88	TBI control unit

1987 fuel-injected models

Code	Probable cause
11	Ignition pulse/crank angle sensor
12	Starter switch or circuit
13	Crank angle sensor or circuit
14	Injectors 1 and 2
15	Injectors 3 and 4
21	Coolant temperature sensor or circuit
22	Knock sensor or circuit
23	Air flow meter or circuit
24	Air control
31	Throttle sensor or circuit
32	Oxygen sensor or circuit
33	Vehicle Speed Sensor (VSS) or circuit
34	EGR solenoid valve stuck on or off
35	Purge control solenoid or circuit
41	Lean fuel mixture indicated
42	Idle switch or circuit
45	Kick-down relay or circuit
51	Neutral switch or circuit
61	Parking switch or circuit

1988 and later models with
Single-Point Fuel Injection

Code	Probable cause
11	Crank angle sensor or circuit
12	Starter switch or circuit
13	Crank angle sensor or circuit
14	Fuel injector - abnormal output
21	Coolant temperature sensor or circuit
23	Air flow meter or circuit
24	Air control valve or circuit
31	Throttle sensor or circuit
32	Oxygen sensor or circuit
33	Vehicle Speed Sensor (VSS) or circuit
34	EGR solenoid or circuit
35	Purge control solenoid or circuit
42	Idle switch or circuit
45	Kick-down control relay or circuit
51	Neutral switch continuously in the on position
55	EGR temperature sensor or circuit
61	Parking switch or circuit

1988 and later models with
Multi-Point Fuel Injection

Code	Probable cause
11	Crank angle sensor or circuit
12	Starter switch or circuit
13	Cam position sensor or circuit (TDC sensor on Justy)
14	Fuel injector no. 1 (Legacy, Impreza, Justy, SVX)
14	Fuel injector nos. 1 and 2 (XT, Loyale, GL, DL)
15	Fuel injector no. 2 (Legacy, Impreza, Justy, SVX)
15	Fuel injector nos. 3 and 4 (Loyale, GL, DL)
15	Fuel injector nos. 5 and 6 (XT6)

Code	Probable cause
16	Fuel injector no. 3 (Legacy, Impreza, Justy, SVX)
16	Fuel injector nos. 3 and 4 (XT)
17	Fuel injector no. 4 (Legacy, Impreza, SVX)
17	Fuel injector nos. 1 and 2 (XT6)
18	Fuel injector no. 5 (SVX)
19	Fuel injector no. 6 (SVX)
21	Coolant temperature sensor or circuit
22	Knock sensor or circuit (right side on SVX)
23	Airflow meter or circuit (exc. Justy)
23	Pressure sensor (Justy)
24	Air control valve or circuit (exc. Justy)
24	Idle Speed Control solenoid valve (Justy)
25	Fuel injector nos. 3 and 4 (XT6)
26	Air temperature sensor (Justy)
28	Knock sensor no. 2 (SVX, left side)
29	Crank angle sensor (SVX, no. 2)
31	Throttle position sensor or circuit
32	Oxygen sensor or circuit (no. 1, right side, on SVX)
33	Vehicle Speed Sensor (VSS) or circuit
34	EGR solenoid valve
35	Canister purge solenoid or circuit
36	Air suction solenoid valve (Impreza)

Code	Probable cause
36	Igniter circuit (Justy)
37	Oxygen sensor (no. 2, left side, SVX)
38	Engine torque control (SVX)
41	Air/fuel adaptive control
42	Idle switch or circuit
43	Throttle switch (Justy)
44	Wastegate duty solenoid (turbo)
45	Pressure sensor duty solenoid (turbo)
45	Atmospheric pressure sensor or circuit (non-turbo)
49	Airflow sensor
51	Neutral switch (MT); inhibitor switch (AT)
52	Parking brake switch (exc. Justy)
52	Clutch switch (Justy)
55	EGR temperature sensor
56	EGR system
61	Parking brake switch (Loyale)
61	Fuel tank pressure control solenoid valve (Impreza)
62	Fuel temperature sensor (Impreza)
62	Electric load signal (Justy)
63	Fuel tank pressure sensor (Impreza)
63	Blower fan switch (Justy)
65	Vacuum pressure sensor

Toyota

CHECK   MIL   SERVICE ENGINE SOON   CHECK   CHECK ENGINE LIGHT

Camry (1983 through 1986 models), Corolla (1987 models), Pick-ups and 4-Runner (1984 through 1987 models)

Code	Probable cause	Code	Probable cause
		3	Air Flow Meter Signal (1984 Trucks, 1983 through 1985 Camry)
1	Normal	3	No ignition signal from igniter
2	Air Flow Meter Signal	4	Coolant temperature sensor or circuit

Code	Probable cause	Code	Probable cause
5	Oxygen sensor or circuit	11	Switch signal - air conditioning, TPS or Neutral start
6	No ignition signal (1984 trucks, 1983 through 1985 Camry)	11	ECU main relay (Cressida, Supra, Celica 3S-GE)
6	RPM signal (no signal to ECU)	12	Knock sensor or circuit (distributor or circuit on Cressida, Supra, Celica 3S-GE)
7	Throttle Position Sensor (TPS) or circuit	13	Knock sensor/CPU (ECU) faulty
8	Intake Air Temperature sensor or circuit	14	Turbocharger pressure (22R-TE/Turbo 22R models) - over-boost (abnormalities in air flow meter may also be detected)
9	Vehicle Speed Sensor (VSS) or circuit		
10	Starter signal	14	Ignitor (Cressida, Supra, Celica 3S-GE)

Camry (1987 through 1990 models), all other models (1988 through 1990)

Code	Probable cause
11	Momentary interruption in power supply to ECU
12	RPM signal/no NE or G Signal to ECU within several seconds after engine is cranked
13	RPM Signal/no signal to ECU when engine speed is above 1500 RPM
14	No ignition signal to ECU
21	Oxygen sensor circuit or oxygen sensor heater circuit failure
22	Coolant temperature sensor circuit
23/24	Intake air temperature circuit
25	Air fuel ratio - lean condition indicated
26	Air fuel ratio - rich condition indicated
27	Oxygen sensor circuit (open or shorted)
31	Air flow meter or circuit
31	1989 and 1990 Corolla - vacuum sensor signal
32	Air flow meter or circuit
41	Throttle position sensor or circuit
42	Vehicle Speed Sensor (VSS) or circuit
43	Starter signal/no start signal to ECU
51	Switch signal/Neutral start switch off or air conditioning on during diagnostic check
51	Switch signal - no IDL signal, NSW or air conditioning signal to ECU (1988 through 1990 Corolla, 1988-1/2 through 1990 Camry models)

Code	Probable cause
52	Knock sensor circuit
53	Knock sensor signal/faulty ECU
71	Exhaust Gas Recirculation (EGR) system malfunction

All models (1991 on)

Code	Circuit or system	Diagnosis	Probable cause
Code 1	Normal	This appears when none of the other codes are identified.	
Code 11	ECM	Interruption of power supply to ECM	
Code 12	RPM signal	No "Ne" signal to the ECM within several seconds after the engine is cranked. No "G" signal to the ECM two times in succession when engine speed is between 500 rpm and 4000 rpm.	Distributor circuit Distributor Igniter Igniter circuit Starter circuit ECM
Code 13	RPM signal	No "Ne" signal to the ECM engine speed is above 1500 rpm.	Distributor circuit Distributor Igniter Igniter circuit ECM
Code 14	Ignition signal	No "IGN" signal to the ECM 8 times in succession.	Igniter Igniter circuit ECM
Code 16	Transmission ECM	Fault in ECM signal.	Transmission ECM ECM
Code 21	Main oxygen sensor and heater	Problem in the main oxygen sensor circuit. Open or Short in the main oxygen heater circuit	Main oxygen sensor circuit ECM Main oxygen sensor heater sensor
Code 22	Coolant temperature sensor	Open or short in the coolant sensor circuit	Coolant temperature sensor circuit Coolant temperature sensor ECM
Code 23 or Code 24	Intake air temperature sensor	Open or short in the intake air sensor circuit.	Intake air temperature sensor Intake air temperature sensor circuit
Code 25	Air/fuel ratio lean malfunction	The air/fuel ratio feedback correction value or adaptive control value continues at the upper (lean) or lower (rich) limit for a certain period of time.	Injector circuit Oxygen sensor or circuit ECM Oxygen sensor Fuel line pressure (injector blockage or leakage) Air temperature sensor or circuit Air leak Air flow meter Air intake system Ignition system

Toyota (continued)

All models (1991 on) (continued)

Code	Circuit or system	Diagnosis	Probable cause
Code 26	Air/fuel ratio rich malfunction	The air/fuel ratio is overly rich. Open or short circuit in the oxygen sensor.	Injector or Injector circuit Coolant temperature sensor or circuit Air temperature sensor or circuit Airflow meter Oxygen sensor or circuit Cold start injector ECM
Code 27	Sub-oxygen sensor	Open or shorted circuit in the sub-oxygen sensor circuit.	Sub-oxygen sensor circuit ECM
Code 28	No. 2 Oxygen sensor signal or heater signal	Open or short in Oxygen sensor circuit or in sensor heater circuit	Oxygen sensor Oxygen signal or heater Sensor heater circuit
Code 31	Airflow meter	Open or short circuit in Vc to E2.	Airflow meter circuit
Code 31	MAP sensor, vacuum sensor signal	Open or short circuit in Vc to E2.	MAP sensor-to-ECM circuit
Code 31	Volume Air Flow (VAF) sensor or circuit (1995)	No VAF signal for 2 seconds after starting	VAF sensor or circuit
Code 32	Airflow meter	Open or short circuit in Vs to Vc or E2.	Airflow meter circuit/ECM
Code 34/35	Turbocharger	Pressure abnormal	Open or short circuit in turbocharger pressure or BARO sensor(s)
Code 35	High altitude compensation (HAC) sensor	Incorrect signal	Open or short in HAC sensor circuit
Code 36	Turbocharger (1992 through 1994)	Pressure sensor signal circuit	Open or short for at least 0.5 seconds in turbocharging pressure sensor
Code 41	Throttle position sensor	Open or short in the throttle position sensor circuit.	Throttle position sensor or circuit ECM
Code 42	Vehicle speed sensor	No "SPD" signal for 8 seconds when the engine speed is above 2000 rpm.	Vehicle speed sensor or circuit sensorECM
Code 43	Starter signal	No "STA" signal to the ECM until engine speed reaches 800 rpm with the vehicle not moving.	Starter signal circuit Ignition switch Main relay switch ECM
Code 47	TPS signal	Sub-throttle position sensor	Open or short circuit in sub-throttle position sensor

Code	Circuit or system	Diagnosis	Probable cause
Code 51	Switch condition signal	No IDL signal or no NSW signal or A/C signal to the ECM when the test connector E1 and TE1 are connected.	A/C switch or circuit A/C amplifier Neutral start switch (A/T) Throttle position sensor Throttle position sensor circuit
Code 52	Knock sensor signal	Open or short circuit in knock sensor circuit.	Knock sensor ECM
Code 53	Knock control signal	Problem with knock control system in ECM.	ECM
Code 55	Knock control signal	Open or short circuit in knock sensor circuit	Knock sensor ECM
Code 71	EGR	EGR gas temperature signal is too low.	EGR system (EGR valve, hoses, etc.) EGR gas temperature sensor or circuit . Vacuum switching valve for the EGR circuit ECM
Code 72	Fuel cut solenoid or circuit	Circuit open	Faulty solenoid or circuit
Code 78	Fuel pump	Open or short circuit in fuel pump control circuit.	Fuel pump electronic control unit (ECM) Fuel pump control circuit
Code 81	Transmission to ECM	Open in ECT1 circuit for at least 2-seconds.	ECM Transmission control module (TCM)
Code 83	Transmission to ECM	Open in ESA1 circuit for 1/2-second after the engine idles at least 1/2-second.	ECM Transmission control module (TCM)
Code 84	Transmission to ECM	Open in ESA1 circuit for 1/2-second after the engine idles at least 1/2-second.	ECM Transmission control module (TCM)
Code 85	Transmission to ECM	Open in ESA1 circuit for 1/2-second after the engine idles at least 1/2-second.	ECM Transmission control module (TCM)

Volkswagen

  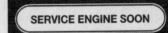 CHECK ENGINE LIGHT

Code	Location or description of fault	Probable cause
1111	Control unit	a) Defective control unit
1231	Speed sender	a) Open circuit b) Faulty sender
1232	Throttle actuator solenoid	a) Open or short circuit b) Faulty solenoid

Code	Location or description of fault	Probable cause
2111	Engine speed sensor	a) Open circuit b) Faulty sender
2112	Ignition reference sensor	a) Open circuit b) Faulty sensor
2113	Hall sender	a) No signal or faulty signal from Hall sender
2121	Idle switch	a) Open circuit or short to ground b) Switch faulty or misadjusted
2123	Full throttle switch	a) Open circuit b) Faulty switch
2141	Knock sensor	a) Engine knock b) Fuel of incorrect octane c) Incorrect ignition timing d) Damaged shield on knock sensor wiring
2142	Knock sensor	a) Open or short circuit in knock sensor wiring b) Faulty knock sensor c) Faulty control unit
2142 (Eurovan)	Transmission control module	a) Open circuit to control module b) Faulty module
2144	Knock sensor II	a) Open or short circuit in knock sensor wiring b) Faulty knock sensor c) Faulty control unit
2212	Throttle Position Sensor	a) Open or short circuit to ground or battery voltage b) Faulty sensor
2214	Maximum rpm exceeded	a) Engine rpm exceeded fuel injection cut-off point b) Interference on signal wire
2222 (Eurovan)	Manifold Absolute Pressure	a) No vacuum to ECM (check the hose) b) Faulty ECM
2231	Idle speed stabilizer system has exceeded adaptive range	a) Throttle valve basic adjustment incorrect b) Incorrect ignition timing c) Evaporative emission control system faulty d) Intake air leaks
2232	Air flow sensor Potentiometer	a) Open circuit or short to ground b) Potentiometer faulty
2234	System voltage out of range	a) Check battery b) Check charging system
2242	Throttle valve potentiometer	a) Open or short circuit b) Faulty potentiometer

Code	Location or description of fault	Probable cause
2243	Fuel consumption signal	a) Short circuit to battery voltage in instrument panel
2312	Coolant temperature sensor	a) Faulty sensor b) Open circuit or short to ground
2314	Transmission control signal	a) Short to ground in transmission control module circuit
2214	Full consumption signal	
2322	Intake air	a) Sensor faulty
2323	Airflow sensor signal is missing	a) Open circuit b) Faulty sensor
2324	Mass Airflow Sensor	a) Open or short circuit b) Faulty sensor
2341	Oxygen sensor control range exceeded	a) Idle mixture (%CO) incorrectly adjusted b) Faulty oxygen sensor wiring c) Leaking cold-start valve d) Evaporative emission control system faulty e) Intake air leaks
2342	Oxygen sensor system (faulty signal or exceeding adjustment range)	a) Open circuit b) Faulty oxygen sensor c) Incorrect idle speed d) Intake air leaks (leaking
2411	Exhaust Gas Recirculation (EGR) system (California cars only)	a) Intake air temperature sensor faulty b) Open circuit or short circuit to ground c) EGR system faulty or plugged
2412	Intake air temperature sensor	a) Open or short circuit b) Faulty sensor
2413	Fuel mixture out of limit	a) Fuel pressure too low or high b) Fuel injector(s) faulty c) Leak in intake or exhaust system d) Faulty EGR frequency valve
3434	Heated oxygen sensor relay	a) Open or short circuit b) Faulty relay
4312	EGR frequency valve	a) Open or short circuit b) Faulty valve
4332	ECM	a) Connectors at ECM loose b) Faulty ECM
4343	EVAP frequency valve	a) Open or short circuit b) Faulty valve
4411 (exc. Eurovan)	Injector no. 1	a) Open or short circuit b) Faulty injector

Volkswagen (continued)

Code	Location or description of fault	Probable cause
4411 (Eurovan)	Injector driver circuit	a) Open or short circuit b) Faulty injector
4412	Injector no. 2	a) Open or short circuit b) Faulty injector
4413	Injector no. 3	a) Open or short circuit b) Faulty injector
4414	Injector no. 4	a) Open or short circuit b) Faulty injector
4421 (VR6)	Injector no. 5	a) Open or short circuit b) Faulty injector
4422 (VR6)	Injector no. 6	a) Open or short circuit b) Faulty injector
4431	Idle air control valve	a) Open circuit or short circuit to ground b) Control unit faulty c) Faulty IAC valve
4433	Fuel pump relay	a) Open or short circuit b) Faulty relay
4444	No faults stored in memory	
0000	End of code output sequence	

Volvo

 CHECK MIL 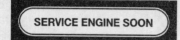 SERVICE ENGINE SOON CHECK | CHECK ENGINE LIGHT

Code	Probable cause
1-1-1	No Faults
1-1-2	ECU fault
1-1-3	Fuel Injectors
1-1-3 (1994 on)	Heated oxygen sensor at maximum enrichment unit
1-1-5	Injector no. 1 – open or short circuit
1-2-1	Mass airflow signal missing or faulty (MAF) or air pressure sensor
1-2-2	Air temperature sensor signal missing or faulty

Code	Probable cause
1-2-3	Coolant temperature sensor signal faulty or missing
1-2-5	Injector no. 2 open or short circuit
1-3-1	Ignition system RPM signal open or short circuit
1-3-2	Battery voltage out of range
1-3-3	Throttle switch signal (incorrect idle setting)
1-3-5	Injector no. 3 open or short circuit
1-4-2	ECU faulty
1-4-3	Knock sensor signal missing or sensor defective
1-4-4	Fuel system load signal (missing or defective)
1-4-5	Injector no. 4 open or short circuit
1-5-3	Rear heated oxygen sensor signal open or short circuit
1-5-4	EGR system - leakage or excessive flow
1-5-5	Injector no. 5 open or short circuit
2-1-2	Oxygen Sensor Signal (front sensor on 1994 and later models) faulty or missing
2-1-3	Throttle switch signal (incorrect wide open setting)
2-1-4	Ignition rpm signal erratic
2-2-1	Lambda (oxygen sensor) running rich at part throttle
2-2-1	Heated oxygen sensor running rich at part throttle
2-2-2	Main relay signal missing or faulty
2-2-3	Idle valve signal missing or faulty
2-2-4	Coolant temperature sensor signal missing or faulty
2-2-5	A/C pressure sensor signal 3 sensor or circuit faulty
2-3-1	Lambda adjustment
2-3-1 (1994 on)	Heated oxygen sensor (mixture too lean under part throttle)
2-3-2	Lambda adjustment
2-3-2 (1994 on)	Adaptive heated oxygen sensor control lean or rich
2-3-3	Idle valve - closed, or intake air leak
2-3-4	Throttle switch signal missing
2-4-1	EGR malfunction
2-4-5	Idle Air Control valve - closing signal
3-1-1	Speedometer Signal
3-1-2	Knock/Fuel Enrichment signal missing
3-1-4	Camshaft position signal missing or defective

Code	Probable cause
3-1-5	EVAP emission control system
3-2-1	Cold start valve - signal missing or circuit shorted
3-2-2	Airflow meter hot wire burn-off signal missing
3-2-4	Camshaft position signal erratic
3-2-5	ECU memory failure
3-3-5	TCM request for MIL (CHECK ENGINE light)
3-4-2	A/C blocking relay high current
4-1-1	Throttle switch signal faulty or missing
4-1-3	EGR temperature sensor signal incorrect or missing
4-1-4	Turbo boost regulation
4-1-6	Turbo boost reduction from TCM – faulty TCM circuit
4-2-1	Boost pressure sensor in control – faulty
4-2-3	Throttle position sensor signal faulty or missing
4-2-5	Temperature warning level no. 1
4-3-1	EGR temperature sensor faulty or missing
4-3-2	High temperature warning inside ECU
4-3-3	No rear knock sensor signal
4-3-5	Front heated oxygen sensor - slow response
4-3-6	Rear heated oxygen sensor compensation
4-4-3	Catalytic converter efficiency – faulty converter
4-4-4	Acceleration sensor signal – sensor or circuit faulty
4-5-1	Misfire, cylinder no. 1
4-5-2	Misfire, cylinder no. 2
4-5-3	Misfire, cylinder no. 3
4-5-4	Misfire, cylinder no. 4
4-5-5	Misfire, cylinder no. 5
5-1-1	Adaptive oxygen sensor control, provides leaner mixture at idle
5-1-2	Oxygen sensor at maximum lean running limit
5-1-3	High temperature warning inside ECU
5-1-4	Engine cooling fan - low speed signal faulty
5-2-1	Oxygen sensor preheating, front
5-2-2	Oxygen sensor preheating, rear

Code	Probable cause
5-3-1	Power stage, group A – fuel injectors evap canister purge solenoid, circuit or ECU
5-3-2	Power stage; group B – fuel injectors, EVAP canister, purge solenoid circuit or ECU
5-3-3	Power stage; group C - fuel injectors, EVAP canister, purge solenoid circuit or ECU
5-3-4	Power stage; group D - fuel injectors, EVAP canister, purge solenoid circuit or ECU
5-3-5	TC wastegate control valve signal – open or short circuit
5-4-1	EVAP canister purge solenoid signal – faulty solenoid or open or circuit short
5-4-2	Misfire on more than one cylinder
5-4-3	Misfire on at least one cylinder
5-4-4	Misfire on more than one cylinder, catalytic converter damage
5-4-5	Misfire on at least one cylinder, catalytic converter damage
5-5-1	Misfire on cylinder no. 1, catalytic converter damage
5-5-2	Misfire on cylinder no. 2, catalytic converter damage
5-5-3	Misfire on cylinder no. 3, catalytic converter damage
5-5-4	Misfire on cylinder no. 4, catalytic converter damage
5-5-5	Misfire on cylinder no. 5, catalytic converter damage

OBD II Powertrain Diagnostic Trouble Codes

Note: *The following list of OBD II trouble codes is a generic list applicable to all models equipped with an OBD II system, although not all codes apply to all models.*

P0100	Mass air flow or volume air flow circuit malfunction
P0101	Mass air flow or volume air flow circuit, range or performance problem
P0102	Mass air flow or volume air flow circuit, low input
P0103	Mass air flow or volume air flow circuit, high input
P0104	Mass air flow or volume air flow circuit, intermittent
P0105	Manifold absolute pressure or barometric pressure circuit malfunction
P0106	Manifold absolute pressure or barometric pressure circuit, range or performance problem
P0107	Manifold absolute pressure or barometric pressure circuit, low input
P0108	Manifold absolute pressure or barometric pressure circuit, high input
P0109	Manifold absolute pressure or barometric pressure circuit, intermittent
P0110	Intake air temperature circuit malfunction
P0111	Intake air temperature circuit, range or performance problem

P0112	Intake air temperature circuit, low input
P0113	Intake air temperature circuit, high input
P0114	Intake air temperature circuit, intermittent
P0117	Engine coolant temperature circuit, low input
P0118	Engine coolant temperature circuit, high input
P0119	Engine coolant temperature circuit, intermittent
P0120	Throttle position or pedal position sensor/switch circuit malfunction
P0121	Throttle position or pedal position sensor/switch circuit, range or performance problem
P0122	Throttle position or pedal position sensor/switch circuit, low input
P0123	Throttle position or pedal position sensor/switch circuit, high input
P0124	Throttle position or pedal position sensor/switch circuit, intermittent
P0125	Insufficient coolant temperature for closed loop fuel control
P0126	Insufficient coolant temperature for stable operation
P0130	O2 sensor circuit malfunction (cylinder bank no. 1, sensor no. 1)
P0131	O2 sensor circuit, low voltage (cylinder bank no. 1, sensor no. 1)
P0132	O2 sensor circuit, high voltage (cylinder bank no. 1, sensor no. 1)
P0133	O2 sensor circuit, slow response (cylinder bank no. 1, sensor no. 1)
P0134	O2 sensor circuit - no activity detected (cylinder bank no. 1, sensor no. 1)
P0135	O2 sensor heater circuit malfunction (cylinder bank no. 1, sensor no. 1)
P0136	O2 sensor circuit malfunction (cylinder bank no. 1, sensor no. 2)
P0137	O2 sensor circuit, low voltage (cylinder bank no. 1, sensor no. 2)
P0138	O2 sensor circuit, high voltage (cylinder bank no. 1, sensor no. 2)
P0139	O2 sensor circuit, slow response (cylinder bank no. 1, sensor no. 2)
P0140	O2 sensor circuit - no activity detected (cylinder bank no. 1, sensor no. 2)
P0141	O2 sensor heater circuit malfunction (cylinder bank no. 1, sensor no. 2)
P0142	O2 sensor circuit malfunction (cylinder bank no. 1, sensor no. 3)
P0143	O2 sensor circuit, low voltage (cylinder bank no. 1, sensor no. 3)
P0144	O2 sensor circuit, high voltage (cylinder bank no. 1, sensor no. 3)
P0145	O2 sensor circuit, slow response (cylinder bank no. 1, sensor no. 3)
P0146	O2 sensor circuit - no activity detected (cylinder bank no. 1, sensor no. 3)
P0147	O2 sensor heater circuit malfunction (cylinder bank no. 1, sensor 3)
P0150	O2 sensor circuit malfunction (cylinder bank no. 2, sensor no. 1
P0151	O2 sensor circuit, low voltage (cylinder bank no. 2, sensor no. 1)
P0152	O2 sensor circuit, high voltage (cylinder bank no. 2, sensor no. 1)

P0153	O2 sensor circuit, slow response (cylinder bank no. 2, sensor no. 1)
P0154	O2 sensor circuit - no activity detected (cylinder bank no. 2, sensor no. 1)
P0155	O2 sensor heater circuit malfunction (cylinder bank no. 2, sensor no. 1)
P0156	O2 sensor circuit malfunction (cylinder bank no. 2, sensor no. 2)
P0157	O2 sensor circuit, low voltage (cylinder bank no. 2, sensor no. 2)
P0158	O2 sensor circuit, high voltage (cylinder bank no. 2, sensor no. 2)
P0159	O2 sensor circuit, slow response (cylinder bank no. 2, sensor no. 2)
P0160	O2 sensor circuit - no activity detected (cylinder bank no. 2, sensor no. 2)
P0161	O2 sensor heater circuit malfunction (cylinder bank no. 2, sensor no. 2)
P0162	O2 sensor circuit malfunction (cylinder bank no. 2, sensor no. 3)
P0163	O2 sensor circuit, low voltage (cylinder bank no. 2, sensor no. 3)
P0164	O2 sensor circuit, high voltage (cylinder bank no. 2, sensor no. 3)
P0165	O2 sensor circuit, slow response (cylinder bank no. 2, sensor no. 3)
P0166	O2 sensor circuit - no activity detected (cylinder bank no. 2, sensor no. 3)
P0167	O2 sensor heater circuit malfunction (cylinder bank no. 2, sensor 3)
P0170	Fuel trim malfunction (cylinder bank no. 1)
P0171	System too lean (cylinder bank no. 1)
P0172	System too rich (cylinder bank no. 1)
P0173	Fuel trim malfunction (cylinder bank no. 2)
P0174	System too lean (cylinder bank no. 2)
P0175	System too rich (cylinder bank no. 2)
P0176	Fuel composition sensor circuit malfunction
P0177	Fuel composition sensor circuit, range or performance problem
P0178	Fuel composition sensor circuit, low input
P0179	Fuel composition sensor circuit, high input
P0180	Fuel temperature sensor A circuit malfunction
P0181	Fuel temperature sensor A circuit, range or performance problem
P0182	Fuel temperature sensor A circuit, low input
P0183	Fuel temperature sensor A circuit, high input
P0184	Fuel temperature sensor A circuit, intermittent
P0185	Fuel temperature sensor B circuit malfunction
P0186	Fuel temperature sensor B circuit, range or performance problem
P0187	Fuel temperature sensor B circuit, low input
P0188	Fuel temperature sensor B circuit, high input
P0189	Fuel temperature sensor B circuit, intermittent
P0190	Fuel rail pressure sensor circuit malfunction

OBD II Powertrain Diagnostic Trouble Codes (continued)

P0191	Fuel rail pressure sensor circuit, range or performance problem
P0192	Fuel rail pressure sensor circuit, low input
P0193	Fuel rail pressure sensor circuit, high input
P0194	Fuel rail pressure sensor circuit, intermittent
P0195	Engine oil temperature sensor malfunction
P0196	Fuel rail pressure sensor circuit, range or performance problem
P0197	Fuel rail pressure sensor circuit, low input
P0198	Fuel rail pressure sensor circuit, high input
P0199	Fuel rail pressure sensor circuit, intermittent
P0200	Injector circuit malfunction
P0201	Injector circuit malfunction - cylinder no. 1
P0202	Injector circuit malfunction - cylinder no. 2
P0203	Injector circuit malfunction - cylinder no. 3
P0204	Injector circuit malfunction - cylinder no. 4
P0205	Injector circuit malfunction - cylinder no. 5
P0206	Injector circuit malfunction - cylinder no. 6
P0207	Injector circuit malfunction - cylinder no. 7
P0208	Injector circuit malfunction - cylinder no. 8
P0209	Injector circuit malfunction - cylinder no. 9
P0210	Injector circuit malfunction - cylinder no. 10
P0211	Injector circuit malfunction - cylinder no. 11
P0212	Injector circuit malfunction - cylinder no. 12
P0213	Cold start injector no. 1 malfunction
P0214	Cold start injector no. 2 malfunction
P0215	Engine shut-off solenoid malfunction
P0216	Injection timing control circuit malfunction
P0217	Engine overheating condition
P0218	Transmission overheating condition
P0219	Engine overspeed condition
P0220	Throttle position or pedal position sensor/switch B circuit malfunction
P0221	Throttle position or pedal position sensor/switch B, range or performance problem
P0222	Throttle position or pedal position sensor/switch B circuit, low input
P0223	Throttle position or pedal position sensor/switch B circuit, high input
P0224	Throttle position or pedal position sensor/switch B circuit, intermittent

P0225	Throttle position or pedal position sensor/switch C circuit malfunction
P0226	Throttle position or pedal position sensor/switch C, range or performance problem
P0227	Throttle position or pedal position sensor/switch C circuit, low input
P0228	Throttle position or pedal position sensor/switch C circuit, high input
P0229	Throttle position or pedal position sensor/switch C circuit, intermittent
P0230	Fuel pump primary circuit malfunction
P0231	Fuel pump secondary circuit, low
P0232	Fuel pump secondary circuit, high
P0233	Fuel pump secondary circuit, intermittent
P0234	Engine overboost condition
P0235	Turbocharger boost sensor A circuit malfunction
P0236	Turbocharger boost sensor A circuit, range or performance problem
P0237	Turbocharger boost sensor A circuit, low
P0238	Turbocharger boost sensor A circuit, high
P0239	Turbocharger boost sensor B circuit malfunction
P0240	Turbocharger boost sensor B circuit, range or performance problem
P0241	Turbocharger boost sensor B circuit, low
P0242	Turbocharger boost sensor B circuit, high
P0243	Turbocharger wastegate solenoid A malfunction
P0244	Turbocharger wastegate solenoid A, range or performance problem
P0245	Turbocharger wastegate solenoid A, low
P0246	Turbocharger wastegate solenoid A, high
P0247	Turbocharger wastegate solenoid B malfunction
P0248	Turbocharger wastegate solenoid B, range or performance problem
P0249	Turbocharger wastegate solenoid B, low
P0250	Turbocharger wastegate solenoid B, high
P0251	Injection pump fuel metering control A malfunction (cam/rotor/injector)
P0252	Injection pump fuel metering control A, range or performance problem (cam/rotor/injector)
P0253	Injection pump fuel metering control A, low (cam/rotor/injector)
P0254	Injection pump fuel metering control A, high (cam/rotor/injector)
P0255	Injection pump fuel metering control A, intermittent (cam/rotor/injector)
P0256	Injection pump fuel metering control B malfunction (cam/rotor/injector)
P0257	Injection pump fuel metering control B, range or performance problem (cam/rotor/injector)
P0258	Injection pump fuel metering control B, low (cam/rotor/injector)
P0259	Injection pump fuel metering control B, high (cam/rotor/injector)
P0260	Injection pump fuel metering control B, intermittent (cam/rotor/injector)

OBD II Powertrain Diagnostic Trouble Codes (continued)

P0261	Cylinder no. 1 injector circuit, low
P0262	Cylinder no. 1 injector circuit, high
P0263	Cylinder no. 1 contribution/balance fault
P0264	Cylinder no. 2 injector circuit, low
P0265	Cylinder no. 2 injector circuit, high
P0266	Cylinder no. 2 contribution/balance fault
P0267	Cylinder no. 3 injector circuit, low
P0268	Cylinder no. 3 injector circuit, high
P0269	Cylinder no. 3 contribution/balance fault
P0270	Cylinder no. 4 injector circuit, low
P0271	Cylinder no. 4 injector circuit, high
P0272	Cylinder no. 4 contribution/balance fault
P0273	Cylinder no. 5 injector circuit, low
P0274	Cylinder no. 5 injector circuit, high
P0275	Cylinder no. 5 contribution/balance fault
P0276	Cylinder no. 6 injector circuit, low
P0277	Cylinder no. 6 injector circuit, high
P0278	Cylinder no. 6 contribution/balance fault
P0279	Cylinder no. 7 injector circuit, low
P0280	Cylinder no. 7 injector circuit, high
P0281	Cylinder no. 7 contribution/balance fault
P0282	Cylinder no. 8 injector circuit, low
P0283	Cylinder no. 8 injector circuit, high
P0284	Cylinder no. 8 contribution/balance fault
P0285	Cylinder no. 9 injector circuit, low
P0286	Cylinder no. 9 injector circuit, high
P0287	Cylinder no. 9 contribution/balance fault
P0288	Cylinder no. 10 injector circuit, low
P0289	Cylinder no. 10 injector circuit, high
P0290	Cylinder no. 10 contribution/balance fault
P0291	Cylinder no. 11 injector circuit, low
P0292	Cylinder no. 11 injector circuit, high
P0293	Cylinder no. 11 contribution/balance fault
P0294	Cylinder no. 12 injector circuit, low

P0295	Cylinder no. 12 injector circuit, high
P0296	Cylinder no. 12 contribution/balance fault
P0300	Random/multiple cylinder misfire detected
P0301	Cylinder no. 1misfire detected
P0302	Cylinder no. 2 misfire detected
P0303	Cylinder no. 3 misfire detected
P0304	Cylinder no. 4 misfire detected
P0305	Cylinder no. 5 misfire detected
P0306	Cylinder no. 6 misfire detected
P0307	Cylinder no. 7 misfire detected
P0308	Cylinder no. 8 misfire detected
P0309	Cylinder no. 9 misfire detected
P0310	Cylinder no. 10 misfire detected
P0311	Cylinder no. 11 misfire detected
P0312	Cylinder no. 12 misfire detected
P0320	Ignition/distributor engine speed input circuit malfunction
P0321	Ignition/distributor engine speed input circuit, range or performance problem
P0322	Ignition/distributor engine speed input circuit, no signal
P0323	Ignition/distributor engine speed input circuit, intermittent
P0325	Knock sensor no. 1 circuit malfunction (cylinder bank no. 1 or single sensor)
P0326	Knock sensor no. 1 circuit, range or performance problem (cylinder bank no. 1 or single sensor)
P0327	Knock sensor no. 1 circuit, low input (cylinder bank no. 1 or single sensor)
P0328	Knock sensor no. 1 circuit, high input (cylinder bank no. 1 or single sensor)
P0329	Knock sensor no. 1 circuit, intermittent (cylinder bank no. 1 or single sensor)
P0330	Knock sensor no. 2 circuit malfunction (cylinder bank no. 2)
P0331	Knock sensor no. 2 circuit, range or performance problem (cylinder bank no. 2)
P0332	Knock sensor no. 2 circuit, low input (cylinder bank no. 2)
P0333	Knock sensor no. 2 circuit, high input (cylinder bank no. 2)
P0334	Knock sensor no. 2 circuit, intermittent (cylinder bank no. 2)
P0335	Crankshaft position sensor A circuit malfunction
P0336	Crankshaft position sensor A circuit, range or performance problem
P0337	Crankshaft position sensor A circuit, low input
P0338	Crankshaft position sensor A circuit, high input
P0339	Crankshaft position sensor A circuit, intermittent
P0340	Camshaft position sensor circuit malfunction

P0341	Camshaft position sensor circuit, range or performance problem
P0342	Camshaft position sensor circuit, low input
P0343	Camshaft position sensor circuit, high input
P0344	Camshaft position sensor circuit, intermittent
P0350	Ignition coil primary or secondary circuit malfunction
P0351	Ignition coil A primary or secondary circuit malfunction
P0352	Ignition coil B primary or secondary circuit malfunction
P0353	Ignition coil C primary or secondary circuit malfunction
P0354	Ignition coil D primary or secondary circuit malfunction
P0355	Ignition coil E primary or secondary circuit malfunction
P0356	Ignition coil F primary or secondary circuit malfunction
P0357	Ignition coil G primary or secondary circuit malfunction
P0358	Ignition coil H primary or secondary circuit malfunction
P0359	Ignition coil I primary or secondary circuit malfunction
P0360	Ignition coil J primary or secondary circuit malfunction
P0361	Ignition coil K primary or secondary circuit malfunction
P0362	Ignition coil L primary or secondary circuit malfunction
P0370	Timing reference high resolution signal A malfunction
P0371	Timing reference high resolution signal A, too many pulses
P0372	Timing reference high resolution signal A, too few pulses
P0373	Timing reference high resolution signal A, intermittent/erratic pulses
P0374	Timing reference high resolution signal A, no pulse
P0375	Timing reference high resolution signal B malfunction
P0376	Timing reference high resolution signal B, too many pulses
P0377	Timing reference high resolution signal B, too few pulses
P0378	Timing reference high resolution signal B, intermittent/erratic pulses
P0379	Timing reference high resolution signal B, no pulse
P0380	Glow plug/heater circuit A malfunction
P0381	Glow plug/heater indicator circuit malfunction
P0382	Glow plug/heater circuit B malfunction
P0385	Crankshaft position sensor B circuit malfunction
P0386	Crankshaft position sensor B circuit, range or performance problem
P0387	Crankshaft position sensor B circuit, low input
P0388	Crankshaft position sensor B circuit, high input

P0389	Crankshaft position sensor B circuit, intermittent
P0400	Exhaust gas recirculation flow malfunction
P0401	Exhaust gas recirculation, insufficient flow detected
P0402	Exhaust gas recirculation, excessive flow detected
P0403	Exhaust gas recirculation circuit malfunction
P0404	Exhaust gas recirculation circuit, range or performance problem
P0405	Exhaust gas recirculation sensor A circuit low
P0406	Exhaust gas recirculation sensor A circuit high
P0407	Exhaust gas recirculation sensor B circuit low
P0408	Exhaust gas recirculation sensor B circuit high
P0410	Secondary air injection system malfunction
P0411	Secondary air injection system, incorrect flow detected
P0412	Secondary air injection system switching valve A, circuit malfunction
P0413	Secondary air injection system switching valve A, open circuit
P0414	Secondary air injection system switching valve A, shorted circuit
P0415	Secondary air injection system switching valve B, circuit malfunction
P0416	Secondary air injection system switching valve B, open circuit
P0417	Secondary air injection system switching valve B, shorted circuit
P0418	Secondary air injection system, relay A circuit malfunction
P0419	Secondary air injection system, relay B circuit malfunction
P0420	Catalyst system efficiency below threshold (cylinder bank no. 1)
P0421	Warm-up catalyst efficiency below threshold (cylinder bank no. 1)
P0422	Main catalyst efficiency below threshold (cylinder bank no. 1)
P0423	Heated catalyst efficiency below threshold (cylinder bank no. 1)
P0424	Heated catalyst temperature below threshold (cylinder bank no. 1)
P0430	Catalyst system efficiency below threshold (cylinder bank no. 2)
P0431	Warm-up catalyst efficiency below threshold (cylinder bank no. 2)
P0432	Main catalyst efficiency below threshold (cylinder bank no. 2)
P0433	Heated catalyst efficiency below threshold (cylinder bank no. 2)
P0434	Heated catalyst temperature below threshold (cylinder bank no. 2)
P0440	Evaporative emission control system malfunction
P0441	Evaporative emission control system, incorrect purge flow
P0442	Evaporative emission control system, small leak detected
P0443	Evaporative emission control system, purge control valve circuit malfunction
P0444	Evaporative emission control system, open purge control valve circuit

P0445	Evaporative emission control system, short in purge control valve circuit
P0446	Evaporative emission control system, vent control circuit malfunction
P0447	Evaporative emission control system, open vent control circuit
P0448	Evaporative emission control system, shorted vent control circuit
P0449	Evaporative emission control system, vent valve/solenoid circuit malfunction
P0450	Evaporative emission control system, pressure sensor malfunction
P0451	Evaporative emission control system, pressure sensor range or performance problem
P0452	Evaporative emission control system, pressure sensor low input
P0453	Evaporative emission control system, pressure sensor high input
P0454	Evaporative emission control system, pressure sensor intermittent
P0460	Fuel level sensor circuit malfunction
P0461	Fuel level sensor circuit, range or performance problem
P0462	Fuel level sensor circuit, low input
P0463	Fuel level sensor circuit, high input
P0464	Fuel level sensor circuit, intermittent
P0465	Purge flow sensor circuit malfunction
P0466	Purge flow sensor circuit, range or performance problem
P0467	Purge flow sensor circuit, low input
P0468	Purge flow sensor circuit, high input
P0469	Purge flow sensor circuit, intermittent
P0470	Exhaust pressure sensor malfunction
P0471	Exhaust pressure sensor, range or performance problem
P0472	Exhaust pressure sensor, low
P0473	Exhaust pressure sensor, high
P0474	Exhaust pressure sensor, intermittent
P0475	Exhaust pressure control valve malfunction
P0476	Exhaust pressure control valve, range or performance problem
P0477	Exhaust pressure control valve, low
P0478	Exhaust pressure sensor, high
P0479	Exhaust pressure sensor, intermittent
P0480	Cooling fan no. 1, control circuit malfunction
P0481	Cooling fan no. 2, control circuit malfunction
P0482	Cooling fan no. 3, control circuit malfunction
P0483	Cooling fan rationality check malfunction

P0484	Cooling fan circuit, high current
P0485	Cooling fan power/ground circuit malfunction
P0500	Vehicle speed sensor malfunction
P0501	Vehicle speed sensor, range or performance problem
P0502	Vehicle speed sensor circuit, low input
P0503	Vehicle speed sensor circuit, intermittent, erratic or high input
P0505	Idle control system malfunction
P0506	Idle control system, rpm lower than expected
P0507	Idle control system, rpm higher than expected
P0510	Closed throttle position switch malfunction
P0520	Engine oil pressure sensor/switch circuit malfunction
P0521	Engine oil pressure sensor/switch circuit, range or performance problem
P0522	Engine oil pressure sensor/switch circuit, low voltage
P0523	Engine oil pressure sensor/switch circuit, high voltage
P0530	A/C refrigerant pressure sensor, circuit malfunction
P0531	A/C refrigerant pressure sensor, range or performance problem
P0532	A/C refrigerant pressure sensor, low input
P0533	A/C refrigerant pressure sensor, high input
P0534	A/C refrigerant charge loss
P0550	Power steering pressure sensor, circuit malfunction
P0551	Power steering pressure sensor circuit, range or performance problem
P0552	Power steering pressure sensor circuit, low input
P0553	Power steering pressure sensor circuit, high input
P0554	Power steering pressure sensor circuit, intermittent input
P0560	System voltage malfunction
P0561	System voltage unstable
P0562	System voltage low
P0563	System voltage high
P0565	Cruise control on signal malfunction
P0566	Cruise control off signal malfunction
P0567	Cruise control resume signal malfunction
P0568	Cruise control set signal malfunction
P0569	Cruise control coast signal malfunction
P0570	Cruise control accel signal malfunction
P0571	Cruise control/brake switch A, circuit malfunction

P0572	Cruise control/brake switch A, circuit low
P0573	Cruise control/brake switch A, circuit high
P0600	Serial communication link malfunction
P0601	Internal control module, memory check sum error
P0602	Control module, programming error
P0603	Internal control module, keep alive memory (KAM) error
P0604	Internal control module, random access memory (RAM) error
P0605	Internal control module, read only memory (ROM) error
P0606	PCM processor fault
P0608	Control module VSS, output A malfunction
P0609	Control module VSS, output B malfunction
P0620	Generator control circuit malfunction
P0621	Generator lamp L, control circuit malfunction
P0622	Generator lamp F, control circuit malfunction
P0650	Malfunction indicator lamp (MIL), control circuit malfunction
P0654	Engine rpm output, circuit malfunction
P0655	Engine hot lamp output control, circuit malfunction
P0656	Fuel level output, circuit malfunction
P0700	Transmission control system malfunction
P0701	Transmission control system, range or performance problem
P0702	Transmission control system, electrical
P0703	Torque converter/brake switch B, circuit malfunction
P0704	Clutch switch input circuit malfunction
P0705	Transmission range sensor, circuit malfunction (PRNDL input)
P0706	Transmission range sensor circuit, range or performance problem
P0707	Transmission range sensor circuit, low input
P0708	Transmission range sensor circuit, high input
P0709	Transmission range sensor circuit, intermittent input
P0710	Transmission fluid temperature sensor, circuit malfunction
P0711	Transmission fluid temperature sensor circuit, range or performance problem
P0712	Transmission fluid temperature sensor circuit, low input
P0713	Transmission fluid temperature sensor circuit, high input
P0714	Transmission fluid temperature sensor circuit, intermittent input
P0715	Input/turbine speed sensor circuit malfunction

P0716	Input/turbine speed sensor circuit, range or performance problem
P0717	Input/turbine speed sensor circuit, no signal
P0718	Input/turbine speed sensor circuit, intermittent signal
P0719	Torque converter/brake switch B, circuit low
P0720	Output speed sensor malfunction
P0721	Output speed sensor circuit, range or performance problem
P0722	Output speed sensor circuit, no signal
P0723	Output speed sensor circuit, intermittent signal
P0724	Torque converter/brake switch B circuit, high
P0725	Engine speed input circuit malfunction
P0726	Engine speed input circuit, range or performance problem
P0727	Engine speed input circuit, no signal
P0728	Engine speed input circuit, intermittent signal
P0730	Incorrect gear ratio
P0731	Incorrect gear ratio, first gear
P0732	Incorrect gear ratio, second gear
P0733	Incorrect gear ratio, third gear
P0734	Incorrect gear ratio, fourth gear
P0735	Incorrect gear ratio, fifth gear
P0736	Incorrect gear ratio, reverse gear
P0740	Torque converter clutch, circuit malfunction
P0741	Torque converter clutch, circuit performance or stuck in off position
P0742	Torque converter clutch circuit, stuck in on position
P0743	Torque converter clutch circuit, electrical problem
P0744	Torque converter clutch circuit, intermittent
P0745	Pressure control solenoid malfunction
P0746	Pressure control solenoid, performance problem or stuck in off position
P0747	Pressure control solenoid, stuck in on position
P0748	Pressure control solenoid, electrical problem
P0749	Pressure control solenoid, intermittent operation
P0750	Shift solenoid A malfunction
P0751	Shift solenoid A, performance problem or stuck in off position
P0752	Shift solenoid A, stuck in on position
P0753	Shift solenoid A, electrical problem
P0754	Shift solenoid A, intermittent operation
P0755	Shift solenoid B malfunction

P0756	Shift solenoid B, performance problem or stuck in off position
P0757	Shift solenoid B, stuck in on position
P0758	Shift solenoid B, electrical problem
P0759	Shift solenoid B, intermittent operation
P0760	Shift solenoid C malfunction
P0761	Shift solenoid C, performance problem or stuck in off position
P0762	Shift solenoid C, stuck in on position
P0763	Shift solenoid C, electrical problem
P0764	Shift solenoid C, intermittent operation
P0765	Shift solenoid D malfunction
P0766	Shift solenoid D, performance problem or stuck in off position
P0767	Shift solenoid D, stuck in on position
P0768	Shift solenoid D, electrical problem
P0769	Shift solenoid D, intermittent operation
P0770	Shift solenoid E malfunction
P0771	Shift solenoid E, performance problem or stuck in off position
P0772	Shift solenoid E, stuck in on position
P0773	Shift solenoid E, electrical problem
P0774	Shift solenoid E, intermittent operation
P0780	Shift malfunction
P0781	First-to-second shift malfunction
P0782	Second-to-third shift malfunction
P0783	Third-to-fourth shift malfunction
P0784	Fourth-to-fifth shift malfunction
P0785	Shift/timing solenoid malfunction
P0786	Shift/timing solenoid, range or performance problem
P0787	Shift/timing solenoid, low
P0788	Shift/timing solenoid, high
P0789	Shift/timing solenoid, intermittent
P0790	Normal/performance switch circuit malfunction
P0801	Reverse inhibit control circuit malfunction
P0803	First-to-fourth upshift (skip shift) solenoid control circuit malfunction
P0804	First-to-fourth upshift (skip shift) lamp control circuit malfunction

8 Component check and replacement

Introduction

This chapter will help you diagnose and replace the various components that make up your particular engine management system. There are so many different types and versions of engine management systems, depending upon the year, make and manufacturer of the vehicle, that it is impossible to give specific tests and exact specifications. Instead, this chapter will go into detail concerning the functions and the similarities of the various components to allow the home mechanic to make correct conclusions and repairs. Modern engine management systems may seem very complicated at first, but with a little working knowledge and a few tools, the home mechanic can easily repair many of the most common problems that occur. This chapter is separated into sections that deal with the different areas of the engine management system. The easiest and most obvious problems involved with the electrical circuit of the fuel system are covered first, followed by a section that covers components used in feedback carburetor systems. Section 3 covers all the component checks and replacement procedures for electronic fuel injection systems. Finally, Section 4 will give general information and checks on modern ignition systems.

1 Fuel pump electrical circuit

The first test will determine if the fuel pump is actually operating. In the event the engine cranks but will not start, the most obvious test would be to find out if the fuel pump is pumping! The easiest place to hear the fuel pump in action is directly at the fuel filler cap. Simply remove the cap from the filler neck and have someone turn the ignition over and crank the engine. Most electric fuel pumps will activate for a few seconds just by turning the ignition key ON without the engine running. It should be relatively quiet when this test is performed. You should hear a whirring sound that lasts for at least a couple of seconds. If the

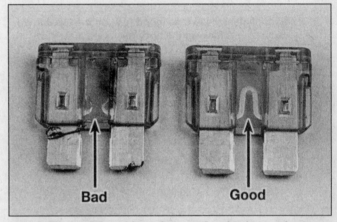

1.1 To check for a blown fuse on the plastic type fuses, activate the circuit and probe the exposed blades at the top of the fuse with a test light; if power is available on one terminal but not the other, the fuse is blown

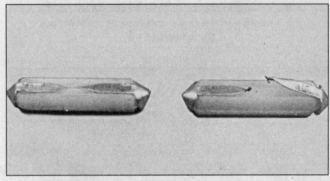

1.2 Ceramic fuses are often used on European cars (good fuse on the left, blown fuse on the right)

pump is working and the engine still does not start, go back and check for a clogged fuel line or a defective ignition module or igniter. Remember, fuel, spark and compression are necessary to make combustion! Most likely the engine will not start because of an ignition system problem. If the fuel pump does not run, then you will need to continue down the list. Next check the fuel pump fuse.

The second test will determine if the fuse that protects the fuel pump circuit is blown **(see illustrations)** or cor-

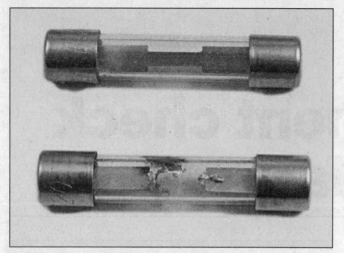

1.3 Traditional glass case fuse (good fuse on the top, blown fuse on the bottom)

1.4 Location of the fuel pump fuse on Toyota Previa minivans

1.5 Location of the fuel pump fuse on a BMW 318i (fuse number 11)

1.6 The fuel pump fuse on the Saturn is located in slot number 12, adjacent to the relay panel under the center console

1.7 The fuel pump relay on late a model Ford Crown Victoria is located in a special relay assembly near the brake master cylinder. The designations are molded onto the cover

roded to the point of malfunctioning the fuel pump. Locate the fuse panel - they're usually located under the dash area or in the engine compartment in a fuse/relay center. If necessary, consult your owner's manual or a *Haynes Automotive Repair Manual* for the correct location. Here are some typical fuel pump fuse locations on selected modern vehicles **(see illustrations)**. Carefully inspect the fuse to make sure it is intact. If the fuse is blown, replace it with a new one. Also check for corrosion on the fuel pump fuse terminals. Here is a good example of a fuse problem in a late model vehicle. Many 240 Volvos will crank and turn over but not start until 20 or 30 seconds later. Down the road, the engine will hesitate slightly but continue to run. This intermittent problem gives the owner fits until the fuel pump fuse from the panel (driver's kick panel) is removed and cleaned. Carefully clean the blades on the fuse as well as the terminals on the panel.

1.8 The fuel pump relay on many front-wheel drive GM vehicles is located on the right side of the engine compartment (1992 Pontiac Sunbird shown)

1.9 The GM minivan Lumina APV positions the fuel pump relay near the front of the engine compartment

A   Fuel pump relay
B   Cooling fan relay
C   Air conditioning compressor relay

The third test will determine if the fuel pump and/or circuit is operating properly. This check will involve a series of little checks and the process of elimination to resolve the problem. Simply remove the fuel pump relay and check for battery voltage to the relay connector, then jump the relay connector to apply battery voltage to the fuel pump and listen for the sound of the fuel pump activating. This will be the most common series of tests that must be performed on fuel injection systems.

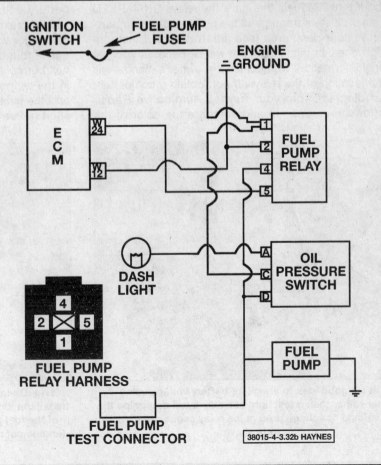

1.10 Schematic of a typical fuel pump relay, fuse and fuel pump circuit

38015-4-3.32b HAYNES

1.11 On GM Lumina APV vans, check for battery voltage on the dark green/white wire on the fuel pump relay connector

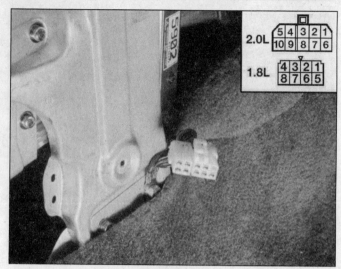

1.12 On Mitsubishi Eclipse, Chrysler Laser and Eagle Talon, remove the EFI relay under the center console and check for battery voltage on terminal number 10 (2.0L engine) or terminal number 8 (1.8L engine)

The toughest part of this step is finding the fuel pump relay. Many manufacturers have the fuel pump relay grouped together with other relays in a fuse/relay center usually located in the engine compartment or under the dash. They sometimes have their designation stamped on the cover **(see illustration)**. This is the easiest case. Now how about those models that have the relays UNMARKED and in small clusters throughout the entire engine compartment and under-dash area **(see illustrations)**. These are the tough ones. In this situation it will be necessary to get additional information. Sometimes the owner's manual will have the location of the relays. If not, obtain a component location diagram from your *Haynes Automotive Repair Manual* or wiring diagram and compare the color of the wires to the ones listed.

Now that you have located the fuel pump relay, remove it from the connector, turn the ignition key ON (engine not running) and check for battery voltage. If you have a wiring schematic for the vehicle, follow the wire directly from the fuel pump relay connector to the ignition key. Check for battery voltage **(see illustrations)**. If you don't have a wiring schematic, probe the terminals of the fuel pump relay connector with the voltmeter or test light until battery voltage is found. If there is NO battery voltage present at the fuel pump connector then there is a bad fuse or a problem in the wiring harness somewhere between the fuse panel and the ignition key and/or battery. Diagnose the electrical short before continuing any further.

1.13 It's a good idea to check for battery voltage using a voltmeter rather than a test light because it will determine the exact voltage or voltage drop at the relay connector (Crown Victoria shown)

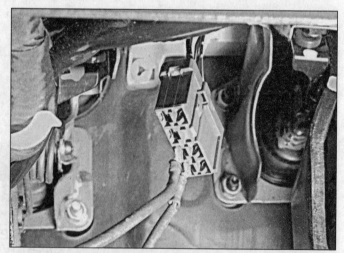

1.14 On late model Honda Accords (1990 through 1994), install the jumper wire into terminals number 5 and number 7 of the fuel pump relay connector with the ignition key ON (engine not running). These models use an EFI relay located under the dash

1.15 On a BMW 325i, use a jumper wire across terminals 30 and 87

1.16 Remove the Saturn fuel pump relay located under the dash near the center console, and jump the top and bottom terminals of the panel

Now that battery voltage is present at the fuel pump relay connector, jump the connector to activate the fuel pump **(see illustrations)**. It will be necessary to check a wiring diagram to determine exactly which two terminals govern the fuel pump. It is possible to check for continuity between the fuel pump harness connector and the relay connector to determine the correct terminal. It is a bit awkward to stretch a jumper lead all the way from the fuel pump relay connector to the fuel pump but it is not impossible. **Caution:** *If the fuse blows when the jumper wire is installed in the relay connector, replace the fuse with a new one and double-check the terminal designation. Most likely, the jumper was inserted into the wrong terminal or it accidentally touched the wrong terminal and overloaded the circuit.* You should hear a whirring sound from the fuel tank area or from under the body. A quick note on jumping the

1.17 Fuel pump jumper location for the Ford Crown Victoria

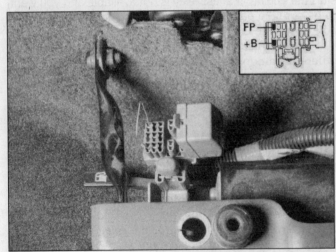

1.18 On Toyota Previa minivans, bridge terminals FP and B+ using a jumper wire or paper clip. The diagnostic terminal box is located under the driver's seat

1.19 On Mitsubishi Eclipse, Chrysler Laser and Eagle Talon, install a jumper wire from the positive (+) terminal of the battery to the fuel pump check terminal taped to the wiring harness on the firewall behind the battery

1.20 The fuel pump test terminal on many GM vehicles is located next to the battery

1.21 On Ford systems, ground terminal FP (top left terminal) to activate the fuel pump

fuel pump; many manufacturers include a special test port to jump the fuel pump. This test connector is usually located in the engine compartment **(see illustrations)**. Most require a jumper wire from the battery to the test port to power the fuel pump, but some use a simple jumper wire from a power source on the test connector. These test ports or test connectors are very handy to quick-check the fuel pump pressure but they do not check the working condition of the fuel pump relay. That is why it is a good idea to go ahead and make all the basic checks without using the test port unless necessary.

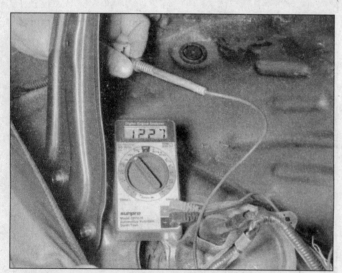

1.22 Check for battery voltage to the fuel pump using a voltmeter. On some vehicles this will require removing the carpet for access to the fuel pump electrical connector (late model Honda Accord shown)

If the fuel pump does not activate, it will be necessary to trace the wiring harness back to the fuel pump and check for battery voltage **(see illustration)**. If battery voltage is available to the fuel pump and the pump is properly grounded, replace the fuel pump with a new one. By carefully and methodically checking the relay and circuit all the way back to the fuel pump, the home mechanic can easily determine, by using the process of elimination, why the fuel pump does not work.

Before finishing the relay diagnostics, let us discuss what to do when battery voltage is available to the relay but the relay does not energize the circuit. In this situation it will be necessary to test the relay. The only easier method would be to replace the relay with a known good relay and start the engine. If a test relay is not available and you want to be sure the part is bad before spending the non-refundable cost, here is a quick check.

The relay testing procedures are subheaded into three different categories; mechanical relays, multiple circuit relays and solid state relays. Mechanical relays that operate a single purpose fuel pump system usually have three or four terminals. The first category covers single circuit **mechanical relays**. The second category covers relays that have more than one circuit involved in their control function. This category is called **multiple circuit relays**. Last category is the **solid state relays**. These relays operate on low voltage signals and they must be diagnosed using different methods. **Note:** *We recommend using the correct wiring diagram for your vehicle to determine the proper terminal designations for the relay you're testing. However, if wiring diagrams are not available, you may be able to determine the test hook-ups from the information that follows.*

Mechanical relays

Note: *The information that follows does not apply to polarity reversing relays, which are used in some power accessory circuits.*

Relays with four terminals

On most relays with four terminals, two of the four terminals are for the relay's control circuit (they connect to the relay's coil). The other two are for the relay's power circuit (they connect to the armature contact and the fixed contact).

If you have wiring diagrams for the vehicle, you can figure out which terminals hook up to which parts of the relay. Often, relay terminals are marked as an aid.

As a general rule, the two thicker gauge wires connected to the relay are for the power circuit; the two thinner gauge wires are for the control circuit.

Remove the relay from the vehicle and check for continuity between the relay's power circuit terminals. There should be no continuity.

Connect a fused jumper wire between one of the two control circuit terminals and the positive battery terminal. Connect another jumper wire between the other control circuit terminal and ground. When the connections are made, the relay should click. On some relays, polarity may be critical, so, if the relay doesn't click, try swapping the jumper wires on the control circuit terminals.

With the jumper wires connected, check for continuity between the power circuit terminals. Now there should be continuity.

If the relay fails any of the above tests, replace it.

Relays with three terminals

If the relay has three terminals, it's a good idea to check the vehicle's wiring diagram to determine which terminals connect to which of the relay's components. Most three-terminal relays are either case-grounded or externally-grounded.

On a case-grounded relay, one side of the relay's control circuit grounds through the relay case, eliminating the need for the fourth terminal. This type of relay requires the case to be securely connected to a good chassis ground. Check this type of relay the same way you would a four-terminal relay, noting that one of the control circuit's terminals is actually the relay case.

On an externally grounded relay, one of the relay's terminals is connected to a positive power source. We'll call this the battery power terminal. Inside the relay, the battery power terminal is connected to one side of both the relay's power and control circuits. Another terminal is connected to the other side of the control circuit; the circuit is completed through a switch to ground. The third terminal is connected to the other side of the power circuit; it's grounded at the circuit's load component. This type of three-terminal relay is sometimes a plug-in type with no connection between the case and ground.

To check an externally grounded relay, remove it from the vehicle and check for continuity between the relay's battery power terminal and it's power circuit terminal. There should be no continuity.

Hook up a fused jumper wire between the battery power terminal and the positive battery terminal. Connect another jumper wire between the relay's control circuit terminal and ground. The relay should click.

With the jumper wires in place, connect a test light between the relay's power circuit terminal and ground. The test light should light. If the relay fails any of these tests, replace it.

Multiple circuit relays

Multiple circuit relays are checked the same way as relays with four terminals. It will be necessary to acquire a wiring diagram for the system to properly identify the exact terminals that govern the fuel pump system. Then it is just a matter of checking the relay within the relay. Follow the previous steps.

Solid state relays

A transistor can act as solid-state relay in a circuit, and this is one of the most important uses of a transistor in automotive electrical systems. They operate differently in theory but function the same as an electromagnetic type relay. The combination of diodes, resistors and zener diodes can control the switching action rapidly and efficiently. Have solid state relays checked by a dealer service department or an electronics repair shop.

2 Feedback carburetor systems

Note: *Because engine management systems may differ depending upon the year and the manufacturer, certain trouble codes may indicate different problems from one year to the next. Be sure to double-check the code number with the exact year of production. Since this is the case, it would be a good idea to consult your dealer or other qualified repair shop before replacing any electrical component, as they are usually expensive and can't be returned once they are purchased.*

The first step in diagnosing any feedback carburetor driveability problem is to use the self-diagnosis system and check for any codes that have been stored in the computer. This system is a big help for the home mechanic because it eliminates many tedious and involved testing procedures and "trial and error" methods of diagnosing a driveability problem. Refer to Chapter 7 for the code accessing procedure and code charts for your particular vehicle.

Here are some simple checks for testing the main components (actuators and sensors) of the feedback carburetor system:

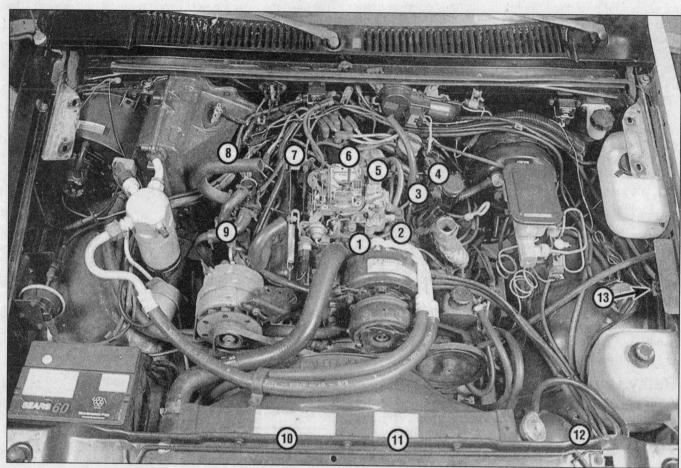

2.2 Feedback carburetor and other related emission system components - 2.8L Chevrolet S-10 pick-up

1	Coolant temperature sensor and Thermal vacuum switch	*6*	Exhaust Gas Recirculation (EGR) valve
2	Throttle Position Sensor	*7*	Electronic Spark Timing (EST) connector
3	Heated EFE grid connector	*8*	Oxygen sensor
4	PCV valve	*9*	Air diverter valve
5	Mixture control solenoid		

10	VECI label
11	Vacuum hose routing diagram
12	Vapor canister
13	Manifold Absolute Pressure (MAP) sensor

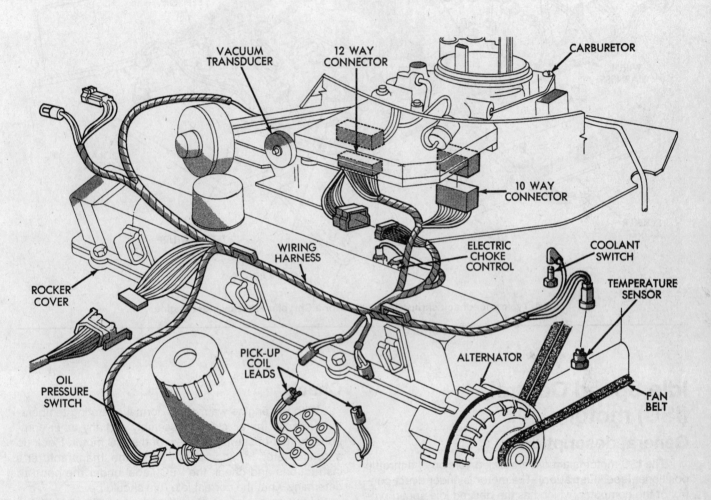

2.3 Typical feedback carburetor system for a Chrysler six-cylinder engine

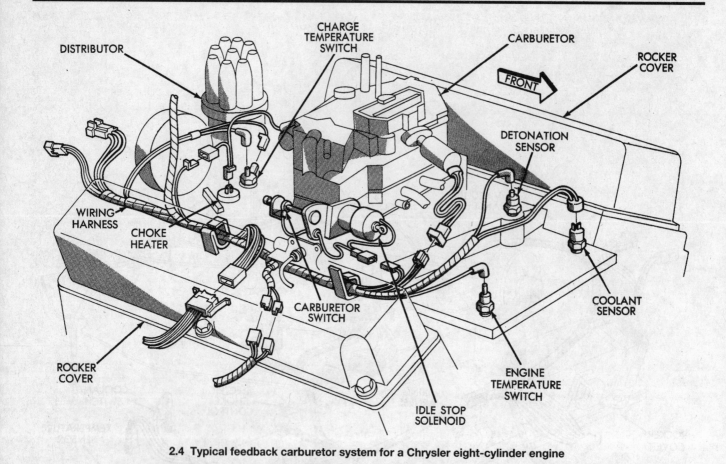

CHARGE TEMPERATURE SWITCH
DISTRIBUTOR
CARBURETOR
ROCKER COVER
FRONT
DETONATION SENSOR
WIRING HARNESS
CHOKE HEATER
CARBURETOR SWITCH
ROCKER COVER
COOLANT SENSOR
IDLE STOP SOLENOID
ENGINE TEMPERATURE SWITCH

2.4 Typical feedback carburetor system for a Chrysler eight-cylinder engine

Idle Speed Control (ISC) motor

General description

The ISC motor is a more advanced version of a throttle positioner **(see illustration)**. The motor is under direct control of the computer, which has the desired idle speed programmed into its memory. The computer compares the actual idle speed from the engine (taken from the distributor or crankshaft position sensor ignition impulses) to the desired rpm reference in memory. When the two do not match, the ISC plunger is moved in or out. This automatically adjusts the throttle to hold the idle speed, regardless of engine loads.

Many ISC motors have a throttle contact switch at the end of the plunger. The position of the switch determines whether or not the ISC should control idle speed. When the throttle lever is resting against the ISC plunger, the switch contacts are closed, at which time the computer moves the ISC motor to the programmed idle speed. When the throttle lever is not contacting the ISC plunger, the switch contacts are open and the ECM stops sending the idle speed commands and the driver controls engine speed.

Check

With the engine warmed to normal operating temperature, remove the air cleaner assembly and any other components that obscure your view of the ISC motor. Hook up a tachometer in accordance with the manufacturer's instructions and check the VECI label under the hood to determine what the correct idle rpm should be.

Have an assistant start the engine. Check that the engine rpm is correct. Have your assistant turn on the air conditioning (if equipped), headlights and any other electrical accessories. If the vehicle is equipped with power steering, have your assistant turn the steering wheel from side-to-side. Note the reading on the tachometer. The engine speed should remain stable at the correct idle speed. If the vehicle is equipped with an automatic transmission, block the wheels and have your assistant set the parking brake, place his/her foot firmly on the brake pedal and place the transmission in Drive. Again the engine rpm should remain stable at the correct speed. **Warning:** *Do not stand in front of the vehicle during this test.*

If the ISC motor is not functioning as it should, first check the condition of the wiring and electrical connector(s). Make sure the connector is securely attached and

2.5 Use a jumper wire (arrow) to connect the tachometer lead to the TACH terminal on the distributor (GM HEI systems only)

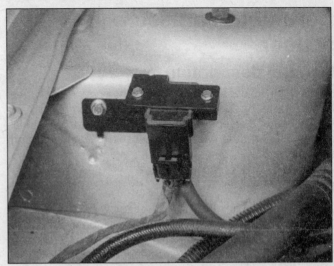

2.6 Typical MAP sensor - they are sometimes mounted on the firewall, like this one, or on the side of the air cleaner housing

there is no corrosion at the terminals. For further diagnosis of this system, refer to factory service manual for your particular vehicle or take the vehicle to a dealer service department or other qualified shop.

Manifold Absolute Pressure (MAP) sensor

General description

The MAP sensor (sometimes referred to as the pressure differential sensor) reports engine load to the computer, which uses the information to adjust spark advance and fuel enrichment **(see illustration)**. The MAP sensor measures intake manifold pressure and vacuum on the absolute scale (from zero instead of from sea-level atmospheric pressure (14.7 psi) as most gauges and sensors do). The MAP sensor reads vacuum and pressure through a hose connected to the intake manifold. A pressure-sensitive ceramic or silicon element and electronic circuit in the sensor generates a voltage signal that changes in direct proportion to pressure.

Under low-load, high-vacuum conditions, the computer leans the fuel/air mixture and advances the spark timing for better fuel economy. Under high-load, low-vacuum conditions, the computer richens the fuel/air mixture and retards timing to prevent detonation. The MAP sensor serves as the electronic equivalent of both a vacuum advance on a distributor and a power valve in the carburetor.

Check

Anything that hinders accurate sensor input can upset both the fuel mixture and ignition timing. This includes the

MAP sensor itself as well as shorts or opens in the sensor wiring circuit and/or vacuum leaks in the intake manifold or vacuum hose. Some of the most typical driveability symptoms associated with problems in the MAP sensor circuit include:

1) Detonation and misfire due to increased spark advance and a lean fuel mixture.
2) Loss of power and/or fuel economy and sometimes even black smoke due to retarded ignition timing and a very rich fuel mixture.
3) Poor fuel economy
4) Hard starts and/or stalling.

Note: *A vacuum leak in the hose to the MAP sensor causes the MAP sensor to indicate a higher than normal pressure (less vacuum) in the manifold, which makes the computer think the engine is under much more load than it really is. As a result, the ignition timing is retarded and the fuel mixture is richened.*

When a MAP sensor trouble code is detected, be sure to first check for vacuum leaks in the hoses or electrical connectors or wiring damage in the MAP sensor circuit. Kinks in the line, blockage or splits can occur and deter the sensor's ability to respond accurately to the changes in the manifold pressure. Check for anything that is obvious and easily repaired before actually replacing the sensor itself.

A MAP sensor will typically produce a voltage signal that will drop with decreasing manifold pressure (rising vacuum). Test specifications will vary according to the manufacturer and engine type. A typical MAP sensor will read 4.6 to 4.8 volts with 0 in-Hg vacuum applied. Raise it to 5 in-Hg vacuum and the reading should drop to about 3.75 volts. Raise it up again to 20 in-Hg and the reading should drop to about 1.1 volts.

Barometric pressure (BARO) sensor

General description

The BARO sensor detects ambient pressure changes that occur as the result of changes in the weather and/or the altitude of the vehicle. It then sends an electronic signal to the ECM that is used to adjust the air/fuel ratio and spark timing.

Check

A problem with the BARO sensor will usually set a Code 32 on GM feedback carburetor systems. To check the sensor, begin by checking the voltage from terminal A to terminal B at the sensor electrical connector. Compare your voltage reading with the chart below.

2.7 Here is a typical Ford TPS - note there are slots in the sensor at the mounting screws that allow for adjustment on carbureted models

Altitude (in feet)	Voltage range
Below 1000	3.8 to 5.5
1000 to 2000	3.6 to 5.3
2000 to 3000	3.5 to 5.1
3000 to 4000	3.3 to 5.0
4000 to 5000	3.2 to 4.8
5000 to 6000	3.0 to 4.6
6000 to 7000	2.9 to 4.5
7000 to 8000	2.8 to 4.3
8000 to 9000	2.6 to 4.2
9000 to 10000	2.5 to 4.0

Connect a hand-held vacuum pump to the port of the sensor (you may have to remove a small filter to do this), apply a vacuum of 10 in-Hg to the sensor and check the voltage again. If the change is more than 2.3 volts, replace the sensor.

If the voltage change is less than 1.2 volts, check for a short between sensor terminals B and C. If there's no short, replace the sensor.

If the voltage change is between 1.2 to 2.3 volts, the problem lies in the wire to ECM terminal no. 1, a bad connection at the ECM or a defective ECM.

Throttle Position Sensor (TPS)

General description

The TPS is either mounted externally on the throttle body or inside of the carburetor (**see illustration**). The TPS output voltage varies according to the angle of the throttle. Its job is to inform the computer about the rate of throttle opening and relative throttle position. A separate Wide Open Throttle (WOT) switch may be used to signal the computer when the throttle is wide open. The TPS consists of a variable resistor that changes resistance as the throttle changes its opening. By signalling the computer when the throttle opens, the computer can richen the fuel mixture to retain the proper air/fuel ratio. The initial setting of the TPS is very important because the voltage signal the computer receives tells the computer the exact position of the throttle at idle.

Check

Throttle Position Sensors typically have their own types of driveability symptoms that can be distinguished from other information sensors. The most common symptom of a faulty or misadjusted sensor is hesitation or stumble during acceleration. The same symptom of a bad accelerator pump in a non-feedback, carbureted engine.

There are basically two voltage checks you can perform to test the Throttle Position Sensor. **Note:** *It is best to have the correct wiring diagram for the vehicle when performing the following checks.*

The first test is for the presence of voltage at the TPS supply wire with the ignition key ON. The sensor cannot

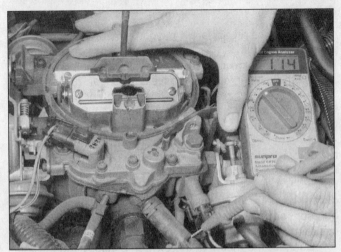

2.8 Check the TPS signal voltage and confirm that as the throttle opens, the signal voltage INCREASES (Rochester carburetor shown)

2.9 First check the TPS resistance with the throttle closed . . .

deliver the correct signal without the proper supply voltage. You can determine the function of each individual wire (ground, supply, signal wire) by probing each one with a voltmeter and checking the different voltages. The voltage that remains constant when the throttle is opened and closed will be the supply voltage. If there's no voltage at any of the wires, there's probably an open or short in the wiring harness to the sensor.

The second check is for the proper voltage change that occurs as the throttle opens and closes. As the throttle goes from closed-to-wide open, the voltage at the signal wire should typically increase smoothly from 1 volt to 5 volts **(see illustration)**.

To check the resistance of the sensor, unplug the electrical connector and hook up an ohmmeter to the supply and signal terminals. With the ignition key OFF, slowly

move the throttle through the complete range **(see illustrations)**. Observe carefully for any unusual changes in the resistance (the change should be smooth) as it increases from low to high.

Also, be sure to check for trouble codes. Be sure you have checked all the obvious items before replacing the TPS.

Oxygen sensor
General description

The oxygen sensor is located in the exhaust manifold (or in the exhaust pipe near the exhaust manifold) and produces a voltage signal proportional to the content of oxygen in the exhaust **(see illustration)**. A higher oxygen con-

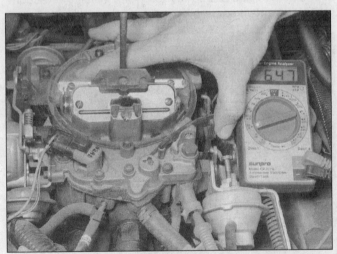

2.10 . . . then with the throttle open. Resistance should INCREASE

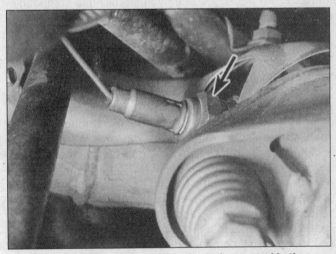

2.11 A typical oxygen sensor (arrow) mounted in the exhaust manifold

tent across the sensor tip will vary the oxygen differential, thereby lowering the sensor's output voltage. On the other hand, lower oxygen content will raise the output voltage. Typically the voltage ranges from 0.10 volts (lean) to 0.90 volts (rich). The computer uses the sensor's input voltage to adjust the air/fuel mixture, leaning it out when the sensor detects a rich condition or enrichening it when it detects a lean condition. When the sensor reaches operating temperature (600-degrees F), it will produce a variable voltage signal based on the difference between the amount of oxygen in the exhaust (internal) and the amount of oxygen in the air directly surrounding the sensor (external). The ideal stochiometric fuel/air ratio (14.7:1) will produce about 0.45 volts.

There are basically two types of oxygen sensors on the market. The most popular type uses a zirconia element in its tip. The latest type of oxygen sensor uses a titania element. Instead of producing its own voltage, the titania element resistance will alter a voltage signal that is supplied by the computer itself. Although the titania element works differently than the zirconia element, the results are basically identical. The biggest difference is that the titania element responds faster and allows the computer to maintain more uniform control over a wide range of exhaust temperatures.

Contamination can directly affect engine performance and life span of the oxygen sensor. There are basically three types of contamination; carbon, lead and silicon. Carbon buildup due to a rich-running condition will cause inaccurate readings and increase the problem's symptoms. Diagnose the fuel injection system or carburetor feedback controls for correct fuel adjustments. Once the system is repaired, run the engine at high rpm without a load (parked in the driveway) to remove the carbon deposits. Avoid leaded gasoline as it causes contamination of the oxygen sensor. Also, avoid using old-style silicone gasket sealant (RTV) that releases volatile compounds into the crankcase which eventually wind up on the sensor tip. Always check to make sure the RTV sealant you are using is compatible with modern emission systems.

Before an oxygen sensor can function properly it must reach a minimum operating temperature of 600-degrees F. The warm-up period prior to this is called "open loop." In this mode, the computer detects a low coolant temperature (cold start) and wide open throttle (warm-up) condition. Until the engine reaches operating temperature, the computer ignores the oxygen sensor signals. During this time span, the emission controls are not precise! Once the engine is warm, the system is said to be in "closed loop" (using the oxygen sensor's input). Some manufacturers have designed an electric heating element to help the sensor reach operating temperature sooner. A typical heated sensor will consist of a ground wire, a sensor output wire (to the computer) and a third wire that supplies battery voltage to the resistance heater inside the oxygen sensor. Be careful when testing the oxygen sensor circuit! Clearly identify the function of each wire or you might confuse the data and draw the wrong conclusions.

Check

Sometimes an apparent oxygen sensor problem is not the sensor's fault. An air leak in the exhaust manifold or a fouled spark plug or other problem in the ignition system causes the oxygen sensor to give a false lean-running condition. The sensor reacts only to the content of oxygen in the exhaust, and it has no way of knowing where the extra oxygen came from.

When checking the oxygen sensor it is important to remember that a good sensor produces a fluctuating signal that responds quickly to the changes in the exhaust oxygen content. To check the sensor you will need a 10 mega-ohm digital voltmeter. Never use an ohmmeter to check the oxygen sensor and never jump or ground the terminals. This can damage the sensor.

Connect the meter to the oxygen sensor circuit. Back-probe the oxygen sensor signal circuit with a sewing pin. Select the mV (millivolt) scale. If the engine is equipped with a later style (heated) oxygen sensor, be sure you are connected to the signal wire and not one of the heater or ground wires. If necessary, consult a wiring diagram for the correct terminal designations. Start the engine and let it idle. Typically, the meter will respond with a fluctuating millivolt reading when connected properly. Also, be sure the engine is in closed loop (warmed-up to operating temperature).

Watch very carefully as the voltage fluctuates. The display will flash values ranging from 100 mV to 900 mV (0.1 to 0.9 volt). The numbers will flash very quickly, so be observant. Record the high and low values over a period of one minute. With the engine operating properly, the oxygen sensor should average approximately 500 mV (0.5 volt) **(see illustration)**.

To further test the oxygen sensor, remove a vacuum line and observe the readings as the engine stumbles from the excessively LEAN mixture. The voltage should LOWER to an approximate value of 200 mV (0.2 volt). Install the vacuum line. Now, obtain some propane gas mixture (bottled) and

2.12 Check for a millivolt signal on the oxygen sensor electrical connector (usually located near the firewall)

connect it to a vacuum port on the intake manifold. Start the engine and open the propane valve (open the propane valve only partially and do so a little at a time to prevent over-richening the mixture). This will create a RICH mixture. Watch carefully as the readings INCREASE. **Warning:** *Propane gas is highly flammable. Be sure there are no leaks in your connections or an explosion could result.* If the oxygen sensor responds correctly to the makeshift lean and rich conditions, the sensor is working properly.

Vehicle Speed Sensor (VSS)

Many feedback carburetor control systems are also equipped with a speed sensor to monitor engine rpm. These sensors function and operate the same as the fuel injected vehicle speed sensors. Refer to Section 3 for complete information and checking procedures.

Torque Converter Clutch (TCC) solenoid

Many feedback control systems are also equipped with the torque converter clutch (TCC) system. This system operates the same as the TCC system on fuel-injected vehicles. Refer to Section 3 for complete information and checking procedures.

Mixture Control (M/C) solenoid

General description

The mixture control (M/C) solenoid is a device that controls fuel flow from the bowl to the main well and at the same time controls the idle circuit air bleed. There are several different types of mixture control solenoids depending upon the manufacturer. Motorcraft and Carter carburetors use an air pulsing solenoid. Holley carburetors use vacuum to control a fuel control valve assembly. The most common type is the plunger style installed on Rochester feedback carburetors.

Motorcraft and Carter feedback carburetors

On Motorcraft and Carter feedback carburetors, an electric signal from the computer activates the solenoid and in turn allows fresh air from the air cleaner into the idle and main system air bleed passages. The amount of air that is allowed to enter depends on the duty cycle. 0-percent duty cycle keeps the solenoid closed (no voltage) and the feedback carburetor will go to a maximum rich condition. 100-percent duty cycle opens the solenoid fully, and the feedback system will go into maximum lean condition.

An easy way to check this type of system is to remove a large vacuum line to drive the system to LEAN. Watch carefully as the mixture control solenoid goes RICH to overcompensate for the imbalance. This can be checked with a dwellmeter set on the 6-cylinder scale.

Thermo-quad and Carter BBD feedback carburetors

The Thermo-quad and Carter BBD feedback carburetors are equipped with a plunger style mixture control solenoid that is electronically activated in response to the lean/rich conditions signalled from the oxygen sensor. This is accomplished by metering the main jets in the carburetor. By controlling the duration of this voltage signal, the ratio of power ON-time versus the power OFF-time is called the duty cycle. The mixture control solenoid is of a slightly different design and mounted in different locations depending upon the model and type of feedback system.

To check these type of feedback carburetors, maintain an engine speed of 1,500 rpms. Disconnect the mixture control solenoid connector from the solenoid. The average engine speed should increase a minimum of 50 rpms. Reconnect the feedback solenoid connector. The engine speed should slowly return to 1,500 rpms. If the engine rpm doesn't change, check the operation of the mixture control solenoid and the oxygen sensor (see previous text). If the oxygen sensor is operating correctly, replace the mixture control solenoid.

Holley feedback carburetors

On Holley feedback carburetors, the duty cycle solenoid (mixture control solenoid) regulates vacuum to a fuel control valve assembly. This valve consists of a diaphragm and an actuator in the air horn and metering valve assembly (needle and seat) in the main body of the carburetor. The regulated vacuum directly above the diaphragm moves the actuator which positions a tapered needle in the valve seat, allowing additional fuel to flow through the channel restrictor into the main mixing well. This regulates fuel into the main system thereby controlling off idle and part throttle air/fuel ratios.

An easy way to check this type of mixture control solenoid is to is to tee into the main vacuum lines with a vacuum gauge. Remove a large vacuum line from another source on the engine and drive the system to LEAN. Watch carefully as the vacuum changes and the system compensates by going into full RICH. If the vacuum to the actuator is regulating properly and you suspect problems with the valve assembly not fluctuating, have the system checked by a dealer service department.

Rochester feedback carburetors

On Rochester plunger style mixture control solenoids, the mixture control (M/C) solenoid is located in the float bowl where the power piston used to be. It is equipped with a spring loaded plunger that moves up and down like a power piston, but does so more rapidly. Certain areas on

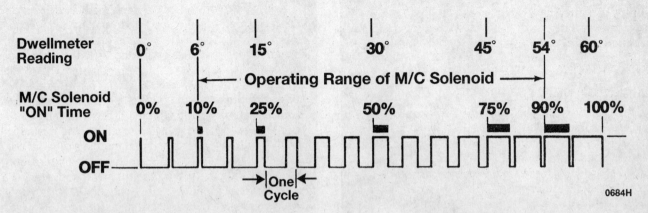

2.17 This chart indicates the relationship of the dwellmeter readings to the mixture control solenoid cycling. It is important to select the 6-cylinder scale on the dwellmeter to obtain the correct reading

the plunger head contact the metering rods and an idle air bleed valve. Plunger movement controls both the metering rods and the idle air bleed valve simultaneously.

When the mixture control solenoid is energized it moves down causing the metering rods to move into the jets and restrict the flow of fuel into the main well. The idle air bleed plunger opens the air bleed and allows air into the idle circuit. Both these movements reduce fuel flow and thereby LEANS out the system.

When the plunger is de-energized, the M/C solenoid moves up, causing the metering rods to move out of the jets and allow more fuel to the main well, less idle air and increased fuel flow. Here the solenoid is in the RICH position.

The mixture control solenoid varies the air/fuel ratio based on the electrical input from the ECM. When the solenoid is ON, the fuel is restricted and the air is admitted. This gives a lean air/fuel ratio (approximately 18:1). When the solenoid is OFF, fuel is admitted and the air/fuel ratio is approximately 13:1. During closed loop operation, the ECM controls the M/C solenoid to approximately 14.7:1 by con-

trolling the ON and OFF time of the solenoid.

As the solenoid "*on time*" changes, the up time and down time of the metering rods also changes. When a lean mixture is desired, the M/C solenoid will restrict fuel flow through the metering jet 90-percent of the time, or, in other words, a lean mixture will be provided to the engine.

This lean command will read as 54-degrees on the dwellmeter (54-degrees is 90-percent of 60-degrees), and means the M/C solenoid has restricted fuel flow 90-percent of the time **(see illustration).** A rich mixture is provided when the M/C solenoid restricts it only 10-percent of the time and allows a rich mixture to flow to the engine. A rich command will have a dwellmeter reading of 6-degrees (10-percent of 60-degrees); the M/C solenoid has restricted fuel flow 10-percent of the time. On some engines dwellmeter readings can vary between 5-degrees and 55-degrees, rather than between 6-degrees and 54-degrees. The ideal mixture would be shown on the dwellmeter with the needle varying or swinging back and forth, anywhere between 10-degrees and 50-degrees. "Varying" means the needle continually moves up and down the scale. The amount it moves

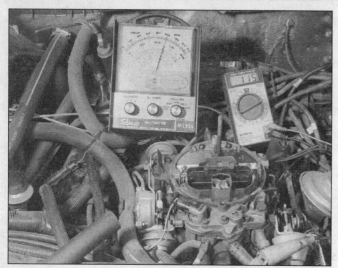

2.18 Connect the dwellmeter connector to the electrical connector (arrow) near the carburetor and observe the engine rpm on the one meter (right side) and the M/C solenoid dwell on the other meter (left side)

2.19 Place a rag over the carburetor air horn and watch the dwell go lean to compensate for a rich running condition

does not matter, only the fact that it does move. The dwell is being varied by the signal sent to the ECM by the oxygen sensor in the exhaust manifold.

The following checks assume the engine has been tuned and the ignition system is in order.

The dwellmeter is used to diagnose the M/C solenoid system. This is done by connecting a dwellmeter to the pigtail connector in the M/C solenoid wiring harness **(see illustration)**.

In the older style contact-points ignition systems, the dwellmeter reads the period of time that the points were closed (or "dwelled" together). That period of time was when voltage flowed to the ignition coil. In the feedback carburetor system, the dwellmeter is used to read the time that the ECM closes the M/C solenoid circuit to ground, allowing voltage to operate the M/C solenoid. Dwell, as used in feedback system performance diagnosis, is the time that the M/C solenoid circuit is closed (energized). The dwellmeter will translate this time into degrees. The "6-cylinder" (0-degrees to 60-degrees) scale on the dwellmeter is used for this reading. The ability of the dwellmeter to make this kind of conversion makes it an ideal tool to check the amount of time the ECM internal switch is closed, thus energizing the M/C solenoid. The only difference is that the degree scale on the meter is more like percent of solenoid **"*on time*"** rather than "degrees of dwell".

First set the dwellmeter on the 6-cylinder position, then connect it to the M/C solenoid dwell lead to measure the output of the ECM. Do not allow the terminal to touch ground, including hoses. You must use the 6-cylinder position when diagnosing all engines, whether the engine you're working on is a 4, 6, or 8 cylinder engine. **Note:** *Some older dwellmeters may not work properly on the feedback carburetor systems. Don't use any dwellmeter which causes a change in engine operation when it is connected to the solenoid lead.*

The 6-cylinder scale on the dwellmeter provides evenly divided points, for example:

15-degrees = 1/4 scale
30-degrees = midscale
45-degrees = 3/4 scale

Connect the positive clip lead of the dwellmeter to the M/C solenoid pigtail connector. Attach the other dwellmeter clip lead to ground. Do not allow the clip leads to contact other conductive cables or hoses which could interfere with accurate readings.

After connecting the dwellmeter to a warm, operating engine the dwell at idle and part throttle will read between 5-degrees and 55-degrees and will be varying. That is, the needle will move continuously up and down the scale. What matters is that the needle does move, not how much it moves. Typical needle movement will occur between the 30 and 35-degree range in a normal operating feedback system. Needle movement indicates that the engine is in "closed-loop," and that the dwell is being varied by signals from the ECM. However, if the engine is cold, has just been restarted, or the throttle is wide open, the dwell will be fixed and the needle will be steady. Those are signs that the engine is in "open-loop."

Diagnostic checks to find a condition without a trouble code are usually made on a warm engine (in "closed-loop"). This is easily checked by making sure the upper radiator hose is hot. There are three ways of distinguishing "open" from "closed-loop" operation.

1) A variation in dwell will occur only in "closed loop".
2) Test for closed loop operation by restricting airflow to the carburetor to choke the engine **(see illustration)**. **Warning:** *Use a thick rag (not your bare hand) and keep your face away from the carburetor. If the dwellmeter moves up scale, that indicates "closed-loop".*

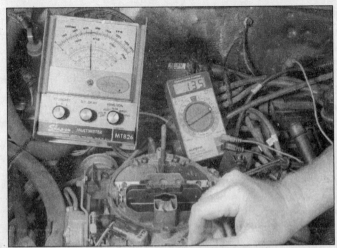

2.20 Disconnect a vacuum line and observe the dwell "on time" indicate rich (low reading) to compensate for the lean running condition

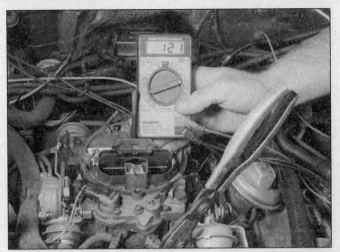

2.21 Install a clamp onto the purge hose from the charcoal canister to prevent entrance of vapors into the carburetor

3) If you create a large vacuum leak and the dwell drops down, that also indicates "closed-loop" **(see illustration)**.

Basically, "closed loop" indicates that the ECM is using information from the exhaust oxygen sensor to influence operation of the Mixture Control (M/C) solenoid. The ECM still considers other information such as, engine temperature, RPM, barometric and manifold pressure and throttle position along with the exhaust oxygen sensor information.

During "open-loop" all information except the exhaust oxygen sensor input is considered by the ECM to control the M/C solenoid. Accurate readings from the oxygen sensor are not attained until the sensor is completely hot (600-degrees F).

It is important to note that the exhaust oxygen sensor may cool below its operational temperature during prolonged idling. This will cause an open loop condition, and make the diagnostic information not usable during diagnosis. Engine RPM must be increased to warm the exhaust oxygen sensor, and again re-establish "closed loop". Diagnosis should begin over at the first step after "closed-loop" is resumed.

System performance test

First, start the engine and ground the diagnostic terminal (terminals A and B of the ALDL connector) using a small jumper wire **(see illustration 7.4a in Chapter 7A)**. This will allow the feedback system to run on the preset default values, thereby not allowing the computer to make any running adjustments. **Caution:** *It is important NOT to crank the engine while the diagnostic connector is grounded.* Disconnect the purge hose from the charcoal canister and plug it (or simply clamp it shut) **(see illustration)**. Disconnect the bowl vent hose at the carburetor and plug the hose on the canister side. These two steps will not allow any recirculated crankcase vapors to enter the carburetor during testing. Connect a tachometer according to the manufacturers' instructions. Disconnect the M/C solenoid and ground the

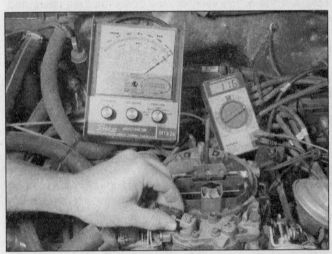

2.22 With the dwellmeter and tachometer properly installed, disconnect the M/C solenoid connector and observe the gauge. Rpm should drop below 300 from the normal level

M/C solenoid dwell lead **(see illustration)**. Run the engine at 3,000 rpm and while holding the throttle steady, reconnect the M/C solenoid and observe the rpm. If the engine is equipped with an electric cooling fan, the rpm may lower when it turns on. Remove the dwell lead before returning to idle.

The test results will be either:

a) the engine will drop below 300 rpm

b) the engine will NOT drop below 300 rpm and may increase rpm

If the engine does not drop below 300 rpm, check the wiring on the M/C solenoid for any damaged connectors and if they are OK, make sure the carburetor adjustments are properly set (refer to the *Haynes Rochester Carburetor Manual*).

If the engine drops below 300 rpm, connect a dwellmeter to the M/C solenoid dwell lead **(see illustration 2.19)**. Be sure to read the information on "closed loop" operation and dwellmeters in the preceding sections. Set the carburetor on the high step of the fast idle cam and run the engine for one minute or until the dwell starts to vary (whichever happens first). Return the engine to idle and observe the dwell. In most cases the dwell should vary between 10 and 50-degrees but there are several types of problems that may occur. **Note:** *The following tests must be performed with the diagnostic connector still grounded (terminals A and B) unless otherwise indicated.*

Fixed dwell under 10-degrees

This condition indicates that the feedback system is responding RICH to offset a very lean condition in the engine. One way to separate the problem is to choke the carburetor with the engine at part throttle. This will either increase or decrease the dwell.

If the dwell increases, check for a vacuum leak in the hoses, gaskets, AIR system etc. Also, check for an exhaust leak near the oxygen sensor, any hoses that are misrouted and an EGR valve that is not operating or that is leaking.

If the dwell does not increase, check the oxygen sensor, the wiring harness from the ECM to the oxygen sensor, TPS, TPS voltage and/or the ECM. If necessary, have the system diagnosed by a dealer service department or other repair shop.

Fixed dwell between 10 and 50-degrees

This condition indicates that the feedback system is stuck in one mode (open loop) because of a faulty coolant temperature sensor, oxygen sensor or TPS. Start the diagnosis by running the engine at part throttle for one minute. Then with the engine idling, observe the dwell, remove the connector from the coolant sensor and jump the terminals on the connector. This will ground the signal and indicate to the ECM that the sensors are functioning (grounded). The dwell reading should not be fixed with the sensor grounded. Check each sensor for the correct resistance and voltage signal from its respective electrical connector.

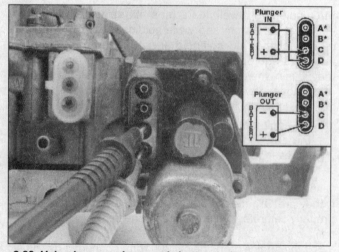

2.23 Using jumper wires, apply battery voltage to terminal C while grounding D to retract the ISC solenoid plunger

Fixed dwell over 50-degrees

This condition indicates that the feedback system is responding LEAN to offset a very rich condition in the engine. Start the diagnosis by running the engine at fast idle for about two minutes and then let it return to idle. This procedure makes sure that the feedback system is in closed-loop (warmed-up). Next, disconnect the large vacuum hose to the PCV valve and cause a major vacuum leak. Do not allow the engine to stall. The dwell should drop by approximately 20-degrees. If it does, check the carburetor on-vehicle adjustments (refer to the *Haynes Rochester Carburetor Manual*). Also, check the evaporative canister for fuel overload or leaks in the purge control system that would cause an over-rich condition in the carburetor.

If the dwell does not drop, check the oxygen sensor, oxygen sensor signal voltage and their respective wiring circuits for any problems.

Feedback carburetor adjustments (Rochester feedback carburetors only)

Depending upon the engine size and year of the vehicle, feedback carburetor systems require several on-vehicle adjustments to fine-tune engine performance.

Idle speed control (ISC) system

If the carburetor has just been overhauled, the ISC solenoid has just been replaced with a new one or the vehicle is having a fluctuating idle problem, it is necessary to check the ISC system adjustments.

1   First, place the transmission in Neutral, set the parking brake and block the drive wheels. Connect a tachometer according to the manufacturer's instructions.

2   With the A/C off (if equipped), start the engine and warm it up to normal operating temperature (closed loop).

3   Turn the ignition OFF and unplug the electrical connector from the ISC motor.

4   Fully retract the ISC plunger by applying 12 volts to terminal C (run a fused jumper wire from the battery's positive terminal) of the ISC motor connector and grounding terminal D **(see illustration). Note 1**: *Do not allow the battery voltage (12V) to contact terminal C any longer than necessary to retract the ISC plunger. Prolonged contact will cause damage to the motor. Also, it is very important to never connect a voltage source across terminals A and B, as it may damage the internal throttle contact.*

Note 2: *If the ISC solenoid does not respond when battery voltage is applied to the C and D terminals, it is faulty and should be replaced.*

5   Start the engine and allow it to return to normal operation (closed loop). Have an assistant place his foot firmly on the brake and place the transmission in DRIVE (automatic) or Neutral (manual).

6   With the plunger completely retracted (from Step 4), turn the idle stop screw **(see illustration)** to attain the minimum idle speed. The minimum base idle speed is usually about 450 rpm in DRIVE. Consult your VECI label under the hood of the engine compartment to verify the idle specifications.

7   Now, with the transmission in DRIVE or Neutral and an

2.24 Location of the idle stop screw (arrow) on feedback carburetors

2.25 Adjust the ISC plunger by turning the plunger end with pliers (carburetor removed for clarity)

2.26 Do not unscrew the plunger end more than 5/16-inch from its completely retracted position

2.27 Be sure to protect the carburetor when drilling out the air bleed cover rivets (otherwise, metal chips could fall into the carburetor throat)

assistant depressing the brake pedal firmly, fully extend the plunger by applying battery positive voltage (12V) to terminal D of the ISC connector and grounding terminal C. **Note**: *Do not allow the battery voltage (12V) to contact terminal D any longer than necessary to retract the ISC plunger. Prolonged contact will cause damage to the motor. Also, it is very important to never connect a voltage source across terminals A and B as it may damage the internal throttle contact switch.*

8   With the ISC plunger fully extended, check the idle speed, which should be approximately 900 rpm in DRIVE or NEUTRAL. If necessary, adjust the plunger length **(see illustrations)**. Consult your VECI label under the hood of the engine compartment to verify the idle specifications. **Note**: *When the ISC plunger is in the fully extended position, the plunger must also be in contact with the throttle lever (on carburetor) to prevent possible internal damage to the ISC solenoid.*

9   If the ISC motor was removed and the plunger length changed, double-check the maximum allowable speed (see

Step 8). If necessary, readjust the plunger until the correct speed is obtained.

10   Reconnect the harness connector to the ISC motor.

Idle air bleed valve (E2ME and E4ME carburetors)

To gain access to the idle air bleed valve, it is necessary to first remove the idle air bleed valve cover. Often, if the carburetor has been overhauled before, the cover has already been removed. If it has not been removed before, the air bleed is probably still at its factory setting and should not be tampered with unless it's known to be incorrect.

1   With the engine off, cover all the bowl vents, air inlets and air intakes with masking tape to prevent any metal chips from falling into the carburetor.

2   Carefully align a Number 35 drill bit (0.110 inches) on one end of the steel rivet heads and drill only enough to remove the rivet head from the carburetor. Use a drift and hammer to remove the remaining rivet from the assembly **(see illustration)**.

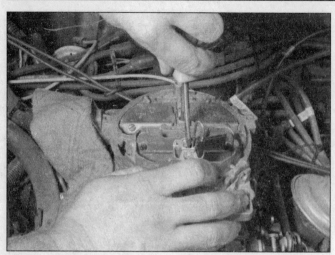

2.28 The special gauging tool shown is necessary to check the idle air bleed valve adjustment. Use a large screwdriver, as shown here, to adjust the valve

2.29 Do not adjust the ILC plunger to a point where the screw is extending more than one inch

3　Lift off the cover and remove any pieces of metal, rivets or debris from the carburetor body. Discard the idle air bleed valve cover.

4　Using compressed air (if available) blow out any remaining pieces of metal from the carburetor area. **Warning:** *Be sure to wear safety goggles whenever using compressed air.*

5　Install a special gauging tool (available from auto parts stores and automotive tool suppliers) into the "D"-shaped vent hole **(see illustration)**. The upper end of the tool should be positioned over the open cavity next to the idle air bleed valve.

6　While holding the gauging tool down lightly, engage the solenoid plunger against the solenoid stop. Adjust the idle air bleed valve so that the gauging tool will pivot over and just contact the top of the valve.

7　Remove the gauging tool. Next, it will be necessary to check the duty cycle **(on-time)** of the mixture control solenoid to verify that the air bleed is adjusted properly or if the idle mixture must be adjusted (see the *System performance check*).

8　Disconnect the canister purge hose and plug the end (canister side). Start the engine and allow it to reach normal operating temperature (closed loop). Follow the procedure for checking the M/C solenoid duty cycle as described in the *System performance check*. If the dwell average is not within 25 to 35 degrees, then it will be necessary to adjust the idle mixture (refer to the procedure in this chapter).

Idle load compensator (ILC) (some later 5.0L engines)

The idle load compensator (ILC) is used instead of an ISC solenoid on some later 5.0L engines to control curb idle speed. The ILC uses manifold vacuum to sense changes in engine load and compensates by changing the idle speed. The idle load compensator is adjusted at the factory. It is not necessary to make any adjustments unless the curb idle speed is out of adjustment or the ILC solenoid was faulty

and had to be replaced. Before adjusting the ILC, make sure the vacuum lines to the anti-diesel solenoid, vacuum regulator, ILC solenoid and all the components that require vacuum are in order and not leaking. Check the vacuum schematic on the VECI label under the hood for the correct vacuum routing.

1　Connect a tachometer according to the manufacturer's instructions. Remove the air cleaner and plug the hose to the thermal vacuum valve (TVV). Disconnect and plug the vacuum hose to the EGR valve. Disconnect and plug the vacuum hose to the canister purge port. Disconnect and plug the vacuum hose to the ILC.

2　Back out the idle-stop screw on the carburetor three turns.

3　Turn the A/C system OFF (if equipped). Place the transmission in PARK (automatic) or NEUTRAL (manual), apply the emergency brake and place a block under each of the drive wheels.

4　Start the engine and allow it to reach normal operating temperature. On automatic transmission models, have an assistant place his foot firmly on the brake pedal and place the transmission in DRIVE. The ILC plunger should be fully extended with no vacuum applied. Using back-up wrenches, adjust the ILC plunger to obtain 750 rpm, plus or minus 50 rpm.

5　Next, measure the distance from the jam nut to the tip of the plunger **(see illustration)**. It should not exceed one inch. If the plunger measures more than one inch, check for other carburetor problems.

6　Remove the plug from the vacuum hose and reconnect it to the ILC and observe the idle speed. Idle speed should be 450 rpm (vehicle in NEUTRAL(manual) or DRIVE with the brake applied). If the idle speed is correct, proceed to Step 9).

7　If the idle speed is not correct, it will be necessary to adjust the ILC diaphragm. Stop the engine and remove the ILC. Remove the center cap from the center outlet tube. Using a 3/32-inch Allen wrench, insert it through the open center tube to engage the idle speed adjusting screw inside

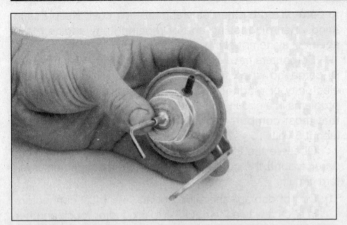

2.30 Use a 3/32-inch Allen wrench to adjust the ILC solenoid (removed from vehicle for clarity)

2.31 To adjust the TPS, drill out and remove the access plug

(see illustration). If the idle speed was low, turn the adjusting screw counterclockwise ONE turn to increase the idle speed approximately 75 rpm. Conversely, turn the screw clockwise ONE turn to lower the idle speed about 75 rpm. **Note**: *Turn the adjusting screw TWO full turns to raise or lower the idle speed approximately 150 rpm and consequently use the same ratio to calculate the necessary rpm change desired for the situation.*

8   Re-install the ILC onto the carburetor and attach the springs and other related parts. Recheck the idle speed. Make sure the engine is completely warmed up (closed loop). If it is not correct, repeat the ILC adjustment procedure.

9   The last adjustment must be performed on the engine after the TPS value has been reset by the ECM. This can be accomplished by turning off the ignition for 10 seconds or more. Using a hand-held vacuum pump, apply vacuum to the ILC vacuum tube inlet to fully retract the plunger.

10   Adjust the idle stop screw on the carburetor to obtain 450 rpm with the vehicle in NEUTRAL (manual) or DRIVE with the brake applied.

11   Place the vehicle in PARK and stop the engine. Remove the plug from the ILC vacuum hose and install the hose onto the ILC. Reconnect all the vacuum hoses, install the air cleaner and gaskets.

Throttle position sensor (TPS)

The throttle position sensor is equipped with an adjustment screw that is covered by a factory-installed plug. Do not remove the plug unless it has been determined with careful testing that the TPS is out of adjustment. This is a critical adjustment that must be performed correctly.

1   Using a 0.076-inch drill bit, carefully drill a hole in the aluminum plug covering the TPS adjustment screw **(see illustration)**. Drill only enough metal to start a self-tapping screw.

2   Start a number 8 X 1/2-inch long self-tapping screw into the drilled hole in the plug, turning the screw just enough to ensure good thread engagement in the hole.

3   Place a wide blade section of screwdriver between the screw head and the air horn casting. Carefully pry against the screw head to remove the plug. It is also possible to use a slide hammer.

4   Disconnect the TPS electrical connector, install jumper wires, as shown **(see illustration)**, then connect a digital voltmeter between the wires connected to the B (center) and C (bottom) terminals of the TPS connector on the carburetor.

5   With the engine and ignition off and the throttle closed, turn the screw until the voltage reading is approximately 0.48 volts **(see illustration)**.

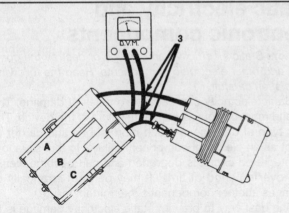

2.32 Disconnect the TPS connector and hook up a digital voltmeter, as shown . . .

2.33 . . . then use a small screwdriver to turn the adjusting screw until the readings are correct

6   Make sure the voltage is correct, then install a new plug into the air horn. Drive the plug into place until it is flush with the raised boss on the casting.

3 Fuel injection engine management sensors and output actuators

Note: *Some of the procedures in this Section require you to operate the vehicle after disconnecting a portion of the engine management system (such as a sensor or a vacuum line). This may set trouble codes in the computer. Be sure to clear any trouble codes (see Chapter 7A) before returning the vehicle to normal service.*

This Section deals with the engine management systems used on modern, computer-controlled vehicles to meet new low-emission regulations. The system's computer, information sensors and output actuators interact with each other to collect, store and send data. Basically, the information sensors collect data (such as the intake air mass and/or temperature, coolant temperature, throttle position, exhaust gas oxygen content, etc.) and transmit this data, in the form of varying electrical signals, to the computer. The computer compares this data with its "map," which tells what these data should be under the engine's current operating conditions. If the data does not match the map, the computer sends signals to output actuators (fuel injectors or throttle body injector, Electronic Air Control Valve (EACV), Idle Speed Control (ISC) motor, etc.) which correct the engine's operation to match the map **(see illustration).**

When the engine is warming up (and sensor input is not precise) or there is a malfunction in the system, the system operates in an "open loop" mode. In this mode, the computer does not rely on the sensors for input and sets the fuel/air mixture rich so the engine can continue operation until the engine warms up or repairs are made. **Note:** *The engine's thermostat rating and proper operation are critical to the operation of a computer-controlled vehicle. If the thermostat is rated at too low a temperature, is removed or stuck open, the computer may stay in "open loop" operation and emissions and fuel economy will suffer.*

The automotive computer

Automotive computers come in all sizes and shapes and are generally located under the dashboard, around the fenderwells or under the front seat. The Environmental Protection Agency (EPA) and the Federal government require all automobile manufacturers to warranty their emissions systems for 5 years or 50,000 miles. This broad emissions warranty coverage will allow most computer malfunctions

to be repaired by the dealership at their cost. Keep this in mind when diagnosing and/or repairing any engine management system/fuel injection problems.

Computers have delicate internal circuitry which is easily damaged when subjected to excessive voltage, static electricity or magnetism. When diagnosing any electrical problems in a circuit connected to the computer, remember that most computers operate at a relatively low voltage (about 5 volts).

Observe the following precautions whenever working on or around the computer and engine management system circuits:

1) Do not damage the wiring or any electrical connectors in such a way as to cause it to ground or touch another source of voltage.
2) Do not use any electrical testing equipment (such as an ohmmeter) that is powered by a six-or-more-volt battery. The excessive voltage might cause an electrical component in the computer to burn or short. Use only a ten mega-ohm impedance multimeter when working on engine management circuits.
3) Do not remove or troubleshoot the computer without the proper tools and information, because any mistakes can void your warranty and/or damage components.
4) All spark plug wires should be at least one inch away from any sensor circuit or control wires. An unexpected problem in computer circuits is magnetic fields that send false signals to the computer, frequently resulting in hard-to-identify performance problems. Although there have been cases of high-power lines or transformers interfering with the computer, the most common cause of this problem in the sensor circuits is the position of the spark plug wires (too close to the computer wiring).
5) Use special care when handling or working near the computer. Remember that static electricity can cause computer damage by creating a very large surge in voltage (see *Static electricity and electronic components* below).

Static electricity and electronic components

Caution: *Static electricity can damage or destroy the computer and other electronic components. Read the following information carefully.*

Static electricity can cause two types of damage. The first and most obvious is complete failure of the device. The other type of damage is much more subtle and harder to detect as an electrical component failure. In this situation, the integrated circuit is degraded and can become weakened over a period of time. It may perform erratically or appear as another component's intermittent failure.

The best way to prevent static electricity damage is to drain the charge from your body by grounding your body to the frame or body of the vehicle and then working strictly on

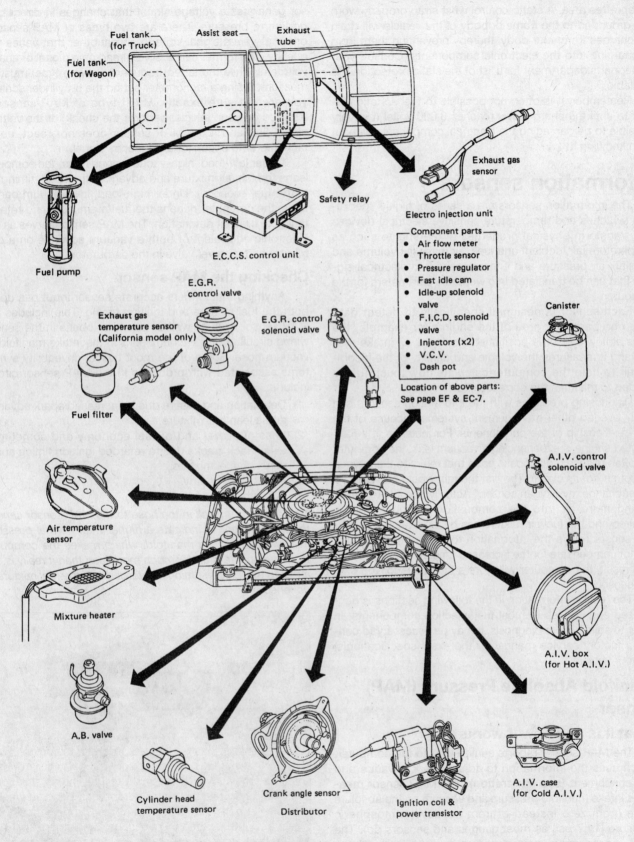

Fuel tank (for Truck)

Fuel tank (for Wagon)

Assist seat

Exhaust tube

Exhaust gas sensor

Safety relay

Electro injection unit

Component parts
- Air flow meter
- Throttle sensor
- Pressure regulator
- Fast idle cam
- Idle-up solenoid valve
- F.I.C.D. solenoid valve
- Injectors (x2)
- V.C.V.
- Dash pot

Location of above parts:
See page EF & EC-7.

Fuel pump

E.C.C.S. control unit

E.G.R. control valve

E.G.R. control solenoid valve

Canister

Exhaust gas temperature sensor (California model only)

Fuel filter

Air temperature sensor

A.I.V. control solenoid valve

Mixture heater

A.I.V. box (for Hot A.I.V.)

A.B. valve

Cylinder head temperature sensor

Crank angle sensor

Distributor

Ignition coil & power transistor

A.I.V. case (for Cold A.I.V.)

3.1 Overall view of a fuel injection system, including the computer, information sensors and output actuators (Nissan pick-up shown)

a static-free area. A static-control wrist strap properly worn and grounded to the frame or body of the vehicle will drain the charges from your body, thereby preventing them from discharging into the electronic components. Consult your dealer parts department for a list of the static protection kits available.

Remember, it is often not possible to feel a static discharge until the charge level reaches 3,000 volts! It is very possible to be damaging the electrical components without even knowing it!

Information sensors

The information sensors are a series of highly specialized switches and temperature-sensitive electrical devices that transform physical properties of the engine such as temperature (air, coolant and fuel), air mass (air volume and density), air pressure and engine speed into electrical signals that can be translated into workable parameters for the computer.

Each sensor is designed specifically to detect data from one particular area of the engine; for example, the mass airflow sensor is positioned inside the air intake system and it measures the volume and density of the incoming air to help the computer calculate how much fuel is needed to maintain the correct air/fuel mixture.

Diagnosing problems with the information sensors can easily overlap other management systems because of the inter-relationship of the components. For instance, if a fuel-injected engine is experiencing a vacuum leak, the computer will often release a diagnostic code that refers to the oxygen sensor and/or its circuit. The first thought would be "Well, I'd better change my oxygen sensor." Actually, the intake leak is forcing more air into the combustion chamber than is required and the fuel/air mixture has become lean. The oxygen sensor relays the information to the computer which cannot compensate for the increased amount of oxygen and, as a result, the computer will store a fault code for the oxygen sensor.

The testing information in the following sections is generalized and applies to most fuel injection components. In order to solidify your diagnosis, it may be necessary to consult a factory service manual for the exact specification(s) for your vehicle.

Manifold Absolute Pressure (MAP) sensor

What it is and how it works

The MAP sensor reports engine load to the computer, which uses the information to adjust spark advance and fuel enrichment (see illustration). The MAP sensor measures intake manifold pressure and vacuum on the absolute scale (from zero instead of from sea-level atmospheric pressure [14.7 psi] as most gauges and sensors do). The MAP sensor reads vacuum and pressure through a hose connected to the intake manifold. A pressure-sensitive ceramic or silicon element and electronic circuit in the sen-

sor generates a voltage signal that changes in direct proportion to pressure. There are two types of MAP sensors; one that varies signal voltage and another that varies frequency. The former can easily be read on a digital or analog voltmeter while the latter (frequency varying type) must be measured using a tachometer set on the 6-cylinder scale. If you are not sure exactly which type of MAP sensor is installed on your vehicle, perform the check for the voltage signal first and if the MAP sensor does not react, use a tachometer to check for a frequency signal.

Under low-load, high-vacuum conditions, the computer leans the fuel/air mixture and advances the spark timing for better fuel economy. Under high-load, low-vacuum conditions, the computer richens the fuel/air mixture and retards timing to prevent detonation. The MAP sensor serves as the electronic equivalent of both a vacuum advance on a distributor and a power valve in the carburetor.

Checking the MAP sensor

Anything that hinders accurate sensor input can upset both the fuel mixture and ignition timing. This includes the MAP sensor itself as well as shorts or opens in the sensor wiring circuit and/or vacuum leaks in the intake manifold or vacuum hose. Some of the most typical driveability symptoms associated with problems in the MAP sensor circuit include:

1) Detonation and misfire due to increased spark advance and a lean fuel mixture.
2) Loss of power and/or fuel economy and sometimes even black smoke due to retarded ignition timing and a very rich fuel mixture.
3) Poor fuel economy.
4) Hard starts and/or stalling.

Note: *A vacuum leak in the hose to the MAP sensor causes the MAP sensor to indicate a higher than normal pressure (less vacuum) in the manifold, which makes the computer think the engine is under much more load than it really is. As a result, the ignition timing is retarded and the fuel mixture is richened.*

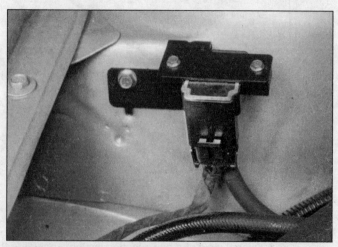

3.2 Here's a typical MAP sensor (voltage varying type) - this one is from a Plymouth Sundance

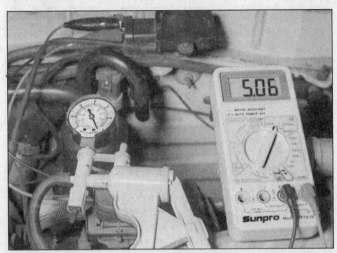

3.3 The MAP sensor voltage (measured at the signal wire) will decrease as vacuum is applied to the sensor

3.4 To check a frequency varying MAP sensor, with no vacuum applied, the sensor should read between 300 and 320 rpm on the tachometer scale (6-cylinder selection)

When the MAP sensor trouble code is detected, be sure to first check for vacuum leaks in the hoses or electrical connectors or wiring damage in the MAP sensor circuit. Kinks in the line, blockage or splits can occur and deter the sensor's ability to respond accurately to the changes in the manifold pressure. Check for anything that is obvious and easily repaired before actually replacing the sensor itself.

To check the MAP sensor it will be necessary to install the negative probe of the voltmeter/tachometer onto the ground wire of the MAP sensor connector and the positive probe onto the signal wire. The ground wire is typically black in color. The signal wire can be distinguished from the reference wire by checking for a 5.0 volt reference signal (ignition key ON [engine not running]) and by the process of elimination, each wire can be designated. Remember, the signal wire will vary voltage or frequency as vacuum is applied to the MAP sensor. If there is ant doubt, consult a wiring diagram for the correct terminal designations.

A MAP sensor will typically produce a voltage signal that will drop with decreasing manifold pressure (rising vacuum). Test specifications will vary according to the manufacturer and engine type. A typical MAP sensor (voltage varying type) will read 4.6 to 4.8 volts with 0 in-Hg vacuum applied to it **(see illustration)**. Raise it to 5 in-Hg vacuum and the reading should drop to about 3.75 volts. Raise it up again to 20 in-Hg and the reading should drop to about 1.1 volts. A typical MAP sensor (frequency varying type) will read 300 to 320 rpm with 0 in-Hg vacuum applied to it **(see illustration)**. Raise it to 5 in-Hg vacuum and the reading should drop to about 275 to 295 rpm. Raise it up again to 20 in-Hg and the reading should drop to about 200 to 215 rpm **(see illustration)**. All tests should be performed with the ignition key ON, engine NOT running.

MAF (Mass Air Flow) sensor

What it is and how it works

The MAF sensor is positioned in the air intake duct **(see illustration)**, and it measures the amount of air entering the

3.5 Now apply vacuum (20 inches Hg) and the tach should read between 200 and 230 rpm

3.6 Here's a typical airflow sensor (this one's from a Nissan Maxima) - to remove it, remove the bolts (arrows)

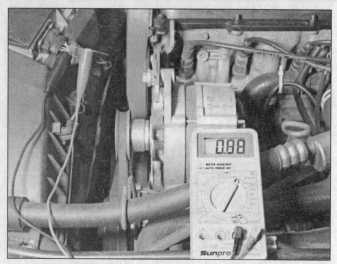

3.7 The signal voltage on a typical Bosch MAF sensor will read 0.60 to 0.80 volts at idle and . . .

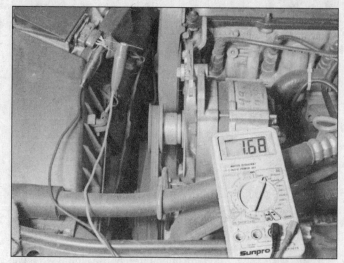

3.8 . . . when the engine speed is raised to 2,500 to 3,500 rpm, the voltage increases to approximately 1.50 to 2.20 volts

engine. Mass airflow sensors come in two basic varieties; hot wire and hot film. Both types work on the same principle, though they are designed differently. They measure the volume and density of the air entering the engine so the computer can calculate how much fuel is needed to maintain the correct fuel/air mixture. MAF sensors have no moving parts. Unlike the vane air flow sensors that use a spring-loaded flap, MAF sensors use an electrical current to measure airflow. There are two types of sensing elements; platinum wire (hot wire) or nickel foil grid (hot film). Each one is heated electrically to keep the temperature higher than the intake air temperature. With hot-film MAF sensors, the film is heated 170-degrees F warmer than the incoming air temperature. On hot-wire MAF sensors, the wire is heated to 210-degrees F above the incoming air temperature. As air flows past the element it cools the element and thereby increases the amount of current necessary to heat it up again. Because the necessary current varies directly with the temperature and the density of the air entering the intake, the amount of current is directly proportional to the air mass entering the engine. This information is fed into the computer and the fuel mixture is directly controlled according to the conditions.

Checking the MAF sensor

The most effective method for testing the MAF sensor is measuring the sensor's output or its effect on the injector pulse width. On Bosch or Ford hot-wire systems, the voltage output can be read directly with a voltmeter by probing the appropriate sensor terminals **(see illustrations)**. Refer to your factory service manual for the correct terminal designations and specifications. If the voltage readings are not within range or the voltage fails to INCREASE when the throttle is opened with the engine running, the sensor is faulty and must be replaced with a new part. A dirty wire or a contaminated wire (a direct result of a faulty self-cleaning circuit) will deliver a slow response of the changes in airflow to the computer. Also, keep in mind that the self-cleaning

circuit is controlled by relays. So, check the relays first if the MAF sensor appears to be sluggish or not responsive. Proper diagnosis of the MAF sensor is very important because this part is usually somewhat expensive. Be sure to check for diagnostic codes, if possible. If the wiring checks out and all other obvious areas are checked carefully, replace the sensor.

Another way to check MAF sensor output is to see what effect it has on injector pulse width (if this specification is available). Using a multimeter or oscilloscope that reads milliseconds, connect the positive probe directly to any injector signal wire and the negative probe to a ground terminal **(see illustration)**. Remember that one injector terminal is connected to the supply voltage (battery voltage) and the other is connected to the computer (signal wire) which varies the amount of time the injector is grounded. **Note:** *Typically, if by chance you connect to the wrong side of the injector connector, one wire will give you a steady*

3.9 Checking a MAF sensor (this one's on a Ford) - this test requires a special multimeter that detects pulse width variations

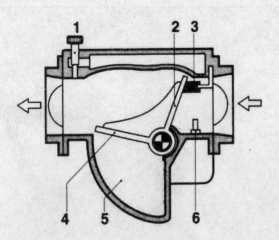

3.10 A cross-sectional diagram of a vane airflow sensor

1	Idle mixture screw	4	Compensation flap
2	Airflow sensor flap	5	Damping chamber
3	Stop	6	Intake air temperature sensor

3.11 Here's a typical MAT sensor (1985 Corvette shown) - it is located in the underside of the air intake plenum

reading (battery voltage) while the signal wire will fluctuate slightly. Look at the pulse width at idle or while cranking the engine. The injector pulse width will vary with different conditions. If the MAF sensor is not producing a signal, the pulse width will typically be FOUR times longer than the correct width. This will indicate an excessively rich fuel/air mixture.

VAF (Vane Air Flow) sensor

What it is and how it works

VAF sensors are positioned in the air intake stream ahead of the throttle, and they monitor the volume of air entering the engine by means of a spring-loaded flap **(see illustration)**. The flap is pushed open by the air entering the system and a potentiometer (variable resistor) attached to the flap will vary the voltage signal to the computer according to the volume of air entering the engine (angle of the flap). The greater the airflow, the further the flap is forced open.

VAF sensors are used most commonly on Bosch L-Jetronic fuel injection systems, Nippondenso multi-port fuel injection systems and certain Ford multi-port fuel injection systems.

Checking the VAF sensor

Diagnosing VAF sensors is quite different from diagnosing MAF or MAP sensors. Vane airflow sensors are vulnerable to dirt and grease. Unfiltered air that gets by a dirty or torn air filter will build up on the flap hinge or shaft, causing the flap to bind or hesitate as it swings. Remove the air intake boot and gently push open the flap with your finger; it should open and close smoothly. If necessary, spray a small amount of carburetor cleaner on the hinge and try to loosen the flap so it moves freely.

Disconnect the electrical connector to the VAF sensor. Connect an ohmmeter to the electrical connector on the VAF sensor; the resistance should vary evenly as the flap opens and closes. If the resistance changes erratically or skips and jumps, you will have to replace the VAF with a new unit. **Note:** *Be sure to use an ANALOG ohmmeter for this check, since a digital meter will not usually register the rapid resistance changes that occur during this test.*

Another common problem to watch out for with VAF sensors is a bent or damaged flap caused by backfiring in the intake manifold. Some VAF sensors incorporate a "backfire" valve in the sensor body that prevents damage to the flap by venting any explosion. If the "backfire" valve leaks, the valve will cause the sensor to read low, consequently causing the engine to run on a rich fuel/air mixture.

The VAF sensor is manufactured as a sealed unit, preset at the factory with nothing that can be serviced except the idle mixture screw. Do not attempt to disassemble the unit if it is still under warranty, because tampering with the unit will void the warranty.

Air temperature sensor

What it is and how it works

The air temperature sensor is also known a a Manifold Air Temperature (MAT) sensor, an Air Charge Temperature (ACT) sensor, a Vane Air Temperature (VAT) sensor, a Charge Temperature Sensor (CTS), an Air Temperature Sensor (ATS) and a Manifold Charging Temperature (MCT) sensor. The sensor is located in the intake manifold or air intake plenum **(see illustration)** and detects the temperature of the incoming air. The sensor usually consists of a temperature sensitive thermistor which changes the value of its voltage signal as the temperature changes. The computer uses the sensor signal to richen or lean-out the fuel/air mixture, and, on some applications, to delay the EGR valve opening until the manifold temperature reaches normal operating range.

3.12 On a typical TPS, the voltage should range from 0.4 to 5.0 volts. Position the positive probe of the voltmeter to the signal wire and the negative probe to the ground wire and slowly open the throttle completely

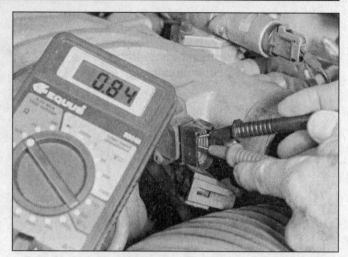

3.13 Slowly move the throttle and observe the resistance readings on the display - there should be a smooth transition as the resistance increases

Checking the ATS

The easiest way to check an air temperature sensor is to remove it from the manifold, then hook up an ohmmeter to its terminals and check the resistance when the sensor is cold. Then warm up the tip of the sensor with a blow drier (never a propane torch!) and watch for a decrease in resistance. No change in resistance indicates the sensor is defective. When reinstalling the sensor, be sure to use sealant on the threads so you don't end up with a vacuum leak.

On most GM vehicles equipped with the MAT sensor, a Code 23 or 25 will indicate a fault in the sensor (see Chapter 7). Be aware that problems with the EGR system might be caused by a defective MAT sensor.

Throttle Position Sensor (TPS)

What it is and how it works

The TPS is usually mounted externally on the throttle body. Some are inside the throttle body. The TPS is attached directly to the throttle shaft and varies simultaneously with the angle of the throttle. Its job is to inform the computer about the rate of throttle opening and relative throttle position. A separate Wide Open Throttle (WOT) switch may be used to signal the computer when the throttle is wide open. The TPS consists of a variable resistor that changes resistance thereby varying the voltage signal as the throttle changes its opening. By signaling the computer when the throttle opens, the computer can richen the fuel mixture to maintain the proper air/fuel ratio. The initial setting of the TPS is very important because the voltage signal the computer receives tells the computer the exact position of the throttle at idle.

Checking the TPS

Throttle position sensors typically have their own types of driveability symptoms that can be distinguished from other information sensors. The most common symptom of a faulty or misadjusted sensor is hesitation or stumble during acceleration (the same symptom of a bad accelerator pump in a carbureted engine).

There are basically two voltage checks you can perform to test the TPS. **Note:** *It is best to have the correct wiring diagram for the vehicle when performing the following checks.*

The first test is for the presence of voltage at the TPS supply wire with the ignition key ON. The throttle position sensor cannot deliver the correct signal without the proper supply voltage. You can determine the function of each individual wire (ground, supply, signal wire) by probing each one with a voltmeter and checking the different voltages. The voltage that remains constant when the throttle is opened and closed is the supply voltage. If there's no voltage at any of the wires, there's probably an open or short in the wiring harness to the sensor. Most systems use 5.0 volts on the supply wire.

The second check is for the proper voltage change that occurs as the throttle opens and closes (signal voltage). As the throttle goes from closed-to-wide open, the voltage at the signal wire should typically increase smoothly from 1 volt to 5 volts **(see illustration)**. **Note:** *An alternate method for checking the range is the resistance test. Hook up an ohmmeter to the supply and signal wires. With the ignition key OFF, slowly move the throttle through the complete range* **(see illustration)**. *Observe carefully for any unusual changes in resistance (the change should be smooth) as it increases from low to high.*

Also, check your diagnostic codes for any differences in the circuit failures versus the actual sensor failure. Be sure you have checked all the obvious items before replacing the throttle position sensor.

Adjusting

TPS's seldom need adjustment. However, many TPS's must be adjusted when they are replaced. Since different

3.14 On a BMW 318i, the TPS is located under the air intake plenum. Both mounting screws must be loosened to adjust the sensor

3.15 This oxygen sensor (arrow) is screwed into the exhaust manifold (GM V6 engine shown)

makes and models of vehicles have different specifications and procedures for adjusting the TPS, we recommend you refer to a service manual for your specific vehicle to adjust the TPS. Also, dealer service departments or other qualified shops can usually adjust the TPS for you for a nominal fee. **Note:** *The adjustment information in the following paragraph may not be applicable to your vehicle. It is only intended to familiarize you with a typical procedure.*

Normally, you'll only need a voltmeter to adjust the TPS. Hook the meter up to the signal (return) and ground terminals (not the five-volt reference wire) and loosen the mounting screws **(see illustration)**. With the throttle in the specified position (usually against the throttle stop), rotate the sensor clockwise or counterclockwise until the specified voltage is obtained (normally about 0.5-volt). Retighten the mounting screws and check the voltage again.

Oxygen sensor

What it is and how it works

The oxygen sensor (also known as a Lambda or EGO sensor) is located in the exhaust manifold (or in the exhaust pipe, near the exhaust manifold) and produces a voltage signal proportional to the content of oxygen in the exhaust **(see illustration)**. A higher oxygen content across the sensor tip will vary the oxygen differential, thereby lowering the sensor's output voltage. On the other hand, lower oxygen content will raise the output voltage. Typically the voltage ranges from 0.10 volts (lean) to 0.90 volts (rich). The computer uses the sensor's input voltage to adjust the air/fuel mixture, leaning it out when the sensor detects a rich condition or enrichening it when it detects a lean condition. When the sensor reaches operating temperature (600-degrees F), it will produce a variable voltage signal based on the difference between the amount of oxygen in the exhaust (internal) and the amount of oxygen in the air directly surrounding the sensor (external). The ideal stoichiometric fuel/air ratio (14.7:1) will produce about 0.45 volts.

There are basically two types of oxygen sensors on the

market. The most popular type uses a zirconia element in its tip. The latest type of oxygen sensor uses a titania element. Instead of producing its own voltage, the titania element resistance will alter a voltage signal that is supplied by the computer itself. Although the titania element works differently than the zirconia element, the results are basically identical. The biggest difference is that the titania element responds faster and allows the computer to maintain more uniform control over a wide range of exhaust temperatures.

Contamination can directly affect the engine performance and life span of the oxygen sensor. There are basically three types of contamination; carbon, lead and silicon. Carbon buildup due to a rich-running condition will cause inaccurate readings and increase the problem's symptoms. Diagnose the fuel injection system for correct fuel adjustments. Once the system is repaired, run the engine at high rpm without a load (parked in the driveway) to remove the carbon deposits. Avoid leaded gasoline as it causes contamination of the oxygen sensor. Also, avoid using old-style silicone gasket sealant (RTV) that releases volatile compounds into the crankcase which eventually wind up on the sensor tip. Always check to make sure the RTV sealant you are using is compatible with modern emission systems. Before an oxygen sensor can function properly it must reach a minimum operating temperature of 600-degrees F. The warm-up period prior to this is called "open loop." In this mode, the computer detects a low coolant temperature (cold start) and wide open throttle (warm-up) condition. Until the engine reaches operating temperature, the computer ignores the oxygen sensor signals. During this time span, the emission controls are not precise! Once the engine is warm, the system is said to be in "closed loop" (using the oxygen sensor's input). Some manufacturers have designed an electric heating element to help the sensor reach operating temperature sooner. A typical heated sensor will consist of a ground wire, a sensor output wire (to the computer) and a third wire that supplies battery voltage to the resistance heater inside the oxygen sensor. Be careful when testing the oxygen sensor circuit! Clearly identify the function of each wire or you might confuse the data and draw the wrong conclusions.

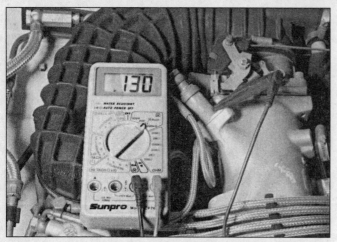

3.16 Very carefully observe the readings as the oxygen sensor cycles - note on paper the high and low values and try to come up with an average - also, if the VOM does not have a millivolt scale, just move the decimal point over; for example, 0.130 volts = 130 millivolts

Checking the oxygen sensor

Sometimes an apparent oxygen sensor problem is not the sensor's fault. An air leak in the exhaust manifold or a fouled spark plug or other problem in the ignition system causes the oxygen sensor to give a false lean-running condition. The sensor reacts only to the content of oxygen in the exhaust, and it has no way of knowing where the extra oxygen came from.

When checking the oxygen sensor it is important to remember that a good sensor produces a fluctuating signal that responds quickly to the changes in the exhaust oxygen content. To check the sensor you will need a 10 megaohm digital voltmeter. Never use an ohmmeter to check the oxygen sensor and never jump or ground the terminals. This can damage the sensor. Connect the meter to the oxygen sensor circuit. Select the mV (millivolt) scale. If the engine is equipped with a later style (heated oxygen sensor), be sure you are connected to the signal wire and not one of the heater or ground wires.

Start the engine and let it idle. Observe the reading on the voltmeter. It should be fixed at approximately 0.2 volts. Allow the engine to warm up and enter "closed loop" operation. This period of time is usually 2 to 3 minutes. **Note:** *Typically once in "closed loop", the meter will respond with a fluctuating millivolt reading (0.1 to 0.9 volts) when connected properly. If the oxygen sensor is slow to respond to the "closed loop" mode, the sensor is not operating efficiently therefore it is termed "lazy". Keep watching the voltmeter. If the oxygen sensor waits more than 1 or 2 minutes after "closed loop" mode (3 to 4 minutes total), replace the oxygen sensor. Be very careful the engine is completely warmed up and actually operating in "closed loop" mode and there is not a problem with the thermostat or cooling system. "Lazy" oxygen sensors will quite often fail emissions testing and if there is any doubt, replace it with a new one.*

Watch very carefully as the voltage oscillates. The display will flash values ranging from 100 mV to 900 mV (0.100 to 0.900 V). The numbers will flash very quickly, so be observant. Record the high and low values over a period of one minute **(see illustration)**. The way the oxygen sensor responds is very important in determining the condition of the sensor. Start the test when the engine is cold (open loop) and confirm that the oxygen sensor is steady at approximately 0.5 to 0.9 volts. As the sensor warms up (closed loop) it will switch suddenly back and forth between 0.1 and 0.9 volts. These signals should be constant and within this range or the sensor is defective. Also, if the engine warms up and the sensor delays before entering into closed loop readings (fluctuating between 0.1 and 0.9 volts), the sensor is defective. Also, if the sensor does not output a voltage signal greater than 0.5 volts, replace it.

To further test the oxygen sensor, remove a vacuum line and observe the readings as the engine stumbles from the excessively LEAN mixture. The voltage should LOWER to an approximate value of 200 mV (0.200 V). Install the vacuum line. Now, obtain some propane gas mixture (bottled) and connect it to a vacuum port on the intake manifold. Start the engine and open the propane valve (open the propane valve only partially and do so a little at a time to prevent over-richening the mixture). This will create a RICH mixture. Watch carefully as the readings INCREASE. **Warning:** *Propane gas is highly flammable. Be sure there are no leaks in your connections or an explosion could result. If the oxygen sensor responds correctly to the makeshift lean and rich conditions, the sensor is working properly.*

EGR Valve Position (EVP) sensor

What it does and how it works

The EGR Valve Position (EVP) sensor **(see illustration)** monitors the position of the EGR valve and keeps the computer informed on the exact amount the valve is open or closed. From this data, the computer can calculate the optimum EGR flow for the lowest NOx emissions and the best driveability, then control the EGR valve to alter the EGR flow by means of the EGR solenoid.

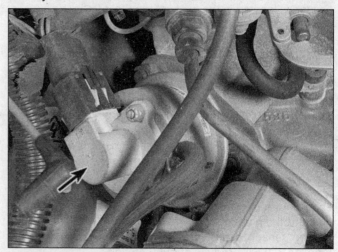

3.17 The EVP sensor is mounted directly on top of the EGR valve (arrow)

3.18 Typical crankshaft position sensor retaining bolts (arrows) (Ford 5.0L V8 shown)

3.19 The crankshaft position sensor pulse rings are mounted on the harmonic balancer (vibration damper)

The EVP sensor is a linear potentiometer that operates very much like a Throttle Position Sensor (TPS). Its electrical resistance changes in direct proportion to the movement of the EGR valve stem. When the EGR valve is closed, the EVP sensor registers maximum resistance. As the valve opens, resistance decreases until it finally reaches a minimum value when the EGR valve is fully open.

Checking

Typical symptoms of a malfunctioning EGR valve position sensor include hesitating during acceleration, rough idling and hard starting. Be sure to distinguish between an EGR valve problem and an EGR valve position sensor problem. Consult the section on EGR valves for additional information on testing the EGR valve itself.

Generally, the EGR valve position sensor should change resistance smoothly as the EGR valve is opened and closed. Be sure to check the appropriate factory service manual to determine which terminals of the sensor to hook the ohmmeter up to (there's often more than two). A typical Ford EVP sensor should have no more than 5,500 ohms resistance when the EGR valve is closed and no less than 100 ohms when the valve is fully open.

Crankshaft position sensor

What it is and how it works

A crankshaft position sensor works very similarly to an ignition pick-up coil or trigger wheel in an electronic distributor **(see illustration)**. The crankshaft position sensor provides an ignition timing signal to the computer based on the position of the crankshaft. The difference between a crankshaft position sensor and a pick-up coil or trigger wheel is that the crankshaft position sensor reads the igni-

3.20 On Ford V6 engines, the pulse rings are directly behind the crankshaft pulley, easily detected by the sensor

tion timing signal directly off the crankshaft or harmonic balancer instead of from the distributor. This eliminates timing variations from backlash in the timing chain or distributor shaft. Crankshaft position sensors are necessary in most modern distributorless ignition (DIS) systems. Basically, the sensor reads the position of the crankshaft by detecting when pulse rings on the crankshaft or harmonic balancer pass by it **(see illustrations)**.

Checking the crankshaft position sensor

Most crankshaft position sensor problems can be traced to a fault in the wiring harness or connectors. These problems can cause a loss of the timing signal and consequently the engine will not start. When troubleshooting a crankshaft position sensor problem, it is advisable to follow the diagnostic flow chart in a factory service manual to isolate the faulty

3.21 Here's a typical knock sensor mounted low on the side of the engine block

3.22 On many GM models, information from the knock sensor is sent to the Electronic Spark Control (ESC) module (arrow), which retards ignition timing if detonation is evident

component. The problem could be in the ignition module, computer, wiring harness or crankshaft position sensor. Be aware of the interrelationship of these components.

If it is necessary to replace the sensor, be sure to install it correctly, paying attention to the alignment. Any rubbing or interference will cause driveability problems. Also, on variable reluctance type crankshaft position sensors, be sure to adjust the air gap properly. Consult a factory service manual for the correct specification.

Vehicle Speed Sensor (VSS)

What it is and how it works

Vehicle Speed Sensors (VSS) are used in modern vehicles for a number of different purposes. One purpose is to monitor the vehicle speed so the computer can determine the correct time for torque converter clutch (TCC) lock-up. The sensor may also provide input to the computer to control the function of various other emissions systems components based on vehicle speed. On some GM vehicles, the signal from the VSS is used by the computer to reset the Idle Air Control valve as well as the canister purge valve. Another purpose is to assist with the power steering. Here, the sensor input is used by the electronic controller to vary the amount of power assist according to the vehicle speed. The lower the speed, the greater the assist for easier maneuverability for parking. The higher the speed, the less the assist for better road feel. Another purpose is to change the position of electronically adjustable shock absorbers used in ride control systems. The ride control systems in Mazda 626's and Ford Probes automatically switch the shocks to a "firm" setting above 50 mph in the AUTO mode and "extra firm" in the SPORT mode. Also, vehicle speed sensors replace the mechanical speedometer cable in some modern vehicles.

Checking the VSS

The driveability symptoms of a faulty vehicle speed sensor depend on what control functions require an accurate speed input. For example, on some GM vehicles, the

idle quality may be affected by a faulty sensor. Other symptoms include hard steering with increased speed, premature torque converter lock-up or fluctuating or inaccurate speedometer readings.

Different vehicles require different testing techniques. It is best to consult a factory service manual for the specific test procedures for your particular vehicle. Also, it is rare, but sometimes the output shaft on the transmission has broken or missing teeth that affect the accuracy of the sensor's reading.

Knock sensor

What it is and how it works

The knock sensor (sometimes called an Electronic Spark Control [ESC] sensor) is an auxiliary sensor that is used to detect the onset of detonation (see illustrations). Although the knock sensor influences ignition timing, it doesn't have direct impact on the fuel and emission systems. It affects ignition timing only.

The sensor, which is usually mounted on the intake manifold or engine block, generates a voltage signal when the engine vibrations are between 6 to 8 Hz. The location of the sensor is very critical because it must be positioned so it can detect any vibrations from the most detonation-prone cylinders. On some engines, it is necessary to install two knock sensors.

When the knock sensor detects a pinging or knocking vibration, it signals the computer to momentarily retard ignition timing. The computer then retards the timing a fixed number of degrees until the detonation stops.

This system is vital on turbocharged vehicles to achieve maximum performance. When the knock control system is working properly, the maximum timing advance for all driving conditions is achieved.

Checking the knock sensor

The most obvious symptom of knock sensor failure will be an audible pinging or knocking, especially during acceleration under a light load. Light detonation usually does not

3.23 Use an automotive-type stethoscope to listen for the sounds of the injector solenoids cycling

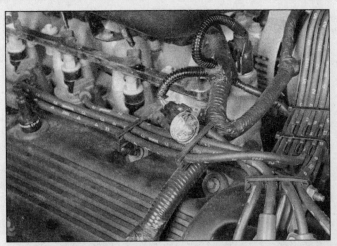

3.24 Plug a "noid light" into the fuel injector electrical connector and confirm that the light blinks as the engine is cranking or running

cause harm, but heavy detonation over a period of time will cause engine damage. Knock sensors sometimes are fooled by other sounds such as rod knocks or worn timing chains. Reduced fuel economy and poor performance result from the constantly retarded timing.

Another thing to keep in mind is that most engine detonation has other causes than the knock sensor. Some causes include:

1) Defective EGR valve
2) Too much compression due to accumulated carbon in the cylinders
3) Overadvanced ignition timing
4) Lean fuel/air mixture; possible vacuum leak
5) Overheated engine
6) Low-octane fuel

To check the knock sensor, use a wrench to rap on the intake manifold (not too hard or you may damage the manifold!) or cylinder block near the sensor while the engine is idling. Never strike the sensor directly. Observe the timing mark with a timing light. The vibration from the wrench will produce enough of a shock to cause the knock sensor to signal the computer to back off the timing. The timing should retard momentarily. If nothing happens, check the wiring, electrical connector or computer for any obvious shorts or problems. If the wiring and connectors are OK, the sensor is probably faulty.

The knock sensor is a sealed unit. If it is defective, replace it with a new part.

Output actuators

The output actuators receive commands from the computer and actuate the correct engine response after all the data and parameters have been analyzed by the computer. Output devices can be divided into three categories: Solenoids, electric motors and controller modules.

Solenoids include the EGR solenoid, Canister Purge (CANP) solenoid, carburetor feedback solenoid (FBC), Electronic Air Control Valve (EACV), Torque Converter Clutch (TCC) solenoid and fuel injectors.

Electric motors include the Idle Speed Control motor (ISC), the fuel pump and cooling fan.

Controller modules are used to control more than one device. Modules can control air conditioner and cooling fan response as well as ignition functions.

The following discusses operation and diagnosis of the most common types of output actuators.

Fuel injectors

Electronic Fuel Injection (EFI)

Check the pulse type fuel injectors (electrical) on the engine. On most TBI systems it is possible to observe the injector spray pattern while the engine is running. Remove the air cleaner assembly from the throttle body and while the engine is running, point the end of a strobe-type timing light into the throat of the throttle body. Observe the spray pattern as the light illuminates the droplets of fuel passing into the manifold. The spray pattern should be an even, conical shaped pattern extending into the venturi area of the throttle body. Now accelerate the engine and observe how the pattern will surge slightly but not change shape or form. This is a very important test to determine how the throttle body injector is performing. **Warning:** *Be sure all loose clothing, ties, shop towels and other miscellaneous items are clear of the fan blades during the test procedure.*

If your engine is equipped with EFI port fuel injection, there are several alternative methods to check the performance of the fuel injectors. First, with the engine running, place the tip of an automotive-type stethoscope on the main body of the injector **(see illustration)**. There should be a distinct clicking sound as the solenoid activates and deactivates from the voltage signal. If there is no sound heard, install a "noid light" into the fuel injector electrical connector and confirm that the light flashes **(see illustration)**. The noid light is simply a small bulb that lights up when the computer supplies voltage to the injector. This test will confirm the presence of the injector voltage. If the

3.25 Hook up a vacuum gauge to the EGR valve side of the solenoid - with the engine running at about 2,000 rpm, the gauge should register at least ten inches-Hg of vacuum

3.26 Connect a test light across the EGR solenoid connector terminals with the ignition key ON (engine not running) - the light should come on

noid light does not activate, there is a problem with the computer or wiring harness back to the computer. Tracking down a wiring problem may become difficult so if necessary, have the fuel injection system wiring repaired by a dealer service department or qualified repair shop.

Any further testing of the fuel injectors is beyond the scope of this manual. Refer to the *Haynes Fuel Injection Diagnostic Manual* for fuel pressure testing, injector spray pattern tests and injector cleaning.

Continuous Injection System (CIS)

Injector checking procedures for the CIS systems, along with fuel pressure testing and injector cleaning, can be found in the *Haynes Fuel Injection Diagnostic Manual*.

EGR valve solenoid

What it is and how it works

On computer-controlled vehicles, the action of the EGR valve is usually controlled by commanding the EGR control solenoid(s). Refer to the information earlier in this Chapter on EGR valve position sensors for additional information concerning these systems. The EGR valve solenoid is computer controlled and located in the vacuum line between the EGR valve and vacuum source. It opens and closes electrically to maintain finer control of EGR flow than is possible with ported-vacuum-type systems. The computer uses information from the coolant temperature, throttle position and manifold pressure sensors to regulate the EGR valve solenoid.

During cold operation and at idle, the solenoid circuit is grounded by the computer to block vacuum to the EGR valve. When the solenoid circuit is not grounded by the computer, vacuum is allowed to the EGR valve.

Checking the EGR valve solenoid

First, inspect all vacuum hoses, wires and electrical connectors associated with the EGR solenoid and system. Make sure nothing is damaged, loose or disconnected.

Locate the vacuum line that runs from the vacuum source to the EGR solenoid. Disconnect it at the solenoid and hook up a vacuum gauge to the hose. Start the engine, bring it to normal operating temperature and observe the vacuum reading. There should be at least ten in-Hg of vacuum. If not, repair the hose to the vacuum source. Disconnect the gauge and re-connect the hose.

If there is at least ten in-Hg vacuum to the EGR solenoid, locate the vacuum hose running from the EGR solenoid to the EGR valve. Disconnect and plug the hose at the solenoid and hook up a vacuum gauge to the solenoid. Open the EGR solenoid by starting the engine and raising the speed to about 2,000 rpm. With the solenoid open, the vacuum gauge should read at least ten in-Hg **(see illustration)**. If there is no vacuum, either the solenoid valve is defective or there is a problem in the wiring circuit or computer.

To check the wiring circuit, disconnect the electrical connector from the EGR solenoid. With the ignition on and the engine off, connect a test light across the two terminals of the connector **(see illustration)**. The test light should come on. If it does not, there is a problem in the wiring or computer. If the light does come on, but there is no vacuum from the EGR solenoid to the EGR valve, the solenoid is probably defective. Check the solenoid's resistance. Normally, it should not be less than about 20 ohms.

Electronic Air Control Valve (EACV)

What it is and how it works

The EACV (sometimes called an Idle Air Control [IAC] valve) changes the amount of air bypassed (not flowing through the throttle valve) into the intake manifold in response to the changes in the electrical signals from the computer. EACV's are usually located on the throttle body, although some are mounted remotely. After the engine starts, the EACV opens, allowing air to bypass the throttle and thus increase idle speed. While the coolant temperature is low, the EACV remains open to obtain the proper

3.27 Observe the voltage reading at the EACV connector

fast idle speed. As the engine warms up, the amount of bypassed air is controlled in relation to the coolant temperature. After the engine reaches normal operating temperature, the EACV is opened, as necessary, to maintain the correct idle speed.

Checking the EACV

To check the EACV valve circuit, connect the positive probe of a voltmeter to the signal wire in the EACV connector and the negative probe to ground **(see illustration)**. Check the voltage as the engine starts to warm up from cold to warm conditions. Most EACV valves will indicate an increase in voltage as the system warms and the valve slowly cuts off the additional air. Consult a factory service manual for the correct voltage specifications for your vehicle. If the voltage is correct, but the EACV valve is not opening or closing to provide the correct airflow, replace the valve.

Torque Converter Clutch (TCC) solenoid

What it is and how it works

Lock-up torque converters are installed on newer vehicles to help eliminate torque converter slippage and thus reduce power loss and poor increase fuel economy. The torque converter is equipped with a clutch that is activated by a solenoid valve. The computer determines the best time to lock up the clutch device based on data it receives from various sensors and switches.

When the vehicle speed sensor indicates speed above a certain range and the coolant temperature sensor is warm, the Throttle Position Sensor (TPS) determines the position of the throttle (acceleration or deceleration) and the transmission sensor relays the particular gear the transmission is operating in to the computer for a complete analysis of operating parameters. If all parameters are within a certain range, the computer sends an electrical signal to the clutch, telling it to lock up. Needless to say, diagnosing a problem in this system can become complicated.

Checking the TCC solenoid

One symptom of TCC failure is a clutch that will not disengage, causing the engine to stall when slowing to a stop. Another symptom is an increase in engine rpm at cruising speed, resulting in decreased fuel economy (this usually means the converter is not locking up). If the converter is not locking up, the driver might not notice any differences unless he/she checks fuel consumption and the increase in tachometer readings. Without the TCC operating, the engine will turn an additional 300 to 500 rpm at cruising speed to maintain the same speed. Also, when the converter is not locking up, there is a chance the transmission will overheat and become damaged due to the higher operating temperatures.

Before diagnosing the TCC system as defective, make some preliminary checks. Check the transmission fluid level, linkage adjustment and the condition of the vacuum lines. After you've checked that all the basics are in order, check for any trouble codes (see Chapter 7). Further diagnosis should be referred to a dealer service department or other qualified repair shop.

4 Ignition control systems

General description

The job of the ignition system is to ignite the fuel/air charge entering each cylinder at just the right moment. It does this by producing a high voltage spark between the electrodes of each spark plug.

While ignition systems have changed dramatically in detail since the days of breaker points-type ignition (which date from 1912), their operation is basically the same. Breaker points are simply an ON and OFF switch that physically opens and closes, grounding the coil primary circuit voltage which induces high voltage in the coil secondary windings, which is then directed to the spark plugs via the ignition rotor, distributor cap and spark plug wires.

The first major step toward the development of modern computer-controlled ignition systems was transistorized ignition. These used a transistor as the switching device between the coil and breaker points, prolonging points life. It didn't eliminate breaker points, however, so development continued. The capacitive discharge ignition system was the next major step toward "electronic" ignition. These systems replaced the breaker points with a magnetic pulse pick-up and an armature device and eventually evolved into the fully electronic ignition system of today.

Electronics have simplified ignition system design while providing extremely accurate and precise ignition timing throughout the engine operating range. The efficiency of electronic ignition systems proved to be a perfect match for computerized engine controls, allowing the sensors (tem-

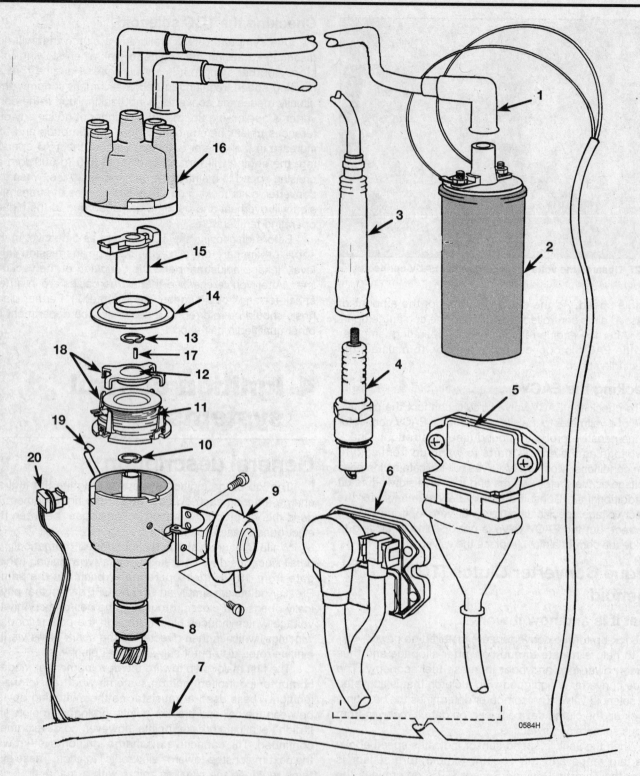

4.1 Typical Bosch pick-up coil type ignition system (BMW)

1	Coil wire	7	Wiring harness	14	Dust shield
2	Ignition coil	8	Distributor housing	15	Ignition rotor
3	Spark plug wire	9	Vacuum diaphragm	16	Distributor cap
4	Spark plug	10	Snap-ring	17	Roll-pin
5	Bosch ignition control unit	11	Pick-up coil	18	Alignment tabs
6	Siemens/Telefunken ignition	12	Reluctor	19	Retaining clip
	control unit	13	Snap-ring	20	Pick-up coil electrical connector

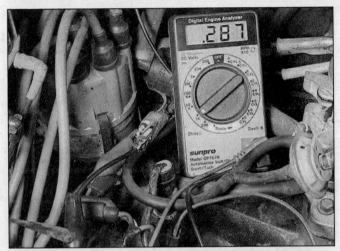

4.2 Disconnect the electrical connector and check the resistance of the pick-up coil at the distributor (Chrysler)

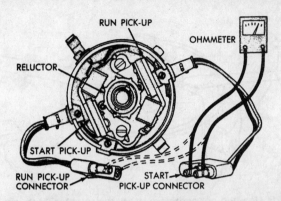

4.3 On Chrysler dual pick-up coil systems, the resistance should be about the same for the START pick-up coil as the RUN pick-up coil

perature, air volume, speed etc.) to control the ignition timing (output actuator). The result was smooth operating, low emissions engine operation.

This section deals with the various types of modern ignition systems used on engines equipped with engine management systems. It covers the simple checks and component replacement procedures for the most common problems involved with electronic ignition systems.

Types of electronic ignition

All ignition systems have the same function: To produce a high voltage spark between the electrodes of each spark plug, but they use different ways to do this. The various designs generally are classified by the particular method used to direct the coil primary circuit voltage to the spark plugs. These are:

Pick-up coil
Hall Effect switch
Crankshaft sensor photo optic type
Distributorless Ignition System (DIS)

Pick-up coil type ignition
General information

The pick-up coil type ignition uses a toothed wheel (reluctor), magnet and pick-up coil mounted in the distributor **(see illustration)**. As the reluctor teeth pass near the magnet, a weak current is produced in the pick-up coil. This current is sent to the electronic control unit to turn the coil primary circuit current ON and OFF and trigger the electronic control unit. Spark timing is constantly adjusted by the control unit and computer depending on engine speed.

Pick-up coil type ignition is widely used on Chrysler, Ford (Duraspark and TFI) and General Motors (HEI) vehicles as well as some Japanese and European (Bosch) models. This ignition system basically controls the ignition spark without any timing advance or retard capabilities. These systems include a module (electronic control unit), coil and

one or two magnetic pick-up coils mounted in the distributor and, on some systems, a ballast resistor.

Pick-up coil(s) - check and replacement

Note: *This is a general check and replacement procedure which will work for most pick-up coils.*

Disconnect the electrical connector(s) from the pick-up coil(s) at the distributor and using an ohmmeter, check for resistance **(see illustrations)**. There should be 500 to 1200 ohms resistance.

If the readings are incorrect, or there is no resistance at all, replace the pick-up coil(s).

Remove the distributor and carefully clamp it in a vise equipped with soft jaws (don't apply excessive pressure). **Note:** *On some models, the pick-up coil can be detached after removing the mounting screw and separating the wires from the retainers on the upper plate and distributor housing. On other models, it will be necessary to remove a snapring before the reluctor can be removed* **(see illustration)**.

Using two screwdrivers not more than 7/16-inch wide, remove the reluctor by prying it up **(see illustration)**. Be careful not to damage the reluctor teeth.

Remove the two mounting screws from the vacuum

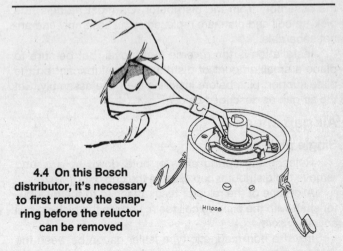

4.4 On this Bosch distributor, it's necessary to first remove the snapring before the reluctor can be removed

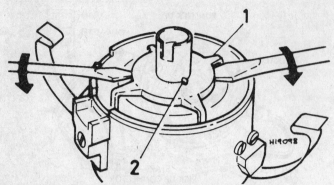

4.5 Use two screwdrivers to pry the reluctor (1) up off the distributor shaft (2)

4.6 On a single pick-up coil distributor, check the air gap as shown here (Chrysler)

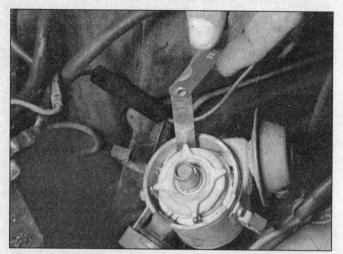

4.7 Use a feeler gauge to check the air gap - make sure the gauge rubs lightly against the reluctor teeth as well as the locating pin (Bosch distributor)

advance unit, if equipped. Disconnect the control arm from the pick-up plate. Remove the pick-up coil leads from the distributor housing and the mounting screws from the pick-up plate.

Lift out (do not completely remove) the pick-up coil and plate as an assembly. Depress the retainer clip on the underside of the plate assembly (some models) and detach the assembly from the distributor. On most models, the pick-up coil and plate are replaced as an assembly and are not separable.

Installation is the reverse of removal, but be sure to place a small amount of distributor cam lubricant on the plate support pins before installing the plate assembly. Set the air gap as described below.

Air gap check

Single pick-up coil

Release the spring clips or hold down screws and remove the distributor cap. Secure the cap out of way.

Align one of the reluctor teeth attached to the distributor shaft with the pick-up coil tooth. Loosen the pick-up coil adjusting screw.

Insert a non-magnetic type feeler gauge between the

reluctor and pick-up coil (see illustrations). Refer to the Specifications listed in the Haynes manual for your vehicle for the correct gap.

Move the pick-up coil until light contact is made with the feeler gauge. Tighten the pick-up coil adjusting screw. Remove the feeler gauge. No force should be required to remove the gauge.

Using a feeler gauge 0.002-inch larger than specified, check the air gap. The feeler gauge should not fit between the teeth (do not force it). Reset the air gap if necessary.

Replace the distributor cap.

Dual pick-up coils

Some Chrysler models equipped with electronic ignition systems from 1976 through 1989 are equipped with dual pick-up coils. These systems include ELB I, Combustion Computer, SC computer and Electronic Fuel Control computer systems. The ignition module or computer is separated into two integral units contained within the computer housing; the program schedule unit and the ignition control unit. The program schedule regulates the RUN pick-up coil (running condition) while the ignition control unit controls the START pick-up coil (starting condition) within the distributor. The air gap for each pick-up coil is set to a different specification designed for the different functions. Release the spring clips or hold-down screws and remove the distributor cap. Secure the cap out of way.

Align one of the reluctor teeth attached to the distributor shaft with the pick-up coil tooth. **Note:** *First adjust the START pick-up coil and then the RUN pick-up coil* **(see illustration)**. *The procedure is the same for both but the air gap specifications are usually different. The START pick-up coil electrical connector is the larger of the two connectors.*

Loosen the pick-up coil adjusting screw.

Insert a non-magnetic type feeler gauge. It will be necessary to refer to the Specifications listed in the *Haynes Automotive Repair Manual* for your vehicle for the correct gap thickness.

Move the pick-up coil until light contact is made with the feeler gauge.

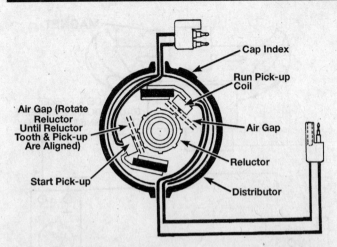

4.8 Dual pick-up coil checking details (Chrysler)

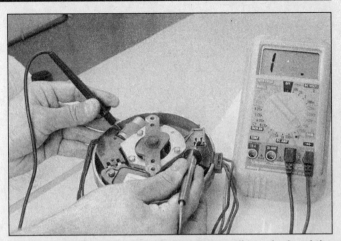

4.9a Connect the ohmmeter to a pick-up coil terminal and the distributor body. If continuity is indicated, there is a short from the pick-up coil wiring to the distributor body

Tighten the pick-up coil adjusting screw.

Remove the feeler gauge. No force should be required to remove the gauge.

Using a feeler gauge 0.002-inch larger than specified, check the air gap. The feeler gauge should not fit between the teeth (do not force it). Reset the air gap if necessary.

Replace the distributor cap.

General Motors HEI type

Pick-up coil - check and replacement

Detach the cable from the negative terminal of the battery.

Remove the distributor cap and rotor.

Remove the distributor from the engine. **Note:** *This Step may be necessary on some models, since it is difficult to gain access to the pick-up coil wires in the distributor. If access on your vehicle is relatively unrestricted, this Step may not be necessary.*

Detach the pick-up coil wires from the module. Connect one lead of an ohmmeter to the terminal of the pick-up coil lead and the other to ground as shown **(see illustrations)**. Flex the leads by hand to check for intermittent opens. The ohmmeter should indicate infinite resistance at all times. If it doesn't, the pick-up coil is defective and must be replaced.

Connect the ohmmeter leads to both terminals of the pick-up coil wires. Flex the wires by hand to check for intermittent opens. The ohmmeter should read one steady value between 500 and 1500 ohms as the leads are flexed by hand. If it doesn't, the pick-up coil is defective and must be replaced.

Remove the distributor, if not already done, then remove the spring from the distributor shaft. Mark the distributor gear drive and shaft so that they can be reassembled in the same position.

Carefully mount the distributor in a soft-jawed vise and, using a hammer and punch, remove the roll pin from the distributor shaft and gear **(see illustration)**. Pull the shaft out of the distributor body. **Caution:** *If the shaft binds when*

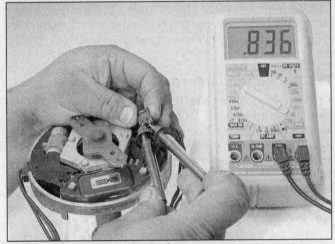

4.9b Connect the ohmmeter to the pick-up coil terminals as shown and measure the resistance of the pick-up coil. It should be between 500 and 1,500 ohms

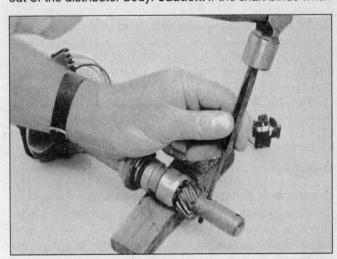

4.10 To remove the distributor shaft assembly, place the distributor assembly in a soft-jawed vise then knock out the roll pin with a punch and hammer

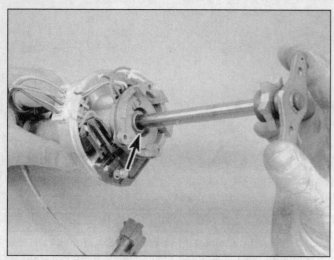

4.11 Remove the shaft, then remove the "C" washer (arrow)

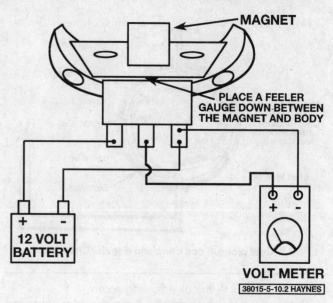

4.12 Hall Effect switch test connections

being pulled out, you may need to lightly sand the lower shaft area so it will pull through without binding.

To remove the pick up coil, remove the thin "C" washer **(see illustration)**. **Note:** *On some models, you may have to unbolt a shield to gain access to the "C" washer.*

Lift the pick-up coil assembly straight up and remove it from the distributor. Reassembly is the reverse of disassembly. Installation is the reverse of removal.

Hall effect switch (HEI system) - check and replacement

Some HEI distributors are equipped with a Hall Effect switch which is located above the pick-up coil assembly. The Hall Effect switch is used in place of the R terminal of the HEI distributor to send engine speed information to the computer.

Test the switch by connecting a 12-volt power supply and voltmeter as shown **(see illustration)**. Check the polarity markings carefully before making any connections.

When the knife blade is not inserted as shown, the voltmeter should read less than 0.5 volts. If the reading is more, the Hall Effect switch is faulty and must be replaced by a new one. With the knife blade inserted, the voltmeter should read within 0.5 volts of battery voltage.

Replace the switch with a new one if the reading is more. Remove the Hall Effect switch by unplugging the connector and removing the retaining screws. Installation is the reverse of removal.

Ford

Duraspark II - general information

These systems are equipped with a gear driven distributor with a die cast base housing a "Hall Effect" vane switch stator assembly and a device for fixed octane adjustment.

Duraspark distributors have a two piece cap. When removing the cap, the upper half is removed, then the rotor is removed, then the lower half of the cap is removed. TFI-

IV distributors have a conventional one piece cap.

However, there are a few differences between various distributors. The distributors on some earlier models, for example, are equipped with centrifugal and vacuum advance mechanisms which control the actual point of ignition based on engine speed and load. As engine speed increases, two weights move out and alter the position of the armature in relation to the distributor shaft, advancing the ignition timing. As engine load increases (when climbing hills or accelerating, for example), a drop in intake manifold vacuum causes the base plate to move slightly in the opposite direction (clockwise) under the action of the spring in the vacuum unit, retarding the timing and counteracting the centrifugal advance. Under light loads (moderate steady speeds, for example), the comparatively high intake manifold vacuum acting on the vacuum advance diaphragm causes the base plate assembly to move in a counterclockwise direction to provide a greater amount of timing advance.

TFI-IV - general information

Later models use the Thick Film Integrated IV (TFI-IV) **(see illustration)** ignition module, which is housed in a molded thermoplastic box mounted on the base of the distributor. "Thick Film" refers to the type of manufactured solid state trigger and power units in the module. The important difference between the DSII and TFI-IV modules is that the TFI-IV module is controlled by the Electronic Engine Control IV (EEC-IV), while the Duraspark II modules are not.

The TFI-IV/EEC-IV type distributor is similar to the Duraspark II model but has neither a centrifugal nor a vacuum advance mechanism because it is computer controlled.

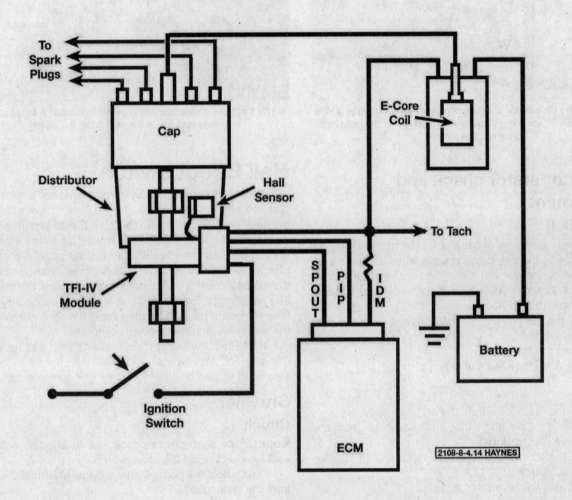

4.14 TFI-IV system layout

4.16a With the distributor shaft housing locked securely in a vise lined with several shop rags (to prevent damage to the housing), drive out the roll pin

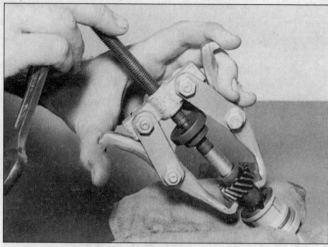

4.16b With the distributor shaft pointing up, use a small puller to separate the drive gear from the shaft

Distributor stator check and replacement

Duraspark II

Check the resistance of the distributor stator. Using an ohmmeter, probe the orange and purple wires at the distributor electrical connector and check the resistance. It should be between 400 and 1,000 ohms. If not, replace the stator assembly within the distributor.

Remove the roll pin and lift the armature from the distributor. Remove the lower plate assembly screws and lift the stator from the distributor.

Installation is the reverse of removal.

TFI-IV

Remove the distributor from the engine.

Remove the roll pin and lift the shaft assembly from the distributor **(see illustrations)**.

Remove the screws that retain the stator and lift the stator from the distributor.

Installation is the reverse of removal.

Hall Effect switch

The Hall Effect switch system consists of a rotor which features shutter blades, Hall Effect switch, electronic control unit and ignition coil. The Hall Effect switch sends a constant electrical signal to a transistor in the electronic control unit. As the rotor shutter blades pass over the Hall Effect switch, the voltage of this signal changes and the transistor turns the coil primary circuit current ON and OFF. The resulting high voltage surge in the coil secondary circuit fires the spark plugs. The plug firing timing is controlled by the electronic control unit and computer.

Hall Effect switch ignition systems are used on various Chrysler and Volkswagen models. Hall Effect switches are also used as part of other types of ignition systems.

Chrysler
Check

Note: *There is no check procedure for models equipped with Multi-Port Fuel Injection (MPFI).*

Disconnect the primary (low voltage) electrical connector from the distributor.

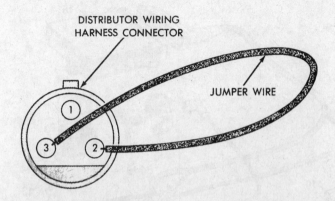

4.17 On Chrysler models, check the Hall Effect switch by connecting a jumper wire between distributor wiring harness connector cavities number 2 and 3

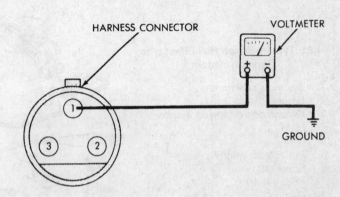

4.18 Check for voltage between the distributor connector cavity number 1 and a good ground

Jump cavity number 2 to cavity number 3 of the connector (see illustration).

Turn the ignition switch to the On position.

While holding the coil wire 1/4-inch from a good ground, make and break the connection at cavity two or cavity three several times. **Warning:** *Be sure to use an insulated tool to hold the coil wire.*

If spark is not present at the coil wire, the circuit connected to cavity number two and/or number three is open, or the coil is bad.

If spark is present at the coil wire, proceed.

Measure voltage at cavity number 1 of the distributor connector - it should be within one volt of battery voltage (see illustration). If it isn't, replace the Hall Effect pick-up. If battery voltage is not present, repair the open in the circuit connected to cavity number one.

Replacement

Four-cylinder models

Disconnect the negative cable at the battery.
Remove the distributor splash shield and cap.

4.19 Lift the Hall Effect pick-up assembly off the distributor shaft (four-cylinder model shown)

Lift the rotor off the shaft, followed by the pick-up assembly (see illustration).

To install the pick-up assembly, place it carefully into position, making sure the wiring grommet is seated in its locating hole. Install the rotor.

Install the distributor cap and splash shield and connect the negative battery cable.

V6 and V8 models

Disconnect the negative cable at the battery.

Remove the distributor cap and rotor. Unscrew the two Hall Effect pick-up screws (located on opposite sides of each other on the distributor housing) (see illustration). Be careful not to drop them.

Carefully lift the Hall Effect pick-up assembly from the distributor housing.

Installation is the reverse of removal.

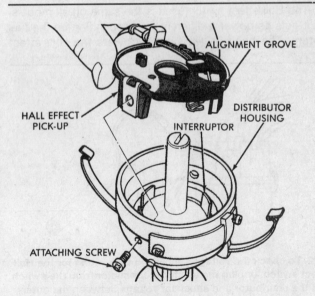

4.20 On this type of distributor, remove the two attaching screws and lift out the Hall Effect pick-up

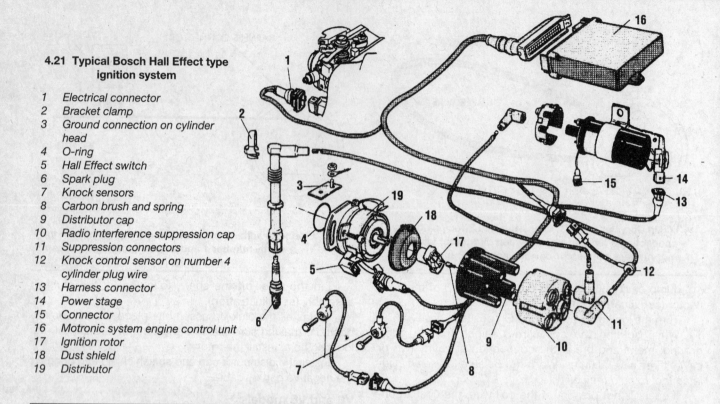

4.21 Typical Bosch Hall Effect type ignition system

1 Electrical connector
2 Bracket clamp
3 Ground connection on cylinder head
4 O-ring
5 Hall Effect switch
6 Spark plug
7 Knock sensors
8 Carbon brush and spring
9 Distributor cap
10 Radio interference suppression cap
11 Suppression connectors
12 Knock control sensor on number 4 cylinder plug wire
13 Harness connector
14 Power stage
15 Connector
16 Motronic system engine control unit
17 Ignition rotor
18 Dust shield
19 Distributor

Volkswagen (Bosch)

The Bosch Hall Effect switch system used on Volkswagens is unique to these models **(see illustration)**. The electronic ignition systems used on these vehicles is generally known as Transistorized Coil Ignition with Hall Effect switch (TCI-h). They have an electronic control unit which, depending on the type of fuel-injection system used, controls parameters such as ignition timing and fuel management.

The Hall effect switch used is the same on all models, but it gets its power a different way depending on the fuel system. The basic TCI-h system powers the Hall effect switch through the ignition control unit. On the TCI-h system with knock sensor, the Hall Effect switch gets power from the knock sensor control unit. On Digifant II systems, the Hall Effect switch gets power from the Digifant II control unit.

If there's no spark at the spark plugs, but the plugs and the ignition coil are in good working order, the problem is either in the Hall Effect switch or the ignition control unit. The Hall Effect switch is located inside the distributor; the connector for the Hall Effect switch is located on the side of the distributor.

To perform the following tests, you'll need to use a high-impedance voltmeter or low-current LED test light. The sequence of the following tests is important. You'll need to stick with the sequence as it's presented to isolate the faulty component.

All systems except CIS-E Motronic

Voltage and ground check

With the ignition off and the ignition control unit connected, unplug the electrical connector from the Hall Effect switch at the distributor. Check for voltage between the outer terminals of the connector **(see illustration)**. Turn on the ignition. There should be voltage present.

If there's no voltage, check the wire harness between the electrical connector for the Hall effect switch and the control unit, and between the control unit and ground. If all of these wires have continuity, but there's still no voltage reaching the Hall Effect switch, the control unit is faulty. Replace it.

4.22 To check the voltage supply and the ground for the Hall Effect switch, unplug the electrical connector from the switch at the distributor and check for voltage between the outer terminals of the connector - when you turn on the ignition, there should be voltage present (CIS, CIS-E and Digifant II systems)

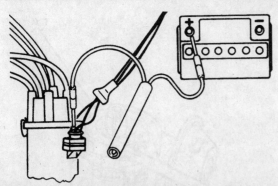

4.23 To check the operation of the switching function of the Hall Effect switch, detach the coil wire from the distributor and ground it with a jumper wire, peel back the boot on the switch connector and connect an LED test light between the center terminal and the positive battery terminal - the LED should flicker (CIS, CIS-E and Digifant II systems)

Switching function check

To check the operation of the Hall Effect switch, you need to verify its ability to switch the primary circuit. Detach the coil wire from the center of the distributor and ground it with a jumper wire. With the Hall Effect switch connected, carefully peel back the rubber connector boot to get at the wires from the back side of the connector. Connect an LED test light between the center terminal and the positive (+) battery terminal **(see illustration)**. Now actuate the starter. The LED should flicker.

If the LED doesn't flicker, the Hall Effect switch is bad. Replace it.

Turn off the ignition, select a 20 volt DC scale on your multimeter and hook up the multimeter test leads to terminals 1 (-) and 15 (+) on the ignition coil **(see illustration)**. Don't disconnect any of the coil wires. On models with the basic TCI-h system, unplug the Hall Effect switch connector from the distributor. On models with TCI-h and knock sensor, unplug the electrical connector from the knock sensor unit. On Digifant II models, unplug the electrical connector from the Digifant II control unit.

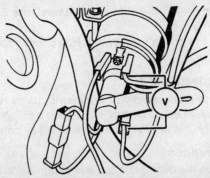

4.24 To check the voltage from the ignition control unit to the coil, hook up the meter test leads to terminals 1 (-) and 15 (+) on the ignition coil, unplug the Hall sender connector (TCI-h), the connector from the knock sensor unit (TCI-h with knock sensor) or the connector from the control unit (Digifant II), then turn on the ignition - the meter should indicate at least 2 volts for 1 to 2 seconds, then drop back to 0 volts (CIS, CIS-E and Digifant II systems)

CIS-E Motronic
Hall effect switch voltage and ground check

With the ignition off, unplug the electrical connector for the Hall Effect switch. Using a voltmeter or multimeter, check for voltage between the outer terminals **(see illustration)**. When the ignition is turned on, there should be at least 9 volts present. Turn off the ignition.

If there's no voltage, check for continuity in the wiring between terminal 3 of the connector for the Hall Effect switch and terminal 30 of the connector for the Motronic control unit, and between terminal 1 of the connector for the Hall Effect switch and ground. Make repairs as necessary, then reattach the connector.

Hall Effect switch switching function check

Peel back the protective boot from the electrical connector for the Hall Effect switch and connect an LED test light between the center terminal and the positive terminal of the battery **(see illustration)**. Disconnect the coil wire from the center of the distributor and ground it with a

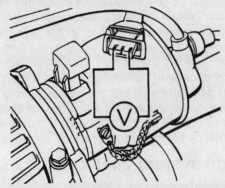

4.25a To check the Hall Effect switch voltage supply and ground, unplug the electrical connector to the switch, hook up a multimeter as shown and check for voltage between the outer terminals - when you turn on the ignition, there should be at least 9 volts present (CIS-E Motronic systems)

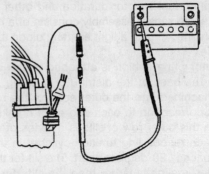

4.25b To check the switching function of the Hall Effect switch, peel back the electrical connector boot, then hook up an LED test light between the switch center terminal battery positive terminal and detach the coil wire from the distributor and ground it with a jumper wire - when you turn on the starter, the LED should flicker (CIS-E Motronic systems)

jumper wire. When the starter is actuated, the LED should flicker.

If the LED doesn't flicker, the Hall Effect switch is bad. Replace it.

Replacement (all)

Note: *Some disassembly of the distributor is required to replace the Hall effect switch. You'll need a pair of snap-ring pliers and, on 16-valve engines, a thin drift or punch.*

8-valve engines

Remove the distributor cap and suppression shield, the rotor and the dust shield. Use a pair of snap-ring pliers to remove the snap-ring which retains the trigger wheel.

To remove the trigger wheel, use a pair of screwdrivers positioned on opposite sides of the wheel and carefully pry it off the distributor shaft **(see illustration)**. Make sure you don't lose the small pin which keys the trigger wheel to the distributor shaft. **Caution**: *Push the screwdrivers in as far as possible and pry up only on the strongest, center portion of the trigger wheel. If you bend the trigger wheel, you'll have to replace it.*

Remove the Hall Effect switch retaining screws and remove the sender unit.

Installation is the reverse of removal.

16-valve engines

Remove the distributor. Using a thin drift or punch, drive out the retaining pin in the distributor drive clutch and pull the distributor shaft, the rotor, the dust shield and the trigger wheel out from the top as a unit. Remove the Hall Effect switch retaining screws and remove the sender unit.

Installation is the reverse of removal.

Crankshaft sensor photo optic type ignition

This design, used on later Nissan models, uses a crankshaft angle sensor inside the distributor to monitor engine speed and piston position, then sends a signal to the computer. The computer uses this signal to determine ignition timing, fuel injector duration and other functions. The crank angle sensor assembly consists of a rotor plate, a "wave forming" circuit, a light emitting diode (LED) and a photo diode.

The rotor plate, which is attached to the distributor shaft, is in the base of the distributor housing. There are 360 slits machined into the outer edge of the rotor plate. These slits correspond to each degree of crankshaft rotation. Within this outer row of slits is a series of six slightly larger slits corresponding to each cylinder in the engine. They are spaced 120-degrees apart. The slit for the number one cylinder is slightly larger than the slits for the other cylinders.

The wave forming circuit is positioned underneath the rotor plate. A small housing attached to one side of the wave forming circuit encloses the upper and lower outer edges of the rotor plate. A light emitting diode (LED) is

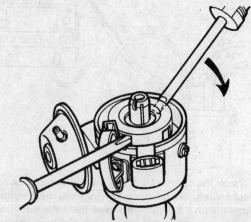

4.26 To remove the Hall Effect rotor, use a pair of screwdrivers wedged under the rotor as shown and carefully pry up to free it from the distributor shaft - make sure you don't lose the small key that locks the rotor in place (eight-valve engines)

located in the upper half and a photo diode is located in the lower half of the small housing. When the engine is running, the LED emits a continuous beam of light directly at the photo diode. As the outer edge of the rotor plate passes through the housing, the slits allow the light beam to pass through to the photo diode, but the solid spaces between the slits block the light beam. This constant interruption generates pulses which are converted into on-off signals by the wave forming circuit and sent to the ECU. The ECU uses the signal from the outer row of slits to determine engine speed and crankshaft position. It uses the signal generated by the inner, larger slits to determine when to fire each cylinder. This information is then relayed to the coil which builds secondary voltage and sends it to the distributor cap in the conventional manner, where it is distributed by the rotor to the appropriate cylinder.

Warning: *Because of the higher voltage generated by the electronic ignition system, extreme caution should be taken whenever an operation is performed involving ignition components. This not only includes the distributor, coil, control module and ignition wires, but related items which are connected to the system as well, such as the plug connections, tachometer and any testing equipment. Consequently, before any work is performed, such as replacing ignition components or even connecting test equipment, the ignition should be turned off and the battery ground cable disconnected. Never disconnect any of the ignition high-tension leads when the engine is running or the transistor ignition unit will be permanently damaged.*

Ignition system check

Crank angle sensor check

Remove the distributor.

Remove the rotor retaining screw and pull the rotor off the shaft.

Remove the sensor dust cover retaining screws **(see**

4.27 Remove the screws (arrows) retaining the crank angle sensor dust cover

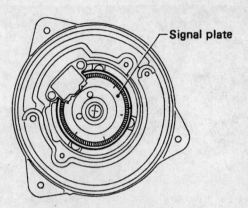

4.28 Inspect the crank angle sensor signal plate for damage and for dirt blocking the slits

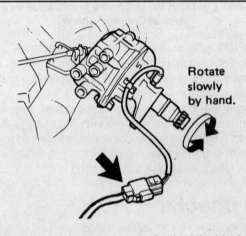

4.29 Insert the test probe into the back of the black wire terminal of the plug (arrow) while it is still connected

illustration) and lift off the cover.

Inspect the crank angle signal plate **(see illustration)** for damage and dirt intrusion. Blow any accumulated dust out of the distributor and reinstall the cover and rotor. Inspect the electrical connections for damage and corrosion and correct any defects.

Attach the ground connector of a high impedance volt-ohm meter to a clean engine ground. Select the ohms scale of approximately 0 to 1,000 ohms and insert the test probe into the black wire terminal in the rear of the distributor connector on the engine side of the harness **(see illustration)**. A reading of approximately zero ohms confirms a good ground connection. **Note:** *Use a thin probe, a stiff wire or a paper clip inserted deeply enough to reach the metal contacts.*

Reconnect the battery and turn the ignition to the On position. **Caution:** *Don't activate the starter.*

Place the volt-ohm meter on a 0 to 15 volt scale (or closest approximation). Working with the same connector, probe the black and white wire connection for voltage. A reading near battery voltage is normal, if little or no voltage is found, trace and repair the wiring.

Rotate the distributor shaft very slowly by hand and probe the green/yellow wire for voltage. The voltage should jump from zero to five volts and back again once every revolution. This provides a top dead center indication to the computer.

Again rotate the distributor shaft very slowly by hand and probe the green/black wire for voltage. The voltage should jump in steps from zero to five volts and back again six times per revolution. This provides a spark plug firing signal to the computer.

Repeat any testing steps that produce inconclusive results to avoid incorrect conclusions. If the voltage pulses fail to occur, replace the distributor. **Note:** *The crank angle sensor is usually not available separately.*

If you are still unable to find the problem, take the vehicle to a dealer service department.

Direct Ignition System (DIS)

The Direct Ignition System has no distributor. Depending on model and year, the DIS system can include coil packs, an ignition module, a crankshaft position sensor, a crankshaft position sensor, a camshaft sensor, spark plug wires and the computer. The coils connect directly to the spark plugs.

The signal sent by the rotating crankshaft position sensor goes to the ignition module which then sends a pulse to the computer. The computer uses this pulse to calculate crankshaft position and engine speed and fires the spark plug. The advantage of this system is simplicity: there are no moving parts, maintenance is minimal, there is more coil cool-down between spark plug firing and no mechanical timing adjustments are required.

Another aspect of this simplicity is the ignition coil design. On conventional ignition coils, one end of the secondary winding is connected to the engine ground. On DIS, neither end of the secondary winding is grounded; instead the end of each coil secondary winding is directly attached to the spark plug and its companion.

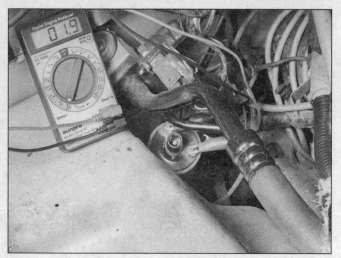

4.30 Checking the coil primary resistance on a typical Chrysler vehicle

4.31 Checking the coil primary resistance on a Ford TFI-IV system

The DIS ignition system uses a "waste spark" method of spark distribution. Each cylinder is paired with its opposing cylinder in the firing order (1-4, 2-5, 3-6) so one cylinder under compression fires simultaneously with its opposing cylinder, where the piston is on the exhaust stroke. Since the cylinder on exhaust requires very little of the available voltage to fire its plug, most of the voltage is used to fire the cylinder on compression.

Checking procedures can be found under *Coil checks*.

Coil checks

The ignition system is separated into two circuits; the primary or low voltage circuit and the secondary or high voltage circuit. Although they are completely separate circuits, they function together and relate closely to each other. The *primary circuit* consists of the battery, ignition switch, ballast resistor, the primary circuit of the ignition coil, primary side of the distributor as well as the electrical wires and vehicle frame necessary to complete the circuit. The *secondary circuit* includes the secondary portion of the ignition coil, the secondary side of the distributor (cap, rotor and wires) and spark plugs.

All ignition systems require an electrical power source or 12 volt battery source. The battery provides the primary voltage.

The ignition coil is designed to change a low primary voltage signal supplied by the battery into a much higher voltage, one capable of jumping the spark plug gap. It consists of an iron core, primary windings, secondary windings and an outside container.

In many cases, ignition problems may originate in the coil. The following coil resistance checks can be used on most electronic ignition coils.

Before testing a coil, these preliminary checks should be made; make sure the coil is mounted securely and all connections are clean and tight. Check for cracked or burned high voltage tower. Check for dents or cracks in the housing. On oil filled types, check for leaks. If the coil has a wiring harness or connecter, check that it is not damaged, and it is securely attached.

A faulty ignition coil may result in a weak spark, intermittent spark,or no spark at all. The engine may misfire, stop running when the coil heats up, or cause a no start problem. The windings inside the coil can break and produce a high resistance or an open in the coil circuit.

Conventional coils for electronic ignition systems

Checks

Most coils can be checked in the same manner. Similar in construction, they all operate in the same manner, receiving low voltage through the primary circuit and discharging high voltage through the secondary system.

At this time let's take the opportunity to check some coils from different manufacturers. Even if your particular

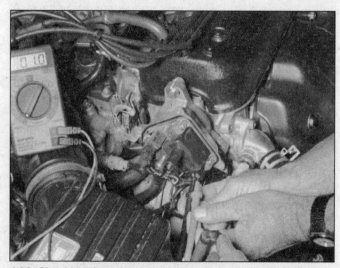

4.32 Checking the primary resistance on a Honda integral coil

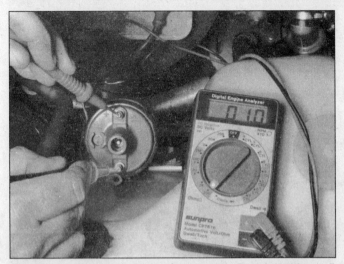

4.33 Checking the primary resistance on a Bosch ignition coil

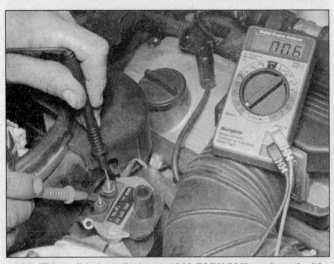

4.34 This coil is installed on a 1989 BMW 535i equipped with the Motronic ignition system

coil appears to look different from other coils in physical appearance, the procedure to check the coil is the same.

Let's take a look at the primary side. Take an ohmmeter and check the resistance from the primary (-) to the primary (+) side of the coil **(see illustrations)**. Typical primary resistance is usually between 0.5 to 15 ohms.

Next, connect the ohmmeter to the secondary tower of the ignition coil and check the resistance between the tower and one of the primary terminals (+) or (-). For example, after taking the reading, move the probe from the primary side (+) and move it to the other terminal of the primary side (-) of the ignition coil and check the resistance. Compare the two resistance values **(see illustrations)**. Secondary coil resistance is usually between 800 and 10,000 ohms. This is a wide range. Refer to the *Haynes Automotive Repair Manual* for your particular vehicle for additional information.

The next step is to check from the secondary tower of the ignition coil to the case of the ignition coil to see if the

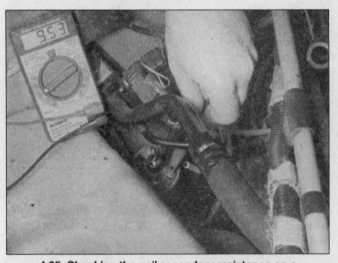

4.35 Checking the coil secondary resistance on a typical Chrysler vehicle

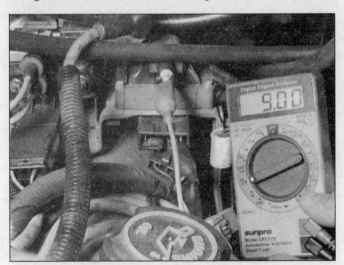

4.36 Checking the coil secondary resistance on a Ford TFI-IV system

4.37 Checking the secondary resistance on a Honda integral coil

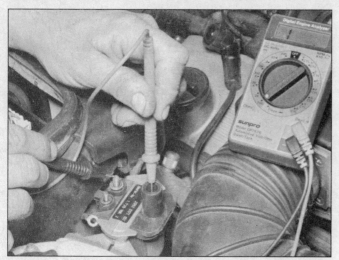

4.38 Checking the secondary resistance on a BMW 535i

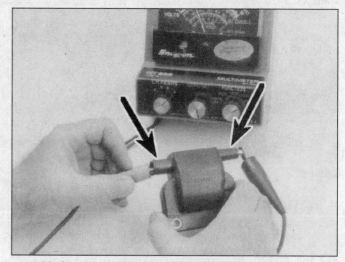

4.39 Checking the secondary coil resistance on a later style Chrysler ignition coil

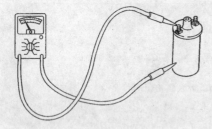

4.40 Primary winding-to-case resistance test

secondary system is shorted out. Also check the resistance from the primary side of the ignition coil to the case of the coil to determine if the primary side has a short to the case **(see illustration)**.

The procedure for removal of the ignition coil varies depending upon the type of coil. Some coils are mounted in a clamp and strapped to the firewall and others are

4.41 Removing the ignition coil on a Honda Accord integral coil system

4.42 Mounting bolt locations (arrows) for the coil on a GM 3.1L V6 engine

4.43 Typical canister-type coil mounting bracket (Toyota)

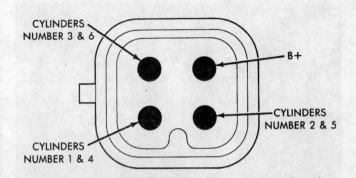

4.44 Here's terminal guide for measuring the primary resistance of the coil pack on Chrysler minivans at the electrical connector (coil pack side of the connector shown) - check between the B+ terminal and each of the other terminals in the connector

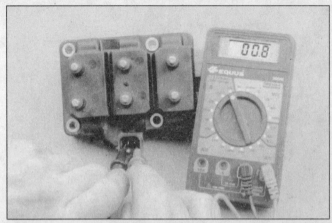

4.45 When measuring the primary resistance of the coil-pack, make sure the test leads are making good contact with the terminals - or you will get an incorrect resistance reading or no reading at all (Chrysler minivans)

mounted inside the distributor and require disassembly of the distributor components **(see illustrations)**. If necessary, consult a *Haynes Automotive Repair Manual* for additional information concerning the removal process.

Remember, these resistance checks will sometimes not diagnose a bad ignition coil. In severe cases, the engine must be tested under load and in actual working conditions. These type of tests will require an automotive oscilloscope and other expensive tools. In the event that your vehicle develops intermittent or "difficult to figure out" driveability problems, have it checked at a qualified repair shop for the correct diagnosis.

DIS style electronic ignition coil pack(s)

The abbreviation DIS stands for distributorless ignition system (or in some cases, *direct* ignition system). This type of ignition coil performs in the same manner as the conventional coil, with one mayor difference - lets take a look at

this difference.

Conventional coils are primarily controlled by the rotation of the distributor, which signals when to break the magnetic field in the ignition coil so that the secondary system in the coil could discharge. Instead of having just one coil, as in a conventional system, the DIS system has a *coil pack*. This coil pack consists of a cluster of coils the number of which depends on the number of cylinders in the engine. A six-cylinder engine typically will have three coils - each coil takes care of two cylinders. Another form of DIS incorporates a separate coil for each cylinder.

As we already know, the conventional versions of ignition coils are controlled by the distributor. The DIS system is controlled by the computer. The computer instructs the coil when to break the primary circuit and discharge the secondary system voltage at the proper time.

Checking the primary and secondary circuits on DIS coil pack(s) is similar to conventional coils. Connect the probes of an ohmmeter to the primary terminals of the coil pack **(see illustrations)** and observe the resistance. Typical

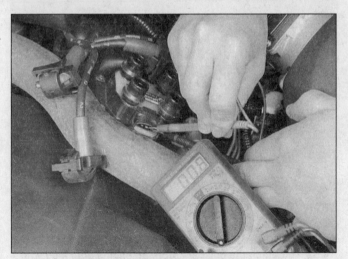

4.46 Checking the primary resistance on a Ford EDIS coil pack

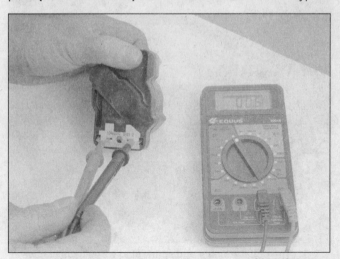

4.47 Measuring the primary resistance of a GM DIS coil

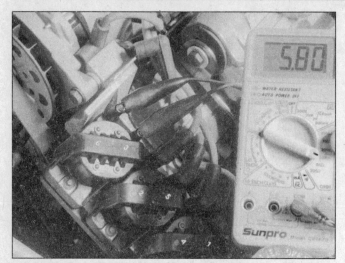

4.48 Next, measure the secondary resistance across both towers of each coil (GM 3.1L V6 engine shown)

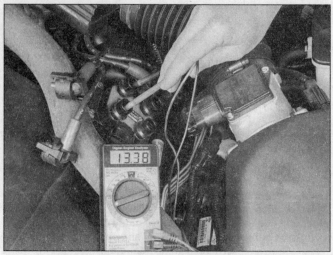

4.49 Checking the secondary resistance on a Ford EDIS system

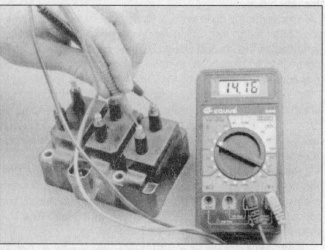

4.50 Checking the secondary resistance on a Chrysler DIS coil

primary resistance values are between 0.2 and 2.0 ohms. Consult the *Haynes Automotive Repair Manual* for your particular vehicle for the exact specification, if necessary.

Now check the secondary resistance of the coil pack(s) **(see illustrations)**. These tests are usually easier because the secondary posts are much more easily accessible than the primary terminals on the DIS coil packs. Secondary resistance for DIS coils range from 4,000 to 7,000 ohms. Here again, the range of resistance is wide so consult your *Haynes Automotive Repair Manual* for additional information.

DIS coils are usually easy to remove from the engine compartment. Locate the bolts that hold it down **(see illustrations)** to the engine or firewall and carefully disconnect all the electrical connectors and remove the bolts from the assembly.

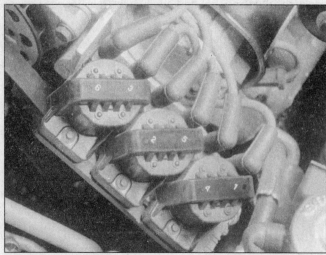

4.51 The coil terminals and spark plug wires usually have corresponding numbers, but if they don't, be sure to mark the positions of the wires before removing them

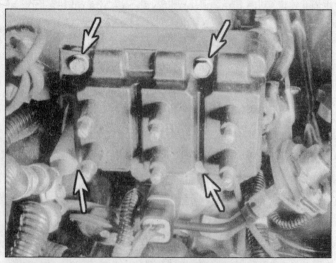

4.52 To detach the coil pack from an engine equipped with DIS, remove the bolts (arrows) (typical Chrysler DIS coil pack shown)

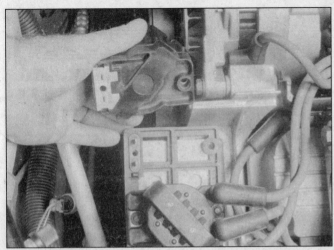

4.53 Carefully lift the coil pack from the ignition module on GM DIS systems

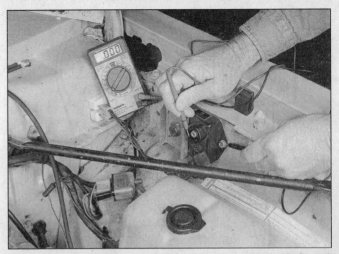

4.54 Check for continuity on the ground circuit (pin number 5) and ground on the ignition module (Chrysler)

Ignition module checks

Introduction

Most ignition modules can only be tested by installing a special electronic ignition module tool into the harness to simulate actual ignition working voltages. Because the tool(s) are very expensive, the home mechanic quite often will not be able to perform the tests. The alternative method for the home mechanic for testing a bad ignition module often involves a complete check of the ignition coil, ignition switch, pick-up coil, Hall Effect switch, the electrical harness and any other additional component or circuit to finally arrive at the conclusion through the process of elimination.

The procedures that follow offer checks and advice concerning the ignition modules on a select group of systems that are designed to be checked with an ohmmeter and voltmeter. If you are not certain about the condition of your ignition module after performing these checks, it is best to have it checked at a dealer service department or other repair shop. Here is a brief list of some of the most common ignition module checks and the main points to look out for in the diagnostic process. **Caution:** *The ignition module is a delicate and relatively expensive electronic component. Failure to follow the step-by-step procedures could result in damage to the module and/or other electronic devices, including the Engine Control Computer (ECU). Additionally, all devices under computer control are protected by a Federally mandated extended warranty. Check with your dealer concerning this warranty before attempting to diagnose and replace the module yourself.*

Pick-up coil and Hall Effect Ignition systems

Chrysler

Connect one ohmmeter lead to a good ground and the other lead to the control unit pin number 5 **(see illustration)**. **Note:** *Early models that are equipped with a 4-pin*

electrical connector on the ignition module also use pin number 5 to check the system ground. If necessary, consult a factory wiring diagram to obtain the correct terminal designations on the module connector. The ohmmeter should show continuity between ground and the control unit pin. If continuity does not exist, try removing the control unit (module), cleaning the back side of the housing and tightening the bolts a little tighter to make a better connection on the firewall. Repeat the continuity check. If continuity still does not exist, replace the control unit.

To replace the module, remove the electrical connector from the control unit (module), remove the bolts and lift the assembly from the engine compartment.

BMW

BMW uses two different styles of pick-up coil ignition systems on their 318i series models. Some use the Bosch system while others are equipped with the Siemens/Telefunken system. The two types can be distinguished by their different electrical connectors at the ignition module **(see illustrations)**. Many of the later model BMW's are equipped

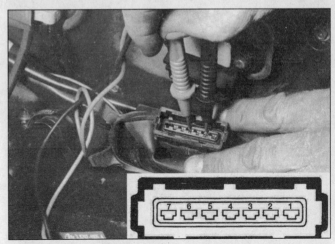

4.55 Check for voltage at terminals number 2 and 4 on the control unit electrical connector (Bosch system shown)

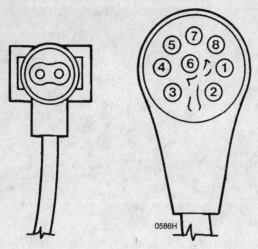

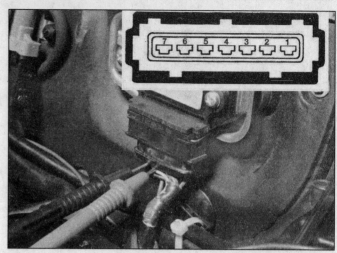

4.56 Check for voltage at terminals number 6 and 3 on the control unit electrical connector (Siemens/Telefunken system shown)

4.57 Backprobe the ignition control unit electrical connector and check for signal voltage on terminals number 5 and 6 (Bosch system shown)

with the Motronic ignition system which is not covered in this book.

With the ignition key OFF, remove the harness connectors from the ignition control unit and connect a voltmeter between terminals number 2 and 4 on the Bosch systems and between numbers 6 and 3 on the Siemens/Telefunken ignition system. Turn the ignition key ON (engine not running). There should be battery voltage available. This will check the voltage available to the ignition control unit.

Now check the continuity between the ignition control unit and body ground. Connect one probe of an ohmmeter to terminal number 2 (Bosch) or terminal number 6 (Siemens/Telefunken) and make sure continuity exists. If not, remove the control unit and clean the backside with

sandpaper to make a better connection.

Next, check for a signal from the impulse generator (ignition module). If the ignition control unit is receiving battery voltage, check the A/C signal coming from the impulse generator (pick-up coil) to the control unit. With the electrical connector in place, backprobe terminals number 5 and 6 on Bosch systems **(see illustration)**. On Siemen/Telefunken systems, connect the positive probe to the (+) terminal on the small electrical connector and the negative probe onto the (-) terminal of the same connector. Have an assistant crank the engine over and observe that there is approximately 1 to 2 volts reading on the voltmeter. This will detect a voltage signal from the module. If the ignition module is not generating a voltage signal, replace it with a new part.

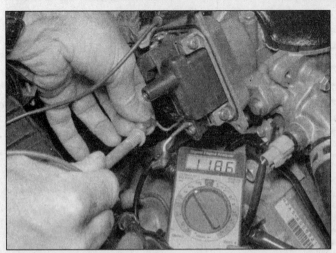

4.59 Check for battery voltage between the black/yellow wire (middle terminal on the igniter) and body ground

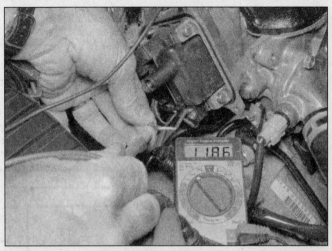

4.60 Check for battery voltage on the yellow/green wire (end terminal) and body ground (1991 Honda Accord shown)

Honda

This procedure covers Honda Accord models equipped with the integral style coil and ignition module. Remove the distributor cap and the igniter cover from the distributor. Disconnect the wires from the igniter unit. With the ignition key turned ON (engine not running), check for voltage between the black/yellow wire (middle terminal off the igniter unit) and body ground **(see illustration)**. There should be battery voltage.

If there is no voltage, check the circuit between the black/yellow wire and the ignition switch. It may be necessary to obtain a wiring diagram to locate the correct terminal designations.

With the ignition key turned ON (engine not running), check for voltage between the yellow/green wire (1990 and 1991 models only) or the light green (1992 and 1993 models) and body ground **(see illustration)**. There should be battery voltage.

Next, check for continuity between the yellow/green wire (1990 and 1991 models) or the light green (1992 and 1993 models) and the ECU. Check for continuity between the blue wire (offset from the igniter) and the tachometer terminal and igniter. There should be 1.1K to 3.3K ohms. If the igniter fails any of the three tests, replace it with a new part.

4.61 Remove the igniter unit straight out from the distributor body on Honda integral coil systems

To replace the igniter on this style distributor, first, remove the distributor cap and cover from the distributor. Remove all the electrical connectors from the igniter unit. Remove the igniter screws and lift the igniter from the distributor **(see illustration)**. Be sure to pack silicone grease into the igniter housing before installing the unit.

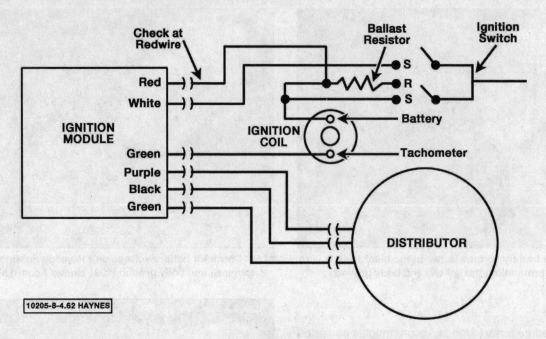

4.62 Check for battery voltage on the red wire on Ford Duraspark II ignition systems

Ford

Duraspark II ignition module - check and replacement

Duraspark II ignition systems are equipped with either a three-connector module or a two-connector module. Do not be confused with these ignition modules but instead follow the same color code for all diagnostic voltage and resistance checks. Check for power to the ignition module.

Using a voltmeter, probe the red wire from the module **(see illustration)**. With the ignition ON (engine not running), there should be battery voltage. Check the ground circuit continuity. Using a voltmeter, probe the black wire from the ignition module **(see illustration)**. With the ignition ON (engine not running), there should be approximately 0.5 volts or greater. If battery voltage is not reaching the ignition module, trace the electrical circuit to the ignition and battery and check for open circuits or a damaged wire har-

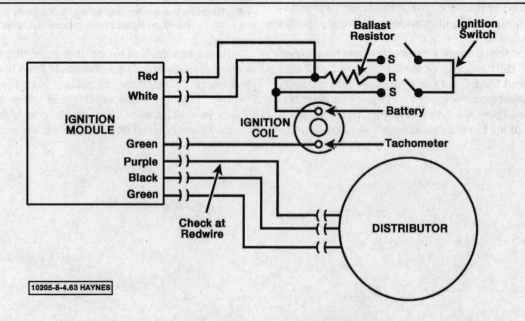

4.63 With the ignition key ON (engine not running), the ground circuit should indicate 0.5 volts (Ford Duraspark II)

4.64 Check the module signal for the primary circuit using a test light on the coil TACH terminal (Ford TFI-IV)

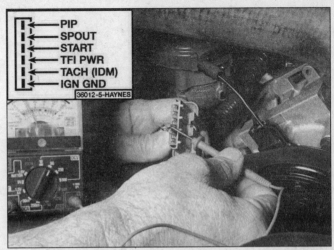

4.65 Check for battery voltage on terminal number 3 (TFI-PWR) (typical Ford TFI system shown) (Ford TFI-IV)

ness. If any of the other test results are incorrect, replace the ignition module with a new part.

Detach the cable from the negative terminal of the battery. Vehicles equipped with a Duraspark II system may have either the universal ignition module or the standard ignition module. If your vehicle is equipped with the standard module, unplug both connectors; if your vehicle is equipped with the U.I.M. module, unplug all three connectors.

Remove the mounting screws and detach the module. Installation is the reverse of removal.

TFI-IV ignition module - check and replacement

First check the ignition coil primary circuit. Unplug the ignition wiring harness connectors and inspect them for dirt, corrosion and damage, then reconnect them. Attach a 12 volt test light between the coil TACH terminal and a good engine ground **(see illustration)**. Remove the coil wire from the ignition coil and use a suitable wire to ground the secondary terminal.

Crank the engine. The test light should flash with each output signal from the coil primary circuit as the engine fires.

Check for power to the ignition module. Using a voltmeter, probe terminal number 3 (TFI PWR) from the module **(see illustration)**. With the ignition ON (engine not running), there should be battery voltage.

Measure the resistance of the stator assembly (pick-up coil) using an ohmmeter (see previous text). If the ohmmeter reads 800 to 975 ohms, then the stator is working but the TFI module is defective. If the ohmmeter reads less than 800 ohms or more than 975 ohms, replace the stator assembly.

Remove the distributor from the engine if access to the module is blocked. Remove the two module mounting screws with a 1/4-inch drive 7/32-inch deep socket **(see illustration)**. Pull straight down on the module to disconnect the spade connectors from the stator connector **(see illustration)**. Whether you are installing the old module or a new one, wipe the back side of the module clean with a

4.66 To remove the TFI-IV ignition module from the distributor base, remove the two screws (arrows) . . .

4.67 . . . then pull the module straight down to detach the spade terminals from the stator connector

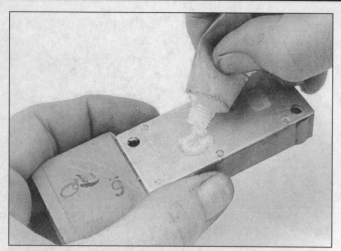

4.68 Be sure to wipe the back side of the module clean and apply a film of dielectric grease (essential for cool operation of the module) - DO NOT use any other type of grease

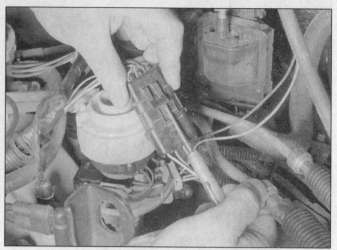

4.69 Use a small screwdriver to release the locking tab on the distributor connector (GM HEI)

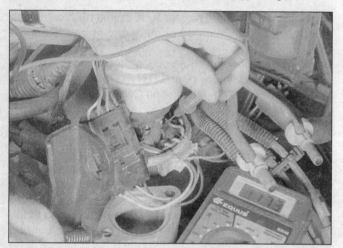

4.70 Check for battery voltage on the + terminal (pink wire) on the ignition module (GM HEI)

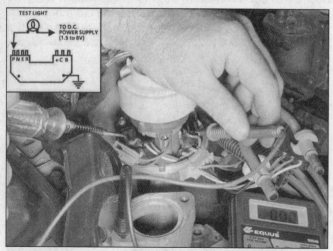

4.71 Check the "C" terminal (brown wire) voltage and watch very carefully for a voltage drop as a test light is momentarily (five seconds or less) connected between the battery positive (+) terminal and the module "P" (pick-up coil) terminal (GM HEI)

soft, clean rag and apply a film of silicone dielectric grease to the back side of the module **(see illustration)**. Installation is the reverse of removal. When plugging in the module, make sure that the three terminals are inserted all the way into the stator connector.

General Motors - High Energy Ignition (HEI) systems

Check

Disconnect the four terminal distributor connector **(see illustration)**. Crank the engine over and check for a spark at the coil and spark plug wires. If there is no spark, remove the distributor cap. Reconnect the four terminal distributor connector. With the ignition switch turned ON, check for voltage at the module positive (+) terminal (pink wire) **(see illustration)**.

If the reading is less than ten volts, there is a fault in the wire between the module positive (+) terminal and the ignition coil positive connector or the ignition coil and primary circuit-to-ignition switch. If the reading is ten volts or more, check the "C" terminal (brown wire) on the module. If the reading is less than one volt, there is an open or grounded lead in the distributor-to-coil "C" terminal connection or ignition coil or an open primary circuit in the coil itself.

If the reading is one to ten volts, replace the module with a new one and check for a spark. If there is a spark the module was faulty and the system is now operating properly. If there is no spark, there is a fault in the ignition coil.

If the reading 10 volts or more, unplug the pick-up coil connector from the module. Check the "C" terminal (brown wire) voltage with the ignition switch ON and watch the voltage reading as a test light is momentarily (five seconds or less) connected between the battery positive (+) terminal and the module "P" (brown wire) (pick-up coil) terminal **(see illustration)**.

a) If there is no drop in voltage, check the module ground and, if it is good, replace the module with a new one.

b) If the voltage drops, check for spark at the coil wire as

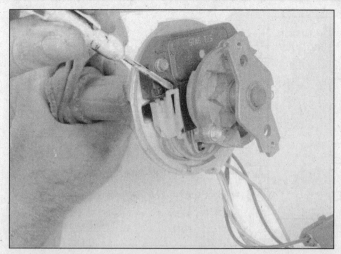

4.72 Unplug both electrical connectors from the module (GM HEI)

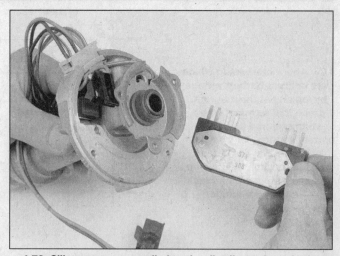

4.73 Silicone grease applied to the distributor base in the areas under the ignition module dissipates heat - the distributor has been removed for clarity (GM HEI)

the test light is removed from the module terminal. If there is no spark, the module is faulty and should be replaced with a new one. If there is a spark, the pick-up coil or connections are faulty or not grounded.

Replacement

Detach the cable from the negative terminal of the battery. Remove the distributor cap and rotor.

Remove both module attaching screws and lift the module up and away from the distributor. Disconnect both electrical leads from the module **(see illustration)**. Note that the leads cannot be interchanged.

Do not wipe the grease from the module or the distributor base if the same module is to be reinstalled. If a new module is to be installed, a package of silicone grease will be included with it. Wipe the distributor base and the new module clean, then apply the silicone grease on the face of the module and on the distributor base where the module seats **(see illustration)**. This grease is necessary for heat dissipation. Install the module and attach both electrical leads. Install the distributor rotor and cap. Attach the cable to the negative terminal of the battery.

Distributorless ignition system (DIS) modules

Introduction

DIS modules are diagnosed in the same way conventional ignition system modules are checked. Some DIS modules are more difficult to locate and connect test equipment to. Follow the procedures for all DIS systems to arrive at the correct diagnosis for your ignition system.

Ignition module checks

First, check for power to the ignition module. Using a voltmeter, probe the power terminal from the battery to check for voltage **(see illustrations)**. It will be necessary to use a factory wiring diagram to identify the correct terminal designation. There should be battery voltage. If battery voltage is not reaching the ignition module, trace the electrical

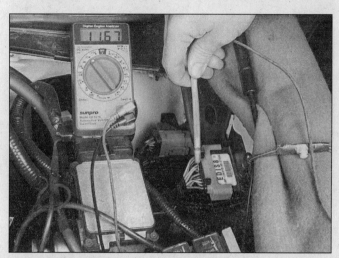

4.74 On Ford EDIS systems, probe terminal number 6 to check for battery voltage from the power relay

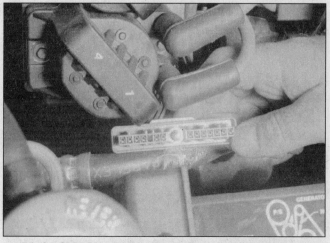

4.75 On GM APV minivans, loosen the electrical connector hold-down bolt and remove the assembly from the ignition module. Follow the color of the wires from a wiring diagram or schematic of the DIS system

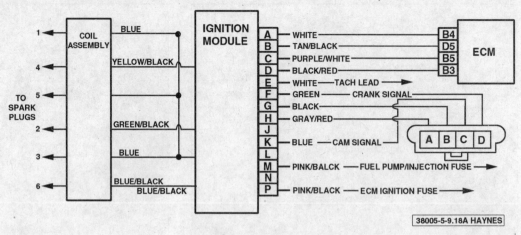

4.76 After determining which wire delivers battery voltage by looking at the diagram, probe that terminal with a voltmeter and check for battery voltage. This diagram indicates that the battery voltage reaches the ignition module from the pink/black wire from the ignition

circuit to the ignition and battery and check for open circuits or a damaged wire harness.

Also, check the ignition coil(s) to make sure they are receiving a pulsing voltage signal from the ignition module. Install a test light onto the positive terminal of the battery and touch the tip of the light to the ignition coil terminal

4.77 On Ford EDIS systems, check for a pulsing signal voltage from the module by attaching the test light to the positive terminal on the battery and probing the electrical terminal (s) on the coil pack(s) with the test light tip. On this particular model (Crown Victoria), probe the outer terminals which govern primary ignition voltage to each coil pack

4.78 GM DIS require the removal of the coil pack(s) from the module (underneath) to expose the module terminals

4.79 Some single type ballast resistors are mounted on the ignition coil (Nissan truck shown)

4.80 To check the ballast resistor, unplug the wires and touch the ohmmeter leads to the resistor terminals

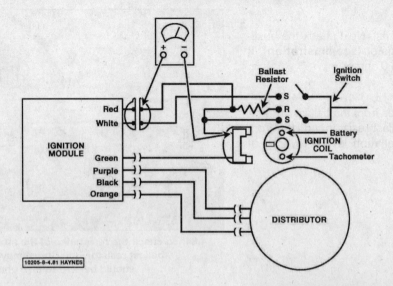

4.81 Some ballast resistors are installed directly into the harness wire that connects the ignition coil and the ignition key (Ford Duraspark system shown)

(see illustrations). Have an assistant crank the engine over and observe that the test light blinks for each firing voltage signal. This test will indicate that the ignition module is producing a primary voltage signal to the coil pack(s). If any of the test results are incorrect, replace the ignition module with a new part.

Replacement

Disconnect the negative cable from the battery. Disconnect the electrical connector from the ignition module. Remove the screws securing the module. Installation is the reverse of the removal procedure. **Note**: *Prior to installing the ignition module, apply a coating of Silicone dielectric grease to the mounting surface of the module.*

Ballast resistor

Check

The ballast resistor limits voltage to the coil during low speed operation but allows it to increase as the engine speed increases. While the engine is cranking, the ballast resistor is by-passed to ensure adequate voltage through the coil.

On models equipped with a dual ballast resistor, voltage is limited by a pair of resistors; the primary resistor and the auxiliary resistor. Voltage to the electronic control unit is limited by the auxiliary side of the ballast resistor. Some earlier models were equipped with speed limiter circuitry to prevent engine damage from excessive rpms.

Disconnect the electrical leads from the ballast resistor and, using an ohmmeter, check the resistance of the ballast resistor. On single ballast resistors, the resistance should be 1.0 to 2.0 ohms **(see illustrations)** (electronic ignition systems) or 0.5 to 0.6 ohms (points type ignition systems). On dual ballast resistors, first check the primary side **(see illustration)**. The primary side is either a thermal type (wire resistor is openly exposed) (it should be 0.5 ohms), or the non-thermal type **(see illustration)** (wire resistor hidden in

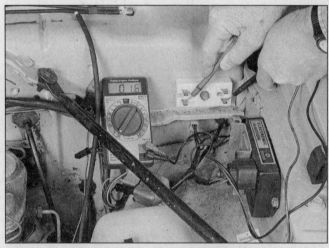

4.82 Checking the primary side of a dual ballast resistor on a typical Chrysler ignition system

4.83 To identify the type of dual ballast resistor, remove the resistor from the firewall and check the backside; non-thermal types will have the resistor coils sealed from the atmosphere (shown) while thermal types will have the resistor coils exposed to the air

case) (it should be 1.0 to 2.0 ohms). Next check the auxiliary side of the dual ballast resistor **(see illustration)**. It should be approximately 5.0 to 6.0 ohms.

Replacement

Disconnect the electrical leads from the ballast resistor. Remove the screws from the ballast resistor and lift it from the engine compartment. Installation is the reverse of removal.

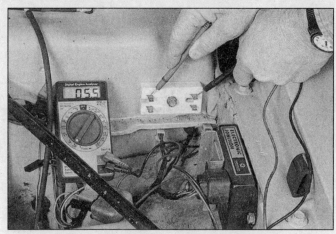

4.84 To check the resistance of the auxiliary side of the ballast resistor - on Chrysler systems it should be 4.75 to 5.75 ohms

Glossary

A

Absolute Pressure - Pressure measured from the point of total vacuum. For instance, absolute atmospheric pressure at sea level is 14.7 psi (1 bar, 100 kpa or 29.92 in. hg) at a temperature of 80 degrees Fahrenheit (26.7 degrees Centigrade.)

Acceleration - The moment the throttle is open with the engine running and the vacuum in the intake manifold drops.

Actuator - One name for any computer-controlled output device, such as a fuel injector, an EGR solenoid valve, an EVAP solenoid purge valve, etc. The term also refers to a specific component, the pressure actuator, used on Bosch KE-Jetronic and KE-Motronic continuous injection systems. See *pressure actuator.*

Adaptive control - The ability of a control unit to adapt its closed-loop operation to changing operating conditions - such as engine wear, fuel quality or altitude - to maintain proper air-fuel mixture control, ignition timing or idle rpm. Also referred to as self-learning.

Adaptive memory - A feature of computer memory that allows the microprocessor to adjust its memory for computing open-loop operation, based on changes in engine operation.

After Top Dead Center (ATDC) - The position of a piston after it has passed top dead center. Usually expressed in degrees.

Air Charge Temperature sensor (ACT) - A thermistor used to measure intake air temperature or air-fuel mixture temperature.

Air-Flow Controlled (AFC) - A Bosch term for early L-Jetronic fuel injection systems, used to distinguish L-Jet from the earlier D-Jetronic, which was a pressure-controlled system. AFC also refers to many other fuel injection systems that measure the amount of air flowing past a sensor to determine engine fuel requirements

Air-fuel ratio - The amount of air compared to the amount of fuel in the air-fuel mixture, almost always expressed in terms of mass. See also *Stoichiometric Ratio.*

Air gap - The space between the spark plug electrodes, motor and generator armatures, field shoes, etc.

Airflow meter - In Bosch systems, any device that measures the amount of air being used by the engine. The control unit uses this information to determine the load on the engine. The two most common examples of airflow meters are the airflow sensor used in the Bosch L-Jetronic and the air mass sensor used in the Bosch LH-Jetronic systems. See *airflow sensor* and *air mass sensor.*

Airflow sensor - A sensor used to measure the volume of air entering the engine on many fuel injection systems. Continuous injection systems use an airflow sensor *plate* to measure airflow volume; electronic systems use a *vane* or flap-type airflow sensor.

Air injection - A way of reducing exhaust emissions by injecting air into each of the exhaust ports of an engine. The air mixes with the hot exhaust gasses and oxidizes the HC and CO to form H_2O and CO_2.

Air mass sensor - An airflow meter that uses the changing resistance of a heated wire in the intake airstream to measure the mass of the air being drawn into the engine. Also referred to as a hot-wire sensor.

Alternating current - A flow of electricity through a conductor, first in one direction, then in the opposite direction.

Air vane - The pivoting flap inside an L-Jetronic or Motronic airflow sensor that swings open in relation to the amount of air flowing through the airflow sensor.

Adjustable timing light - A timing light that delays flashes as an adjusting knob is turned. The delay is displayed as degrees on a meter, usually incorporated in the timing light.

Ambient temperature - The temperature of the surrounding air.

Ammeter - An electric meter used to measure current.

Amperage - The total amount of current (amperage) flowing in a circuit.

Ampere (Amp) - The unit of measure for the flow of current in a circuit. The amount of current produced by one volt acting against one ohm of resistance.

Amplifier - An electronic device (usually an electron tube or transistor) used in a circuit to strengthen or increase an input signal.

Amplitude - The maximum rise (or fall) of a voltage signal from 0 volts.

Analog - A voltage signal or processing action that is that is continuously variable relative to the operation being measured or controlled.

Analog Volt-Ohmmeter (VOM) - A multi-function meter which measures voltage and resistance. Measurements are made with a D'arsenval meter movement (needle) instead of a digital display.

Anti-knock value - The characteristic of gasoline that helps prevent detonation or knocking

Antioxidant inhibitor - A gasoline additive used to prevent oxidation and the formation of gum.

Armature - The spring-loaded part in an injector that's magnetically attracted by the solenoid coil when it is energized. Also another name for the solenoid itself.

Atmospheric pressure - Normal pressure in the surrounding atmosphere, generated by the weight of the air pressing down from above. At sea level, atmospheric pressure is about 14.7 psi, above vacuum or zero absolute, pressure (1 bar, 100 kpa or 29.92 in. hg) at a temperature of 80 degrees Fahrenheit (26.7 degrees Centigrade). See *barometric pressure*.

Atomization - breaking down into small particles or a fine mist.

Auxiliary air valve - A special valve which bypasses the closed throttle valve. The auxiliary air valve admits extra air into the intake manifold during cold engine starting for a higher idle speed during warm-up.

Available voltage - The measured voltage at the source or other point in a circuit with respect to ground.

B

Backfire - The accidental combustion of gasses in an engine's intake or exhaust manifold.

Backpressure - The resistance, caused by turbulence and friction, that is created as a gas or liquid is forced through a passage.

Baffle - A plate or obstruction that restricts the flow of air or liquids. The baffle in a fuel tank keeps the fuel from sloshing as the car moves.

Ballast resistor - A resistor connected in series between the ignition switch and the ignition coil to reduce voltage and current to the coil when the engine is running.

Bar - The metric unit of measurement used in the measurement of both air and fuel. One bar is about 14.7 psi (1 bar, 100 kpa or 29.92 in. hg, at a temperature of 80 degrees Fahrenheit (26.7 degrees Centigrade) at sea level.

Barometric Pressure - Another term for atmospheric pressure, expressed in inches of Mercury (in-Hg). Barometric pressure is determined by how high atmospheric pressure (relative to zero absolute pressure) forces mercury up a glass tube. 14.7 psi = 1 bar, 100 kpa or 29.92 in. hg, at a temperature of 80 degrees Fahrenheit (26.7 degrees Centigrade) at sea level.

Base idle - The idle rpm when the throttle lever rests on the throttle stop and the Idle Speed Control motor or solenoid is fully retracted and disconnected.

Battery - A group of two or more cells connected together for the production of an electric current. It converts chemical energy into electrical energy.

Battery-hot - Refers to a circuit that is fed directly from the starter relay terminal. Voltage is available whenever the battery is charged.

Battery voltage - Voltage measured between the two terminals of a battery.

Binary - A mathematical system consisting of only two digits (0 and 1) which allows a digital computer to read and process input voltage signals.

Bimetal - A spring or strip made of two different metals with different thermal expansion rates. A rising temperature causes a bimetal element to bend or twist one way when it's cold and the other way when it's warm.

Block learn - Long-term recorded memory of air fuel ratios stored in the computer (if electrical power is lost, by disconnecting the battery for example the memory in the block learn will be lost)

Blown - A melted fuse filament caused by electrical overload.

Boost - A condition of over-pressure (above atmospheric) in the intake manifold; caused by intake air being forced in by a turbocharger or supercharger.

Bottom Dead Center - (BDC) - The exact bottom of a piston stroke.

Bypass - A passage inside a throttle body casting that allows air to go around a closed throttle valve.

C

Calibration - The act of determining or rectifying the graduations used on a testing instrument.

Calibration Package - More commonly known as CALPAK is installed in the computer in case of PROM or ECM failure, to give a preset air/fuel ratio and timing so that the vehicle can be driven to a repair facility.

Camshaft overlap - The period of camshaft rotation in degrees during which both the intake and the exhaust valve are open.

Canister - A container in an evaporative emission control system that contains charcoal to trap vapors from the fuel system.

Capacitance - The ability of a condenser (capacitor) to receive and hold an electrical charge.

Capacitor - An electrical device made up of two conductors made of metal foil, separated by a very thin insulating material and rolled up and housed (usually) in a metal container. A capacitor has the ability to store an electrical charge.

Capacity - The quantity of electricity that can be delivered under specified conditions, as from a battery at a given rate of discharge in amp hours.

Carbon dioxide (CO_2) - One of the many by-products of combustion.

Carbon monoxide (CO) - A harmful gas produced during combustion.

Catalyst - A material that starts or speeds up a chemical reaction without being consumed itself.

Catalytic converter - A device mounted in the exhaust system that converts harmful exhaust emissions into harmless gases. Works by catalytic action which promotes additional chemical reaction after combustion

Cavitation - The rapid formation and collapse of gas or vapor-filled cavities in a liquid, in regions of very low pressure (behind the vanes of a fuel pump rotor, for example). The point at which a pump begins to lose efficiency.

Centigrade - Unit of measuring temperature where water boils at 100 degrees and freezes at 0 degrees at sea level altitude (boiling points will decrease as altitude increases).

C Four - (C4) Computer Controlled Catalytic Converter (AMC/GM)

Charge - Any condition where electricity is available. To restore the active materials in a battery cell by electrically reversing the chemical action.

Check Engine Light (CEL) - A dash panel light used either to aid in the identification and diagnosis of a computer system problem.

Check Valve - A one way valve which allows a vacuum or gas to flow in one direction only. Preventing backflow.

Circuit - A circle or unbroken path through which electric current can flow.

Circuit breaker - A device other than a fuse which interrupts a circuit under infrequent abnormal conditions.

Clearance volume - The volume of a combustion chamber when the piston is at top dead center.

Closed circuit - A circuit which is uninterrupted from the current source and back to the current source.

Closed loop - The mode of operation that a system with an oxygen sensor goes into once the engine is sufficiently warmed up. When the system is in closed-loop operation, an oxygen sensor monitors the oxygen content of the exhaust gas and sends a varying voltage signal to the control unit, which alters the air/fuel mixture ratio accordingly.

Cold-start injector - A solenoid-type injector, installed in the intake plenum, that injects extra fuel during cold-engine starts. Also referred to as a cold start valve.

Cold-start valve - See *cold-start injector*.

Combustion - Controlled, rapid burning of the air-fuel mixture in the engine cylinders.

Combustion chamber - Space left between the cylinder head and the top of the piston at TDC; where combustion of the air-fuel mixture takes place.

Compression ratio - The ratio of maximum engine cylinder volume (when the piston is at the bottom of its stroke) to minimum engine cylinder volume (with the piston at TDC). Thus, the theoretical amount that the air-fuel mixture is compressed in the cylinder.

Computer Controlled Coil Ignition (C3I) - General Motors' computerized ignition coil system (a type of distributorless ignition), used on many different engine applications.

Computed timing - The total spark advance in degrees before top dead center. Calculated by the computer based on inputs from a number of sensors.

Condenser - A device for holding or storing an electric charge. See *Capacitor*.

Conductor - A material that allows easy flow of electricity.

Continuity - Little or no resistance in an electrical circuit to the flow of current. A solid electrical connection between two points in a circuit. The opposite of an open circuit.

Continuous Injection System (CIS) - A Bosch-developed fuel injection system that injects fuel continuously. Unlike an electronic injection system, which uses a computer to control the pulse-width of electronic solenoid injectors, CIS uses hydraulic controls to alter the amount of fuel injected. There are four basic types of CIS: K-Jetronic, K-Jetronic with Lambda (oxygen sensor), KE-Jetronic and KE-Motronic.

Controller - One of several names for a solid state micro-computer which monitors engine conditions and controls certain engine functions, i.e. air/fuel ratio, injection and ignition timing, etc. Specific names such as ECM, ECU, Power Module, Logic Module, SBEC and SMEC are generically referred to as controllers in many different instances to refer to all of these computers.

Control module - A transistorized device that processes electrical inputs and produces output signals to control various engine functions. One of several names for a solid-state micro-computer.

Control plunger - In Bosch CIS, the component inside the fuel distributor that rises and falls with the airflow sensor plate lever, which controls fuel flow to the injectors.

Control pressure - In Bosch CIS, the pressurized fuel used as a hydraulic control fluid to apply a counterforce to the control plunger in Bosch CIS. Control pressure alters the air-fuel ratio through the operation of the control-pressure regulator.

Control pressure regulator - In Bosch CIS, the control-pressure regulator is a thermal-hydraulic device that alters the control pressure by returning the excess fuel from the control pressure circuit to the fuel tank. The control pressure regulator controls the counterforce pressure on top of the control plunger. Also referred to as the warm-up regulator.

Control unit - An electronic computer that processes electrical inputs and produces electrical outputs to control a series of actuators which alter engine operating conditions. Also referred to as an electronic control assembly (ECA), electronic control module (ECM), electronic control unit (ECU), logic module, or simply, the computer.

Conventional Theory of Current Flow - The current flow theory which says electricity flows from positive to negative. Also called positive current flow theory.

Converter circuits - Area of the computer where the input data in a form of analog signals coming from sensors are converted into digital signals.

Core - The center conductor part or a wire of the iron magnetic material or a solenoid magnet.

Counterforce - The force of the fuel-pressure applied to the top of the control plunger to balance the force of the airflow pushing against the sensor plate. See *control pressure*.

Cross-circuit short - A current flow path between hot wires in two different circuits.

Current - Amount or intensity of flow of electricity. Measure in amperes.

Current flow - The current flow theory which says electricity flows from positive to negative. Also called positive current flow theory.

Current-limiting resistor - A resistor inserted in a circuit to limit the current.

Cycle - A complete alternation in an alternating current.

D

Dampener - A device, sometimes called an accumulator, installed inline between the fuel pump and the fuel filter on many fuel injection systems, which dampens the pulsations of the fuel pump. The accumulator also maintains residual pressure in the fuel delivery system, even after the engine has been turned off, to prevent vapor lock.

Dead short - A zero-resistance short circuit.

Deceleration - The moment the throttle is released with the engine running and the vacuum in the intake manifold increases.

De-energized - Having the electric current or energy source turned off.

Density- The ratio of the mass of something (air, in this book) to the volume it occupies. Air has less density when it's warm or when the vehicle is operating at higher altitude. It has more density when it's cool, and at lower altitude.

Detonation - See *knock*.

Diagnostic mode - This operation mode is used by the Engine Control Computer (ECU) and provides historical data to the technician that indicates any malfunctions or discrepancies that have been stored in memory.

Diaphragm - A component which moves a control lever accordingly when supplied with a vacuum signal.

Dielectric - The insulating material used between the plates of a capacitor (condenser).

Dieseling - A condition in a gasoline engine in which extreme heat in the combustion chamber continues to ignite fuel after the ignition has been turned off.

Differential pressure - In Bosch KE-Jetronic systems, the difference between actuator fuel pressure in the lower chambers of the differential-pressure valves and the system pressure entering the pressure actuator. See *pressure-drop*.

Differential-pressure regulator - See *pressure actuator*.

Differential-pressure valves- Inside the Bosch CIS fuel distributor, these valves (there's one for each cylinder) maintain a constant pressure drop at each of the control-plunger slits, regardless of changes in the quantity of fuel flow.

Digifant - Volkswagen collaborated with Bosch to develop this electronic injection system. Digifant is similar to a Motronic system, except that its timing control map is less complicated than the Motronic map. And it doesn't have a knock sensor.

Digifant II - A refined version of Volkswagen's Digifant. This system has some control improvements and uses a knock sensor for improved timing control.

Digital - A two-level voltage signal or processing function that is either on/off or high/low.

Digital control - Circuits which handle information by switching the current on and off.

Digital Fuel Injection (DFI) - A General Motors system, similar to earlier electronic fuel injection systems, but with digital microprocessors. Analog inputs from various engine sensors are converted to digital signals before processing. The system is self-monitoring and self-diagnosing. It also has the capabilities of compensating for failed components and remembering intermittent failures.

Digital volt-ohm meter - A highly accurate multimeter. To indicate meter readings, it uses integrated circuits and a digital display instead of conventional needle movement.

D-Jetronic - D-Jetronic is the term used by Bosch to describe a fuel injection system controlled by manifold pressure. The D is short for *druck*, the German word for "pressure." Manifold pressure is measured to indicate engine load (how much air the engine is using). This pressure is an input signal to the control unit (ECU) for calculation of the correct amount of fuel delivery.

Diode - A form of semiconductor that allows electricity to flow only in one direction.

Displacement - A measurement of the volume of air displaced by a piston as it moves from bottom to top of its stroke. Engine displacement is the piston displacement multiplied by the number of pistons in an engine.

Distributor pipe - Another name for the fuel rail.

Draw - The amount of electricity current any load or circuit uses.

Driveability - The operating characteristics of a vehicle.

Duty cycle - Many solenoid-operated metering devices cycle on and off. The duty cycle is a measurement of the amount of time a device is energized, or turned on, expressed as a percentage of the complete on-off cycle of that device. In other words, the duty cycle is the ratio of the pulse width to the complete cycle width.

Dwell - The amount of time that primary voltage is applied to the ignition coil to energize it. Dwell is also a measurement of the duration of time a component is on, relative to the time it's off. Dwell measurements are expressed in degrees (degrees of crankshaft rotation, for example). See *duty cycle*.

Dynamometer - A device used to measure mechanical power, such as the power of an engine.

E

Eccentric - Off center. A shaft lobe which has a center different from that of the shaft.

Electro-hydraulic pressure actuator - See *pressure actuator*.

Electron Theory of Current Flow - The current flow theory which says electricity flows from negative to positive.

Electronic Control Unit (ECU) - One (of many) names for the system computer. Often referred to as simply the "control unit."

Electronic Lean Burn (ELB) - This was the first electronic system introduced by Chrysler Motors to fire an extremely lean air/fuel ratio. This system only controlled ignition timing.

Electromagnetic - Refers to a device which incorporates both electronic and magnetic principles together in its operation.

Electromechanical - Refers to a device which incorporates both electronic and mechanical principles together in its operation.

Electronic - Pertaining to the control of systems or devices by the use of small electrical signals and various semiconductors, devices and circuits.

Emissions - Unburned parts of the air-fuel mixture released in the exhaust. Refers mostly to carbon monoxide (CO), hydrocarbons (HC), and nitrous oxide (NOx)

Energized - Having the electric current or source turned on.

Engine mapping - Vehicle operation simulation procedure used to tailor the onboard computer program to a specific engine/powertrain combination. This program is stored in a PROM or calibration assembly.

Ethanol - Ethyl alcohol distilled from grain or sugar cane.

Evaporative Emission Control (EEC) - A way of controlling HC emissions by collecting fuel vapors from the fuel tank and carburetor fuel bowl vents and directing them through an engine's intake.

F

Fahrenheit - Unit of measuring temperature where water boils at 212 degrees and freezes at 32 degrees at sea level altitude (boiling points decrease as altitude increases).

Fast-burn combustion chamber - A compact combustion chamber with a centrally located spark plug. The chamber is designed to shorten the combustion period by reducing the distance of flame front travel.

Fault codes - A series of numbers representing the results of On-Board Diagnostic or Vehicle Diagnostics. The computer communicates this service information via the Diagnostic Connector as a series of timed pulses read either on a SCAN Tool or as flashes of the "Power Loss/Check Engine" light.

Feed circuit - The power supply or hot wire.

Feedback carburetor - A form of carburetor that has a mixture control solenoid and is controlled by a computer

Firing order - The order in which combustion occurs in the cylinders of an engine.

Flat spot - The brief hesitation or stumble of an engine caused by a momentary overly lean air-fuel mixture due to the sudden opening of the throttle.

Flooding - An excess of fuel in the cylinder, from an over-rich mixture, that prevents combustion.

Flux lines - The lines of magnetic force. Also called Maxwells.

Frequency - The number of cycles (complete alterations) of an alternating current per second.

Frequency valve - In Bosch CIS, a device that regulates pressure in the lower chamber of the differential-pressure valve, in response to a signal from the lambda (oxygen) sensor. Also referred to as a Lambda valve (Bosch's term) or a timing valve.

Fuel distributor - On Bosch CIS, the device that supplies the injectors with pressurized fuel in proportion to air volume, measured by the airflow sensor plate. The fuel distributor houses the control plunger and the differential-pressure valves. All fuel metering takes place inside the fuel distributor.

Fuel filter - Filters fuel before delivery to protect injection system components (on the frame of the vehicle) and the fuel pump (inside the gas tank).

Fuel injector - In all systems (except CIS, CIS/Lambda and CIS-E systems), a spring-loaded, solenoid (electromagnetic) valve which delivers fuel into the intake manifold, in response to electrical signals from the control module. In CIS, CIS/Lambda and CIS-E systems, a spring-loaded, pressure sensitive valve which opens at a preset value.

Fuel metering - Control of the amount of fuel that is mixed with engine intake air to form a combustible mixture.

Fuel pump - Delivers fuel from the tank to the injection system and provides system pressure. On fuel-injected vehicles, the pump is always electric.

Fuel rail - The hollow pipe, tube or manifold that delivers fuel at system pressure to the injectors. The fuel rail also serves as the mounting point for the upper ends of the injectors, and for the damper (if equipped) and the pressure regulator.

Fuel rich/lean - A qualitative evaluation of air/fuel ratio based on an air/fuel value known as stoichiometry or 14.7:1. This is determined by a voltage signal from the oxygen sensor. An excess of oxygen (lean) is a voltage of less than .4 volts. A rich condition is indicated by a voltage of greater than .6 volts.

Full-load - The load condition of the engine when the throttle is wide open. Full-load can occur at any rpm.

Full-load enrichment - The extra fuel injected during acceleration to enrich the mixture when the throttle is wide open. On some systems, the computer goes open-loop during full-load enrichment.

Fuse - A device containing a soft piece of metal which melts and breaks the circuit when it is overloaded.

Fusible link - A device that protects a circuit from damage if a short to ground occurs or if the polarity of the battery or charger is reversed.

G

Galvanic battery - The principle of operation of an oxygen sensor; a galvanic battery generates a direct current voltage as a result of a chemical reaction.

Gasohol - A blend of ethanol and unleaded gasoline, usually at a one to nine ratio.

Generate - To produce electricity by electromagnetic induction.

G-lader - A type of supercharger pump which compresses air by squeezing it through an internal spiral, then forcing it through ports in the engine.

Goose - A brief opening and closing of the throttle (Dynamic Response Test)

Ground - In automobile terms is refer to the negative side of the electrical system, examples are battery negative post and/or cable chassis and engine block.

Gulp valve - A valve used in an air injection system to prevent backfire. During deceleration it redirects air from the air pump to the intake manifold where the air leans out the rich air-fuel mixture.

H

Hall Effect pick-up assembly - This device performs the same job as a pick up coil and reluctor. The Hall Effect pick-up is usually mounted in the distributor and is stationary. Some are used for sensing crankshaft or camshaft position, such as General Motors Computer-Controlled Coil Ignition (C3i) system. The shutter blades (reluctor component) are mounted to the rotor and turn with the rotor. The blades (one for each cylinder) pass through the pick-up switch. As this happens the magnetic field is strengthened, sending a signal to the electronic control unit.

Headers - Exhaust manifolds on high-performance engines that reduce backpressure by using larger passages with gentle curves.

Hertz (Hz) - A measure of frequency, measured in cycles per second.

Hg (Mercury) - A calibration material used as a standard for vacuum measurement.

High impedance DVOM - This voltmeter has high opposition to the flow of electrical current. It is good for reading circuits with low current flow as found in electronic systems. It allows test to be made without affecting the circuit.

High-speed surge - A sudden increase in engine speed caused by high manifold vacuum pulling in an access air-fuel mixture.

High-Swirl Combustion (HSC) chamber - A combustion chamber in which the intake valve is shrouded or masked to direct the incoming air-fuel charge and create turbulence they will circulate the mixture more evenly and rapidly.

Hot start - Starting the engine when it's at or near its normal operating temperature.

Horsepower - The rate of doing work. A common measure of engine output.

Hot-wire sensor - See *air mass sensor*.

Hydrocarbon (HC) - A chemical compound made up of hydrogen and carbon. A major pollutant given off by an internal combustion engine. Gasoline, itself, is a hydrocarbon compound.

I

Ideal air-fuel ratio - See *stoichiometric ratio*.

Idle limiter - A device to control minimum and maximum idle fuel richness. The idler limiter is intended to prevent unauthorized persons from making overly rich idle adjustments.

Idle-speed stabilizer - An electronically-controlled air bypass around the throttle. Also referred to as an idle speed actuator or a constant idle system.

Ignition coil - A device which transfers electrical energy from one circuit to another. Two wound coils of wire with different diameters, usually around an iron core. One coil wire uses more turns than the other coil of wire. This produces an output voltage greater than the input voltage.

Ignition interval (firing interval) - The number of degrees of crankshaft rotation between ignition sparks.

Ignitor - The term used by foreign automobile manufactures for an ignition module.

Impedance - The total opposition a circuit offers to the flow of current. It includes resistance and reactance and is measured in ohms (i.e. 10 megohms).

Impeller - A rotor or rotor blade (vane) used to force a gas or liquid in a certain direction under pressure.

Induction - the production of an electrical voltage in a conductor or coil by moving the conductor or coil through a magnetic field, or by moving the magnetic field past the conductor or coil.

Inductive Discharge Ignition - A method of igniting the air-fuel mixture in an engine cylinder. It is based on the induction of a high voltage in the secondary winding of a coil.

Inert gas - A gas that will not undergo chemical reaction.

Information - Electrical signals received by the computer, sent by the sensors

Infinity reading - A reading of an ohmmeter that indicates an open circuit or an infinite resistance.

In-Hg - Inches of mercury. Used to express the measurement of pressure or vacuum. See *barometric pressure*.

Injection pressure - In Bosch CIS, the pressure of the fuel in the lines between the differential-pressure valves and the injectors. Also referred to as injector fuel.

Injection valve - See *injector*.

Injector - This device opens to spray fuel into the throttle bore (throttle body injection) or into the intake port (electronic port injection systems and continuous injection systems). Electronic injectors are opened by an electric solenoid and closed by a spring; continuous injectors are opened by fuel pressure and closed by a spring. Injectors are also referred to as injection valves.

Injector fuel - See injection pressure.

Input conditioning - The process of amplifying or converting a voltage signal into a form usable by the computer's central processing unit.

Input sensors - A device which monitors an engine operating condition and sends a voltage signal to the control unit. This variable voltage signal varies in accordance with the changes in the condition being monitored. There can be anywhere from half a dozen to two dozen sensors on an engine, depending on the sophistication of the system.

Insulator - Any material which is a poor conductor of electricity or heat.

Integral coil - This is an ignition coil that is build compact enough to be placed inside the distributor cap as opposed to being a separate component from the distributor.

Integrator - The ability of the computer to make short-term corrections in fuel metering.

Integrator - This device is incorporated inside the computer and uses information from the oxygen sensor (O₂) to energize the injectors, to accomplish an air/fuel ratio of 14.7 to 1.

Intercooler - An air-to-air or air-to-liquid heat exchanger used to lower the temperature of the air-fuel mixture by removing heat from the intake air charge.

Intermittent - Occurs now and then (not continuously). In electrical circuits, it refers to an occasional open, short, or ground.

Ionize - To break up molecules into two or more oppositely charged ions. The air gap between the spark plug electrode is ionized when the air-fuel mixture is charged from a nonconductor to a conductor.

J

Jumper wire - Are used to bypass sections of a circuit. The simplest type is a length of electrical wire with a alligator clip at each end.

K

Keep Alive Memory - More frequently known as KAM, Records the trouble codes of a malfunction, also records what is going on in the engine managing system every second, power failure such as disconnecting the battery will erase its memory.

K-Jetronic - K-Jetronic is the term used by Bosch to describe the original continuous injection system. The K is short for *kontinuerlich*, the German word for "continuous." Airflow is measured by a circular plate inside the airflow sensor part of the mixture control unit. Fuel delivery was purely mechanical, in relation to airflow, until 1980, i.e. there were no electronics used in the K-Jet system. VW, Audi and Mercedes refer to K-Jet as CIS.

K-Jetronic with Lambda - This second-generation K-Jet system, which began in 1980, uses a feedback loop consisting of an oxygen sensor and a control unit to provide some electronic control of the air-fuel mixture. This system is also referred to as "CIS with Lambda." "Lambda" is the Bosch term for an oxygen sensor.

KE-Jetronic - This third-generation K-Jet system combines mechanical control with electronic regulation of the mixture. Many of the sensors it uses are the same as those used in L-Jetronic systems. VW, Audi and Mercedes refer to it as CIS-E.

KE-Motronic - This Bosch system is similar to KE-Jetronic, except that it has ignition-timing control and all the other features as any other Motronic system. See *Motronic*.

Kilohertz (kHz) - 1000 Hertz (Hz), the unit of frequency. See *Hertz*.

Kilopascal (kpa) - 1,000 Pascal, a unit of pressure. 100 kpa = Atmospheric Pressure at sea level.

Knock - A sudden increase in cylinder pressure caused by preignition of some of the air-fuel mixture as the flame front moves out from the spark plug ignition point. Pressure waves in the combustion chamber crash into the piston or cylinder walls. The result is a sound known as knock or pinging. Knock can be caused by using fuel with an octane rating that's too low, overheating, by excessively advanced ignition timing, or by a compression ratio that's been raised by hot carbon deposits on the piston or cylinder head.

Knock sensor - A vibration sensor mounted on the cylinder block that generates a voltage when the knock occurs. The voltage signals the control unit, which alters the ignition timing by retarding it and, (on turbocharged vehicles, limits boost) to stop the knock.

L

Lambda (l) - Expresses the air/fuel ratio in terms of the stoichiometric ratio compared to the oxygen content of the exhaust. At the stoichiometric ratio, when all of the fuel is burned with all of the air in the combustion chamber, the oxygen content of the exhaust is said to be at lambda = 1. If there's excess oxygen in the exhaust (a lean mixture), then lambda is greater than 1 (l > 1); if there's an excess of fuel in the exhaust (a shortage of air - a rich mixture), then lambda is less than 1 (l < 1).

Lambda control - Bosch's term for a closed-loop system that adjusts the air-fuel ratio to lambda = 1, based on sensing the amount of excess oxygen in the exhaust.

Lambda control valve - See *frequency valve*.

Lambda sensor - Bosch's term for the oxygen sensor. See *oxygen sensor*.

Lean mixture - A fuel mixture that has more air than required (or not enough fuel) for a stoichiometric ratio.

Lean surge - A change in rpm caused by an extremely lean fuel mixture.

L-Jetronic - L-Jetronic is the term used by Bosch to describe a fuel injection system controlled by the air flowing through a sensor with a movable vane, or flap, which indicates engine load. The L is short for *luft*, the German word for "air." Later versions of L-Jet are equipped with a Lambda (oxygen) sensor for better mixture control. Bosch originally used the term Air-Flow Controlled (AFC) Injection to denote L-Jet systems in order to differentiate them from pressure-controlled D-Jetronic systems.

LH-Jetronic - Bosch LH-Jetronic systems measure air mass (weight of air) with a hot-wire sensor instead of measuring airflow with a vane, or flap, type air *volume* sensor used on L-Jet systems. The H is short for *heiss*, the German word for "hot."

LH-Motronic - This Bosch system is the same as any other Motronic system, except that it uses a hot-wire air-mass sensor (L is short for *luft*, the German word for "air" and H is short for *heiss*, which means "hot," hence hot wire). LH-Motronic systems also have idle stabilization.

"Limp-in", "limp-home" or limp-mode - used by many manufacturers to explain the driveability characteristics of a failed computer system. Many computer systems store information that can be used to get the vehicle to a repair facility. In this mode of operation, driveability is greatly reduced.

Liquid/vapor separator valve - A valve in some EEC fuel systems that separates liquid fuel from fuel vapors.

Light Emitting Diode (LED) - A gallium-arsenide diode that emits energy as light. Often used in automotive indicators.

Linear - Any mathematically expressed relationship whose graphical representation is a straight line in the Cartesian coordinate system.

Load - The amount of work the engine must do. When the vehicle accelerates quickly from a standstill, or from a low speed, the engine is placed under a heavy load.

Lobes - The rounded protrusions on a camshaft that force, and govern, the opening of the intake and exhaust valves.

Logic module - See *control module*.

Logic probe - A simple hand-held device used to confirm the operational characteristics of a logic (On/Off) circuit.

Lucas Bosch - This system, used in Jaguars and Triumphs, is a Bosch L-Jetronic system licensed for production by Lucas.

M

Magnetic field - The area in which magnetic lines of forces exist.

Magnetic pick-up coil - Coil used in the electronic distributor ignition system to determine exactly when to switch off the coil secondary.

Magnetic pulse generator - A signal-generating switch that creates a voltage pulse as magnetic flux changes around a pickup coil.

Magnetic reluctance - That quality in a substance or material which tends to impede the flow of a magnetic field.

Magnetic saturation - The condition when a magnetic field reaches full strength and maximum flux density.

Manifold Absolute Pressure (MAP) - Manifold pressure measured on the absolute pressure scale, an indication of engine load.

Manifold Pressure Controlled (MPC) - A fuel injection system which determines engine load based on intake manifold pressure.

Manifold Tune Valve Solenoid - When engaged, alters the internal shape and air flow of the manifold in order to increase low end engine torque.

Manifold vacuum - low pressure in an engine's intake manifold, located below the carburetor or TBI throttle plate.

Map - A pictorial representation of a series of data points stored in the memory of the control unit of systems with complete engine management. The control unit refers to the map to control variables such as fuel injection pulse width and ignition timing, an indication of engine load.

Mass - The amount of matter contained in an object or a volume. Also a measure of that object's resistance to acceleration. In the field of earth gravity, mass is roughly equivalent to the weight of the object or volume. In fuel injection terms, a measured air volume is corrected for temperature and density to determine its mass.

Metering slits - In Bosch CIS, the narrow slits in the control-plunger barrel of the fuel distributor. Fuel flows through the slits in accordance with the lift of the control plunger and the pressure drop at the slits.

Methanol - Methyl alcohol distilled from wood or made from natural gas.

Micron - A unit of length equal to one millionth of a meter, one one-thousandth of a millimeter.

Milliampere (mA) - One one-thousandth of one ampere. The current flow to the pressure actuator in KE systems is measured in milliamps.

Misfire - Failure of the air-fuel mixture to ignite during the power stroke.

Mixture control unit - In Bosch CIS, the collective term for the airflow sensor plate and the fuel distributor, which are integrated into a single component.

Mixture control (M/C) solenoid - Device, installed in computer controlled carburetors, which regulates the air/fuel ratio.

Mode - A particular state of operation.

Module - A self-contained, sealed unit that houses the solid-state circuits which control certain electrical or mechanical functions.

Monolith - A large block. In a catalytic converter, the monolith is made like a honeycomb to provide several thousand square yards or meters of catalyst surface area.

Motronic - This term is used by Bosch to denote its engine management systems. The original Motronic system combined L-Jetronic with electronic ignition timing control in one control unit. Most Motronic-equipped engines also have electronic idle stabilization. Around 1986, Motronic systems got: Knock regulation by ignition timing of individual cylinders; adaptive circuitry, which adapts fuel delivery and ignition timing to actual conditions; diagnostic circuitry which enables the control unit to recognize system faults and store fault information in its memory. Motronic has also been integrated with KE-Jetronic systems, and is referred to as KE-Motronic.

Multigrade - An oil that has been tested at more than one temperature, and so has more than one SAE viscosity number.

Multi-Point Fuel Injection (MPFI) - A fuel injection system that uses one injector per cylinder, mounted on the engine to spray fuel near the intake valve area or the combustion chamber. Also referred to as Multi-Port Injection.

Mutual induction - The transfer of energy between two unconnected conductors, caused by the expanding or contracting magnetic flux lines of the current carrying conductor.

N

Negative ground electrical system - An automotive electrical system in which the battery negative terminal is connected to ground.

Negative polarity - Also called ground polarity. A correct polarity of the ignition coil connections. Coil voltage is delivered to the spark plugs so that the center electrode of the spark is negatively charged and the grounded electrode is positively charged.

Negative Temperature Coefficient (NTC) - A term used to describe a thermistor (temperature sensor) in which the resistance decreases as the temperature increases. The thermistors used on fuel injection systems are nearly all NTCs.

Noble metals - Metals that resist oxidation, such as platinum and palladium.

Normally aspirated - An engine that uses normal engine vacuum to draw in its air-fuel mixture. Not supercharged or turbocharged.

O

Octane rating - The measurement of the anti-knock value of a gasoline.

Ohm - An electrical unit used for measuring resistance, one ohm is the amount of resistance required for one volt to produce one ampere of electrical current.

Oil galleries - Passages in the block and head that carry oil under pressure to various parts of the engine.

On-Board Diagnostics (OBD) - This term refers to the ability of the computer system to analyze and verify the operational ability of itself.

Open circuit - A circuit which does not provide a complete path for the flow of current.

Open loop - An operational mode during which "default" (pre-programmed) values in the control unit memory are used to determine the air/fuel ratio, injection timing, etc., instead of "real" sensor inputs. The system goes into open loop during cold-engine operation, or when a particular sensor malfunctions and does not respond to feedback signals from the EGO sensor.

Orifice - The calibrated fuel delivery hole at the nozzle end of the fuel injector.

Oscillating - Moving back and forth with a steady rhythm.

Oxidation - The combination of an element with oxygen in a chemical process that often produces extreme heat as a byproduct.

Oxide of Nitrogen (NOx) - Chemical compounds of nitrogen given off by an internal combustion engine. They combine with hydrocarbons to produce smog. NOx formation is affected by combustion chamber temperatures.

Oxygen sensor - A sensor, mounted in the exhaust manifold or exhaust pipe, that reacts to changes in the oxygen content of the exhaust gases. The voltage generated by the oxygen sensor is monitored by the control unit.

P

Parallel circuit - A circuit with more than one path for the current to follow.

Particulates - Liquid or solid particles such as lead and carbon that are given off by an internal combustion engine as pollution.

Part-load - The throttle opening between idle and fully-open.

Part load enrichment - Extra fuel injected during throttle opening to enrich the mixture during transition. Usually occurs during closed-loop operation.

Percolation - The bubbling and expansion of a liquid. Similar to boiling.

Photochemical smog - A combination of pollutants which, when acted upon by sunlight, forms chemical compounds that are harmful to human, animal, and plant life.

Pick-up coil - The pick-up coil is a coil of fine wire mounted to a permanent magnet. The pick-up coil develops a field that is sensitive to ferrous metal (like a reluctor). As the reluctor passes the pick-up coil, a small alternating current is produced. This alternating current is sent to the electronic control unit. The pick-up coil is sometimes called a stator or sensor.

Piezoelectric - Voltage caused by physical pressure applied to the faces of certain crystals.

Piezoresistive - A sensor whose resistance varies in relation to pressure or force applied to it. A piezoresistive sensor receives a constant reference voltage and returns a variable signal in relation to its varying resistance.

Pintle - In an injector, the tip of the needle that opens to allow pressurized fuel through the spray orifice. The shape of the pintle and the orifice determines the spray pattern of the atomized fuel.

Plenum - A chamber that stabilizes the air-fuel mixture and allows it to rise to a pressure slightly above atmospheric pressure.

Plunger - See *control plunger*.

Poppet valve - A valve that plugs and unplugs its opening by axial motion.

Ported vacuum - The low-pressure area (vacuum) just above the throttle in a carburetor.

Port injection - A fuel injection system in which the fuel is sprayed by individual injectors into each intake port, upstream of the intake valve.

Positive Crankcase Ventilation (PCV) - A way of controlling engine emissions by directing crankcase vapors (blow-by) back through an engine's intake system.

Positive ground electrical system - An automotive electrical system in which the battery positive terminal is connected to ground.

Positive polarity - Also called reverse polarity. An incorrect polarity of the ignition coil connections. Coil voltage is delivered to the spark plugs so that the center electrode of the spark plugs is positively charged and the grounded electrode is negatively charged.

Positive Temperature Coefficient (PTC) - A term used to describe a thermistor (temperature sensor) in which the resistance increases as the temperature increases. The thermistors used on most fuel injection systems are negative temperature coefficient (NTC) but a few Chryslers and some mid-80s Cadillacs used PTCs.

Potentiometer - A variable resistor element that acts as a voltage divider to produce a continuously variable output signal proportional to a mechanical position.

Power loss lamp - This was the term given to the instrument panel-mounted lamp on early Chrysler vehicles. It functions in the same manner as the Check Engine Light.

Power module - On Chryslers, the power module works in conjunction with the logic module. The power module is the primary power supply for the EFI system.

Pre-ignition - An engine condition in which the air-fuel mixture ignites prematurely due to excessive combustion chamber temperature.

Pressure actuator - On Bosch KE-Jetronic and KE-Motronic systems, an electronically-controlled hydraulic valve, affixed to the mixture-control unit, that regulates fuel flow through the lower chambers of the differential-pressure valves. The pressure actuator controls all adjustments to basic fuel metering and air-fuel ratio to compensate for changing operating conditions. Also referred to as a differential-pressure regulator and as an electro-hydraulic pressure actuator.

Pressure differential - A difference in pressure between two points.

Pressure drop - The difference in pressure where fuel metering occurs. In electronic injection systems, this is the difference between fuel system pressure and intake manifold pressure. In Bosch CIS, it's the difference between system pressure inside the control plunger and the pressure outside the slits, in the upper-chamber of the differential-pressure valves.

Pressure regulator - A spring-loaded diaphragm-type pressure-relief valve which controls the pressure of fuel delivered to the fuel injector(s) by returning excess fuel to the tank.

Pressure relief - What you must do to all fuel-injection systems before cracking a fuel line and opening up the system.

Pressure relief valve - Another name for the fuel-injection system test port.

Pressure tap - Another name for the fuel-injection system test port.

Primary circuit - The low voltage circuit in the ignition system. Sometimes 6 volts, but usually 12 volts.

Primary pressure - Another name for system pressure in a continuous injection system.

Processing - The computer receives information in the form of voltage and channels it through a logic electronic circuit according with the programmed instructions.

Programmable Read Only Memory - More commonly known as the PROM, carries all the particular information of the vehicle such as (number of cylinder, weight, if is automatic or standard, if it has fuel injection or carburetion, year build etc.) and can't be changed from one vehicle to another, due to its peculiarities.

Pulsed injection - A system that delivers fuel in intermittent pulses by the opening and closing of solenoid-controlled injectors. Also referred to as electronic fuel injection (EFI).

Pulse - An abrupt change in voltage whether positive or negative.

Pulse air system - Part of the emission control system that utilizes a reed-type check valve which allows air to be drawn into the exhaust system as a result of exhaust pulses.

Pulse generator - Term used by foreign automobile manufactures for pick-up coil. It generates signals or pulses, which are fed to the ignitor (ignition control unit). Sometime called signal generator.

Pulse period - The available time, depending on the speed of crankshaft rotation, for opening of pulsed solenoid injectors.

Pulse time - The amount of time that solenoid injectors are open to inject fuel. Also known as pulse width, especially when displayed on an oscilloscope as a voltage pattern.

Pulse width - The amount of time that a fuel injector is energized, measured in milliseconds. The duration of the pulse width is determined by the amount of fuel the engine needs at any time. Also referred to as pulse time.

Purge valve - A vacuum-operated valve used to draw fuel vapors from a vapor canister.

Push valve - In a continuous injection system, the push valve controls the return of fuel from the control-pressure regulator to the system-pressure regulator. When the engine is shut off, the push valve closes the control pressure circuit.

R

Random-Access Memory (RAM) - Temporary short-term or long term computer memory that can be read and changed, but is lost whenever power is shut off to the computer.

Ratio - The proportion of one value divided by another.

Reach - The length of the spark plug shell from the seat to the bottom of the shell.

Read Only Memory (ROM) - The permanent part of a computer's memory storage function. ROM can be read but not changed, and is retained when power is shut off to the computer.

Reciprocating engine - Also called piston engine. An engine in which the pistons move up and down or back and forth, as a result of combustion in the top of the piston cylinder.

Recombinant - A non-gassing battery design in which the oxygen released by the electrolyte recombines with the negative plates.

Rectified - Electrical current changed from alternating (A.C.) to direct (D.C.).

Reduction - A chemical process in which oxygen is taken away from a compound.

Reed valve - A one-way check valve. A reed, or flap, opens to admit a fluid or gas under pressure from one direction, while closing to deny movement from the opposite direction.

Reference voltage - A constant voltage signal (below battery voltage) applied to a sensor by the computer. The sensor alters the voltage according to engine operating conditions and return it as a variable input signal to the computer which adjust the system operation accordingly.

Relative pressure - In electronic injection systems, the difference in pressure between fuel pressure in the injector(s) and pressure in the intake manifold.

Relay - A switching device operated by a low current circuit which controls the opening and closing of another circuit of higher current capacity.

Relief valve - A pressure limiting valve located in the exhaust chamber of the thermactor air pump. It functions to relieve part of the exhaust air flow if the pressure exceeds a calibrated value.

Reluctance - The resistance that a magnetic circuit offers to lines of force in a magnetic field.

Reluctor - This is a piece of ferrous metal that resembles a wheel with spokes or teeth. It is sometimes called an armature, timing core or trigger wheel. Whatever it is called, The function is the same. As it rotates, the spokes or teeth pass a pick-up coil which generates a small alternating current.

Reserve capacity rating - A battery rating based on the number of minutes a battery at 80 degrees F. can supply 25 amperes, with no battery cell falling bellow 1.75 volts.

Residual pressure - Fuel pressure maintained within the system after engine shutdown.

Resistance - Opposition to electrical current flow.

Resistor - Any electrical circuit element that provides resistance in a circuit.

Resistor type spark plugs - A plug that has a resistor in the center electrode to reduce the inductive portion of the spark discharge.

Rest pressure - Fuel pressure maintained within the fuel system after the engine has been shut down.

Rich mixture - Not enough air or too much fuel is drawn into the engine to maintain a stoichiometric ratio. There's still fuel left after the combustion process.

Road draft tube - The earliest type of crankcase ventilation; it vented blow-by gases to the atmosphere.

Runners - The passages in the intake manifold that connects the manifold's plenum chamber to the engine's inlet ports.

S

SAE viscosity grade - A system of numbers signifying an oil's viscosity at a specific temperature; assigned by the Society of Automotive Engineers.

Scavenging - A slight suction caused by a vacuum drop through a well designed exhaust header system. Scavenging helps pull exhaust gases out of an engine cylinder.

Secondary circuit - The high voltage circuit of the ignition system. Usually measured in thousands of volts (10,000 to as high as 80,000 volts).

Semiconductor - A semiconductor is simply a material that conducts electricity only when the conditions are right. Two basic types of semiconductors are used in the automobiles, they are the diodes and transistors types.

Sensor - A device which monitors an engine operating condition and sends a voltage signal to the control unit. This variable voltage signal varies in accordance with the changes in the condition being monitored. There can be anywhere from half a dozen to two dozen sensors on an engine, depending on the sophistication of the system.

Sensor plate - In Bosch CIS, the flat, round plate, bolted to a lever arm, which rises and falls with the flow of air through the airflow sensor, raising and lowering the control plunger in the fuel distributor.

Sensor test mode - This mode of diagnosis is used to read the output signal of a specific sensor when the engine is not running. Specific codes are used to select a specific sensor on the SCAN Tool. The output of this mode is actual output of the selected sensor (temperature, voltage, speed, etc.).

Sequential Electronic Fuel Injection (SEFI), or Sequential Fuel Injection (SFI) - A fuel injection system which uses a micro-computer to determine and control the amount of fuel required by, and injected into, a particular engine in the same sequence as engine firing sequence.

Series circuit - A circuit with only one path for the current to flow.

Series-parallel circuit - A circuit in which some loads are wired in series and some loads are wired in parallel.

Short circuit - An undesirable connection between a circuit and any other point.

Signal - Another name for vacuum transmitted from one location, or component, to another.

Single grade - An oil that has been tested at only one temperature, and so has only one SAE viscosity number.

Sintered - Welded together without using heat to form a porous material, such as the metal disc used in some vacuum delay valves.

Siphoning - The flowing of liquid as a result of pressure differential, without the aid of a mechanical pump.

Slit - See *metering slits*.

"Soft" fault code - A circuit or component failure that does not reappear after you clear the codes and retest the system.

Solenoid - An electromagnetic actuator consisting of an electrical coil with a hollow center and an iron piece, the armature, that moves into the coil when it is energized. Solenoids are used to open fuel injectors and many other output actuators on fuel-injected vehicles.

Solenoid valve - A valve operated by a solenoid.

Solid-state - A method of controlling electrical current flow, in which the parts are primarily made of semiconductor materials.

Spark advance - Causing spark to occur earlier.

Spark retard - Causing less spark advance to be added, resulting in a spark which is introduced later.

Spark timing - A way of controlling exhaust emissions by controlling ignition timing. Vacuum advance is delayed or shut off at low and medium speeds, reducing Nox and HC emissions.

Spark voltage - The inductive portion of a spark that maintains the spark in the air gap between a spark plug's electrodes. Usually about one-quarter of the firing voltage level.

Specific gravity - The ratio of a weight of any volume of a substance to the weight of an equal volume of water. When battery electrolyte (acid) is tested, the result is the specific gravity of the electrolyte.

Starting bypass - A parallel circuit branch that bypasses the ballast resistor during engine cranking.

Starting safety switch - A neutral start switch. It keeps the starting system from operating when a car's transmission is in gear.

Stator - This is another name for a pick-up coil. The stator is sometimes called a pick-up coil, a sensor or a Hall Effect pick-up. See *Pick-up coil*.

Stepper motor - Are digital devices actuators (motors) that work with DC current, that moves in a fixed amount of increments from the off position.

Stoichiometric ratio - The ideal air/fuel mixture ratio (14.7:1) at which the best compromise between engine performance (richer mixture) and economy and low exhaust emissions (leaner mixture) is obtained. All of the air and all of the fuel is burned inside the combustion chamber.

Storage - The programmed instructions are stored in computer electronic memory.

Stratified charge engine - An engine that uses 2-stage combustion: first is the combustion of rich air-fuel mixture in a pre-combustion chamber, then combustion of a leaner air-fuel mixture occurs in the main combustion chamber.

Stroke - One complete top-to-bottom or bottom-to-top movement of an engine piston.

Sub oxygen sensor - The second oxygen sensor (after the catalytic converter), which monitors catalytic converter efficiency.

Substrate - The layer, or honey-comb, of aluminum oxide upon which the catalyst (platinum or palladium) in a catalytic converter is deposited.

Sulfation - The crystallization of lead sulfate on the plates of a constantly discharged battery.

Sulfur oxides - Chemical compounds given off by processing and burning gasoline and other fossil fuels. As they decompose, they combine with water to form sulfuric acid.

Supercharging - Use of an air pump to deliver an air-fuel mixture to the engine cylinders at a pressure greater than atmospheric pressure.

Switches - Are one of the simples ways of sensors, they simply signal a condition of on/off.

Synthetic motor oil - Lubricants formed by artificially combining molecules of petroleum and other materials.

System pressure - The fuel pressure in the fuel lines and at the pressure regulator, created by the fuel pump.

System pressure regulator - In a continuous injection system, holds system fuel pressure constant.

T

Television-Radio-Suppression (TVRS) Cables - High-resistance, carbon-conductor ignition cables that suppress RFI.

Temperature inversion - A weather pattern in which a layer or "lid" of warm air keeps the cooler air beneath it from rising.

Temperature sensor - A special type of solid-state resistor, known as a thermistor. Used to sense coolant and, on some systems, air temperature also. See *thermistor*.

Test port - The Schrader valve fitting located on the fuel rail of a port injection system. Used for relieving fuel pressure and for hooking up a fuel-pressure gauge.

Tetraethyl lead - A gasoline additive used to help prevent detonation.

Thermactor - A system for injection of air into the exhaust system to aid in the control of hydrocarbons and carbon monoxide in the exhaust.

Thermal cracking - A common oil refining process which uses heat to break down (crack) the larger components of the crude oil. The gasoline which is produced usually has a higher sulfur content than gasoline produced by catalytic cracking.

Thermistor - A special kind of resistor whose resistance decreases as its temperature increases. Thermistors are used for air and coolant temperature sensors. Also referred to as a Negative Temperature Coefficient (NTC) resistor. See *temperature sensor*.

Thermostatic - Referring to a device that automatically responds to temperature changes in order to activate a switch.

Throttle body - The carburetor-like aluminum casting that houses the throttle valve, the idle air bypass (if equipped), the throttle position sensor (TPS), the idle air control (IAC) motor, the throttle linkage and, on TBI systems, one or two injectors.

Throttle Body Injection (TBI) - . Any of several injection systems which have the fuel injector(s) mounted in a centrally located throttle body, as opposed to positioning the injectors close to the intake ports.

Throttle valve - The movable plate, inside the throttle body, which is controlled by the accelerator pedal. The throttle valve controls the amount of air that can enter the engine.

Thyristor - A silicon-controlled rectifier (SCR) that normally blocks all current flow. A slight voltage applied to one layer of its semiconductor structure will allow current flow in one direction while blocking current flow in the other direction.

Timing - Relationship between spark plug firing and piston position usually expressed in crankshaft degrees before (BTDC) or after (ATDC) top dead center of the piston.

Timing valve - See *frequency valve*.

Top Dead Center (TDC) - The exact top of a piston's stroke. Also is used for specifications when tuning an engine.

Total ignition advance - The sum of centrifugal advance, vacuum advance, and initial timing; expressed in crankshaft degrees.

T-Pin - A common type of sewing pin which is very useful in probing an electrical connector in order to make a test lead connection.

Transducer - A transducer converts or transduces a form of energy to another. All of the sensors or actuators are transducers.

Transistor - A three-terminal semiconductor used for current switching, detection, and amplification. Low current flows between another pair of terminals, with one common terminal.

Trigger wheel - This is another name for a reluctor or armature. It is a metallic timing device used in a system with a sensor. See *Reluctor* in this Glossary for description.

Tuned Port Injection (TPI) - A General Motors fuel injection system that uses tuned air intake runners for improved airflow.

Turbo lag - The time interval required for a turbocharger to overcome inertia and spin up to speed.

Turbocharger - A supercharging device that uses exhaust gases to turn a turbine that forces extra air-fuel mixture into the cylinders.

V

Vacuum - Anything less than atmospheric pressure.

Vacuum advance - The use of engine vacuum to advance ignition spark timing by moving the distributor breaker plate.

Vacuum lock - A stoppage of fuel flow caused by insufficient air intake to the fuel tank.

Vacuum regulator - Provides constant vacuum output when the vehicle is at idle. Switches to engine vacuum at off idle.

Vaporization - Changing a liquid, into a gas (vapor).

Vapor lock - A condition which occurs when the fuel becomes so hot that it vaporizes, slowing or stopping fuel flow in the fuel lines.

Variable dwell - The ignition dwell period varies in distributor degrees at different engine speeds, but remains relatively constant in duration or actual time.

Variable reluctance sensor - A non-contact transducer that converts mechanical motion into electrical control signals.

Varnish - An undesirable deposit, usually on engine pistons, formed by oxidation of fuel and of motor oil.

Venturi - A restriction in an airflow, such as in a carburetor or TBI, that speeds the airflow and creates a vacuum.

Venturi vacuum - Low pressure in the venturi of a carburetor, caused by the fast air flowing through the venturi.

Viscosity - The tendency of a liquid, such as oil, to resist flowing.

Volatility - The ease with which a liquid changes from a liquid to a gas vapor.

Voltage - The force (electromotive force) that moves electrons through a conductor. It can be visualized as the difference in electrical pressure. One volt moves one ampere of current through one ohm of resistance.

Volt - A unit of electrical pressure (electromotive force), which causes current to flow in a circuit. One volt causes one ampere of current to flow one ohm of resistance.

Voltage decay - The rapid oscillation and dissipation of secondary voltage after the spark in a spark plug air gap has stopped.

Voltage drop - The net difference in electrical pressure when measured across a resistance. Voltage drop is always measured in parallel.

Voltage reserve - The amount of coil voltage available in excess of the voltage required to fire the spark plug.

Volumetric Efficiency (VE) - Describes the efficiency of taking air into the cylinder. Taking 5.0L of air into a 5.0L engine is described as 100% volumetric efficiency. Must engines running at wide open throttle range from 70-80%. With a turbo/supercharger, compressing the intake air can raise it to over 100%.

W

Warm-up regulator - On Bosch CIS, the original name for the control-pressure regulator.

Wastegate control - A solenoid or diaphragm used to control boost output on turbocharged models. The computer varies the duty cycle of the solenoid to match maximum boost to changing engine operating conditions.

Water injector - A method of lowering the air-fuel mixture temperature by injecting a fine spray of water which evaporates as it cools the intake charge.

Water jackets - Passages in the head and block that allow coolant to circulate throughout the engine.

Watt - The unit of measure that indicates electrical power applied in a direct current circuit. Watts are calculated by multiplying the current in amperes by the voltage.

Z

Zero absolute pressure - A total vacuum. Zero on the absolute pressure scale.

Acronyms

A

AAC - Auxiliary Air Control Valve

ACC - A/C Clutch Compressor sensor - Sends information to the computer relating status of the A/C clutch.

ACP - Air Conditioning Pressure sensor - Sends information to the computer about the pressures in the air conditioning lines.

ACT- Air Charge Temperature sensor - Sends information to the computer about the temperature of the air entering the engine.

A/D Converter - Analog-to-digital converter. Converts analog voltage signal from each sensor into digital.

A.I.R. - Air Injection Reaction system - Injects air into the exhaust system to burn any remaining unburned fuel.

AIS - Automatic Idle Speed - Receives a voltage signal from the computer to adjust the engine idle speed.

AISC - Air Induction System Control - Receives a voltage signal from the computer to adjust the air coming into the induction system.

AISM - Automatic Idle Speed Motor

ALDL - Assembly Line Data Link (GM)

APS - Atmospheric Pressure sensor - Sends information to the computer about pressure in the atmosphere to make correct fuel mixture calculations.

AS - Air Switch Solenoid - Receives a voltage signal from the computer to route the air from the air pump to the correct location.

AS - Airflow Sensor - Sends information to the computer about the amount of air entering the engine.

AS - Altitude Sensor

ATDC - After Top Dead Center - After the piston has come to the highest point in the cylinder and starts on its way down (measured in degrees).

ATS - Air Temperature sensor - Sends information to the computer about the temperature of the outside air.

B

BARO - Barometric Pressure sensor - Sends information to the computer about the barometric pressure in the atmosphere.

B+ - Describes voltage or potential of the battery positive terminal.

BATT (+) - Battery positive post or its circuit.

BATT (-) - Battery negative post or its circuit.

BCS - Boost Control Solenoid - Receives a voltage signal from the computer to adjust the amount of boost from the turbocharger.

BTS - Battery Temperature Sensor - Sends information to the computer about the temperature of the battery.

BTDC - Before Top Dead Center - The amount of travel the piston has to move (measured in degrees) before it reaches its highest point in the cylinder.

BVS - Bowl Vent Solenoid - Receives a voltage signal from the computer to control when the carburetor bowl vent must be vented.

C

CANP - Canister Purge Solenoid - Receives a voltage signal from the computer to control when the charcoal canister must be vented.

CAS - Crank Angle sensor - Sends information to the computer about the angle of location of the crankshaft.

CCA - Cluster Control Assembly

CCC - Computer Command Control (GM)

CCD Bus - This is the communication line used by various on-board computers for transmitting data.

CCS - Coast Clutch Solenoid - Receives a voltage signal from the computer to set the transmission clutches in coast mode.

CCS - Converter Clutch Solenoid - Receives a voltage signal from the computer to control when to apply the torque converter clutch in the transmission.

CEC - Computerized Emission Control (AMC)

CFCS - Coasting Fuel Cut Off System - Receives a voltage signal from the computer to cut off the fuel when the engine is coasting.

CFI - Central Fuel Injection. A Ford Motor Company fuel injection system that uses an injector-mounted throttle body assembly.

CID - Cylinder identification

CIS - Continuous Injection System. A Bosch fuel injection system which injects a steady stream of pressurized fuel into each intake port. CIS was once widely used throughout the industry.

CIS-E - A CIS system with electronic controls.

CIS-Lambda - A CIS system with an oxygen sensor.

CKP - Crankshaft Position sensor

CLC - Converter Lockup Solenoid - Receives a voltage signal from the computer to control when to apply the torque converter clutch in the transmission.

CO - Carbon Monoxide

CPI - A GM fuel injection system that uses a centrally located injector and lines running to injector nozzles located at each cylinder.

CPS - Cam Position sensor - Sends information to the computer about the angle of location of the camshaft.

CPS - Canister Purge Solenoid - Receives a voltage signal from the computer to control when the charcoal canister must be vented.

CPS - Crank Position Sensor - Sends information to the computer about the angle of location of the crankshaft.

CRSV - Coasting Richer Solenoid Valve - Receives a voltage signal from the computer to adjust the air/fuel ratio during periods of engine coasting.

CTS - Coolant Temperature sensor - Sends information to the computer about the temperature in the cooling system.

D

DCL - Data Communication Link is a terminal used to access the computer codes.

DIS - Direct Ignition System

DIS - Distributorless Ignition System. An ignition system using individual coils to fire the spark plugs.

DLC - Data Link Connector

DOL - Data Output Link. Fuel calculation data from the EEC-4 control module to the electronic tripminder.

DTC - Diagnostic Trouble Code

DVOM - Digital Volt-Ohm Meter used to measure voltage and resistance. Readings are indicated in a digital display rather than by the sweep of a hand.

E

EACV - Electronic Air Control Valve - Receives a voltage signal from the computer in order to control the air valve when must be applied.

ECA - Electronic Control Assembly (Ford EEC-IV)

ECM - Electronic Control Module

ECT - Engine Coolant Temperature sensor - Sends information to the computer about the temperature in the cooling system.

ECTS - Engine Coolant Temperature sensor - Sends information to the computer about the temperature in the cooling system.

ECU - Electronic Control Unit

EDF - Electrodrive Fan Relay or control citcuit

EDIS - Electronic Distributorless Ignition System

EEC - Electronic Engine Control

EPROM - Erasable Programmable Read Only Memory (GM)

EFC - Electronic Feedback Carburetor (Chrysler)

EFE - Early Fuel Evaporation Solenoid - Receives a voltage signal from the computer to send a signal when to start and finish the early evaporation of the fuel.

EFI - Electronic Fuel Injection. A fuel injection system which uses a microcomputer to determine and control the amount of fuel required by, and injected into, a particular engine.

EGI - Electronic Gasoline Injection. Mazda's fuel injection system for the RX7, RX7 Turbo, 323 and 626 models.

EGO sensor - Exhaust Gas Oxygen sensor

EGR valve - Exhaust Gas Recirculation Valve, allows a small percentage of exhaust gases to enter the combustion area to control detonation and NOx.

EGRVP - Exhaust Gas Recirculation Valve Position sensor - Sends information to the computer about the position of the EGR valve pintle.

EGRC - Exhaust Gases Recirculation Control Solenoid - Receives a voltage signal from the computer to open the EGR.

EGRGTS - Exhaust Gas Recirculation Gas Temperature sensor - Sends information to the computer about the temperature of gases recirculating around the EGR.

EGRPS - Exhaust Gas Recirculation Position sensor - Sends information to the computer about the position of the EGR valve pintle.

EIC - Electronic Instrument Cluster

EHA - Electro Hydraulic Actuator - Receives a voltage signal from the computer to allow the electro hydraulic actuator to open and let hydraulic pressure go by.

EOTS - Engine Oil Temperature Sensor - Sends information to the computer about the temperature of the engine oil.

EPC - Electronic Pressure Control.

EPS - Engine Position Sensor - Sends information to the computer about the crankshafts angle of location.

EPT - EGR Valve Pressure Transducer

ESC - Electronic Spark Control - Receives a voltage signal from the computer to adjust the ignition timing.

ESS - Engine Speed Sensor

EST - Electronic Spark Timing

ETCS - Electronics Throttle Control Solenoid

ETS - Exhaust Temperature Sensor

EVAP - Evaporative Emission system

EVP - EGR Valve Position Sensor or its signal circuit

EVR - Electronic Vacuum Regulator

F

FBC - Feedback carburetor

FCS - Fuel Cutoff Solenoid

FF Sensor - Flexible Fuel Sensor

FKS - Front Knock Sensor - Sends information to the computer about fuel detonation.

FLTVS - Full Load Throttle Valve Switch - Sends information to the computer about when the throttle is at wide open throttle (WOT).

FMEM - Failure Mode Effects Management - An alternative computer mode that maintains vehicle driveability in the event of an EEC-IV component malfunction.

FOS - Front Oxygen sensor - Sends information to the computer about the amount of oxygen in the front exhaust manifold.

FTS - Fuel Temperature Sensor

FTVPV - Fuel Tank Vent Purge Valve

H

HAC - High Altitude Compensation sensor

HACV - High Altitude Compensation Valve

HEDF - High-speed electro-drive fan relay or control circuit

HEGO - Heated Exhaust Gas Oxygen Sensor

HO$_2$S - Heated Oxygen Sensor - Sends information to the computer about the heated oxygen sensor.

I

IAC - Idle Air Control solenoid

IAT - Intake Air Temperature sensor

IC - Ignition Control

ICV - Induction Control Valve - Receives a voltage signal from the computer to adjust the air induction into the engine.

IDM - Ignition Diagnostic Monitor

ILC - Idle Load Compensation solenoid - Receives a voltage signal from the computer to adjust the engine idle when the engine is under load.

IMS - Inferred Mileage Sensor. A circuit using an E-cell which deflates its state with the application of current. As the vehicle ages (in terms of Key-On time) the **EEC**-IV control module compensates for aging of the vehicle by changing calibration parameters (Ford).

ISA - Idle Speed Actuator

ISAV - Idle Speed Air Valve

ISC - Idle Speed Control solenoid

ISCV - Idle Speed Control Valve

ITS - Idle Tracking Switch

ITVS - Idle Throttle Valve Switch

IUSV - Idle UP Solenoid Valve

K

KNOCK - Knock (Detonation) sensor - Sends information to the computer if there is any fuel detonation occurring in the engine.

L

LKS - Left Knock Sensor - Sends information to the computer if there is any detonation occurring in the left side of the engine.

LUCSV - Lockup Control Solenoid Valve - Receives a voltage signal from the computer to lockup the torque converter in the transmission.

M

MAF - Mass Air Flow sensor - Sends information to the computer about the quantity of the mass of air flowing into the engine.

MAM - Mass Airflow Meter - Sends information to the computer by metering the quantity of air flowing into the engine.

MAP sensor - Manifold Absolute Pressure sensor - A device that monitors manifold absolute pressure and sends a varying voltage to the control unit, which alters the air-fuel mixture accordingly.

MAT - Manifold Air Temperature sensor - Sends information to the computer about the air temperature inside the manifold.

MCS - Mixture Control Solenoid - Receives a voltage signal from the computer to adjust the air fuel mixture (air/fuel ratio).

MFI - Multiport Fuel Injection

MIL - Malfunction Indicator Lamp/Light

MLP - Manual Lever Position sensor - Sends information to the computer about which gear the transmission is in.

MRL - Maintenance Reminder Light

MSD - Multiple Spark Discharge

MTVS - Manifold Tune Valve Solenoid - Receives a voltage signal from the computer to adjust the intake manifold flow plenum.

N

NDS - Neutral Drive Sensor - Sends information to the computer about the position of the transmission (neutral or in drive).

NECCS - Nissan Electronic Concentrated Engine Control System.

NOx - Oxide of Nitrogen. Chemical compounds of nitrogen given off by an internal combustion engine. They combine with hydrocarbons to produce smog. NOx formation is affected by combustion chamber temperatures.

O

O₂S - Oxygen sensor

O₂ sensor - Oxygen sensor - Sends information to the computer about the amount of oxygen in the exhaust.

OBD - On Board Diagnostic (can refer to OBD systems I or II)

OL - Open Loop

OS - Overdrive Solenoid - Receives a voltage signal from the computer to energize the overdrive in the transmission.

OSS - Overboost Shutoff Solenoid - Receives a voltage signal from the computer to control the turbocharger when it's producing more boost that recommended.

P

PAIR - Pulsed Air Injection system

PCM - Powertrain Control Module

PCV - Positive Crankcase Ventilation. A system which controls the flow of crankcase vapors into the engine intake manifold where they are burned in combustion rather than being discharged into the atmosphere.

PFE - Pressure Feedback EGR Sensor - Sends information to the computer about how much back pressure is in the exhaust system.

PGM-FI - Programmed Fuel Injection (Honda)

P/N Switch - Park/Neutral Switch

PIP - Profile Ignition Pickup - Sends information to the computer about the reference of the ignition pickup profile (Ford).

PSDS - Pressure Sensor Duty Solenoid

PSI - Pound Per Square Inch - PSI can be a measure of air or fluid pressure.

PSPS - Power Steering Pressure Sensor - Sends information to the computer about the pressure in the power steering lines.

PSPS - Power Steering Pressure Switch - A control module input to regulate idle speed based on power steering load demand.

R

RKS - Rear Knock Sensor - Sends information to the computer if there is any detonation in the rear of the engine.

RKS - Right Knock sensor - Sends information to the computer if there is any detonation in the right side of the engine.

RPM - Revolution Per-Minute - The speed of crankshaft rotation.

RPMS - Revolutions Per Minute Sensor - Sends information to the computer about the speed of the engine (RPM).

S

SCS - Speed Control Solenoid - Receives a voltage signal from the computer to control the engine idle speed.

SEFI - Sequential Electronic Fuel Injection (also known as SPFI or SEFI) - Port fuel injection triggered off ignition timing that fires each injector separately.

SIL - Shift Indicator Light - A system that provides a visual indication to the driver of a vehicle when to shift to the next higher gear to obtain optimum fuel economy.

SM - Stepper Motor - Receives a voltage signal from the computer to control the engine idle speed.

SOS - Sub Oxygen sensor - The second oxygen sensor (after the catalytic converter), which monitors catalytic converter efficiency.

SPOUT - Spark Output Signal from the EEC-IV control module.

SRI - Service Reminder Indicator - This light is used to inform the driver that the vehicle is due for service. Prior to 1993 it was commonly called the Maintenance Reminder Light.

SS - Shift Solenoid - Receives a voltage signal from the computer to shift the transmission from one gear to another.

SS - Speed Sensor

SDS - Speed/Distance Sensor - Sends information to the computer about the distance the vehicle has run since it was reset.

STAR - Self-Test Automatic Readout. A testing device in which the EEC and MCU systems output service codes in a digital format (Ford).

STO - Self Test Output circuit in the EEC and MCU systems that transmits service codes (pulses) to either a VOM (Volt-Ohm Meter) or star tester (Ford).

T

TABS - Thermactor Air By-Pass Solenoid - Receives a voltage signal from the computer in order to control the flow of by-pass air after it has been put into the by-pass mode.

TADS - Thermactor Air Diverter Solenoid - Receives a voltage signal from the computer to route the direction of air from the Thermactor.

TAS - Throttle Angle Sensor - Sends information to the computer about the angle of the throttle opening.

TBI - Throttle Body (fuel) Injection

TCC - Torque Converter Clutch solenoid - Receives a voltage signal from the computer in order to lock-up the torque converter for more efficient operation.

TCM - Transmission Control Module

TDCS - Top Dead Center Sensor

TFT - Transmission Fluid Temperature sensor

TK - Throttle Kicker vacuum solenoid

TKA - Throttle Kicker Actuator - Receives a voltage signal from the computer to adjust the engine idle speed, based upon the load on the engine.

TKR - Throttle Kicker Relay - Receives a voltage signal from the computer sending a signal to the throttle kicker actuator beginning its operation.

TKS - Throttle Kicker Solenoid - Receives a voltage signal from the computer sending a signal to the throttle kicker actuator beginning its operation.

TLV - Transmission Lock Up Solenoid - Receives a voltage signal from the computer to lock up the torque converter for more efficient operation.

TOT - Transmission Oil Temperature Sensor

TP - Throttle Position Sensor

TPS - Throttle Position Sensor - Sends information to the computer about the angle of throttle opening.

TR - Transmission Range sensor

TSS - Transmission Speed Sensor

TTS - Transaxle Temperature Sensor

TVV - Thermal Vacuum Valve

TWC - Three Way Catalyst

V

VAF - Vane Airflow sensor

VAT - Vane Air Temperature sensor

VCRM - Variable Control Relay Module

VOM - Volt-Ohm Meter - Used to measure voltage and resistance for component testing.

VS - Vacuum Sensor

VSS - Vehicle Speed Sensor

W

WAC - Wide-open throttle A/C Cutoff

WCS - Wastegate Control Solenoid - Receives a voltage signal from the computer to control the amount of turbocharger boost the engine receives.

WDS Wastegate Duty Solenoid - Receives a voltage signal from the computer to vary the amount of turbocharger boost the engine receives.

WOT - Wide Open Throttle

WTS - Water Temperature Sensor

WU-TWC - Warm Up Three Way Catalytic Converter

WU-OC - Warm Up Oxidation Catalytic Converter

Notes

Index

Notes

Haynes Automotive Manuals (continued)

NOTE: If you do not see a listing for your vehicle, consult your local Haynes dealer for the latest product information.

GMC
Vans & Pick-ups - see CHEVROLET

HONDA
42010 **Accord CVCC** all models '76 thru '83
42011 **Accord** all models '84 thru '89
42012 **Accord** all models '90 thru '93
42013 **Accord** all models '94 thru '97
42014 **Accord** all models '98 thru '02
42015 **Honda Accord** models '03 thru '07
42020 **Civic 1200** all models '73 thru '79
42021 **Civic 1300 & 1500 CVCC** '80 thru '83
42022 **Civic 1500 CVCC** all models '75 thru '79
42023 **Civic** all models '84 thru '91
42024 **Civic & del Sol** '92 thru '95
42025 **Civic** '96 thru '00, **CR-V** '97 thru '01, **Acura Integra** '94 thru '00
42026 **Civic** '01 thru '05, **CR-V** '02 thru '06
42035 **Honda Odyssey** all models '99 thru '04
42037 **Honda Pilot** '03 thru '07, **Acura MDX** '01 thru '07
42040 **Prelude CVCC** all models '79 thru '89

HYUNDAI
43010 **Elantra** all models '96 thru '06
43015 **Excel & Accent** all models '86 thru '98
43050 **Santa Fe** all models '01 thru '06
43055 **Sonata** all models '99 thru '08

ISUZU
Hombre - see CHEVROLET S-10 (24071)
47017 **Rodeo, Amigo & Honda Passport** '89 thru '02
47020 **Trooper & Pick-up** '81 thru '93

JAGUAR
49010 **XJ6** all 6 cyl models '68 thru '86
49011 **XJ6** all models '88 thru '94
49015 **XJ12 & XJS** all 12 cyl models '72 thru '85

JEEP
50010 **Cherokee, Comanche & Wagoneer Limited** all models '84 thru '01
50020 **CJ** all models '49 thru '86
50025 **Grand Cherokee** all models '93 thru '04
50029 **Grand Wagoneer & Pick-up** '72 thru '91 Grand Wagoneer '84 thru '91, Cherokee & Wagoneer '72 thru '83, Pick-up '72 thru '88
50030 **Wrangler** all models '87 thru '03
50035 **Liberty** '02 thru '04

KIA
54070 **Sephia** '94 thru '01, **Spectra** '00 thru '04

LEXUS
ES 300 - see TOYOTA Camry (92007)

LINCOLN
Navigator - see FORD Pick-up (36059)
59010 **Rear-Wheel Drive** all models '70 thru '05

MAZDA
61010 **GLC Hatchback** (rear-wheel drive) '77 thru '83
61011 **GLC** (front-wheel drive) '81 thru '85
61015 **323 & Protegé** '90 thru '00
61016 **MX-5 Miata** '90 thru '97
61020 **MPV** all models '89 thru '98
Navajo - see Ford Explorer (36024)
61030 **Pick-ups** '72 thru '93
Pick-ups '94 thru '00 - see Ford Ranger (36071)
61035 **RX-7** all models '79 thru '85
61036 **RX-7** all models '86 thru '91
61040 **626** (rear-wheel drive) all models '79 thru '82
61041 **626/MX-6** (front-wheel drive) '83 thru '92
61042 **626, MX-6/Ford Probe** '93 thru '01

MERCEDES-BENZ
63012 **123 Series Diesel** '76 thru '85
63015 **190 Series** four-cyl gas models '84 thru '88
63020 **230/250/280** 6 cyl sohc models '68 thru '72
63025 **280 123 Series** gasoline models '77 thru '81
63030 **350 & 450** all models '71 thru '80
63040 **C-Class**: C230/C240/C280/C320/C350 '01 thru '07

MERCURY
64200 **Villager & Nissan Quest** '93 thru '01
All other titles, see FORD Listing.

MG
66010 **MGB** Roadster & GT Coupe '62 thru '80
66015 **MG Midget, Austin Healey Sprite** '58 thru '80

MITSUBISHI
68020 **Cordia, Tredia, Galant, Precis & Mirage** '83 thru '93
68030 **Eclipse, Eagle Talon & Ply. Laser** '90 thru '94

68031 **Eclipse** '95 thru '05, **Eagle Talon** '95 thru '98
68035 **Mitsubishi Galant** '94 thru '03
68040 **Pick-up** '83 thru '96 & **Montero** '83 thru '93

NISSAN
72010 **300ZX** all models including Turbo '84 thru '89
72011 **350Z & Infiniti G35** all models '03 thru '08
72015 **Altima** all models '93 thru '06
72020 **Maxima** all models '85 thru '92
72021 **Maxima** all models '93 thru '04
72030 **Pick-ups** '80 thru '97 **Pathfinder** '87 thru '95
72031 **Frontier Pick-up, Xterra, Pathfinder** '96 thru '04
72032 **Nissan Frontier & Xterra** '05 thru '08
72040 **Pulsar** all models '83 thru '86
Quest - see MERCURY Villager (64200)
72050 **Sentra** all models '82 thru '94
72051 **Sentra & 200SX** all models '95 thru '04
72060 **Stanza** all models '82 thru '90

OLDSMOBILE
73015 **Cutlass** V6 & V8 gas models '74 thru '88
For other OLDSMOBILE titles, see BUICK, CHEVROLET or GENERAL MOTORS listing.

PLYMOUTH
For PLYMOUTH titles, see DODGE listing.

PONTIAC
79008 **Fiero** all models '84 thru '88
79018 **Firebird** V8 models except Turbo '70 thru '81
79019 **Firebird** all models '82 thru '92
79040 **Mid-size Rear-wheel Drive** '70 thru '87
For other PONTIAC titles, see BUICK, CHEVROLET or GENERAL MOTORS listing.

PORSCHE
80020 **911** except Turbo & Carrera 4 '65 thru '89
80025 **914** all 4 cyl models '69 thru '76
80030 **924** all models including Turbo '76 thru '82
80035 **944** all models including Turbo '83 thru '89

RENAULT
Alliance & Encore - see AMC (14020)

SAAB
84010 **900** all models including Turbo '79 thru '88

SATURN
87010 **Saturn** all models '91 thru '02
87011 **Saturn Ion** '03 thru '07
87020 **Saturn** all L-series models '00 thru '04
87040 **Saturn VUE** '02 thru '07

SUBARU
89002 **1100, 1300, 1400 & 1600** '71 thru '79
89003 **1600 & 1800** 2WD & 4WD '80 thru '94
89100 **Legacy** all models '90 thru '99
89101 **Legacy & Forester** '00 thru '06

SUZUKI
90010 **Samurai/Sidekick & Geo Tracker** '86 thru '01

TOYOTA
92005 **Camry** all models '83 thru '91
92006 **Camry** all models '92 thru '96
92007 **Camry, Avalon, Solara, Lexus ES 300** '97 thru '01
92008 **Toyota Camry, Avalon and Solara and Lexus ES 300/330** all models '02 thru '06
92015 **Celica Rear Wheel Drive** '71 thru '85
92020 **Celica Front Wheel Drive** '86 thru '99
92025 **Celica Supra** all models '79 thru '92
92030 **Corolla** all models '75 thru '79
92032 **Corolla** all rear wheel drive models '80 thru '87
92035 **Corolla** all front wheel drive models '84 thru '92
92036 **Corolla & Geo Prizm** '93 thru '02
92037 **Corolla** models '03 thru '05
92040 **Corolla Tercel** all models '80 thru '82
92045 **Corona** all models '74 thru '82
92050 **Cressida** all models '78 thru '82
92055 **Land Cruiser FJ40, 43, 45, 55** '68 thru '82
92056 **Land Cruiser FJ60, 62, 80, FZJ80** '80 thru '96
92060 **Matrix & Pontiac Vibe** '03 thru '08
92065 **MR2** all models '85 thru '87
92070 **Pick-up** all models '69 thru '78
92075 **Pick-up** all models '79 thru '95
92076 **Tacoma, 4Runner, & T100** '93 thru '04
92077 **Tacoma** all models '05 thru '09
92078 **Tundra** '00 thru '06 & **Sequoia** '01 thru '07
92079 **4Runner** all models '03 thru '09
92080 **Previa** all models '91 thru '95
92081 **Prius** all models '01 thru '08
92082 **RAV4** all models '96 thru '05

92085 **Tercel** all models '87 thru '94
92090 **Toyota Sienna** all models '98 thru '06
92095 **Highlander & Lexus RX-330** '99 thru '06

TRIUMPH
94007 **Spitfire** all models '62 thru '81
94010 **TR7** all models '75 thru '81

VW
96008 **Beetle & Karmann Ghia** '54 thru '79
96009 **New Beetle** '98 thru '05
96016 **Rabbit, Jetta, Scirocco & Pick-up** gas models '75 thru '92 & Convertible '80 thru '92
96017 **Golf, GTI & Jetta** '93 thru '98 & **Cabrio** '95 thru '02
96018 **Golf, GTI, Jetta** '99 thru '05
96020 **Rabbit, Jetta & Pick-up** diesel '77 thru '84
96023 **Passat** '98 thru '05, **Audi A4** '96 thru '01
96030 **Transporter 1600** all models '68 thru '79
96035 **Transporter 1700, 1800 & 2000** '72 thru '79
96040 **Type 3 1500 & 1600** all models '63 thru '73
96045 **Vanagon** all air-cooled models '80 thru '83

VOLVO
97010 **120, 130 Series & 1800 Sports** '61 thru '73
97015 **140 Series** all models '66 thru '74
97020 **240 Series** all models '76 thru '93
97040 **740 & 760 Series** all models '82 thru '88
97050 **850 Series** all models '93 thru '97

TECHBOOK MANUALS
10205 **Automotive Computer Codes**
10206 **OBD-II & Electronic Engine Management**
10210 **Automotive Emissions Control Manual**
10215 **Fuel Injection Manual, 1978 thru 1985**
10220 **Fuel Injection Manual, 1986 thru 1999**
10225 **Holley Carburetor Manual**
10230 **Rochester Carburetor Manual**
10240 **Weber/Zenith/Stromberg/SU Carburetors**
10305 **Chevrolet Engine Overhaul Manual**
10310 **Chrysler Engine Overhaul Manual**
10320 **Ford Engine Overhaul Manual**
10330 **GM and Ford Diesel Engine Repair Manual**
10333 **Engine Performance Manual**
10340 **Small Engine Repair Manual, 5 HP & Less**
10341 **Small Engine Repair Manual, 5.5 - 20 HP**
10345 **Suspension, Steering & Driveline Manual**
10355 **Ford Automatic Transmission Overhaul**
10360 **GM Automatic Transmission Overhaul**
10405 **Automotive Body Repair & Painting**
10410 **Automotive Brake Manual**
10411 **Automotive Anti-lock Brake (ABS) Systems**
10415 **Automotive Detailing Manual**
10420 **Automotive Electrical Manual**
10425 **Automotive Heating & Air Conditioning**
10430 **Automotive Reference Manual & Dictionary**
10435 **Automotive Tools Manual**
10440 **Used Car Buying Guide**
10445 **Welding Manual**
10450 **ATV Basics**
10452 **Scooters, Automatic Transmission 50cc to 250cc**

SPANISH MANUALS
98903 **Reparación de Carrocería & Pintura**
98904 **Carburadores para los modelos Holley & Rochester**
98905 **Códigos Automotrices de la Computadora**
98910 **Frenos Automotriz**
98913 **Electricidad Automotriz**
98915 **Inyección de Combustible 1986 al 1999**
99040 **Chevrolet & GMC Camionetas** '67 al '87
99041 **Chevrolet & GMC Camionetas** '88 al '98
99042 **Chevrolet & GMC Camionetas Cerradas** '68 al '95
99055 **Dodge Caravan & Plymouth Voyager** '84 al '95
99075 **Ford Camionetas y Bronco** '80 al '94
99077 **Ford Camionetas Cerradas** '69 al '91
99088 **Ford Modelos de Tamaño Mediano** '75 al '86
99091 **Ford Taurus & Mercury Sable** '86 al '95
99095 **GM Modelos de Tamaño Grande** '70 al '90
99100 **GM Modelos de Tamaño Mediano** '70 al '88
99106 **Jeep Cherokee, Wagoneer & Comanche** '84 al '00
99110 **Nissan Camioneta** '80 al '96, Pathfinder '87 al '95
99118 **Nissan Sentra** '82 al '94
99125 **Toyota Camionetas y 4Runner** '79 al '95

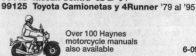

Over 100 Haynes motorcycle manuals also available

6-09

Haynes Automotive Manuals

NOTE: If you do not see a listing for your vehicle, consult your local Haynes dealer for the latest product information.

HAYNES XTREME CUSTOMIZING
11101 Sport Compact Customizing
11102 Sport Compact Performance
11110 In-car Entertainment
11150 Sport Utility Vehicle Customizing
11213 Acura
11255 GM Full-size Pick-ups
11314 Ford Focus
11315 Full-size Ford Pick-ups
11373 Honda Civic

ACURA
12020 Integra '86 thru '89 & Legend '86 thru '90
12021 Integra '90 thru '93 & Legend '91 thru '95
12050 Acura TL all models '99 thru '08

AMC
Jeep CJ - see *JEEP (50020)*
14020 Mid-size models '70 thru '83
14025 (Renault) Alliance & Encore '83 thru '87

AUDI
15020 4000 all models '80 thru '87
15025 5000 all models '77 thru '83
15026 5000 all models '84 thru '88

AUSTIN-HEALEY
Sprite - see *MG Midget (66015)*

BMW
18020 3/5 Series '82 thru '92
18021 3-Series incl. Z3 models '92 thru '98
18022 3-Series, '99 thru '05, Z4 models
18025 320i all 4 cyl models '75 thru '83
18050 1500 thru 2002 except Turbo '59 thru '77

BUICK
19010 Buick Century '97 thru '05
Century (front-wheel drive) - see *GM (38005)*
19020 Buick, Oldsmobile & Pontiac Full-size (Front-wheel drive) '85 thru '05
Buick Electra, LeSabre and Park Avenue; Oldsmobile Delta 88 Royale, Ninety Eight and Regency; Pontiac Bonneville
19025 Buick Oldsmobile & Pontiac Full-size (Rear wheel drive) '70 thru '90
Buick Estate, Electra, LeSabre, Limited, Oldsmobile Custom Cruiser, Delta 88, Ninety-eight, Pontiac Bonneville, Catalina, Grandville, Parisienne
19030 Mid-size Regal & Century all rear-drive models with V6, V8 and Turbo '74 thru '87
Regal - see *GENERAL MOTORS (38010)*
Riviera - see *GENERAL MOTORS (38030)*
Roadmaster - see *CHEVROLET (24046)*
Skyhawk - see *GENERAL MOTORS (38015)*
Skylark - see *GM (38020, 38025)*
Somerset - see *GENERAL MOTORS (38025)*

CADILLAC
21030 Cadillac Rear Wheel Drive all gasoline models '70 thru '93
Cimarron - see *GENERAL MOTORS (38015)*
DeVille - see *GM (38031 & 38032)*
Eldorado - see *GM (38030 & 38031)*
Fleetwood - see *GM (38031)*
Seville - see *GM (38030, 38031 & 38032)*

CHEVROLET
24010 Astro & GMC Safari Mini-vans '85 thru '05
24015 Camaro V8 all models '70 thru '81
24016 Camaro all models '82 thru '92
24017 Camaro & Firebird '93 thru '02
Cavalier - see *GENERAL MOTORS (38016)*
Celebrity - see *GENERAL MOTORS (38005)*
24020 Chevelle, Malibu & El Camino '69 thru '87
24024 Chevette & Pontiac T1000 '76 thru '87
Citation - see *GENERAL MOTORS (38020)*
24027 Colorado & GMC Canyon '04 thru '08
24032 Corsica/Beretta all models '87 thru '96
24040 Corvette all V8 models '68 thru '82
24041 Corvette all models '84 thru '96
10305 Chevrolet Engine Overhaul Manual
24045 Full-size Sedans Caprice, Impala, Biscayne, Bel Air & Wagons '69 thru '90
24046 Impala SS & Caprice and Buick Roadmaster '91 thru '96
Impala - see *LUMINA (24048)*
Lumina '90 thru '94 - see *GM (38010)*
24047 Impala & Monte Carlo all models '06 thru '08
24048 Lumina & Monte Carlo '95 thru '05
Lumina APV - see *GM (38035)*

24050 Luv Pick-up all 2WD & 4WD '72 thru '82
24055 Malibu '97 thru '00 - see *GM (38026)*
Monte Carlo all models '70 thru '88
Monte Carlo '95 thru '01 - see *LUMINA (24048)*
24059 Nova all V8 models '69 thru '79
24060 Nova and Geo Prizm '85 thru '92
24064 Pick-ups '67 thru '87 - Chevrolet & GMC, all V8 & in-line 6 cyl, 2WD & 4WD '67 thru '87; Suburbans, Blazers & Jimmys '67 thru '91
24065 Pick-ups '88 thru '98 - Chevrolet & GMC, full-size pick-ups '88 thru '98, C/K Classic '99 & '00, Blazer & Jimmy '92 thru '94; Suburban '92 thru '99; Tahoe & Yukon '95 thru '99
24066 Pick-ups '99 thru '06 - Chevrolet Silverado & GMC Sierra '99 thru '06, Suburban/Tahoe/ Yukon/Yukon XL/Avalanche '00 thru '06
24070 S-10 & S-15 Pick-ups '82 thru '93, Blazer & Jimmy '83 thru '94,
24071 S-10 & Sonoma Pick-ups '94 thru '04, including Blazer, Jimmy & Hombre
24072 Chevrolet TrailBlazer & TrailBlazer EXT, GMC Envoy & Envoy XL, Oldsmobile Bravada '02 thru '07
24075 Sprint '85 thru '88 & Geo Metro '89 thru '01
24080 Vans - Chevrolet & GMC '68 thru '96
24081 Chevrolet Express & GMC Savana Full-size Vans '96 thru '07

CHRYSLER
25015 Chrysler Cirrus, Dodge Stratus, Plymouth Breeze '95 thru '00
10310 Chrysler Engine Overhaul Manual
25020 Full-size Front-Wheel Drive '88 thru '93
K-Cars - see *DODGE Aries (30008)*
Laser - see *DODGE Daytona (30030)*
25025 Chrysler LHS, Concorde, New Yorker, Dodge Intrepid, Eagle Vision, '93 thru '97
25026 Chrysler LHS, Concorde, 300M, Dodge Intrepid, '98 thru '04
25027 Chrysler 300, Dodge Charger & Magnum '05 thru '07
25030 Chrysler & Plymouth Mid-size front wheel drive '82 thru '95
Rear-wheel Drive - see *Dodge (30050)*
25035 PT Cruiser all models '01 thru '03
25040 Chrysler Sebring, Dodge Avenger '95 thru '05 Dodge Stratus '01 thru 05

DATSUN
28005 200SX all models '80 thru '83
28007 B-210 all models '73 thru '78
28009 210 all models '79 thru '82
28012 240Z, 260Z & 280Z Coupe '70 thru '78
28014 280ZX Coupe & 2+2 '79 thru '83
300ZX - see *NISSAN (72010)*
28018 510 & PL521 Pick-up '68 thru '73
28020 510 all models '78 thru '81
28022 620 Series Pick-up all models '73 thru '79
720 Series Pick-up - see *NISSAN (72030)*
28025 810/Maxima all gasoline models, '77 thru '84

DODGE
400 & 600 - see *CHRYSLER (25030)*
30008 Aries & Plymouth Reliant '81 thru '89
30010 Caravan & Plymouth Voyager '84 thru '95
30011 Caravan & Plymouth Voyager '96 thru '02
30012 Challenger/Plymouth Saporro '78 thru '83
30013 Caravan, Chrysler Voyager, Town & Country '03 thru '06
30016 Colt & Plymouth Champ '78 thru '87
30020 Dakota Pick-ups all models '87 thru '96
30021 Durango '98 & '99, Dakota '97 thru '99
30022 Dodge Durango models '00 thru '03
Dodge Dakota models '00 thru '04
30023 Dodge Durango '04 thru '06, Dakota '05 and '06
30025 Dart, Demon, Plymouth Barracuda, Duster & Valiant 6 cyl models '67 thru '76
30030 Daytona & Chrysler Laser '84 thru '89
Intrepid - see *CHRYSLER (25025, 25026)*
30034 Neon all models '95 thru '99
30035 Omni & Plymouth Horizon '78 thru '90
30036 Dodge and Plymouth Neon '00 thru '05
30040 Pick-ups all full-size models '74 thru '93
30041 Pick-ups all full-size models '94 thru '01
30042 Dodge Full-size Pick-ups '02 thru '08
30045 Ram 50/D50 Pick-ups & Raider and Plymouth Arrow Pick-ups '79 thru '93
30050 Dodge/Plymouth/Chrysler RWD '71 thru '89
30055 Shadow & Plymouth Sundance '87 thru '94
30060 Spirit & Plymouth Acclaim '89 thru '95
30065 Vans - Dodge & Plymouth '71 thru '03

EAGLE
Talon - see *MITSUBISHI (68030, 68031)*
Vision - see *CHRYSLER (25025)*

FIAT
34010 124 Sport Coupe & Spider '68 thru '78
34025 X1/9 all models '74 thru '80

FORD
10355 Ford Automatic Transmission Overhaul
36004 Aerostar Mini-vans all models '86 thru '97
36006 Contour & Mercury Mystique '95 thru '00
36008 Courier Pick-up all models '72 thru '82
36012 Crown Victoria & Mercury Grand Marquis '88 thru '10
10320 Ford Engine Overhaul Manual
36016 Escort/Mercury Lynx all models '81 thru '90
36020 Escort/Mercury Tracer '91 thru '00
36022 Ford Escape & Mazda Tribute '01 thru '07
36024 Explorer & Mazda Navajo '91 thru '01
36025 Ford Explorer & Mercury Mountaineer '02 thru '07
36028 Fairmont & Mercury Zephyr '78 thru '83
36030 Festiva & Aspire '88 thru '97
36032 Fiesta all models '77 thru '80
36034 Focus all models '00 thru '07
36036 Ford & Mercury Full-size '75 thru '87
36044 Ford & Mercury Mid-size '75 thru '86
36048 Mustang V8 all models '64-1/2 thru '73
36049 Mustang II 4 cyl, V6 & V8 models '74 thru '78
36050 Mustang & Mercury Capri '79 thru '86
36051 Mustang all models '94 thru '04
36052 Mustang '05 thru '07
36054 Pick-ups & Bronco '73 thru '79
36058 Pick-ups & Bronco '80 thru '96
36059 F-150 & Expedition '97 thru '03, F-250 '97 thru '99 & Lincoln Navigator '98 thru '02
36060 Super Duty Pick-ups, Excursion '99 thru '06
36061 F-150 full-size '04 thru '06
36062 Pinto & Mercury Bobcat '75 thru '80
36066 Probe all models '89 thru '92
36070 Ranger/Bronco II gasoline models '83 thru '92
36071 Ranger '93 thru '08 & Mazda Pick-ups '94 thru '08
36074 Taurus & Mercury Sable '86 thru '95
36075 Taurus & Mercury Sable '96 thru '05
36078 Tempo & Mercury Topaz '84 thru '94
36082 Thunderbird/Mercury Cougar '83 thru '88
36086 Thunderbird/Mercury Cougar '89 and '97
36090 Vans all V8 Econoline models '69 thru '91
36094 Vans full size '92 thru '05
36097 Windstar Mini-van '95 thru '07

GENERAL MOTORS
10360 GM Automatic Transmission Overhaul
38005 Buick Century, Chevrolet Celebrity, Oldsmobile Cutlass Ciera & Pontiac 6000 all models '82 thru '96
38010 Buick Regal, Chevrolet Lumina, Oldsmobile Cutlass Supreme & Pontiac Grand Prix (FWD) '88 thru '07
38015 Buick Skyhawk, Cadillac Cimarron, Chevrolet Cavalier, Oldsmobile Firenza & Pontiac J-2000 & Sunbird '82 thru '94
38016 Chevrolet Cavalier & Pontiac Sunfire '95 thru '04
38017 Chevrolet Cobalt & Pontiac G5 '05 thru '09
38020 Buick Skylark, Chevrolet Citation, Olds Omega, Pontiac Phoenix '80 thru '85
38025 Buick Skylark & Somerset, Oldsmobile Achieva & Calais and Pontiac Grand Am all models '85 thru '98
38026 Chevrolet Malibu, Olds Alero & Cutlass, Pontiac Grand Am '97 thru '03
38027 Chevrolet Malibu '04 thru '07
38030 Cadillac Eldorado, Seville, Oldsmobile Toronado, Buick Riviera '71 thru '85
38031 Cadillac Eldorado & Seville, DeVille, Fleetwood & Olds Toronado, Buick Riviera '86 thru '93
38032 Cadillac DeVille '94 thru '05 & Seville '92 thru '04
38035 Chevrolet Lumina APV, Olds Silhouette & Pontiac Trans Sport all models '90 thru '96
38036 Chevrolet Venture, Olds Silhouette, Pontiac Trans Sport & Montana '97 thru '05
General Motors Full-size Rear-wheel Drive - see *BUICK (19025)*

GEO
Metro - see *CHEVROLET Sprint (24075)*
Prizm - '85 thru '92 see *CHEVY (24060)*, '93 thru '02 see *TOYOTA Corolla (92036)*
40030 Storm all models '90 thru '93
Tracker - see *SUZUKI Samurai (90010)*

(Continued on other side)

Haynes North America, Inc., 861 Lawrence Drive, Newbury Park, CA 91320-1514 • (805) 498-6703 • http://www.haynes.com